Communications
in Computer and Information Science 425

Editorial Board

Simone Diniz Junqueira Barbosa
   Ponti cal Catholic University of Rio de Janeiro (PUC-Rio),
   Rio de Janeiro, Brazil

Phoebe Chen
   La Trobe University, Melbourne, Australia

Alfredo Cuzzocrea
   ICAR-CNR and University of Calabria, Italy

Xiaoyong Du
   Renmin University of China, Beijing, China

Joaquim Filipe
   Polytechnic Institute of Setúbal, Portugal

Orhun Kara
   TÜBITAK BILGEM and Middle East Technical University, Turkey

Igor Kotenko
   St. Petersburg Institute for Informatics and Automation
   of the Russian Academy of Sciences, Russia

Krishna M. Sivalingam
   Indian Institute of Technology Madras, India

Dominik Ślęzak
   University of Warsaw and Infobright, Poland

Takashi Washio
   Osaka University, Japan

Xiaokang Yang
   Shanghai Jiao Tong University, China

Béatrix Barafort   Rory V. O'Connor
Alexander Poth   Richard Messnarz (Eds.)

Systems, Software and Services Process Improvement

21st European Conference, EuroSPI 2014
Luxembourg, June 25-27, 2014
Proceedings

Volume Editors

Béatrix Barafort
Public Research Center Henri Tudor, Luxembourg
E-mail: beatrix.barafort@tudor.lu

Rory V. O'Connor
Dublin City University, Ireland
E-mail: roconnor@computing.dcu.ie

Alexander Poth
Volkswagen AG, Wolfsburg, Germany
E-mail: alexander.poth@volkswagen.de

Richard Messnarz
ISCN GesmbH, Graz, Austria
E-mail: rmess@iscn.com

ISSN 1865-0929 e-ISSN 1865-0937
ISBN 978-3-662-43895-4 e-ISBN 978-3-662-43896-1
DOI 10.1007/978-3-662-43896-1
Springer Heidelberg New York Dordrecht London

Library of Congress Control Number: 2014941589

© Springer-Verlag Berlin Heidelberg 2014
This work is subject to copyright. All rights are reserved by the Publisher, whether the whole or part of the material is concerned, specifically the rights of translation, reprinting, reuse of illustrations, recitation, broadcasting, reproduction on microfilms or in any other physical way, and transmission or information storage and retrieval, electronic adaptation, computer software, or by similar or dissimilar methodology now known or hereafter developed. Exempted from this legal reservation are brief excerpts in connection with reviews or scholarly analysis or material supplied specifically for the purpose of being entered and executed on a computer system, for exclusive use by the purchaser of the work. Duplication of this publication or parts thereof is permitted only under the provisions of the Copyright Law of the Publisher's location, in its current version, and permission for use must always be obtained from Springer. Permissions for use may be obtained through RightsLink at the Copyright Clearance Center. Violations are liable to prosecution under the respective Copyright Law.
The use of general descriptive names, registered names, trademarks, service marks, etc. in this publication does not imply, even in the absence of a specific statement, that such names are exempt from the relevant protective laws and regulations and therefore free for general use.
While the advice and information in this book are believed to be true and accurate at the date of publication, neither the authors nor the editors nor the publisher can accept any legal responsibility for any errors or omissions that may be made. The publisher makes no warranty, express or implied, with respect to the material contained herein.

Typesetting: Camera-ready by author, data conversion by Scientific Publishing Services, Chennai, India

Printed on acid-free paper

Springer is part of Springer Science+Business Media (www.springer.com)

Preface

This volume comprises the proceedings of the 21st EuroSPI Conference, held during June 25–27, 2014, in Luxembourg.

Since EuroSPI 2010, we have extended the scope of the conference from software process improvement to systems, software, and service-based process improvement. EMIRAcle is the institution for research in manufacturing and innovation, which is a result of the largest network of excellence for innovation in manufacturing in Europe. EMIRAcle key representatives joined the EuroSPI community, and papers as well as case studies for process improvement on systems and product level will be included in future.

Since 2008, EuroSPI partners have packaged SPI knowledge in job role training and established a European certification association (www.ecqa.org) to transport this knowledge Europe wide using standardized certification and exam processes.

Conferences were held in Dublin (Ireland) in 1994, in Vienna (Austria) in 1995, in Budapest (Hungary) in 1997, in Gothenburg (Sweden) in 1998, in Pori (Finland) in 1999, in Copenhagen (Denmark) in 2000, in Limerick (Ireland) in 2001, in Nuremberg (Germany) in 2002, in Graz (Austria) in 2003, in Trondheim (Norway) in 2004, in Budapest (Hungary) in 2005, in Joensuu (Finland) in 2006, in Potsdam (Germany) in 2007, in Dublin (Ireland) in 2008, in Alcala (Spain) in 2009, in Grenoble (France) in 2010, in Roskilde (Denmark) in 2011, in Vienna (Austria) in 2012, and in Dundalk (Ireland) in 2013.

EuroSPI is an initiative with the following major action lines {http://www.eurospi.net}:

- Establishing an annual EuroSPI conference supported by software process improvement networks from different EU countries.
- Establishing an Internet-based knowledge library, newsletters, and a set of proceedings and recommended books.
- Establishing an effective team of national representatives (from each EUcountry) growing step by step into more countries of Europe.
- Establishing a European Qualification Framework for a pool of professions related with SPI and management. This is supported by European certificates and examination systems.

EuroSPI has established a newsletter series (newsletter.eurospi.net), the SPI Manifesto (SPI = Systems, Software and Services Process Improvement), an experience library (library.eurospi.net) that is continuously extended over the years and is made available to all attendees, and a Europe-wide certification for qualifications in the SPI area (www.ecqa.org, European Certification and Qualification Association).

A typical characterization of EuroSPI is reflected in a statement made by a company: "... the biggest value of EuroSPI lies in its function as a European knowledge and experience exchange mechanism for SPI and innovation."

Since its inception in 1994 in Dublin, the EuroSPI initiative has outlined that there is not a single silver bullet with which to solve SPI issues, but that you need to understand a combination of different SPI methods and approaches to achieve concrete benefits. Therefore, each proceedings volume covers a variety of different topics, and at the conference we discuss potential synergies and the combined use of such methods and approaches. These proceedings contain selected research papers under seven headings:

- Section I: SPI and Very Small Entities
- Section II: Process Improvement Frameworks
- Section III: Testing and Improvement Issues
- Section IV: SPI and People Issues
- Section V: SPI and Quality Issues
- Section VI: Software processes in various contexts
- Section VII: Selected Key Notes and Workshop Papers

Section I presents three papers related to "SPI and Very Small Entities" with a particular focus on the international standard ISO/IEC 29110 Process Lifecycle Standard for Very Small Entities (VSEs). In the first of three papers, Moreno-Campos et al. discuss VSE measurement, while in the second paper Laporte and O'Connor introduce the new systems engineering part of ISO/IEC 29110, and finally in the third paper Mesquida et al. discuss project management aspects of VSEs.

Section II presents three papers under the umbrella topic of "Process Improvement Frameworks." Firstly Regan et al. present a methodology for the generation of software process improvement roadmaps within the medical device domain. Barafort et al. present how the Tudor's IT process assessment (TIPA) framework has been designed and improved via a design science research approach in the case of IT service management processes for the IT infrastructure library (ITIL). The final paper of this section by Jaakkola and Thalheim describes a framework for change management of software systems that covers the entire lifecycle and with a focus on change management.

Section IV explores the theme of "SPI and People Issues." In the first of three papers Yilmaz et al. present a study on personality profiling of software developers and its relationship to process improvement. Munoz et al. continue this theme by exploring the human perspective in SPI. In the final paper, O'Connor and Duchonova investigate one people-related issue in SPI, that of the role of agile coaches in agile method adoption.

Section V presents three papers dealing with associated issues surrounding the topic of "SPI and Quality Issues." In the first paper Seth et al. focus on the influence of management on software product quality by describing an empirical study in software development companies. In the second paper, Yli-Huumo et al. focus on a South Korean study of software quality assurance and development methods. Finally de Souza et al. propose to improve a project's cost predictability by using earned value management and quality data techniques.

Section VI discusses issues surrounding "Software Processes in various contexts." In the first paper Osborne O'Hagan et al. present a systematic literature review (SLR) of software development processes used for computer games development. Munoz et al. investigate improving the software requirements gathering process, and in the final paper of this section Regan et al. present a traceability model for use in process assessment in a medical device context.

Section VII presents selected keynotes from EuroSPI workshops concerning the future of SPI. From 2010 EuroSPI has been inviting recognized key researchers to publish new future directions of SPI. These key messages are discussed in interactive workshops and help creating SPI communities based on new topics.

Six invited papers concerning "Creating Environments Supporting Innovation and Improvement" illustrate that SPI is inherently linked to innovation and that innovation requires a transfer of ideas to an exploitation, a strategy for valorization of new ideas and products or services, a long-lasting scope and sustainability, a roadmap for innovation in development and production, and a concept for software process innovation. Georgiadou et al. describe the results of the EU project VALO and how successful innovation has to focus on the value creation for stakeholders. Fistis et al. describe a new EU project LEADSUS, which develops success criteria and a training program to enable European industry to have leadership in sustainability. Morten Elvang outlines that even if everything changes all the time there are some principles an organization can always believe in. Flatscher et al. describe the experiences of a leading automotive supplier in establishing technology and innovation roadmaps. Eva Homolova et al. provide information about the current activities of the EU project "Idea 2 Enterprise" and how an entrepreneurship schema is rolled out in different EU countries. Finally Kouichi Kishida analyzes the principles of how the notations we use in software process innovation and modelling underline an innovation and evolution by themselves and which factors influence this.

Three invited papers concerning "Risk Management and Functional Safety Management" illustrate experiences from the medical device and automotive industry about the implementation of recent risk management and functional safety standards. Messnarz et al. outline the results of the EU project AQUA where a toolbox for the integrated use of functional safety, Automotive SPICE and Six Sigma, has been developed for the automotive industry. Varkoi and Nevalainen analyze how rigorous an assessment should be to be useful in the safety-critical domain, a pure process assessment would not be sufficient. Finally Masao Ito provides insight into a method that helps to analyse hazards in the concept.

Two invited papers concerning "Assessment and Improvement" illustrate new assessment and improvement models and standards. Tomas Schweigert provides insight into the new version of Test SPICE 3.0, while Pries-Heje and Johansen explain how to use the practice of identifying the right change strategy in the new ISO/IEC 33014 standard.

June 2014

Béatrix Barafort
Rory V. O'Connor
Alexander Poth
Richard Messnarz

Recommended Further Reading

In [1] the proceedings of three EuroSPI conferences were integrated into one book, which was edited by 30 experts in Europe. The proceedings of EuroSPI 2005 to 2013 inclusive have been published by Springer in [2], [3], [4], [5], [6], [7], [8], [9], and [10], respectively.

References

1. Messnarz, R., Tully, C. (eds.): Better Software Practice for Business Benefit – Principles and Experience, 409 pages. IEEE Computer Society Press, Los Alamitos (1999)
2. Svensson, H.: A framework for improving soft factors in software development. In: Richardson, I., Abrahamsson, P., Messnarz, R. (eds.) EuroSPI 2005. LNCS, vol. 3792, pp. 202–213. Springer, Heidelberg (2005)
3. Richardson, I., Runeson, P., Messnarz, R. (eds.): EuroSPI 2006. LNCS, vol. 4257. Springer, Heidelberg (2006)
4. Abrahamsson, P., Baddoo, N., Tiziana, M., Messnarz, R.: Software process improvement – EuroSPI 2007 conference. In: Abrahamsson, P., Baddoo, N., Margaria, T., Messnarz, R. (eds.) EuroSPI 2007. LNCS, vol. 4764, pp. 1–6. Springer, Heidelberg (2007)
5. O'Connor, R.V., Baddoo, N., Smolander, K., Messnarz, R. (eds.): EuroSPI 2008. CCIS, vol. 16. Springer, Heidelberg (2008)
6. O'Connor, R.V., Baddoo, N., Cuadrago Gallego, J., Rejas Muslera, R., Smolander, K., Messnarz, R. (eds.): EuroSPI 2009. CCIS, vol. 42. Springer, Heidelberg (2009)
7. Riel, A., O'Connor, R., Tichkiewitch, S., Messnarz, R. (eds.): EuroSPI 2010. CCIS, vol. 99. Springer, Heidelberg (2010)
8. O'Connor, R.V., Pries-Heje, J., Messnarz, R. (eds.): EuroSPI 2011. CCIS, vol. 172. Springer, Heidelberg (2011)
9. Winkler, D., O'Connor, R.V., Messnarz, R. (eds.): EuroSPI 2012. CCIS, vol. 301. Springer, Heidelberg (2012)
10. McCaffery, F., O'Connor, R.V., Messnarz, R. (eds.): EuroSPI 2013. CCIS, vol. 364. Springer, Heidelberg (2013)

Organization

Board Members

EuroSPI board members represent centers or networks of SPI excellence having extensive experience with SPI. The board members collaborate with different European SPINS (Software Process Improvement Networks). The following six organizations have been members of the conference board for the last 13 years:

- ASQ, http://www.asq.org
- ASQF, http://www.asqf.de
- DELTA, http://www.delta.dk
- ISCN, http://www.iscn.com
- SINTEF, http://www.sintef.no
- STTF, http://www.sttf.fi

EuroSPI Scientific Program Committee

EuroSPI established an international committee of selected well-known experts in SPI who are willing to be mentioned in the program and to review a set of papers each year. The list below comprises the Research Program Committee members. EuroSPI also has a separate Industrial Program Committee responsible for the industry/experience contributions.

Alain Abran	ETS-University of Quebec, Canada
Alberto Sillitti	Free University of Bolzano, Italy
Andreas Riel	Grenoble Institute of Technology, France
Antonia Mas Pichaco	Universitat de les Illes Balears, Spain
Antonio De Amescua	Carlos III University of Madrid, Spain
Bee Bee Chua	University of Technology Sydney, Australia
Christiane Gresse von Wangenheim	Federal University of Santa Catarina, Brazil
Dietmar Winkler	Vienna University of Technology, Austria
Fergal McCaffery	Dundalk Institute of Technology, Ireland
Javier Garíca-Guzman	Carlos III University of Madrid, Spain
Jose Antonio Calvo-Manzano	Universidad Politecnica de Madrid, Spain
Kerstin Siakas	Alexander Technological Educational Institute of Thessaloniki, Greece
Luigi Buglione	Engineering Ingegneria Informatica, Italy

Marion Lepmets	Dundalk Institute of Technology, Ireland
Michael Reiner	IMC Fachhochschule Krems, Austria
Paul Clarke	Dundalk Institute of Technology, Ireland
Paula Ventura Martins	FCT-University of Algarve, Portugal
Ricardo Colomo Palacios	Ostfold University College, Norway
Rory V. O'Connor	Dublin City University, Ireland
Serge Tichkiewitch	Grenoble Institute of Technology, France
Timo Mäkinen	Tampere University of Technology, Finland
Timo Varkoi	Tampere University of Technology, Finland
Torgeir Dingsøyr	SINTEF ICT, Norway

General Chair

Richard Messnarz

Scientific Chairs

Béatrix Barafort
Rory V. O'Connor
Alexander Poth

All four chairs, the general and the research chairs, have a complementary and interesting profile. Dr. Richard Messnarz works in close collaboration with Austrian research institutions (universities of applied sciences) and large German automotive companies. Béatrix Barafort is the manager of the Business Process & Service Engineering research unit in the Centre de Recherche Public Henri Tudor in Luxembourg. Dr. Rory O'Connor is Head of the School of Computing and a senior lecturer at Dublin City University and also a senior researcher with Lero, the Irish Software Engineering Centre. Alexander Poth is an improvement expert and assessor at one of the world-leading automotive companies and with experience in implementing improvement programs in industry.

Acknowledgments

Some contributions published in this book have been funded with support from the European Commission. European projects (supporting ECQA and EuroSPI) contributed to this Springer book including I2E (Idea to Enterprise), AQUA (Knowledge Alliance for Training Quality and Excellence in Automotive), LEADSUS (Leading Sustainability), and LSSH (Lean Six Sigma for Health Care).

In this case the publications reflect the views only of the author(s), and the Commission cannot be held responsible for any use which may be made of the information contained therein.

Table of Contents

SPI and Very Small Entities

Towards Measuring the Impact of the ISO/IEC 29110 Standard:
A Systematic Review 1
    *Euclides Moreno-Campos, Mary-Luz Sanchez-Gordón,
Ricardo Colomo-Palacios, and Antonio de Amescua Seco*

A Systems Process Lifecycle Standard for Very Small Entities:
Development and Pilot Trials 13
    Claude Y. Laporte and Rory V. O'Connor

An Integrated Environment to Support Project Management in
VSEs 25
    Antoni-Lluís Mesquida, Antonia Mas, and Adelaida Delgado

Process Improvement Frameworks

A Critical Evaluation of a Methodology for the Generation of Software
Process Improvement Roadmaps 36
    Derek Flood, Fergal Mc Caffery, Gilbert Regan, and Val Casey

How to Design an Innovative Framework for Process Improvement?
The TIPA for ITIL Case 48
    Béatrix Barafort, Anne Rousseau, and Eric Dubois

A Framework for Systematic Change Management 60
    Hannu Jaakkola and Bernhard Thalheim

Testing and Improvement Issues

Engineering Process Improvement in Heterogeneous Multi-disciplinary
Environments with Defect Causal Analysis 73
    *Olga Kovalenko, Dietmar Winkler, Marcos Kalinowski,
Estefania Serral, and Stefan Biffl*

Information Sources and Their Importance to Prioritize Test Cases in
the Heterogeneous Systems Context 86
    *Ahmad Nauman Ghazi, Jesper Andersson, Richard Torkar,
Kai Petersen, and Jürgen Börstler*

Software Process Assessment Validation and Improvement
Prioritization 99
    Sven Richter and David Escorial Rico

SPI and People Issues

An Exploration of Individual Personality Types in Software
Development 111
   Murat Yilmaz, Rory V. O'Connor, and Paul Clarke

Covering the Human Perspective in Software Process Improvement 123
   *Mirna Muñoz, Jezreel Mejia, Gloria Piedad Gasca-Hurtado,
Claudia Valtierra, and Brenda Duron*

Assessing the Value of an Agile Coach in Agile Method Adoption 135
   Rory V. O'Connor and Natalia Duchonova

SPI and Quality Issues

The Influence of Management on Software Product Quality:
An Empirical Study in Software Developing Companies 147
   Frank Philip Seth, Erja Mustonen-Ollila, and Ossi Taipale

Software Development Methods and Quality Assurance: Special Focus
on South Korea 159
   Jesse Yli-Huumo, Ossi Taipale, and Kari Smolander

A Proposal for the Improvement of Project's Cost Predictability Using
Earned Value Management and Quality Data – An Empirical Study 170
   *Adler Diniz de Souza, Ana Regina Cavalcanti Rocha,
Djenane Cristina, and Bruno Augusto Constantino*

Software Processes in Various Contexts

Software Development Processes for Games: A Systematic Literature
Review 182
   Ann Osborne O'Hagan, Gerry Coleman, and Rory V. O'Connor

Software Requirements Development: A Path for Improving Software
Quality 194
   *Gloria Piedad Gasca-Hurtado, Mirna Muñoz, Jezreel Mejia, and
Jose A. Calvo-Manzano*

A Traceability Process Assessment Model for the Medical Device
Domain 206
   *Gilbert Regan, Miklos Biro, Fergal Mc Caffery, Kevin Mc Daid, and
Derek Flood*

Selected Key Notes and Workshop Papers

Creating Environments Supporting Innovation and Improvement

Project Valorisation through Agility and Catering for Stakeholder
Expectations 217
    Elli Georgiadou, Kerstin Siakas, and Richard Messnarz

Leadership in Sustainability 231
    *Gabriela Fistis, Tomislav Rozman, Andreas Riel, and
Richard Messnarz*

Game Changing Beliefs for the Product Developing Organization 246
    Morten Elvang

The Need for a Structured Approach towards Production Technology
Roadmaps in Innovation-Driven Industries 251
    Martina Flatscher, Andreas Riel, and Tobias Kösler

Empowering Entrepreneurship in Europe: Going from the Idea to
Enterprise in 4 EU Countries 262
    *Eva Homolová, Andreas Riel, Marek Gavenda,
Ana Azevedo, Marisa Pais, Jiří Balcar, Alessandra Antinori,
Giuseppe Metitiero, Giorgos Giorgakis, Photis Photiades,
Damjan Ekert, Richard Messnarz, and Serge Tichkiewitch*

Linguistic Analogy for Software Process Innovation 271
    Kouichi Kishida

Risk Management and Functional Safety Management

Finding Threats with Hazards in the Concept Phase of Product
Development 277
    Masao Ito

Integrating Functional Safety, Automotive SPICE and Six Sigma – The
AQUA Knowledge Base and Integration Examples 285
    *Richard Messnarz, Christian Kreiner, Andreas Riel,
Serge Tichkiewitch, Damjan Ekert, Michael Langgner, and
Dick Theisens*

Compliance and Rigour in Process Assessment for Safety-Critical
Domain 296
    Timo Varkoi and Risto Nevalainen

SPI and Assessments and Improvement

The Feature Set of TestSPICE 3.0 309
  Tomas Schweigert, Andreas Nehfort, and Mohsen Ekssir-Monfared

Change Strategy for ISO/IEC 33014: A Multi-case Study on Which
Change Strategies Were Chosen.................................... 317
  Jan Pries-Heje and Jørn Johansen

Author Index 331

Towards Measuring the Impact of the ISO/IEC 29110 Standard: A Systematic Review

Euclides Moreno-Campos[1], Mary-Luz Sanchez-Gordón[1],
Ricardo Colomo-Palacios[2], and Antonio de Amescua Seco[1]

[1] Universidad Carlos III de Madrid, Computer Science Department
Av. Universidad 30, Leganés, 28911, Madrid, Spain
`100289251@alumnos.uc3m.es, mary_sanchezg@hotmail.com, amescua@inf.uc3m.es`
[2] Østfold University College, Faculty of Computer Sciences
B R A Veien 4, 1783 Halden, Norway
`Ricardo.colomo-palacios@hiof.no`

Abstract. The software industry recognizes the value of VSEs in contributing valuable products and services. Unfortunately current ISO/IEC standards do not completely address the needs of VSEs. Due to this, the ISO/IEC 29110 standard has been developed. The aim of this paper is to analyze the impact of the initiative by means of a systematic literature review of the ISO/IEC 29110 standard. This analysis was conducted using the most significant bibliographic databases. The result of the analysis reflects some tendencies in research that target the development of software process assessment and SIP models for supporting the standard, the performance, creation and utilization of deployment packages, pilot projects and ISO/IEC 29110 standard implementation approaches, the encouragement on concluding the remaining profiles or the creation of new profiles and the design, development and implementation of documentation and knowledge management tools in order to support the adoption of the standard by VSEs.

Keywords: VSE, ISO/IEC 29110, SLR, systematic literature review, very small entity, software engineering.

1 Introduction

The software industry recognizes the value of Very Small Entities (VSEs[1]) in contributing valuable products and services [2, 3]. In fact, certain VSEs provide software components that are being assembled in larger software companies in order to generate critical and intensive software configurations [4]. According [2], the OECD (Organization for Economic Co-operation and Development) SME and Entrepreneurship

---

[1] The terms "very small entity" and "very small entities" (VSE/VSEs) have been defined by the ISO/IEC JTC1/SC7 Working Group 24 (WG24) as being "an entity (enterprise, organization, department or project) having up to 25 people" and have subsequently been adopted for the use in the ISO/IEC 29110 standard [1].

Outlook report (2005) *"SMEs constitute the dominant form of business organization in all countries world-wide, accounting for over 95 % and up to 99 % of the business population depending on country"*.

From studies and surveys conducted, it is clear that the majority of International Standards do not address the needs of VSEs. Conformance with these standards is difficult, if not impossible. Subsequently VSEs have no, or very limited, ways to be recognized as entities that produce quality software in their domain. Therefore, VSEs are often cut off from some economic activities. It has been discovered that VSEs find it difficult to relate International Standards to their business needs and to justify the application of the standards to their business practices. Most VSEs can neither afford the resources, in terms of number of employees, budget and time, nor do they see a net benefit in establishing software life cycle processes. To rectify some of these difficulties, a set of standards and guides has been developed according to a set of VSE characteristics. The guides are based on subsets of appropriate standards elements, referred to as VSE Profiles such as ISO/IEC 12207 and ISO/IEC 15289) [2, 4]. The so-called guides are gathered into the ISO/IEC 29110 *Software engineering — Lifecycle profiles for Very Small Entities standard*, which describes processes for project management and software implementation [5] and pretends to facilitate access to, and utilization of, ISO software engineering standards in VSEs [3].

The ISO/IEC 29110 Software engineering — Lifecycle profiles for Very Small Entities standard is aimed to approach Software Engineering and Project Management good practices to VSEs. According to [2], the ISO/IEC 29110 standard is divided in five parts as follow:

ISO/IEC TR 29110-1 defines the business terms common to the VSE Profile Set of Documents. It introduces processes, lifecycle and standardization concepts, and the ISO/IEC 29110 series. It also introduces the characteristics and requirements of a VSE, and clarifies the rationale for VSE-specific profiles, documents, standards and guides.

ISO/IEC 29110-2 introduces the concepts for software engineering standardized profiles for VSEs, and defines the terms common to the VSE Profile Set of Documents. It establishes the logic behind the definition and application of standardized profiles. It specifies the elements common to all standardized profiles (structure, conformance, assessment) and introduces the taxonomy (catalogue) of ISO/IEC 29110 profiles.

ISO/IEC TR 29110-3 defines the process assessment guidelines and compliance requirements needed to meet the purpose of the defined VSEs Profiles. ISO/IEC TR 29110-3 also contains information that can be useful to developers of assessment methods and assessment tools. ISO/IEC TR 29110-3 is addressed to people who have direct relation with the assessment process, e.g. the assessor and the sponsor of the assessment, who need guidance on ensuring that the requirements for performing an assessment have been met.

ISO/IEC 29110-4-1 provides the specification for all the profiles of the Generic Profile Group. The Generic Profile Group is applicable to VSEs that do not develop critical software products. The profiles are based on subsets of appropriate standards elements. VSEs' Profiles apply and are targeted to authors/providers of guides and authors/providers of tools and other support material.

ISO/IEC 29110-5-1 provides an implementation management and engineering guide for both the Entry and Basic Profile of the Generic Profile Group described in ISO/IEC 29110-4-1. The Entry Profile describes software development of a single application by a single project team with no special risk or situational factors for start-up VSEs (i.e. VSEs who started their operation less than 3 years) and/or for VSEs working on small project (e.g. project size of less than 6 person-months). The Basic Profile describes software development of a single application by a single project team with no special risk or situational factors.

As far as authors can see, the impact or, in other words, the actual adoption of the ISO/IEC 29110 standard in the literature has been increasing since the time of its publication (and even before), although there is no formal systematic literature review (SRL) on the impact of the standard in the research field [4]. Thus, the main purpose of this paper is to review the existent literature regarding ISO/IEC 29110 standard with the detection of potential improvements and developments on this subject.

2 Research Methodology

2.1 Motivation and Objectives

The literature presents a lack of studies on the adoption and implementation of the standard. At the present time, there are few documented and published research work regarding to the implementation of the standard in small organizations[4]. Therefore, this study will facilitate the understanding of the current status of research in different areas and address further investigation.

2.2 Research Method

According to [6], in order to achieve an overview of the state of the question, a research must be carried out following Kitchenham and Charters' guidelines on Systematic Literature Review (SLR). An SLR is defined as a methodical way to synthesize existing work in a manner that is fair. An SLR is a means of identifying, evaluating and interpreting all available research relevant to a definite research question or topic area or phenomenon of interest. After reviewing the literature on SLR for similar research objectives, it can be identified that there is no previously published search on the topic. This section presents each step followed to carry out this systematic review study, based on the guidelines provided by Kitchenham and Charters.

2.3 Planning

The goal of the study is to achieve an overview of the current status of the ISO/IEC 29110 standard in scientific literature. An SLR protocol was adapted to describe the plan for the review. The protocol includes research background, research questions, search strategy, study selection criteria and procedures, data extraction, and data synthesis strategies to ensure that the study is undertaken as planned and reduce the possibility of researcher bias. In this review protocol, the whole study timetable was not decided from the beginning, but rather the actual timetable of the study and results produced were recorded as the study progressed [6].

2.4 Research Questions

The research question is threefold:

1. What is the impact of the ISO/IEC 29110 standard in the scientific literature?
2. Which areas of research are more influenced by the ISO/IEC 29110 standard?
3. Which research trends are revealed from the systematic review of the ISO/IEC 29110 standard?

The keyword used to find an answer to the research question was: ISO/IEC 29110. The results expected at the end of the systematic review were, among other things, to discover what surveys exist as well as to identify the implications of the ISO/IEC 29110 standard in scientific literature. Authors also expected to see which applied researches had been carried out on the topic, as well as which trends are revealed from the performance of the systematic review.

2.5 Search Strategy and Search Process

The search strategy includes search resources and a search process as follows:

2.5.1 Search Resources
This study was planned to find all the literature available about the ISO/IEC 29110 standard. Given the diversity of sources to be consulted electronically via the web, five electronic databases of established literature resources were used for the actual SLR, namely IEEEXplore, Web of Science (WOS), ACM Digital Library, ScienceDirect and SpringerLink. It is important to highlight that a manual search on the EuroSPI's industrial proceedings conferences was also performed in order to find relevant literature.

2.5.2 Search Process
The overall search process is depicted in figure 1. *First*, the search string was applied in December 2013, returning 86 papers in total. Duplicate documents were removed, remaining with a set of 62 unique papers. After this, the EuroSPI's industrial proceedings conferences (from 2011 to 2013) were manually searched in January 2014, at the time that a second review of electronic databases was performed. In these books, three more papers were found, so the number of total unduplicated papers increased from 62 to 65. *Second*, the papers were reviewed based on titles, abstracts, conclusions, references and keywords, and then were classified into three different types:

- Relevant papers: if the paper satisfies the inclusion criterion (depicted further in this sub-section).
- Process assessment papers: if the paper is somehow related to the ISO/IEC 29110 standard and could be relevant for this study.
- Excluded papers: other papers, which are not relevant to the topic.

When there was doubt about the classification of a paper, it was included in the relevant group, leaving the possibility of discarding the paper during the next phase when the full texts of the papers were studied.

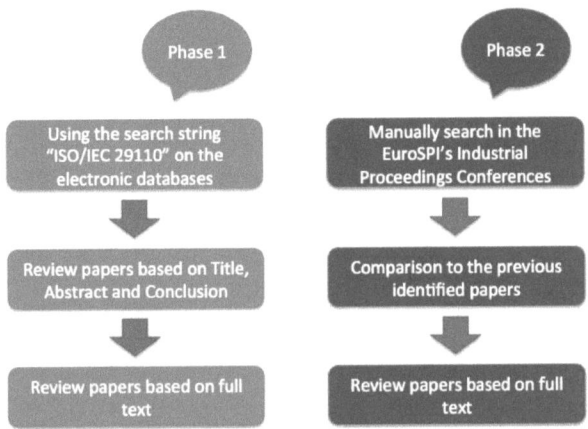

Fig. 1. Search Process Description

Third, each full article was retrieved and read to verify its inclusion or exclusion. The reason for exclusion or inclusion in this third phase was documented.

Fourth, in order to check the consistency of the inclusion/exclusion decisions, a test-retest approach and re-evaluation of a random sample of the primary studies was made. A paper is kept in this mapping study if it satisfies one of the two criteria:

- The paper is explicitly related to the ISO/IEC 29110 standard.
- The paper is relevant to software engineering research.

The documents were first reviewed based on titles, abstracts, and keywords and they were classified into three different types:

- Relevant papers: if the paper satisfies the inclusion criteria.
- Process assessment papers: if the paper is related to the ISO/IEC 29110 standard because it is used as a reference.
- Excluded papers: other papers which do not satisfy one of the two inclusion criteria.

The authors reviewed all 65 papers and other documentation and put them into three different groups according to the previously mentioned criteria. This list was reviewed in order to check for inconsistencies. When there was disagreement about the classification of a paper, it was included in the relevant group, leaving the possibility to discard the paper during the next phase when the full papers were read. The result of this stage was that 24 publications were classified as relevant. There is a risk that some papers have been missed. Therefore, this study cannot guarantee completeness, but it can still be trusted to give a good overview of the relevant literature on the ISO/IEC 29110 standard.

2.6 Data Extraction

The data extracted from each paper was documented and kept in a reference manager. After identification of the papers, the following data was extracted: (i) Source (journal or conference), (ii) Title, (iii) Authors, (iv) Publication Year, (v) Classification, according to topics in Table 2, and (vi) Summary of the research, including which questions were solved. Based on the papers classification criteria, all these were reviewed, and the corresponding data was extracted. To be able to analyze the 24 papers, there was a need to classify and sub-classify them in more ways than just according to the framework defined in Section 2. For this purpose, further criteria for classifying the papers were defined based on what information was available in the papers (i.e. research areas and trends). When needed, the topics were updated or clarified during the classification and sub-classification processes.

2.7 Results

The data required for analysis was extracted by exploring the full-text of each paper. Table 1 presents the results of the search and the source of the documents. As mentioned before, after the papers exclusion process, total number of publications remained in 24. Table 2 includes the classification of papers with regards to the knowledge area.

Table 1. Results with and without filtering

Source	Relevant literature
EuroSPI Industrial Proceedings	3
ScienceDirect	6
ACM Digital Library	14
WOS (Web of Science)	14
IEEE Digital Library	25
SpringerLink	27
Total (with duplication)	89
Total (without duplication)	65
Total (after the inclusion/exclusion criteria)	24

Table 2. Classification of papers with regards to the knowledge area

Area	Topic	Relevant Studies	#
Education	Dissemination	[7], [8], [9]	3
Research	Generate further study proposals	[10], [11]	2
Research	New contributions	[12], [13], [14], [15], [16], [17], [18], [19], [20], [21], [22], [23], [24]	13
Research	Importance of the ISO/IEC 29110 in other related issues	[25]	1
Research	Validate the results of the study	[26], [27], [28], [29], [30]	5
		Total	24

3 Topics Influenced by the ISO/IEC 29110 Standard

3.1 Dissemination

In 2008, Laporte et al. [7] highlighted the importance of VSE. They summarized the efforts taken place in the ISO/IEC JTC1/SC7 Working Group in order to obtain the Technical Report TR 29110. Thereafter, separate documents were developed as part of the new ISO/IEC 29110 standard (e.g. ISO 29110-2, ISO 29110-4). Afterwards, Weiß et al. [8] included a brief description of the standard, and Buchalcevova [9] presented an Enterprise Architecture (EA) framework for VSEs and the ISO/IEC 29110. The latter author also outlined the existing relationships between EA and SPI (Software Process Improvement).

3.2 Generate Further Study Proposals

Ribaud et al. [10] proposed the incursion in new process areas, such as "Infrastructure and Support" for including in the future evolution of ISO/IEC 29110 Process Profiles. Meanwhile O'Connor and Laporte [11] highlighted the need for creating a lightweight flexible approach to the ISO/IEC 29110 standard process assessment.

3.3 New Contributions

Cruz Mendoza et al. [12] focused on the development of a e-learning-based tool, in order to help VSEs to get to know and understand SPI models, through the creation of a Deployment Package (DP) set in accordance to ISO/IEC 29110. The developed tool also serves as a mean for spreading and disseminating COMPETISOFT[2] as SPI model and the ISO/IEC 29110-5-1 as Software Process Development Model. Ribaud et al. [13] provided a simple knowledge management system intended to gather, link, and reuse knowledge about Software Engineering activities related to the ISO/IEC 29110. Varkoi [14] proposed a process assessment method for VSEs according to ISO/IEC 29110. Likewise, Ribaud and Saliou [15] presented the establishment a set of Base Practices conforming to the ISO/IEC 29110 Basic Profile and reduced from ISO 15504-5. Contribution made by O'Connor and Laporte [16] is centered on DPs and pilot projects initiatives, to evaluate these DPs and assist VSEs in understanding and exploring the potential of the ISO/IEC 29110. Ribaud and Saliou [17] proposed the use a semantic wiki for documentation management in VSEs, in the scope of the ISO/IEC 29110; to assist them both unlock the potential benefits of using software engineering standards and improve the documentation management infrastructure and processes. They also pretend to implement this proposition in the form of a pilot project. Takeuchi et al. [18] designed and developed a process assessment method based on the ISO/IEC 29110 and the ISO/IEC 15504 as framework. This method was later implemented in a VSE in order to evaluate its effectiveness. The assessments

---

[2] COMPETISOFT provides the Latin American software industry with a reference framework for improvement and certification of its software processes [4].

results were useful for identifying problems, issues and risks in low efforts. O'Connor and Laporte [19] presented the design and development of project management support documentation and their associated usage in early trials of ISO/IEC 29110. Boucher et al. [20] described an approach based on configurable workflows to assist VSEs in adopting ISO/IEC 29110 compliant processes. Wen and Rout [21] used Composition Trees (CT) as formal notation to compare ISO/IEC 29110 to its counterpart, the ISO/IEC 12207. They also proposed this approach to study, develop and implement software processes, such as the ones depicted in ISO/IEC 29110. Mas and Mesquida [22] proposed the use of the ISO/IEC 29110-5-1-2 Project Management process, complemented by the PMBOK (Project Management Body of Knowledge) Guide. Mas and Mesquida [23] also described the results obtained and lessons learned from the implementation of the ISO/IEC 29110 in four VSEs, grouped in a process improvement program. Finally, Garzás et al. [24] presented the use and adaptation of some ISO models to the creation of an organizational maturity model for the Spanish software industry using the latest versions of the ISO/IEC 15504, ISO/IEC 12207 and ISO/IEC 17021. According the authors this model has been created to comply with ISO standards such as ISO 9001 and ISO/IEC 27001, 20000 and 29110.

3.4 Provide Evidence of the Importance of the ISO/IEC 29110 in Other Related Issues

IEEE P730™/D8 Draft Standard for Software Quality Assurance Processes [25], in annex G, provides a mapping between IEEE 730 and ISO/IEC 29110 for VSEs. That means a description of the coverage of the IEEE 730 tasks by the ISO/IEC 29110 Basic profile. Authors evidenced that most of IEEE 730 software quality assurance activities are covered by ISO/IEC 29110 objective 7.

3.5 Validate the Results of the Study

Basri and O'Connor [26] presented a series of industry data collection studies. They concluded: (i) The acceptance level of any type or model of software quality or lifecycle standard in VSEs is a very low priority item, but the level of awareness of standards and potential benefits was high. (ii) The main reason for not adopting standards was a lack of customer requirement, a lack of resources and the perceived difficulties in defining an organizational process. (iii) The acceptance level of quality standard such as ISO among VSEs is still low even though the staff and management are knowledgeable and aware about the benefits of adopting such standards.

O'Connor and Laporte [27] outlined the ISO/IEC 29110 standard and the implementation of a series of pilot project initiative harnessing the DPs to assist VSEs in understanding the potential usage of this software process standard. They also highlighted the need for a lightweight flexible approach to process assessment. O'Connor [28] presented the results of a set of interviews with senior management in a series of development VSEs in Ireland, which were conducted to gauge their opinion, software attitude and sentiment towards the ISO/IEC 29110 standard. As result, none of the VSEs had plans to adopt any particular standard in their software development process, arguing either lack of acceptance or priority. Kasurinen et al. [29] presented a study made on seven game software development organizations. They concluded that these organizations mostly work ad hoc however the applicability of the ISO/IEC 29110 could be possible, but the model should support iterations, because the model might change throughout the development process. O'Connor and Sanders [30] presented results of implementing ISO/IEC 29110 (Basic profile part 5-1-2), using DPs in seven Irish VSEs. They concluded that VSEs have too much work to do, with too little time and people to do it; even more, some VSEs viewed the standard as an add-on task, not a way to do business. They also indicated the need of enhancing the mentoring and assessment labor with VSEs in order to adequately implement this type of programs.

4 Summary of Results

The relevance of the ISO/IEC 29110 standard leads to consider two major areas: education (dissemination) and research (validate the results of the study, new contributions, provide evidence of the importance of the standard in other related issues and generate further study proposals). In Figure 2, out of a total of 24 relevant studies, these can be classified as *new contributions* (54%), *validate the results of the study* (21%), *dissemination* (13%), *generate further study proposals* (8%), and *provide evidence of the importance of the ISO/IEC 29110 in other related issues* (4%). In figure 3, after reviewing the existent literature and classifying the papers on areas, one can also sub-classify them and see specific subject trends inside the analyzed publications. Around 42% of publications make special emphasis on developing *Software Process Assessment and Software Process Improvement models or methods for supporting the standard*. 58% refer to *deployment packages, pilot projects or implementation approaches*, 17% of *assessed articles encourage to the conclusion of remaining profiles or the creation of new profiles*, and finally, a 17% of publications refer to the *design, development or implementation of documentation and knowledge management (KM) tools* in order to support the adoption of the ISO/IEC 29110 standard by VSEs.

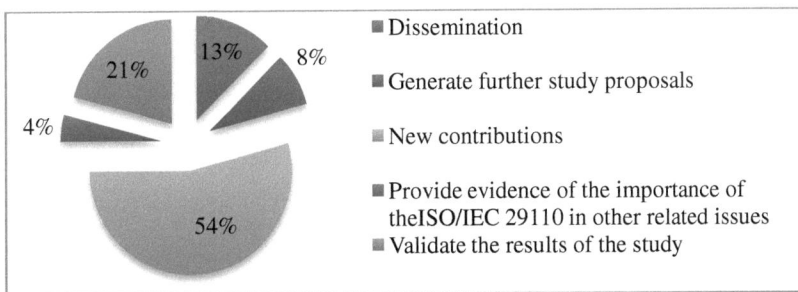

Fig. 2. Distribution of papers in various topics

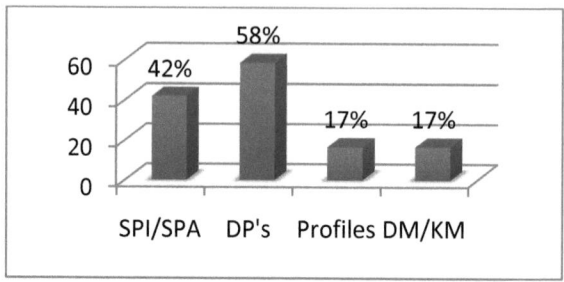

Fig. 3. Distribution of specific subject trends found on evaluated papers

5 Conclusions and Future Work

This paper presents a SLR of the ISO/IEC 29110 standard. The rigor of the search process is one factor that distinguishes this review from traditional ones. In order to perform an exhaustive search, a variety of sources were inspected. Nevertheless, one of the issues that could threaten the validity of results of this SLR is that other papers, which can report other types of scientific research, might be excluded because they are not available in the sources analyzed. As a result, almost all the papers selected are written by the authors of the standard thus may be slightly biased. However, the sources used are enough to generalize the findings in our study.

Results obtained from this SLR have allowed us obtaining a global vision of this standard, which should be investigated in detail due to its potential impact on the software industry. In fact, there is an increasing interest on the standard, although only the degree of adoption among VSEs will determine its scope and validity. As the papers reviewed during the performance of this study have evidenced, there is still too much work to be done. In this context, a clear finding of the review is that we need to increase both the number and quality of studies on ISO/IEC 29110 standard. Excluded papers provide an idea of the closely related areas: dynamic team, software development process knowledge, managerial commitment, task management, effort estimation methods, certification of VSE, integrated framework to guide SPI. Moreover, there are several challenges related to knowledge transfer [17].

Finally, despite the efforts that have been made, we see there is a backlog of research issues to be addressed such as the ones regarding to (i) Software Process Assessment & SPI, (ii) DPs/Pilot & implementation Projects, (iii) Conclusion of remaining profiles/Creation of new profiles and (iv) Documentation & KM tools for supporting the adoption of the standard.

References

1. Laporte, C., O'Connor, R., Fanmuy, G.: International systems and software engineering standards for very small entities. CrossTalk J. Def. Softw. Eng. 26, 28–33 (2013)
2. ISO/IEC: ISO/IEC TR 29110-5-1-1:2012 Software engineering – Lifecycle profiles for Very Small Entities (VSEs) Part 5-1-1: Management and engineering guide: Generic profile group: Entry profile, Geneva (2012)

3. Laporte, C.Y., April, A., Renault, A.: Applying ISO/IEC software engineering standards in small settings: historical perspectives and initial achievements. In: Proceedings of SPICE Conference, Luxembourg (2006)
4. Moreno-Campos, E.J., Sanchez-Gordón, M.-L., Colomo-Palacios, R.: ISO/IEC 29110: Current overview of the standard. Revista Procesos y Métricas 10, 24–40 (2013)
5. Varkoi, T., Mäkinen, T.: A Process Assessment Model for Very Small Software Entities. In: Rout, T., et al. (eds.) Proceedings of SPICE Conference, Italy (2010)
6. Sánchez Gordón, M.L., Colomo-Palacios, R., Amescua Seco, A.: Towards measuring the impact of the SPI Manifesto: a systematic review. In: Messnard, R., Ekert, D., Johansen, J., Christof, E. (eds.) 20th EuroSPI Industrial Proceedings, DELTA, Denmark (2013)
7. Laporte, C.Y., Alexandre, S., O'Connor, R.V.: A software engineering lifecycle standard for very small enterprises. In: O'Connor, R.V., Baddoo, N., Smolander, K., Messnarz, R. (eds.) EuroSPI 2008. CCIS, vol. 16, pp. 129–141. Springer, Heidelberg (2008)
8. Weiß, G., Pomberger, G., Beer, W., Buchgeher, G., Dorninger, B., Pichler, J., Prähofer, H., Ramler, R., Stallinger, F., Weinreich, R.: Software engineering–processes and tools. In: Hagenberg Research, pp. 157–235. Springer (2009)
9. Buchalcevova, A.: Software Process Improvement in Small Companies as a Path to Enterprise Architecture. In: Information Systems Development, pp. 243–253. Springer, New York (2013)
10. Ribaud, V., Saliou, P., O'Connor, R.V., Laporte, C.Y.: Software Engineering Support Activities for Very Small Entities. In: Riel, A., O'Connor, R., Tichkiewitch, S., Messnarz, R. (eds.) EuroSPI 2010. CCIS, vol. 99, pp. 165–176. Springer, Heidelberg (2010)
11. O'Connor, R.V., Laporte, C.Y.: Deploying Lifecycle Profiles for Very Small Entities: An Early Stage Industry View. In: O'Connor, R.V., Rout, T., McCaffery, F., Dorling, A. (eds.) SPICE 2011. CCIS, vol. 155, pp. 227–230. Springer, Heidelberg (2011)
12. Cruz Mendoza, R., Morales Trujillo, M., Morgado, C., Oktaba, H., Ibarguengoitia, G.E., Pino, F.J., Piattini, M.: Supporting the software process improvement in very small entities through e-learning: the HEPALE! Project. In: Mexican International Conference on Computer Science (ENC). IEEE Press, New York (2009)
13. Ribaud, V., Saliou, P., Laporte, C.Y.: Experience Management for Very Small Entities: Improving the Copy-paste Model. In: Fifth International Conference on Software Engineering Advances. IEEE Press, New York (2010)
14. Varkoi, T.: Process Assessment In Very Small Entities-An ISO/IEC 29110 Based Method. In: Seventh International Conference QUATIC. IEEE Press, New York (2010)
15. Ribaud, V., Saliou, P.: Process Assessment Issues of the ISO/IEC 29110 emerging standard. In: Proceedings of the 11th International Conference on Product Focused Software. ACM, New York (2010)
16. O'Connor, R.V., Laporte, C.Y.: Towards the provision of assistance for very small entities in deploying software lifecycle standards. In: Proceedings of the 11th International Conference on Product Focused Software. ACM, New York (2010)
17. Ribaud, V., Saliou, P.: Using a semantic wiki for documentation management in very small projects. In: Sánchez-Alonso, S., Athanasiadis, I.N. (eds.) MTSR 2010. CCIS, vol. 108, pp. 119–130. Springer, Heidelberg (2010)
18. Takeuchi, M., Kohtake, N., Shirasaka, S., Koishi, Y., Shioya, K.: Report on an assessment experience based on ISO/IEC 29110. In: 18th EuroSPI Industrial Proceedings. DELTA, Denmark (2011)
19. O'Connor, R.V., Laporte, C.Y.: Software Project Management in Very Small Entities with ISO/IEC 29110. In: Winkler, D., O'Connor, R.V., Messnarz, R., et al. (eds.) EuroSPI 2012. CCIS, vol. 301, pp. 330–341. Springer, Heidelberg (2012)

20. Boucher, Q., Perrouin, G., Deprez, J.-C., Heymans, P.: Towards Configurable ISO/IEC 29110-Compliant Software Development Processes for Very Small Entities. In: Winkler, D., O'Connor, R.V., Messnarz, R. (eds.) EuroSPI 2012. CCIS, vol. 301, pp. 169–180. Springer, Heidelberg (2012)
21. Wen, L., Rout, T.: Using Composition Trees to Validate an Entry Profile of Software Engineering Lifecycle Profiles for Very Small Entities (VSEs). In: Mas, A., Mesquida, A., Rout, T., O'Connor, R.V., Dorling, A. (eds.) SPICE 2012. CCIS, vol. 290, pp. 38–50. Springer, Heidelberg (2012)
22. Mas, A., Mesquida, A.L.: Software project management in small and very small entities. In: 8th Iberian Conference on Information Systems and Technologies (CISTI). IEEE Press, New York (2013)
23. Mesquida, A.L., Mas, A.: A Project Management improvement programme according to ISO/IEC 29110 and PMBOK. In: EuroSPI Industrial Proceedings. DELTA, Denmark (2013)
24. Garzás, J., Pino, F.J., Piattini, M., Fernández, C.M.: A Maturity Model for the Spanish Software Industry based on ISO standards. Comput. Stand. Interfaces 35, 616–628 (2013)
25. The Institute of Electrical and Electronics Engineers, Inc. (IEEE): IEEE P730™/D8 Draft Standard for Software Quality Assurance Processes, New York (2013)
26. Basri, S., O'Connor, R.V.: Understanding the perception of very small software companies towards the adoption of process standards. In: Riel, A., O'Connor, R., Tichkiewitch, S., Messnarz, R. (eds.) EuroSPI 2010. CCIS, vol. 99, pp. 153–164. Springer, Heidelberg (2010)
27. O'Connor, R.V., Laporte, C.Y.: Using ISO/IEC 29110 to Harness Process Improvement in Very Small Entities. In: O'Connor, R.V., Pries-Heje, J., Messnarz, R. (eds.) EuroSPI 2011. CCIS, vol. 172, pp. 225–235. Springer, Heidelberg (2011)
28. O'Connor, R.V.: Evaluating Management Sentiment towards ISO/IEC 29110 in Very Small Software Development Companies. In: Mas, A., Mesquida, A., Rout, T., O'Connor, R.V., Dorling, A. (eds.) SPICE 2012. CCIS, vol. 290, pp. 277–281. Springer, Heidelberg (2012)
29. Kasurinen, J., Laine, R., Smolander, K.: How Applicable Is ISO/IEC 29110 in Game Software Development? In: Heidrich, J., Oivo, M., Jedlitschka, A., Baldassarre, M.T. (eds.) PROFES 2013. LNCS, vol. 7983, pp. 5–19. Springer, Heidelberg (2013)
30. O'Connor, R.V., Sanders, M.: Lessons from a Pilot Implementation of ISO/IEC 29110 in a Group of Very Small Irish Companies. In: Woronowicz, T., Rout, T., O'Connor, R.V., Dorling, A. (eds.) SPICE 2013. CCIS, vol. 349, pp. 243–246. Springer, Heidelberg (2013)

A Systems Process Lifecycle Standard for Very Small Entities: Development and Pilot Trials

Claude Y. Laporte[1] and Rory V. O'Connor[2,3]

[1] École de technologie supérieure, Montréal, Canada
[2] Lero, the Irish Software Engineering Research Centre, Ireland
[3] Dublin City University, Dublin, Ireland
`Claude.Y.Laporte@etsmtl.ca`, `roconnor@computing.dcu.ie`

Abstract. Very small entities, organizations with up to 25 people, are very important to the worldwide economy. The products they develop are either developed specifically for a customer or are integrated into products made by larger enterprises. To address the needs of Very small entities, a set of standards and guides have been developed using the systems engineering lifecycle standard ISO/IEC/IEEE 15288 as the main framework. The systems engineering handbook, developed by the International Council on Systems Engineering (INCOSE), is used as the reference for the development of a set of systems engineering deployment packages. Two pilot projects, using the new ISO/IEC 29110 guide for systems engineering, are presented as well as a cost and savings analysis. Finally, the certification scheme is discussed as well as the future developments.

Keywords: VSE, ISO/IEC 29110, ISO, Standards.

1 Introduction

Today, the ability of organizations to compete, adapt, and survive depends increasingly on software. In 2010 a cellular phone contained 20 million lines of code and some cars had up to 100 million lines of code. Manufacturers depend increasingly on the components produced by their suppliers. A manufacturing chain of large mass-market products often has a pyramidal structure, for example, a large mass product manufacturer recently integrated into one of its products a part with an unknown software error that was produced by one of its 6,000 lower-level producers. This defective part resulted in a loss of over $200 million by the mass product manufacturer.

The term Very Small Entities (VSEs) has been defined as being *"an enterprise, organization, department or project having up to 25 people"* [1]. VSEs have unique characteristics, which make their business styles different to SMEs and therefore most of the management processes are performed through a more informal and less documented manner [2]. Furthermore there is an acknowledged lack of adoption of standards in small and very small companies, as the perception is that they have been developed for large software companies and not with the small organisation in mind

[3]. Accordingly the new standard ISO/IEC 29110 "Lifecycle profiles for Very Small Entities" is aimed at meeting the specific needs of VSEs [4]. The overall objective of this new standard is to assist and encourage small software organization in assessing and improving their software process and it is predicted that this new standard could encourage and assist small software companies in assessing their software development process. The approach [5] used to develop ISO/IEC 29110 started with the pre-existing international standards ISO/IEC 12207 and ISO/IEC 15504.

The working group behind the development of this standard is advocating the use of pilot projects as a mean to accelerate the adoption and utilization of ISO/IEC 29110 by VSEs [6]. Pilot projects are an important mean of reducing risks and learning more about the organizational and technical issues associated with the deployment of new software engineering practices [7]. To date a series of pilot projects for the software engineering profile standard have been completed in several countries with the results published in a variety of literature [8, 9, 10].

2 The Development of Systems Engineering Standards for VSEs

In 2008, after a presentation at the annual International Council on Systems Engineering (INCOSE) symposia it was agreed by the INCOSE Board of Directors, to setup up a working group to develop a set of standards and guides, for systems engineering VSEs, similar to the one developed for software VSEs. A new INCOSE working group, the Very Small and Medium-sized Enterprise (VSME) working group, was mandated in 2009 to apply systems engineering to product development for small and very small entities. The working group, created in April 2009, co-chaired by one co- author, is composed of INCOSE members from mainly from Canada, France, Germany, and the US. At the first meeting of the INCOSE WG, the project editor of ISO/IEC 29110 proposed an approach similar to that developed by WG24, i.e. the conducting of a survey, the development of a set of requirements, the creation of profiles (e.g. roadmaps), the development of deployment packages to facilitate the implementation of the standards and guides, and the conduct of pilot projects. The members of the working group agreed with this proposition. The initial goals of the INCOSE WG were to [11]:

- Improve or make product development efficient by using systems engineering methodology,
- Elaborate tailored practical guidance to apply to VSMEs in the context of the prime contractor or subcontractor of commercial products,
- Contribute to standardization

At the SC7 Plenary meeting in France in May 2011, the ISO/IEC 29110 project editor submitted, on behalf of Canada, a formal project proposal to develop a set of systems engineering standards for VSEs similar to the set developed for software VSEs. A draft systems engineering Management and Engineering guide for the Basic profile was attached to the formal proposal. The scope of this work includes the current scope of ISO/IEC/IEEE 15288, the associated guidance documents and other relevant SC7 Standards such as ISO/IEC/IEEE 15289 and ISO/IEC 29110. The project will produce Standards and Technical Reports (Guides), similar to the ISO/IEC 29110 set of Software documents for the Generic profile group (i.e. for VSEs developing non critical system), which establishes a common framework for describing assessable system engineering life cycle profiles for Very Small Entities (VSEs).

In August 2011, the proposal, as well as a draft systems engineering management and engineering guide for the Basic profile, were circulated for approval by the members of SC7. In September 2011, the proposal to develop SE standards for VSEs has been accepted by twenty countries. Nine countries made a commitment to participate in the development of the new ISO Systems Engineering standard.

Instead of developing a complete set of 5 documents, as illustrated in table 3, similar to the ones developed for software, it was proposed by the project editor to broaden scope of existing Part 1- Overview, Part 2- Framework and Part 3- Assessment guide to cover also systems engineering while Part 4- Profile specifications and Part 5- Management and engineering guide would be specific to systems engineering.

In November 2011, WG24 met in Ireland to launch the official development of the systems engineering ISs and TRs for VSEs. Delegates from Brazil, Canada, France, Japan, Thailand, United States and INCOSE participated to the first meeting. A draft was sent for a round of review within ISO in January 2012. More than 450 comments have been submitted by seven countries. A new version was sent for a second round of review in December 2012. Less than 150 comments have been submitted. The Management and engineering guide for the Basic Profile has been published by ISO in 2014.

The Basic profile, as illustrated in Figure 1, is composed of two processes: a Project Management (PM) process and a System definition and Realization (SR) process. The PM process uses the Acquirer's Statement of Work to elaborate the Project Plan. If there is no statement of work available from the customer, the PM, in collaboration with the Work Team, has to clarify the basis to develop the Statement of Work. The PM project assessment and control tasks compare the project progress against the Project Plan and actions are taken to eliminate deviations or incorporate changes to the Project Plan. The PM project closure activity ensures delivery of the product (new or modified product), produced by SR (System definition and Realization) process, and gets the Acquirer's acceptance to formalize the end of the project. A Project Repository is established to save the work products and to control its versions during the project.

It is to be noted that the ISO/IEC 29110 SE standards and guides are not intended to dictate the use of different lifecycles such as: waterfall, iterative, incremental, evolutionary or agile. The ISO/IEC 29110 systems engineering standards and guides have been developed to work hand-in-hand with the published ISO/IEC 29110 software engineering standards and guides.

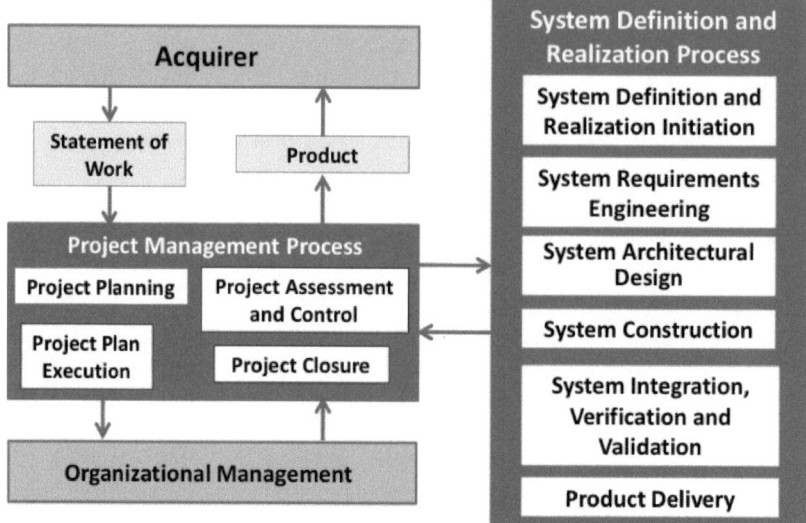

Fig. 1. Processes of the systems engineering Basic Profile

2.1 Project Management Process of the Systems Engineering Basic Profile

As defined in ISO/IEC 29110, the purpose of the Project Management (PM) process is to establish and carry out in a systematic way the tasks of the system development, which allows complying with the project's objectives in the expected quality, time and cost. The objectives of the ISO/IEC 29110-5-62 Project Management Process of the Basic profile are:

- **PM.O1.** The Project Plan, the Statement of Work (SOW) and commitments are reviewed and accepted by both the Acquirer and the Project Manager. The Tasks and Resources necessary to complete the work are sized and estimated.
- **PM.O2.** Progress of the project is monitored against the Project Plan and recorded in the Progress Status Record. Corrections to remediate problems and deviations from the plan are taken when project targets are not achieved. Closure of the project is performed to get the Acquirer acceptance documented in the Acceptance Record.
- **PM.O3.** Change Requests are addressed through their reception and analysis. Changes to system requirements are evaluated by the project team for cost, schedule, risks and technical impact.
- **PM.O4.** Review meetings with the Work Team and the Acquirer, suppliers are held. Agreements are registered and tracked.
- **PM.O5.** Risk Management Approach is developed. Risks are identified, analyzed, prioritized, and monitored as they develop and during the conduct of the project. Resources to manage the risks are determined.

- **PM.O6.** A Product Management Strategy is developed. Items of Product are identified, defined and baselined. Modifications and releases of the items are controlled and made available to the Acquirer and Work Team. The storage, handling and delivery of the items are controlled.
- **PM.O7.** Quality Assurance is performed to provide assurance that work products and processes comply with the Project Plan and System Requirements Specifications.
- **PM.O8.** A Disposal Management Approach is developed to end the existence of a system entity.

To show the links between ISO/IEC/IEEE 15288 and the objectives of the PM process, we illustrate in table 1 the outcomes of the project planning process and the measurement process of ISO15288 used to develop objective 1 of the PM Process of ISO/IEC 29110. Notice that just a subset of the Project Planning and Measurement processes of ISO 15288 has been selected for the Basic profile.

Table 1. Links between the ISO15288 outcomes and the PM.01 process

6.3.1 Project Planning Process
a) Project plans are available;
e) Plans for the execution of the project are activated.
6.3.7 Measurement Process
a) The information needs of technical and management
[ISO/IEC 15288, 6.3.1, 6.3.7]

2.2 Modifications to the Software PM process of the ISO 29110 Software Engineering Basic Profile

Few modifications/additions were made to the Software engineering Basic profile to develop the PM process of the SE Basic profile. The role of Customer was replaced by the role of Acquirer. Two tasks were added: *Define the system breakdown structure* and *Identify and document a disposal management approach*. Two tasks were modified: *Identify and document risks* was replaced by *Identify and document a Risk Management Approach*; the *Version Control Strategy* was replaced by *Configuration Management Strategy*.

2.3 System Definition and Realization Process of the Systems Engineering Basic Profile

The purpose of the System Definition and Realization (SR) process is the systematic performance of the analysis, design, construction, integration, verification, and validation activities for new or modified system according to the specified requirements. The seven objectives of the SR process are [12]:

- **SR.O1.** Tasks of the activities are performed through the accomplishment of the current Project Plan.
- **SR.O2.** System requirements are defined, analyzed for correctness and testability, approved by the Acquirer, baselined and communicated.
- **SR.O3.** The System architectural design is developed and baselined. It describes the System elements and internal and external interfaces of them. Consistency and traceability to system requirements are established.
- **SR.O4.** System elements defined by the design are produced or acquired. Acceptance tests are defined and performed to verify the consistency with requirements and the design. Traceability to the requirements and design are established.
- **SR.O5.** System elements are integrated. Defects encountered during integration are corrected and consistency and traceability to System Architecture are established.
- **SR.O6.** A System Configuration, as agreed in the Project Plan, and that includes the engineering artifacts is integrated, baselined and stored at the Project Repository. Needs for changes to the Product are detected and related change requests are initiated.
- **SR.O7.** Verification and Validation Tasks of all required work products are performed using a defined criteria to achieve consistency among output and input products in each activity. Defects are identified, and corrected; records are stored in the Verification/Validation Reports.

2.4 Modifications to the Software Implementation Process of the ISO 29110 Software Basic Profile

Some significant changes were made to the software implementation (SI) process of the ISO 29110 basic profile to produce the System Definition and Realization process (SR) of the SE basic profile: new system activities and tasks were added, irrelevant SW activities were suppressed, new system roles were defined. Also, new system documents were added as the result of the addition/modification to the tasks.

2.5 Roles for Systems Engineering and Management

The Analyst role was replaced by the Systems Engineer role. The Customer was replaced by the Acquirer and the Stakeholders. The Programmer was replaced by the Developer. Two new roles were also defined: the IVV (Integration, Verification and Validation) Engineer and the Supplier.

2.6 Product Description

Product descriptions are based on ISO/IEC/IEEE 15289 [13] Information Items with some exceptions. Nine product descriptions were added to the software basic profile: Data Model, Disposed System, Integration Report, IVV Plan, IVV Procedure, Justification Document, Systems Engineering Management Plan, System Design

Document, System Element, System Element Requirements Specification, and System Maintenance Document. The product descriptions were modified to align them with the system engineering context.

2.7 Deployment Packages to Support the Systems Engineering Basic Profile

Members of the INCOSE VSME working group defined a set of guidelines explaining in more detail the processes defined in the Basic profile. These guidelines are freely accessible to VSEs on the internet as a collection of Deployment Packages. Since the INCOSE Handbook is a 'how to' document, it has been used to develop the set of DPs. Figure 8 illustrates the proposed set of SE Deployment Packages for the Basic Profile which are available, at no cost to members of INCOSE, on the Internet and on the INCOSE VSME working group page.

A first commercial software solution, using the deployment packages, has been developed to facilitate the implementation of the Basic Profile. The tool is based on the well-known Atlassian tool suite. The solution facilitates the role of the project manager and enhances team collaboration. It has the following characteristics:

- Project artifacts shared in one place
- Project documentation is managed
- Project progress dashboard can be generated
- Integrated with Model-based solutions

The solution provides project artifacts and documentation templates. It enforces the project management process, the system definition, the realization process and it facilitates progress tracking. When using a model-based approach, project artifacts such as: requirements, tests, changes and model artifacts, can be integrated and traced. The solution is already available in different languages such as English, French and Spanish.

3 Pilot Projects Conducted in Engineering Enterprises

So far, two systems engineering organizations implemented the ISO/IEC 29110. We shortly describe below two applications of the Engineering and Management Guide: one in a start-up VSE and one in a large engineering firm.

A first implementation project has been conducted in a start-up VSE specialized in the integration of interactive, communication systems such as Public Address, Visual Information and Media, Vehicle Wayside Communications, Networking and Radio and safety systems such as CCTV, Fire Management, Access Control and Intrusion Detection, Perimeter Protection, Emergency Intercom, in the public transportation field such as trains and buses. In this domain, customers often require a CMMI® maturity level (SEI 2010), such as a CMMI level 2 for sub-system suppliers. In 2012, the VSE was composed of just 4 professionals. It was felt that implementing the process areas of the level 2 of CMMI was too demanding at that time. The company decided to implement the draft version of ISO/IEC 29110 systems engineering Basic profile as a foundation for its development work. It was felt that, once the processes would have been documented and implemented in a few projects, the VSE could, if required, perform a gap analysis between the CMMI level 2 practices and the Basic profile and implement the practices needed for a level 2 assessment.

A large engineering firm has implemented a program to define and implement project management processes for their small-scale and medium-scale projects. The firm already had a robust and proven process to manage their large-scale projects. Their projects are classified into three categories as illustrated in Table 2.

Table 2. Classification of projects by the engineering firm [10]

	Small project	Medium project	Large project
Duration	< 2 months	>2 and <8 months	>8 months
Team size	<= 4 people	4-8 people	>8 people
No. engineering specialties	1	>1	Many
Engineering fees	$5,000 - $70,000	$50,000 - $350,000	>$350,000

The engineering firm documented the business goals, as illustrated in Table 3, as well as the problems that one division of the company wished to solve. The division used the project management process of the Entry profile of ISO/IEC 29110 to document their small-scale project management process and they used the project management process of the Basic profile to document their medium-scale project management process.

Table 3. Division's business goals [10]

ID No.	Description
O-1	Facilitate the integration of new project managers
O-2	Achieve a global customer satisfaction level of 80 %.
O-3	Meet the deadlines and costs planned for the projects, within a margin of 5%.
O-4	Reduce resource overload by 10 %.
O-5	Reduce time delays to one week and cost overruns to 5 % of the initial budget.
O-6	Reduce corrective work during the quality control phase by 10 %.
O-7	Reduce non-chargeable time for resources by 10 %.

ISO has developed "The ISO Methodology to assess and communicate the economic benefits of standards" [14]. This methodology was used, by the engineering firm, to estimate the anticipated costs and benefits over a period of three years. The estimates were made by the sponsors of this process definition project. Figure 2 illustrates the value chain of the company.

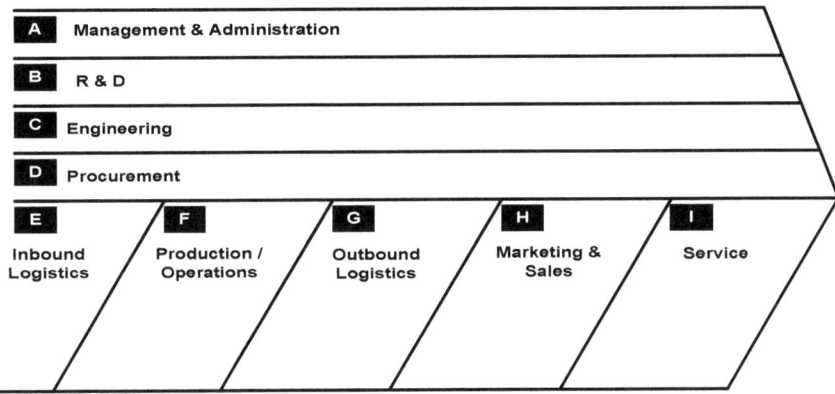

Fig. 2. Value chain of the company

An estimate of anticipated costs and benefits over a period of three years was made by the improvement program project sponsors. Table 4 shows the results for the first three years of this cost/benefit estimation.

Table 4. Costs (in $CAD) and benefits estimations from implementing ISO/IEC 29110 [10]

	Year 1	Year 2	Year 3	Total
Cost to implement &maintain	59,600	50 100	50,100	159,800
Net benefits	255,500	265,000	265,000	785,500

The engineering firm is planning to document and implement their systems engineering processes for the small-scale and medium scale projects once the ISO/IEC 29110 systems engineering guide of the Basic profile gets published by ISO.

4 ISO/IEC 29110 Certification of VSEs

For most enterprises, but in particular for VSEs, international certifications can enhance credibility, competitiveness and access to national and international markets. Brazil has led the development of an ISO/IEC 29110 certification process. An ISO/IEC 29110 auditor should be competent in auditing techniques, have expertise in ISO/IEC 29110 and have experience in systems or software development. For VSEs, such a certification should not be too expensive and short. The certification process has been successfully piloted in a few Brazilian VSEs. For these pilots, it took about 4 staff-days of work by the auditors. A first auditor course was conducted in English in Dublin in November 2013.

The certification scheme, described in ISO/IEC 29110-3-2 document [15] is based on ISO Standards on Conformity Assessment. As illustrated in figure 3, it is a four-stage certification process.

WG24 has initially developed the Systems Engineering and Management Guide since this document describes in a useful way for VSEs wishing to implement the project management and system definition and realization processes. WG24 has started, in 2014, the development of the Systems Engineering Basic profile specification document, i.e. ISO/IEC 29110-4-6. This document will be an international standard and will be required by the auditors when they perform an ISO/IEC 29110 audit. This standard should reach publication stage in 2015.

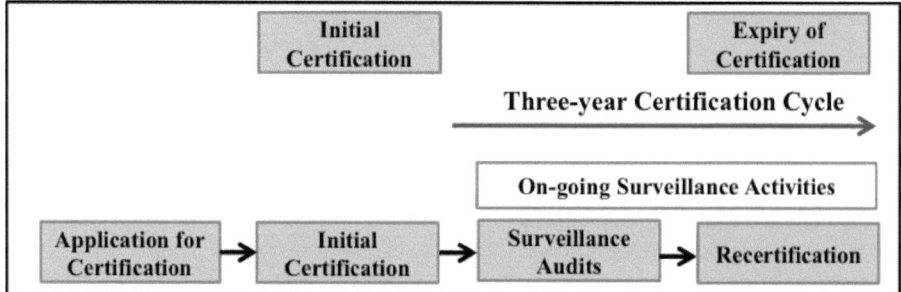

Fig. 3. ISO/IEC 29110 Four-Stage Certification Process (adapted [15])

5 Development of the Entry Profile for Systems Engineering

VSEs targeted by the Entry Profile are VSEs working on small projects (e.g. at most six person-months effort) and for start-up VSEs. The approach used by WG24 to develop this profile was to use, as the baseline, the published software Entry Profile and the published systems engineering Basic profile keeping in mind that the 2 Entry profiles should be about of the same size and should have the same structure. Also, if a VSE develops a system having a software component, it could use the SE Entry profile to guide the development of the system and use the software Entry profile to guide the development of the software component.

At the November 2013 WG24 meeting in Dublin, the delegates, of the systems engineering sub-working group of ISO WG24, have reviewed the 2 tables and made modifications based on consensus. Then, they analyzed the PM and SR processes of the SE Basic profile and deleted/added/modified text of the activities, tasks, roles and products to produce a first draft of the SE Engineering and Management guide Entry profile. The document has been sent for a first review cycle within ISO at the beginning of 2014. The comments received have been processed at the May 2014 meeting of WG24 in Australia. A new version of the Entry profile will be sent for a second review cycle in August 2014. We expect this second review cycle to generate only minor comments. These comments will be processed and the document should be ready for publication by ISO in 2015.

6   Conclusions and Future Work

Industry recognizes the contribution of VSEs in terms of the valuable products and services they offer. A large majority of organisations worldwide have up to 25 people. The collection of ISO/IEC JTC1 SC7 standards was not easily applied in VSEs, which generally found standards difficult to understand and implement.

After having developed ISs and TRs for VSEs involved in the development of software, WG24 developed the ISO/IEC 29110 systems engineering Basic profile management and engineering guide. Then members of the INCOSE VSME WG developed a set of Deployment Packages to help implement the Basic profile. WG24 started the development of the Entry profile for systems engineering. Once a stable version of the SE Entry profile is available, the INCOSE VSME working group will be able to start the development of the deployment packages to support the Systems Engineering Entry Profile. Once the ISO/IEC 29110 software Intermediate and Advanced profiles are ready, the development of the two matching systems engineering profiles for VSEs will start [16].

Since many VSEs developing systems are also involved in the development of critical systems, WG24 and the INCOSE VSME Working Group will conduct an analysis to determine if a set of systems/software engineering standards for VSEs developing critical systems should be developed.

Additional information: The following website provides more information, as well as articles by WG24 members and deployment packages for software and systems engineering: http://profs.logti.etsmtl.ca/claporte/English/VSE/index.html

Acknowledgments. This work is supported, in part, by Science Foundation Ireland grant 03/CE2/I303_1 to Lero, the Irish Software Engineering Research Centre (www.lero.ie).

References

1. Laporte, C.Y., Alexandre, S., O'Connor, R.V.: A Software Engineering Lifecycle Standard for Very Small Enterprises. In: O'Connor, R.V., Baddoo, N., Smolander, K., Messnarz, R. (eds.) EuroSPI 2008. CCIS, vol. 16, pp. 129–141. Springer, Heidelberg (2008)
2. O'Connor, R.V., Basri, S., Coleman, G.: Exploring Managerial Commitment towards SPI in Small and Very Small Enterprises. In: Riel, A., O'Connor, R., Tichkiewitch, S., Messnarz, R. (eds.) EuroSPI 2010. CCIS, vol. 99, pp. 268–279. Springer, Heidelberg (2010)
3. O'Connor, R.V., Coleman, G.: Ignoring 'Best Practice': Why Irish Software SMEs are rejecting CMMI and ISO 9000. Australasian Journal of Information Systems 16(1) (2009)
4. O'Connor, R.V., Laporte, C.Y.: Deploying Lifecycle Profiles for Very Small Entities: An Early Stage Industry View. In: O'Connor, R.V., Rout, T., McCaffery, F., Dorling, A. (eds.) SPICE 2011. CCIS, vol. 155, pp. 227–230. Springer, Heidelberg (2011)

5. O'Connor, R.V., Laporte, C.Y.: Using ISO/IEC 29110 to Harness Process Improvement in Very Small Entities. In: O'Connor, R.V., Pries-Heje, J., Messnarz, R. (eds.) EuroSPI 2011. CCIS, vol. 172, pp. 225–235. Springer, Heidelberg (2011)
6. O'Connor, R.V., Laporte, C.Y.: Towards the provision of assistance for very small entities in deploying software lifecycle standards. In: Proceedings of the 11th International Conference on Product Focused Software (PROFES 2010). ACM (2010)
7. Laporte, C.Y., O'Connor, R.V., Fanmuy, G.: International Systems and Software Engineering Standards for Very Small Entities. CrossTalk - The Journal of Defense Software Engineering 26(3), 28–33 (2013)
8. O'Connor, R.V.: Evaluating Management Sentiment Towards ISO/IEC 29110 in Very Small Software Development Companies. In: Mas, A., Mesquida, A., Rout, T., O'Connor, R.V., Dorling, A. (eds.) SPICE 2012. CCIS, vol. 290, pp. 277–281. Springer, Heidelberg (2012)
9. Ribaud, V., Saliou, P., O'Connor, R.V., Laporte, C.Y.: Software Engineering Support Activities for Very Small Entities. In: Riel, A., O'Connor, R., Tichkiewitch, S., Messnarz, R. (eds.) EuroSPI 2010. CCIS, vol. 99, pp. 165–176. Springer, Heidelberg (2010)
10. Laporte, C.Y., Chevalier, F., Maurice, J.-C.: Improving Project Management for Small Projects, ISO Focus+. International Organization for Standardization, pp. 52–55 (February 2013)
11. INCOSE VSME Project Charter (2009), https://connect.incose.org/tb/vsme/default.aspx
12. ISO/IEC TR 29110-5-6-2:2014 - Systems and Software Engineering – Systems Engineering Lifecycle Profiles for Very Small Entities (VSEs) - Management and engineering guide: Generic profile group: Basic profile, International Organization for Standardization/International Electrotechnical Commission: Geneva, Switzerland. Available at no cost from ISO at: http://standards.iso.org/ittf/PubliclyAvailableStandards
13. ISO/IEC/IEEE 15289:2011, Systems and software engineering - Content of systems and software life cycle process information products (Documentation), International Organization for Standardization/International Electrotechnical Commission: Geneva, Switzerland
14. ISO/IEC 29110-2:2011 Software Engineering - Lifecycle Profiles for Very Small Entities (VSEs) - Part 2: Framework and Taxonomy, Geneva: International Organization for Standardization (ISO) (2011), Available from ISO at: http://www.iso.org/iso/iso_catalogue/catalogue_tc/catalogue_detail.htm?csnumber=51151
15. ISO/IEC PDTR 29110-3-2 - Systems and Software Engineering – Systems and software engineering– Lifecycle profiles for Very Small Entities (VSEs) - Part 3-2: Conformity assessment guide, International Organization for Standardization/International Electrotechnical Commission: Geneva, Switzerland
16. Laporte, C.Y., Marvin, J., Houde, R.: Systems Engineering International Standards and Support Tools for Very Small Enterprises. In: 24th Annual International Symposium of INCOSE (International Council on Systems Engineering), Las Vegas, USA, June 30-July 3 (2014)

An Integrated Environment to Support Project Management in VSEs

Antoni-Lluís Mesquida, Antonia Mas, and Adelaida Delgado

University of the Balearic Islands
Ctra. de Valldemossa, Km. 7.5. 07122 Palma de Mallorca, Spain
{antoni.mesquida,antonia.mas,adelaida.delgado}@uib.es

Abstract. Small software development companies need to have simple but useful tools in order to perform an efficient management of their projects and become more productive in their daily work. From the demand of four small software development companies, clustered in a joint process improvement programme for the implementation of the ISO/IEC 29110 standard, we selected, proposed and agreed a set of software tools to support both collaborative work and project management tasks. In this paper, an integrated environment for project management that brings together a set of tools supporting some of the PMBOK® Guide good practices is presented. This environment is composed of both transversal tools, such as office suites, social bookmarking services or virtual storage services, and specific applications for managing project scope, time and communications.

Keywords: Project Management, Tools, Very Small Entities (VSE), Software Process Improvement (SPI), ISO/IEC 29110, PMBOK®.

1 Introduction

Software development small and very small enterprises (VSEs) have the challenge of handling multiple small-scale, fast-moving projects allowing little room for unwieldy management processes, but still requiring an efficient and straightforward monitoring process [1]. Moreover due to the small number of people involved in the project and the organization, most of the management processes are performed through an informal way and less documented [2]. The perception of heavyweight processes, especially in terms of documentation, cost and nonalignment with current development process, are among the reasons why the companies did not plan to adopt a lifecycle standard in the short to medium term [3].

VSEs use project management both to manage operations, to deliver tailored or bespoke products to customers, and manage innovation and growth [4]. However, these companies usually do not have efficient tools or project management processes suited to managing small-scale projects [1]. Project management tools and techniques are being used to a limited extent by high-technology SMEs [5].

We have been able to validate and be aware of all these distinctive features of software development projects in VSEs during our participation in a joint process improvement programme involving a set of four very small companies. Our initial aim was to support them both in the definition of the best practices that should follow their software development processes, and in the management of their projects [6]. From our experience in implementing process improvement programmes in VSEs [7-9] and, given the nature of these organizations, we suggested to adopt the ISO/IEC 29110 international standard for software process improvement, since it is specific for VSEs and completely fitted their needs [10, 11].

The ISO/IEC 29110-5-1-2 standard [12] is aimed at providing a management and engineering guide which is applicable to the vast majority of small and very small entities that do not develop critical software. This standard defines two processes, Software Implementation and Project Management. The purpose of the Software Implementation process is the systematic performance of the analysis, design, construction, integration and tests activities for new or modified software products according to the specified requirements. The purpose of the Project Management process is to establish and carry out in a systematic way the tasks of the software implementation project, which allows complying with the project's objectives in the expected quality, time and cost. Since the companies participating in this programme did already perform many of the tasks proposed by the Software Implementation process, the main goal of our work supporting these organizations was focused on establishing the project management activities.

The main results of the joint process improvement programme were on the one hand, the definition of a standardized set of processes and procedures and, on the other, the development of a Process Asset Library to support project management good practices. In order to provide detailed knowledge about project management inputs, outputs and best techniques, the Project Management Body of Knowledge (PMBOK®) Guide [13] was used to complement the ISO/IEC 29110-5-1-2 standard.

The PMBOK® Guide is a collection of recognised good practices that are widely applied by project management professionals and practitioners for the successful management of projects around the world. The project management good practices in the PMBOK® Guide cover the entire project lifecycle, from proposal to delivery, final acceptance and closing. The standard defines 47 project management processes which are grouped into five categories known as Project Management Process Groups: Initiating, Planning, Executing, Monitoring and Controlling, and Closing. Moreover, the PMBOK® Guide recognises ten Knowledge Areas typical of almost all projects: Project Integration management, scope management, time management, cost management, quality management, human resources management, communications management, risk management, procurement management and stakeholder management.

In parallel with the implementation of the ISO/IEC 29110-5-1-2 standard, and from the demand to provide the participant companies with supporting software tools, we were trying different software to facilitate the development and management of the assets in the Process Asset Library. These tools should follow the techniques recommended by the PMBOK® Guide. Currently, in the scope of the joint programme, which is still in force, we have developed a pilot project in which 11 project managers in the 4 participant companies use the proposed software supporting toolset for managing projects.

As an individual can design and create a Personal Learning Environment (PLE) that integrates a set of tools, services and links needed to achieve different goals linked to the acquisition of new skills, a project manager can also create a personal environment for project management that integrates the most useful software tools to support the entire project life cycle.

This paper presents an *Integrated environment to support project management in VSEs*, which has been defined using Symbaloo [14]. This environment has been designed to operate, from a single interface, all digital resources and Web 2.0 tools that regularly use a project manager either from the computer, tablet or mobile phone.

The paper is structured as follows: section 2 presents the software tools to support the project management process asset creation and the application of some techniques recommended by the PMBOK® Guide. Section 3 describes the integrated environment that brings together all the identified software tools. Finally, in section 4 the conclusions are presented.

2   Tools to Support Project Management in VSEs

The tools that the *Integrated environment to support project management in VSEs* brings together can be grouped into different categories. On the one hand, some of these tools are transversal, that is, they have a general purpose and can be used in any management area. More specifically, we refer to:

- Office tools. Word processors to elaborate templates (such as a communications plan or a progress status record), tools to create presentations (such as the kick-off presentation), spreadsheets, among others. Some of the office tools we recommend are Zoho Docs [15] and OpenOffice [16].
- Social bookmarking tools. They allow saving and sharing links to blogs and websites of interest. This category includes Diigo [17], Mister Wong [18] and Citeulike [19].
- Cloud computing tools. They offer storage and resource sharing services. The most commonly used are Dropbox [20], Google Drive [21] and OneDrive (formerly SkyDrive) [22].

However, other tools are specific for a particular management area. Concretely, we have compiled software to support processes of the following areas: scope management, time management and communications management. The following subsections details the selected tools for each of these three management areas.

2.1   Tools for Scope Management

One of the actions proposed by the PMBOK® Guide related to defining the scope of a project consists in collecting all the relations with other past or future projects in the organizational portfolio. To capture these relations among projects is recommended to develop flow charts and relations diagrams using a tool such as Flowchart [23]. Flowchart is an online multi-user and real-time collaboration service.

The next action to be carried out to define the project scope is to identify the requirements of the project, including both the project restrictions (infrastructure needs, deadlines, etc.) and the product requirements. All these requirements can be collected using the Mind Mapping technique. A very simple and intuitive mind mapping tool is FreeMind [24]. Figure 1 presents an example of mind map with all the requirements of a software development project.

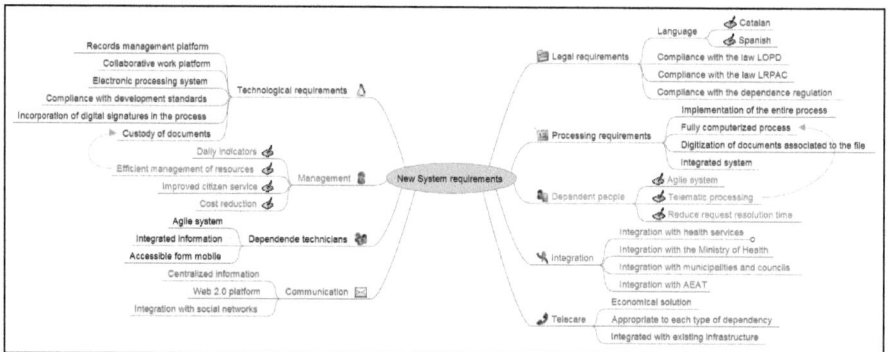

Fig. 1. Example of mind map created in FreeMind

Another action of this management area consists in defining groups of tasks to be performed by the team, both for executing all software engineering tasks and for managing their execution. The PMBOK® Guide recommends using the Work Breakdown Structure (WBS) technique in order to obtain a hierarchical representation in work packages for all the project tasks. A software tool for this type of diagrams is WBS Chart Pro [25]. Figure 2 shows a WBS created in this tool.

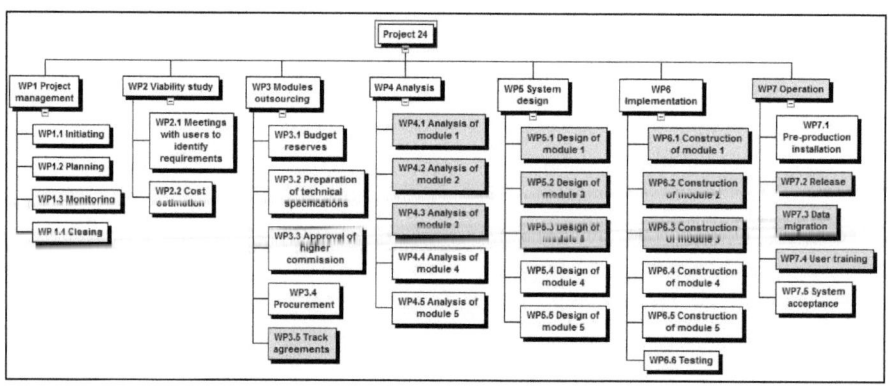

Fig. 2. Example of WBS created in WBS Chart Pro

2.2 Tools for Time Management

The work packages identified in the WBS must be broken down into more specific tasks. In addition, milestones should be set, which can match with the provision of a product or service by a contracted provider or with the delivery of a release to the customer. Once the tasks list is established, these tasks must be sequenced and distributed on the calendar. The end result of this process is a schedule diagram showing the timing of all planned tasks.

Google Calendar [26] can be used to set the work calendar. This tool allows generating diverse calendars containing all work days for different project stakeholders. These calendars can be shared with internal project team members (who will be able to edit and make changes on them) and other guests (with only query options).

A free tool for sequencing tasks and setting milestones is Gantter [27]. This tool can be used to develop a Gantt chart with all temporal dependencies between tasks. Additionally, it allows allocating resources to tasks in order to indicate the team member who is going to execute it or the stakeholder who will supervise it. Even the project manager can also assign materials and infrastructure resources that the assigned member must have to perform that task. Figure 3 shows the Gantt diagram created in Gantter with the tasks and milestones for a software development project.

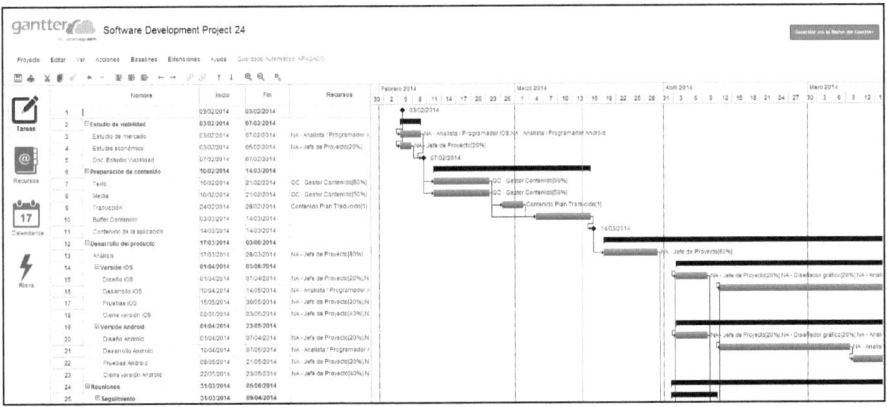

Fig. 3. Example of Gantt diagram created in Gantter

Other tools for managing task and time assignments are Asana [28] and Trello [29], both with web and mobile devices applications. Asana is a collaborative tool to facilitate users or teams planning and managing their projects and tasks. Each team has a workspace. Workspaces contain projects and these, in turn, contain tasks. Asana provides many features, such as personal projects, tasks, tags, notes, comments and a mailbox that organizes and updates information in real time. Figure 4 shows the list of tasks in a project (on the left side of the image) and detailed information for the selected task (right side).

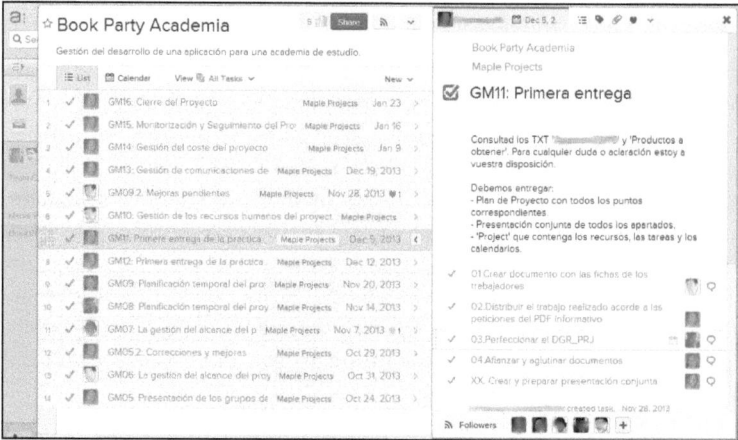

Fig. 4. General view of a project in Asana

Trello uses the Kanban project management paradigm. Projects are represented by boards containing lists. These lists contain cards (matching with the project tasks on the Gantt chart). The cards are moved from one list to another reflecting, for example, the flow of a task since it is planned until it has been executed. Users can be assigned to cards. Each card can store different attributes of a task such as: description, deadline, list of activities, comments, etc. Trello also allows attaching files required for the execution of the identified tasks, linking them to a Dropbox or Google Drive account. Figure 5 shows the board for a project with four tasks lists.

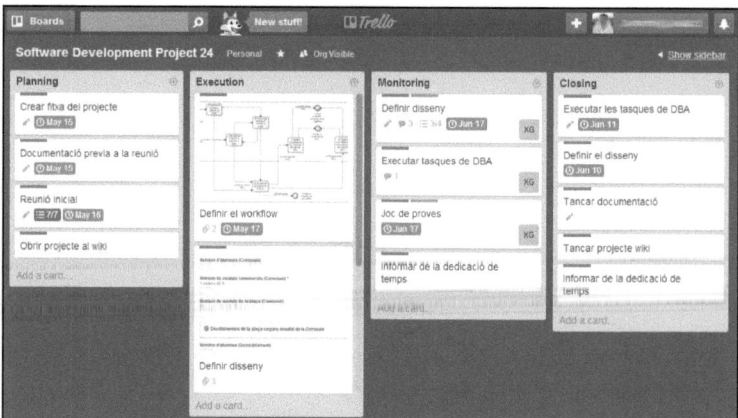

Fig. 5. A project board in Trello

2.3 Tools for Communication Management

Another need when planning a project is to define all communication procedures both internal within the team and external with customers and other stakeholders.

Doodle [30] is a very useful tool when planning meetings, such as requirements elicitation meetings with customers or internal coordination meetings. This tool allows users to create a poll to determine the best date and time for the meeting. The survey administrator receives email alerts with votes and comments. Doodle can operate with several external calendar systems as Google Calendar, Microsoft Outlook, IBM Lotus Notes and Apple iCal. Figure 6 shows an example of a survey to plan a coordination meeting.

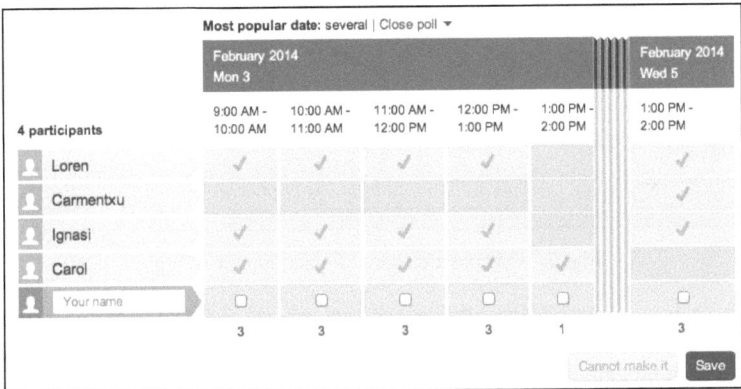

Fig. 6. Example of a survey for a coordination meeting in Doodle

Other tools that can be used for daily communication between the team components are Skype [31] and Google Hangouts [32]. These tools allow text, voice and video communications and file sending between users. They also offer screen sharing and remote desktop features.

There are different collaborative work tools that can be used to support and enhance communication and coordination among stakeholders. These tools can be used with two different objectives: to organize the internal tasks of the team, and to track the work progress of the different providers or other stakeholders. Some of the collaborative work tools that can be used to manage projects in VSEs are Wiggio [33], Redbooth (previously known as Teambox) [34] and TeamLab [35].

Wiggio is a free tool that is divided into three main sections: the groups and members bar, the work area and the utilities bar (providing different communication tools, document creation features and survey creation tools). The work area contains three tabs: *feed*, summarizing the activities that have taken place in the group, *folder*, with all files shared in the group, and *calendar*, which stores information about activities, meetings and planned or held events. A very useful feature is the alert system, which prior to a scheduled event occurs, reports it by email to the affected users. Wiggio supports integration with the calendars of Google Calendar, Microsoft Outlook, etc. Figure 7 shows the working area for a project team in Wiggio.

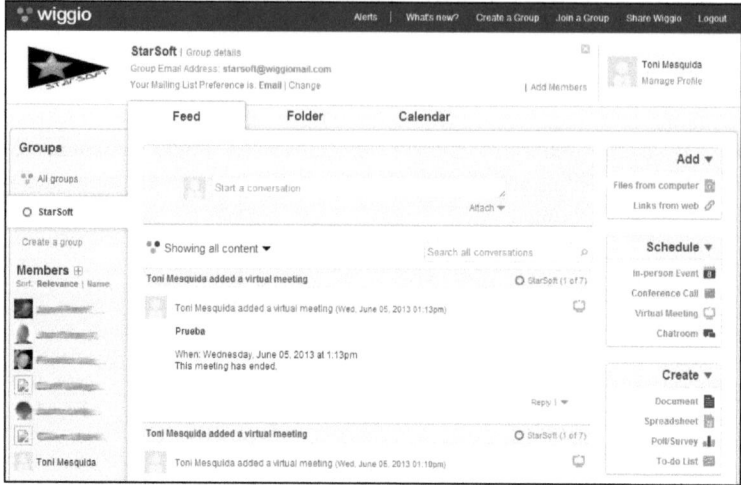

Fig. 7. Working area for a project team in Wiggio

Redbooth is another collaborative work tool which is free for teams of up to five users. It supports the creation of task lists to structure projects and, also, the definition of conversations that can be converted into activities, and, in turn, into deliverables. Notes feature allow sharing documentation within the team like a Wiki. In order to perform time control of each task, Redbooth has a time tracking system. It also allows file sharing in Dropbox or Google Drive. Figure 8 shows a view of the conversation feature.

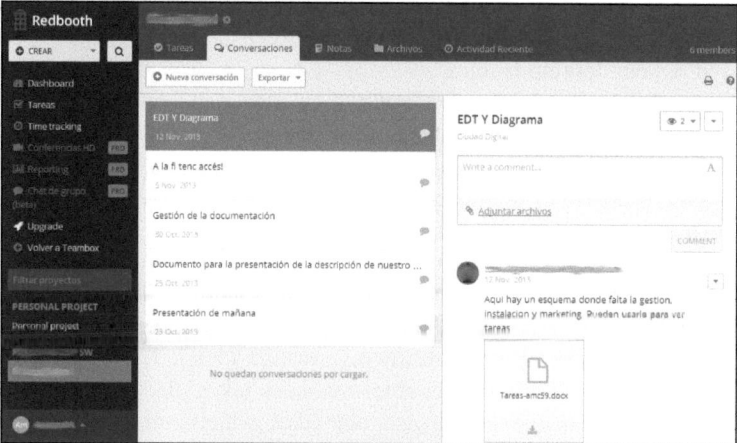

Fig. 8. Example of a team conversation in Redbooth

3 Integrated Environment to Support Project Management in VSEs

The *Integrated environment to support project management in VSEs* has been developed using the Symbaloo tool [14], which provides very useful features to visually create and organize links. This management environment integrates all the tools listed above for each of the knowledge areas described (Scope, Time and Communication Management). In addition, it also incorporates the transversal tools, such as office suites, social bookmarking tools, virtual storage services, content generators and social networks.

The Integrated environment is organized into blocks, to which the link to the resource is attached: video, feed, RSS news reader, etc. Each block can have a color, a title and an icon assigned. As many block pages (called *webmix*) as desired can be created. The *webmix* background can be customized. All blocks can be easily moved by dragging them with the mouse, offering the possibility to design the *webmix* as the company likes the most. An extension can be installed in the browser in order to automatically add links while browsing. The *webmix* can be kept private or be shared both publicly (appearing on Google and Bing search results) and with specific stakeholders.

Figure 9 provides a view of the *Integrated environment to support project management in VSEs* developed in Symbaloo. The transversal tools are grouped in the lower rows. The other tools are grouped by rows, one for each project management knowledge area.

Fig. 9. Main view of the Integrated environment to support project management in VSEs

4 Conclusion and Lessons Learned

In this paper, an *Integrated environment to support project management in VSEs* has been presented. This integrated environment is the result of a research in which we selected, proposed and agreed a set of tools to support both collaborative work and project management tasks.

The Integrated environment has been developed with a double objective. On the one hand, to promote project management good practices in small and very small software development companies. The authors of this article truly believe that planning in detail the scope of a project, estimating the time for each work package and task, and deciding which team member is better able to perform each task, provides an invaluable support not only so that every member can control the own work and be coordinated with the entire team, but also for the customer or other key stakeholders to know in detail all aspects of the progress of the project and, ultimately, to obtain results that comply with the scope, time and quality restrictions.

On the other hand, we pursue a second objective which is to validate, expand and improve the set of project management procedures, tools and process assets in our Process Asset Library [6] to support the implementation of the ISO/IEC 29110-5-1-2 standard.

The valuation of the Integrated environment in the context of the currently ongoing pilot project is totally positive. Each company selected, from the list we had proposed, the subset of tools that best suited their needs. From the feedback offered by the participant project managers, working in different companies, with different ways to manage their work, we have been able to identify the most effective software tools.

Participant VSEs all agreed on the need to have simple but useful tools to become more productive in their daily projects. It seems that this kind of companies is willing to bet on free software tools, mainly for economic reasons. However, they have traditionally found difficulties, due to the lack of knowledge of the existing tools, to decide which ones could better fit to its internal organization. It has to be noted that, during the last years, there has been an increasing proliferation of software tools to address specific project management aspects.

The results presented in this paper represent one more step on the road to developing a method with the necessary guidelines for the implementation of ISO/IEC 29110-5-1-2 project management good practices reducing the amount of effort. Further work is expected to be performed to determine what more tools should be added to the Integrated environment in order to meet different management needs, in other PMBOK® Guide knowledge areas not covered so far.

Acknowledgments. This research has been supported by CICYT-TIN2010-20057-C03-03 "Simulación aplicada a la gestión de equipos, procesos y servicios", Sim4Gest.

References

1. Laporte, C.Y., O'Connor, R.V., Fanumy, G.: International Systems and Software Engineering Standards for Very Small Entities. CrossTalk, The Journal of Defense Software Engineering 26(3), 28–33 (2013)
2. Basri, S., O'Connor, R.V.: A Study of Knowledge Management Process Practices in Very Small Software Companies. American Journal of Economics and Business Administration 3(4), 636–644 (2012)
3. O'Connor, R.V.: Evaluating Management Sentiment towards ISO/IEC 29110 in Very Small Software Development Companies. In: Mas, A., Mesquida, A., Rout, T., O'Connor, R.V., Dorling, A. (eds.) SPICE 2012. CCIS, vol. 290, pp. 277–281. Springer, Heidelberg (2012)

4. Turner, R., Ledwith, A., Kelly, J.: Project management in small to medium-sized enterprises: Matching processes to the nature of the firm. International Journal of Project Management 28, 744–755 (2010)
5. Murphy, A., Ledwith, A.: Project management tools and techniques in high-technology SMEs. Management Research News 30(2), 153–166 (2007)
6. Mesquida A.L., Mas, A.: A Project Management improvement programme according to ISO/IEC 29110 and PMBOK®. In: EuroSPI 2013, Industrial Proceedings (2013)
7. Amengual, E., Mas, A.: Software Process Improvement in Small Companies: An Experience. In: EuroSPI 2007, Industrial Proceedings, pp. 11.11–11.18 (2007)
8. Mas, A., Mesquida, A.L., Fluxà, B.: The long way to maturity: a road map to success. In: EuroSPI 2012 Industrial Proceedings (2012)
9. Mas, A., Fluxà, B., Amengual, E.: Lessons learned from an ISO/IEC 15504 SPI programme in a company. Journal of Software Maintenance and Evolution-Research and Practice 24(5), 493–500 (2012)
10. O'Connor, R.V., Laporte, C.Y.: Software Project Management in Very Small Entities with ISO/IEC 29110. In: Winkler, D., O'Connor, R.V., Messnarz, R. (eds.) EuroSPI 2012. CCIS, vol. 301, pp. 330–341. Springer, Heidelberg (2012)
11. Boucher, Q., Perrouin, G., Deprez, J.-C., Heymans, P.: Towards Configurable ISO/IEC 29110-Compliant Software Development Processes for Very Small Entities. In: Winkler, D., O'Connor, R.V., Messnarz, R. (eds.) EuroSPI 2012. CCIS, vol. 301, pp. 169–180. Springer, Heidelberg (2012)
12. ISO/IEC TR 29110-5-1-2:2011 Software engineering - Lifecycle profiles for Very Small Entities (VSEs) - Part 5-1-2: Management and engineering guide: Generic profile group: Basic profile. International Organization for Standarization, Mayo (2011)
13. A Guide to the Project Management Body of Knowledge (PMBOK® Guide) - 5th edn. Project Management Institute (January 2013)
14. Symbaloo, http://www.symbaloo.com
15. Zoho Docs, http://www.zoho.com/docs
16. OpenOffice, http://www.openoffice.org
17. Diigo, https://www.diigo.com
18. Mister Wong, http://www.mister-wong.com
19. Citeulike, http://www.citeulike.org
20. Dropbox, http://www.dropbox.com
21. Google Drive, http://www.google.com/drive
22. OneDrive, https://onedrive.live.com
23. Flowchart, http://flowchart.com
24. FreeMind, http://freemind.sourceforge.net
25. WBS Chart Pro, http://www.criticaltools.com/wbsmain.html
26. Google Calendar, https://www.google.com/calendar
27. Gantter, http://www.gantter.com
28. Asana, http://www.asana.com
29. Trello, https://trello.com
30. Doodle, http://doodle.com
31. Skype, http://www.skype.com
32. Google Hangouts, https://www.google.com/hangouts
33. Wiggio, http://wiggio.com
34. Redbooth, https://redbooth.com
35. TeamLab, http://www.teamlab.com

A Critical Evaluation of a Methodology for the Generation of Software Process Improvement Roadmaps

Derek Flood, Fergal Mc Caffery, Gilbert Regan, and Val Casey

{gilbert.regan,fergal.mccaffery,
kevin.mcdaid,derek.flood}@dkit.ie

Abstract. For medical device organisations to market their devices in specific geographic regions they must adhere to the regulations of that region. These regulations often recommend that organisations adhere to specific standards and guidance documents which specify "what" must be achieved without specifying "how" this may be done. Due to changes to the medical device directive, which governs the development of medical devices within the EU, in March 2010, software can now in its own right be considered a medical device. This change has meant that a number of software organisations developing software for the medical device domain must now adhere to the same regulations as other medical device manufacturers. In this work we present a concept for a Software Process Improvement (SPI) roadmap to guide such organisations through the task of implementing medical device standards and guidance documents. In addition we present and evaluate a methodology that can be used to create a SPI roadmap from a set of requirements such as the aforementioned standards and guidance documents.

Keywords: software process improvement roadmaps, medical device standards, software, usability, risk management, research method.

1 Introduction

Software can be easily used to configure a medical device without the need for expensive and time consuming hardware changes [1]. In 2006, Faris et al. [2] estimated that approximately half of all medical devices on the US market contained software. Complexity of software has been increased dramatically, posing higher risks of software malfunction and miss-application. Between 2005 and 2009, 87 models of infusion pumps were recalled due to safety problems [3]. In response to this, a whitepaper on the use of infusion pumps produced by the FDA, reports that "many of the problems that have been reported are related to software defects".

Although this is only one example, recent trends show that an increasing number of medical devices are being recalled due to software failures. Due to the increasingly important role of software in these devices, software is now included in the EU's definition of a medical device [4] subjecting it to the same processes and standards as other medical devices.

To ensure compliance, organisations are facing the challenge of implementing a number of medical device standards and guidance documents. These standards and guidance documents clearly define what must be achieved without providing specific methods for achieving them [5].

In this work we aim to alleviate this problem through the use of a series of software process improvement roadmaps. These roadmaps will not only outline what an organisation must do and when it should be introduced (in line with the software development lifecycle), but will also provide specific guidance on the best way to achieve these requirements for individual organisations.

Previous work by the authors [6] has outlined the structure of these roadmaps and proposed a methodology for their development. In this paper we aim to re-evaluate this methodology in light of its application to two medical device standards, IEC 62366[7] and ISO 14971[8], and to share our experiences in the application of the methodology to allow future researchers learn from these experiences.

The remainder of this paper is structured as follows: Section 2 outlines the background to this work and discusses the importance of software to the medical device domain. Section 3 examines the role of software processes and software process improvement within the medical device domain. In section 4 we describe the structure of the roadmaps and a methodology for their development. Section 5 then discusses how the roadmap development methodology was applied to two international standards and discusses the impact this will have on the methodology in the future. Section 6 then concludes the paper with an outline of how this work will progress.

2 Medical Device Regulations, Standards and Guidance Documents

In order to sell a medical device within the European Union (EU), the medical device organisation must demonstrate that they are compliant with the regulations set forth by the EU. Similarly, to sell medical devices within the US the organisation must demonstrate compliance with the FDA regulations [9]. In order to help organisations achieve compliance with these regulations, the EU and FDA have published standards and guidance documents that address specific aspects of the regulations and also recommend compliance with harmonised and consensus international standards, such as IEC 62304 [12] and ISO 13485 [10]. ISO 13485 Quality management system (QMS) ensures that the processes used during the development and production of a medical device are defined and monitored to ensure high quality products are developed. This standard is referred to by the European regulations and has recently been accepted by the FDA as adequate fulfilment of the requirements of a QMS.

As part of the QMS, organisations must perform risk management activities. ISO 14971:2007 [8] describes the requirements of a risk management process for medical device development. This standard identifies 6 key stages of a risk management; risk analysis, risk evaluation, risk control, evaluation of overall residual risk acceptability, risk management report, and production and post-production information.

During the development of a medical device, it is important to consider how the user will interact with it. Usability (the extent to which a product can be used by specified users to achieve specified goals with effectiveness, efficiency and satisfaction in a specified context of use [11]) can be a source of great risk. The IEC 62366 [7] standard defines a usability engineering process that can help medical device developers produce usable products thereby reducing the risk of use errors.

IEC 62304:2006 – Medical device software – Software life cycle processes [12] provides specific guidance on how to perform software development activities for software that is to be incorporated in a medical device. It is therefore used to develop medical device software for both the European and US markets.

3   Software Process Improvement within the Medical Device Domain

There has been very limited adoption of software process improvement within the medical device domain [4]. In addition existing generic SPI models, such as the CMMI® and ISO/IEC 15504-5:2012 (SPICE), do not provide sufficient coverage to achieve medical device regulatory compliance [15] [2] [13] [1]. To address this issue a medical device specific SPI framework, titled Medi SPICE, is being developed [16].

The objective of undertaking a Medi SPICE assessment is to determine the state of a medical device organisation's software processes and practices, in relation to regulatory requirements and best practices with the goal of identifying areas for undertaking process improvement [15] [13]. It can also be used as part of the supplier selection process [17].

Medi SPICE is based on ISO/IEC 15504-5:2012 [14], IEC 62304:2006 [12] and ISO/IEC 12207:2008 [18]. It is being developed in line with the requirements of ISO/IEC 15504-2:2003 [19] and contains a Process Reference Model (PRM) and Process Assessment Model (PAM). It also incorporates the requirements of the relevant medical device regulations, standards, technical reports and guidance documents.

The Medi SPICE PRM consists of 44 processes and 15 sub-processes with clearly defined purpose and outcomes that must be accomplished to achieve that purpose. The Medi SPICE PAM which is related to the PRM, forms the basis for collecting evidence that may be used to provide a rating of process capability.

4   Software Process Improvement Roadmaps

In this work we propose the use of a software process improvement framework for the implementation of medical device standards. Unlike traditional SPI models, the goal of the roadmap implementation framework is not to improve existing processes but to implement the processes necessary to meet the requirements of a specific standard. Initially this work will focus on the development of SPI roadmaps for key medical device standards; IEC 62366, ISO 14971, ISO 13485 and IEC 62304.

For the purposes of this work we define a roadmap as: A series of milestones, comprised of goals, that will guide an organisation, through the use of specific activities, towards compliance with regulatory standards.

The roadmap is divided into two levels. The first level defines the goals, grouped into milestones that the organisation should achieve throughout the SPI initiative. And contains no detail relating to how the goals should be achieved. This is done for two reasons. Firstly, by presenting the roadmap as a series of goals traceability to the relevant standard can be easily achieved. Secondly, the high-level roadmap can form a basis for communication across the industry as the same high-level roadmap can be applied to all organisations. The second level roadmap contains specific guidance for organisations on how to achieve the goals outlined in the high level roadmap and is comprised of multiple activities that can achieve each goal so that the most suitable activity can be presented to an organisation wanting to implement the roadmap.

4.1 Roadmap Development Methodology

The following approach is similar to the transformation method presented in [20] for the construction of ISO/IEC 15504-2 compliant process assessment and process reference models. The goal of the transformation methodology presented in [20] was to develop a process reference model and a process assessment model. As the goal of this methodology is to develop a roadmap for implementing medical device standards it was necessary to alter the methodology to account for the order of implementation and the distinction between the goals and activities (or practices in ISO 15504) in the roadmap.

The methodology used for the development of the roadmaps is as follows:

1. **Identify requirements of the standard**: (The requirements will henceforth be known as 'goals' to differentiate the roadmap from the standard). This will be achieved through manual analysis of the standard.
2. **Logically group all goals.** Goals are grouped based on the stage of the software development lifecycle at which they occur. However as some goals are performed throughout the lifecycle, these goals should be grouped together and placed at or before the first stage at which they are performed.
3. **Separate grouped goals in line with ISO/IEC 15504 capability levels.** These groups are separated based on the capability level at which the requirements should be performed. These groups form the milestones of the roadmap.
4. **Order the milestones based on the capability level and logical groups.** All milestones containing level 1 goals should be implemented first in the order in which they will occur in the development process, followed by all milestones containing level 2 goals, and subsequently by all milestones containing level 3 goals until all of the milestones are in order.
5. **Validate generated roadmap.** The generated roadmap should be validated with industry experts. Members of the standards committee could also assist with the validation. Interviews or workshops are methods that could be used. A Delphi study could also be used. The validation should aim to ensure that:

- The goals are correctly grouped
- The milestones are in the correct order for implementation
6. **Identify activities that can meet the identified goals.**. This can be done through a systematic literature review and/or case studies with organisations already implementing the standard.
7. **Validate activities in host organisation.** This will involve the generation of a roadmap for the host organisation and then undertaking a software process improvement initiative to implement the roadmap.

5 Evaluation

This section presents two case studies that have used the roadmap development methodology to develop and validate a high-level roadmap for two medical device standards (IEC 62366 and ISO 14971). A full description of the developed roadmaps is beyond the scope of this experience report.

5.1 Validation Methodology

To validate each of the roadmaps an expert evaluation was used. There were two aims established for each validation:

1. To determine if the goals are appropriately grouped into milestones
2. To determine if the ordering of the milestones is appropriate for implementation in a medical device organisation.

Experienced personnel within each of the two domains, risk management and usability of medical devices, were asked to complete the on-line questionnaire illustrated in Figure 1. The questionnaire showed participants each milestone in turn and asked them to state whether they thought each goal belonged in the milestone it was included in. In addition the participants were asked to rate on a 5 point likert scale (where 1 = strongly disagree and 5 = strongly agree) whether they agreed with the following statement; *The order of this milestone within the roadmap is correct.* The participants were also provided with the opportunity to add any additional comments they felt were relevant.

In addition to this, the online questionnaire also provides the user with the opportunity to state at what capability level, in line with 15504-2, each goal should be accomplished at. As the participants who took part in the study were experts in medical device standards and not software process improvement these results were not included in the study. However we did manage to recruit 1 software process improvement expert whose feedback is included.

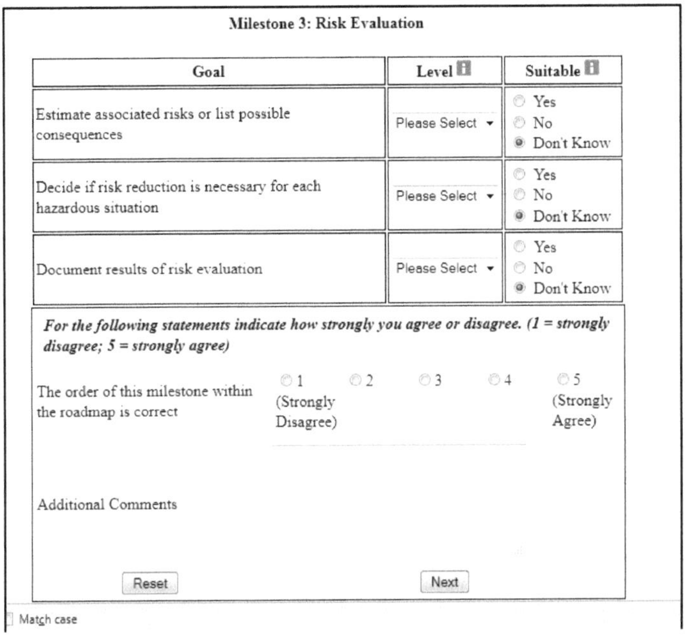

Fig. 1. Screenshot from online questionnaire

5.2 Case Study 1- IEC 62366

The first case study conducted applied the roadmap development methodology to the IEC 62366 standard. This standard outlines the requirements for a usability engineering process and describes what needs to be done to minimise use related risks. The standard requires the development of a number of documents, including a usability engineering file which should at least reference all of the documentation relating to the usability engineering process.

Step 1 of the methodology identified 44 goals, that were separated into 10 milestones (step 3) that are implemented throughout the software development lifecycle. Table 1 shows the number of goals that were included in each of the milestones for the IEC 62366 roadmap. It can be seen that the number of goals range from 2 to 7 per milestone.

Table 1. Initial IEC 62366 Roadmap

Milestone	# of goals	Milestone	# of goals
Task	5	Training	4
Usability Specification	5	Verification	4
Risk Management	7	Validation	4
Implementation	2	Validation Management	3
Documentation	6	Process	4

Once the roadmap was produced it was validated by 5 participants with experience of usability engineering for medical devices. In total 18 individuals were contacted in relation to the validation however, only 5 agreed to participate in the study. Overall the participants felt that the initial roadmap was well structured, however they did feel that the last two milestones should be implemented earlier. It was felt that the Process milestone should be the first milestone as it defines and maintains the overall process of usability engineering.

Although a full overview of the results is beyond the scope of this paper, it is important to mention that the results obtained in relation to the capability level of each goal provided little agreement among the participants. This result may be explained by the participants' area of expertise being in the area of usability engineering and not in ISO 15504 capability levels.

As a result of the validation, the roadmap was revised to include only 39 goals (some of the original goals were merged where the documentation of an activity and the activity itself were separate goals) divided into 9 milestones. Two milestones, validation and validation management, were merged to form a single goal as these were originally separated based on their capability level. Table 2 shows the number of goals by milestone for the revised roadmap.

Table 2. # of goals in the revised IEC 62366 roadmap by milestone

Milestone	# of goals	Milestone	# of goals
Process	3	Documentation	6
Task	3	Training	4
Usability specification	4	Verification	4
Risk Management	6	Validation	7
Implementation	2		

5.3 Case Study 2 – Roadmap for ISO14971

The second case study applied the roadmap development methodology to the ISO 14971 standard. ISO 14971 describes the risk management process that should be applied during the development of medical devices. The standard itself is not limited to software but can apply to any type of medical device. The standard outlines a 6 phase risk management process ranging from risk analysis, which is the identification of possible risks posed by the medical device to Production and post-production management of any residual risks.

The roadmap generated by the roadmap development methodology contained 51 goals divided among 14 milestones. Table 3 shows that there are between 1 and 7 goals per milestone in the roadmap. As risk management is an on-going activity with each stage being repeated throughout the software development lifecycle, the roadmap should be used to introduce the goals early in the product lifecycle so that the necessary activities are in place when needed.

Table 3. # of goals per milestone

Milestone	# of Goals	Milestone	# of Goals
Initial Planning	6	Pre-Production	1
Risk Analysis	4	Post-Production	2
Risk Evaluation	3	Management Planning	4
Risk Control	3	Staff Planning	4
Verification of Risk Control	5	Final Review	2
Residual Risk	7	Risk Management System Review	3
Pre-Release	6	Traceability	1

As was found in case study 1, the validation of the roadmap found that a number of the milestones, which contained goals believed to be at capability level 2 (Managed process- the process meets the requirements for capability level 1 where the process is *performed*, and is now implemented in a *managed* fashion), were introduced too late in the roadmap and as such should be introduced earlier. In addition it was also found that in a number of cases the separation of an activity from its documentation was unnecessary and these goals should be grouped into a single goal.

The validation resulted in a number of changes to the roadmap. The resulting roadmap contains 44 goals divided among 14 milestones. Three of the final 4 milestones were moved so that they would be implemented at the beginning of the implementation process. The final number of goals and order of the milestones can be seen in table 4 (read from top to bottom, then left to right).

Table 4. # of goals per milestone in the ISO 14971 Roadmap

Milestone	# of Goals	Milestone	# of Goals
Initial Planning	6	Verification of risk Control	3
Management Planning	3	Residual Risk	7
Staff Planning	3	Pre-Release	6
Traceability	1	Pre-Production	1
Risk Analysis	4	Post-Production	1
Risk Evaluation	3	Risk Management System Review	3
Risk Control	2	Final Review	1

6 Discussion

The case studies described above have provided a lot of insight into the methodology and have highlighted a number of issues that can arise when applying it to medical device standards.

The first stage is to determine the requirements of the standards. The standards contain a lot of supporting information which can be difficult to discern from the requirements. The authors judgement was used in determining this and the validation found that these judgements were correct. Additionally, it was found that the standards use consistent terminology to describe what needs to done in order to be in compliance with the standard.. This consistency could also allow for the use of Natural Language Processing (NLP) techniques to identify the requirements from the standard.

During the application of step 2 (logically group all goals) it was identified that not all processes can adhere to the software development lifecycle. In the cases outlined above it was found that there were logical groupings that could be easily identified however, some requirements would not easily fit into these groupings. For example in case study 2 it can be seen that 2 of the milestones contained only a single goal. Although the methodology itself can be quite flexible it was found in both case studies that dividing the goals based on their capability level provided little benefit as most of the goals should be implemented by a level 1 organisation. During case study 1, an ISO 15504-2 expert was asked to review the goals to determine if they were assigned an appropriate capability level. This expert remarked that as they are a requirement of the standard they should all be assigned a capability level of 1. For this reason it has been determined that this step (step 3) should be removed from the methodology.

In the cases outlined above it was found that the logical groupings provided a clear path to implementation. The use of the ISO 15504 capability levels in this step however, did cause problems. Some of the goals that were determined to be implemented at level 2 are necessary at the start of the implementation, for example the development of a standard operating procedure. Including these levels in the ordering of the milestones lead to the development of inaccurate roadmaps that was quickly identified by the experts. The case studies also revealed that it is important to select the correct method for validation. In both cases an online form was used to collect the opinions of the validators on the roadmap. Although this approach provided sufficient validation for the two standards selected, this may not scale well due to the large number of inputs that would need to be completed. In case study 2 one participant opted to email their comments directly to the author instead of completing the online form. To address this issue future validation studies may instead opt to take on a different format. One possibility is the use of a workshop whereby the participants are co-located and presented with the roadmap and provided an opportunity to discuss the roadmap in much more detail.

During the case studies it was found that the separation of the documentation of an activity from the activity itself, as was done in a number of cases, should not be done. One of the validators remarked that "If it's not documented, it's not done", and suggested that the documentation of an activity should not be a separate goal but incorporated into the activity that is being performed.

7 Revised Roadmap Development Methodology

As a result of the validation the methodology now consists of:

1. **Identify requirements of the standard**: It is important to ensure that requirements of the standard are identified and distinguished form supporting advice. These requirements should then be phrased as goals of the roadmap.

2. **Logically group all goals.** Each group should not contain too many goals. If this is the case they may be separated into multiple sub-groups. The resulting groups will form the milestones for implementation.
3. **Order the milestones based on the logical groups.** The milestones should ordered in a way that is compatible with implementation in a software development process to ensure that organisations suffer limited disruption due to the implementation.
4. **Validate generated roadmap.** The validation should be performed with industry experts and evaluate the roadmap to answer the following questions:
   - Are the goals appropriately grouped into milestones?
   - Is the ordering of the milestones appropriate for implementation in a medical device organisation?
5. **Identify activities that can meet the identified goals..** This may be done through a systematic literature review and/or case studies with organisations already implementing the standard.
6. **Validate activities in host organisation..** Generate a roadmap for the host organisation through collaboration between the organisation and industry experts and then undertaking a software process improvement initiative to implement the roadmap.

8 Limitations

The validation described above did not include development of the activities repository or industry validation of a complete roadmap. For this reason the validation presented above is limited to the first 5 steps of the methodology which can be used to develop a high-level roadmap. This in itself in a vital aspect to the development of software process improvement roadmaps.

The development methodology has been applied to two standards within the medical device domain. Before it can be established that the methodology can be applied as is to other domains, such as the automotive or aerospace domains, it must be validated within these domains.

9 Conclusions and Future Work

The implementation of any standard required in the development of medical devices can be a complex and time consuming issue. SPI roadmaps provide specific activities, in-line with the medical device standards, for an organisation to implement the chosen standard in a way that complements existing software development lifecycle processes.

This paper outlines how such roadmaps can be developed through the use of the roadmap development methodology and report on the application of this methodology to two medical device standards, IEC 62366 and ISO 4971. In light of these case studies it was deemed that the methodology can be used to develop high level software process improvement roadmaps that would be well received by the medical device community.

In the future this work will examine the use of Natural Language Processing (NLP) techniques to assist in the development of such roadmaps, in line with the roadmap development methodology. NLP techniques could be used to automatically identify the requirements of a medical device standard, the first step in the presented methodology. This could greatly simplify the process of roadmap development as the identification of such requirements can be a time consuming task.

Using the roadmaps presented here, it is intended to recruit a number of medical device organisations to implement the roadmaps to evaluate how well the proposed roadmaps work in an industry setting. After an initial evaluation of the organisations existing processes, a customised roadmap will be developed for the organisation and they will be guided through its implementation, until they have met all of the requirements of the medical device standard

Acknowledgement. This research is supported by the Science Foundation Ireland (SFI) Stokes Lectureship Programme, grant number 07/SK/I1299, the SFI Principal Investigator Programme, grant number 08/IN.1/I2030 (the funding of this project was awarded by Science Foundation Ireland under a co-funding initiative by the Irish Government and European Regional Development Fund), and supported in part by Lero - the Irish Software Engineering Research Centre (http://www.lero.ie) grant 10/CE/I1855.

References

[1] Lee, I., Pappas, G., Cleaveland, R., Hatcliff, J., Krogh, B., Lee, P., Rubin, H., Sha, L.: High-Confidence Medical Device Software and Systems. Computer 39(4), 33–38 (2006)

[2] Faris, T.H.: Safe and Sound Software: Creating an Efficient and Effective Quality System for Software Medical Device Organizations. ASQ Quality Press (2006)

[3] Food and Drugs Administration (FDA), Infusion Pumps Improvement Initiative (2010), http://www.fda.gov/medicaldevices/productsandmedicalprocedures/GeneralHospitalDevicesandSupplies/InfusionPumps/ucm205424.html (accessed December 7, 2012)

[4] McHugh, M., McCaffery, F., Casey, V.: Standalone Software as an Active Medical Device. In: O'Connor, R.V., Rout, T., McCaffery, F., Dorling, A. (eds.) SPICE 2011. CCIS, vol. 155, pp. 97–107. Springer, Heidelberg (2011)

[5] McCaffery, F., Dorling, A., Casey, V.: Medi SPICE: An update. In: International Conference on Software Process Improvement and Capability Determinations (SPICE), Pisa, Italy, May 18-20, pp. 195–198 (2010)

[6] Flood, D., Mc Caffery, F., Casey, V., Regan, G.: A Methodology for Software Process Improvement Roadmaps for Regulated Domains – Example with ISO 62366. In: McCaffery, F., O'Connor, R.V., Messnarz, R. (eds.) EuroSPI 2013. CCIS, vol. 364, pp. 25–35. Springer, Heidelberg (2013)

[7] IEC 62366:2007 "Medical Devices – Application of usability engineering to medical devices" Switzerland, ISO

[8] ISO 14971 – Medical Devices – Application of risk management to medical devices, Switzerland, ISO (2007)

[9] Burton, J., McCaffery, F., Richardson, I.: A risk management capability model for use in medical device companies. In: International Workshop on Software quality (WoSQ 2006). ACM, Shanghai (2006)
[10] ISO 13485:2003, Medical devices — Quality management systems — Requirements for regulatory purposes, 2nd edn. Geneva, Switzerland, ISO (2003)
[11] ISO/IEC, ISO 9241: Ergonomic requirements for office work with visual display terminals (VDT)s - Part 11 Guidance on usability (1998)
[12] IEC 62304:2006, Medical device software—Software life cycle processes. Geneva, Switzerland, IEC (2006)
[13] Humphrey, W.S., Snyder, T.R., Willis, R.R.: Software process improvement at Hughes Aircraft. IEEE Software 8(4), 11–23 (1991)
[14] ISO/IEC 15504-5:2012, Information technology - Process Assessment - Part 5: An Exemplar Process Assessment Model. Geneva, Switzerland, ISO (2012)
[15] McCaffery, F., Dorling, A.: Medi SPICE Development. Software Process Maintenance and Evolution: Improvement and Practice Journal 22, 255–268 (2010)
[16] Casey, V., McCaffery, F.: Development of the medi SPICE PRM. In: Mas, A., Mesquida, A., Rout, T., O'Connor, R.V., Dorling, A. (eds.) SPICE 2012. CCIS, vol. 290, pp. 265–268. Springer, Heidelberg (2012)
[17] Casey, V.: Virtual Software Team Project Management. Journal of the Brazilian Computer Society 16, 83–96 (2010)
[18] ISO/IEC 12207:2008, Systems and software engineering - Software life cycle processes. Geneva, Switzerland, ISO (2008)
[19] ISO/IEC 15504-2 (2003) - Software engineering — Process assessment — Part 2: Performing an assessment, Geneva, Switzerland (2003)
[20] Barafort, B., Renault, A., Picard, M., Cortina, S.: A transformation process for building PRMs and PAMs based on a collection of requirements – Example with ISO/IEC 20000. In: SPICE 2008, Nuremberg, Germany (2008)

How to Design an Innovative Framework for Process Improvement? The TIPA for ITIL Case

Béatrix Barafort, Anne Rousseau, and Eric Dubois

Public Research Centre Henri Tudor,
29 J.F.Kennedy ave., Luxembourg, Luxembourg
{beatrix.barafort,anne.rousseau,eric.dubois}@tudor.lu

Abstract. A design science research method can be applied for designing innovative services. In our research and technology organization, a macro-process model underlying activities of this method is formalized for governing innovative services. It is refined continuously according to current Research, Development and Innovation (RDI) activities such as the Tudor's IT Process Assessment (TIPA®): an open framework for assessing and improving IT service management processes. The TIPA for ITIL (IT Infrastructure Library) case illustrates how this innovative framework has gone through all over the innovation chain.

Keywords: service design, innovative service, service system, science-based sustainable service innovation process model, process assessment, process improvement, IT service management.

1 Introduction

Luxembourg country is concentrating a lot of service industries and suppliers, like in many other European countries, in the United States and Japan. Actually, more than 90% of the Luxembourg GNP is based on services. The financial sector is an important target for services in Luxembourg, but other sectors such as logistics, construction and telecommunication are also expanding. They contribute largely to the service supply. The progressive mutation of the traditional industry can also be observed: once focused on products, towards a more service-oriented industry Finally, beyond the services of a commercial nature, there are also services of a public nature for the benefit of society in general and for the citizens in particular.

Innovation is essential for Luxembourg and IT is largely recognised as a driving force for service innovation. It is even more the case in the new governmental programme [1]. According to OECD, innovation can be classified in several types. These include: a pure technological innovation, a process innovation (like TIPA® , the Tudor's IT Process Assessment tackled in this paper, with a process reference model and a process assessment model, and its associated process assessment method applied to IT Service Management) and an innovation based on the development of new human competences. Ultimately, the innovation can be at the level of a complete information system delivered as a service system, defined by Spohrer et al. as "a configuration of people, processes, technology and shared information connected through a value proposition with the aim of a dynamic co-creation of value through the participation in the exchanges with customers and external/internal service systems" [2]. Finally IT can also be considered as a vector for other types of innovations like those related to new business models or to new regulations and standards.

In this context, it is very important for Luxembourg to propose innovative IT-related services. The application of design science principles guarantees the value chain linking research and technological activities. As a Research and Technology Organization (RTO), the Public Research Centre Henri Tudor (hereinafter referred to as Tudor) proposes to align on Design Science approaches [3], and particularly to a Design Science Research Method (DSRM) [4] with six sets of activities founding the approach. Then in the context of service systems, Tudor enhances its process framework formerly known as S2IP (standing for Sustainable Service Innovation Process) [5, 6] to S3IP: Science-based Sustainable Service Innovation Process.

The paper firstly presents the features of Tudor's S3IP aligned with the Peffer's DSRM in Section 2. Then Section 3 illustrates the approach in the innovative context of the Process-based framework dedicated to IT Service Management: the ITIL® 2011 based framework named TIPA® for ITIL (TIPA stands for Tudor IT Service Management). The paper concludes on the enhancements provided by S3IP, and what innovation the TIPA framework introduces on the market.

2 A Design Science Research Method Meeting Tudor's RTO Goals

According to Wikipedia, the term Design Science was introduced in 1963 by R. Buckminster Fuller [7] who defined it as a systematic form of designing. The concept of design science was taken up in S. A. Gregory's 1966 book of the 1965 Design Methods Conference [8] where he drew the distinction between scientific method and design method. Design science is a "problem-solving paradigm and seeks to create innovations that define the ideas, practices, technical capabilities and products through which the analysis, design, implementation, management and use of Information Systems can be effectively and efficiently accomplished" [9]. Design Science attempts to "create things that serve human purposes, and then to create new and innovative artifacts" [10] such as constructs, models, methods, and instantiations.

Thus in the Tudor's RTO context, we have the twofold mission to produce technological innovations in response to market needs and goals, and to contribute to the scientific theory underlying these innovations. Our focus is on service-based innovations for an enterprise or a network of enterprises: we are targeting systems of services.

A service system design science research method, adapted to the context of a RTO like Tudor has been investigated [3], with the goal to demonstrate a science based approach applied to services.

Peffers et al. proposes a process model consisting of six activities in a nominal sequence [4]. They indicate that the need of relevance in service science finds a multidisciplinary response with a design based approach which enable to bring closer research and practice [11, 12]. Each set of activities of the nominal process sequence is presented in table 1:

Table 1. DSRM activities

1. Problem identification and motivation.
This activity aims at defining the specific research problem and justifying the value of a solution. The problem definition will be used to develop an artifact that can provide a solution. In order to motivate the value of a solution, this set of activities includes knowledge of the state of the problem and the importance of its solution.
2. Define the objectives for a solution
This activity aims at inferring the objectives of a solution from the problem definition and knowledge of what is possible and feasible.
3. Design and development
This activity aims at creating the artifact(s). These artifacts can be "constructs, models, methods, or instantiations" [13] or "new properties of technical, social, and/or informational resources" [14]. A design research artifact can be any designed object in which a research contribution is embedded in the design.
4. Demonstration
This activity aims at demonstrating the use of the artifact to solve one or more instances of the problem. This can be done via the experimentation of the artifact's use.
5. Evaluation
This activity aims at observing and measuring how well the artifact supports a solution to the problem. This activity involves comparing the objectives of a solution to actual observed results from use of the artifact in the demonstration. It requires knowledge of relevant metrics and analysis techniques.
6. Communication
This activity aims at communicating the problem and its importance, the artifact, its utility and novelty, the rigor of its design, and its effectiveness to researchers and other relevant audiences such as practicing professionals, when appropriate.

2.1 The Science-Based Sustainable Service Innovation Process Model

The DSRM principles that were presented previously are jointly applicable to service systems. Because of the specific nature of services, a particular attention should be paid to service systems features. This is the reason why a dedicated process model (S3IP) has been proposed in Tudor in order to illustrate the appropriate application of a DSRM into our RTO context and innovation mission dedicated to service systems. This process model highlights the influence of intensive networking and internal collaborations within an organization. It also emphasizes the alliances with key beneficiaries and end-users of the proposed innovations.

Our S3IP framework was defined on empirical basis in order to support especially service innovation projects taking into account the market and technical uncertainty implied. Of course, as highlighted by Herstatt & Verworn [15], it depends on the degree of newness of an innovation project. The main characteristics of services have been largely discussed in the literature: intangibility, co-production/interactivity, simultaneity, heterogeneity, perishability, transferabi-lity, cultural specificity and information-intensity [16, 17, 18, 19]. Although we are speaking here about incremental innovations with a lower market and technical uncertainty as this is about process improvements that could also result in a considerable competitive advantage. Our S3IP is well a process model but not a stage gate one [20]; it mobilizes not only engineers as we are in an open innovation perspective. So we use for example as well as persona and scenario to extract the requirements of the service design in order to involve collaboration between multi stakeholders within an iterative design process [21].

Figure 1 presents the overall picture associated with our proposed Science-based Sustainable Service Innovation Process model (S3IP).

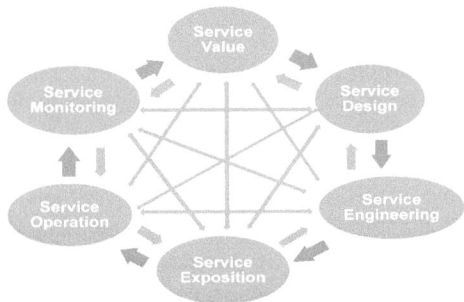

Fig. 1. The Science-based Sustainable Service Innovation Process model (S3IP)

This is a process model composed of six processes, with interactions between the processes and no frozen temporality. Several iterations can happen for a single process.

- **Service Value - Problem identification**

  This process aims at identifying an unsolved problem and/or an opportunity for a new service innovation from a general perspective. An instantiated problem should be analyzed and isolated from a general point of view (generalization) via the identification of a gap in terms of technological/scientific knowledge associated with the proposed innovation. State of the art technologies and scientific results that would play the role of enablers for the innovative service solution are investigated. A preliminary identification of the business model and of the value proposition is also performed.

- **Service Design – Solution objectives**

  This process aims at defining services in terms of business functional objectives, quality criteria and rationale for acceptance. If necessary, constraints are identified (e.g. regulations). Requirements as properties of

the service are formulated (they can be expressed in terms of a service contract such as a Service Level Agreement).

- **Service Engineering – Development of the artifact(s) and demonstration of its(their) use**
  This process aims at developing the solution according to its requirements. The solution should be a class of solutions bringing an answer to a class of problems. It is corresponding to the development of an artifact (or several artifacts) contributing to demonstrate the feasibility of a service: prototypes, complete specification of the service (e.g. architecture model).

- **Service Exposition – Communication**
  This process aims at validating the service contract with early adopters and at promoting the service to other potentially interested parties. It can be via marketing related to the socio-economical sustainability of the service, branding of the new service through some label definition and associated certification schemes (that can be professional and sector-based certifications), and standardization at the national or international levels (e.g. ISO).

- **Service Operation – Evaluation**
  This process aims at deploying the service. This process implementation is not in the scope of a RTO like Tudor where it should be performed by companies on the market. This is nevertheless supported by Tudor by defining and providing tools for service providers intended to check and to measure the correctness of its implementation (in particular measures of quality and degree of appropriation).

- **Service Monitoring – Communication**
  This process aims at collecting feedbacks associated with the measures as well as from the assessment performed with the end-users. This is a starting point for incremental innovation in terms of improvement, optimization and new requirements of the service.

3   TIPA's Innovation Case Illustrated with the S3IP Model

After having introduced the Design Science approach reflected in the Tudor's S3IP, this section is analysing the TIPA's framework. The origin of TIPA appeared in 2002 [22] with the idea of combining the ISO/IEC 15504 standard series requirements and guidance [23] for Process Assessment, and the ITIL® [24] *de facto* standard (IT Service Management best practices) in order to enable **end-users and consultants to improve ITSM processes with the support of a standard-based, objective, repeatable and trustful method**. The overall TIPA framework is composed of the following set of artifacts:

- Process models: Process Reference Models (PRM) and Process Assessment Models (PAM) transforming the set of requirements and practices respectively included in the ITIL *de facto* standard, into a set of

processes described with their purpose and outcomes (in the PRM) and assessment indicators based on the process reference model and a measurement framework providing measurable maturity levels (in the PAM);
- Process Assessment Method: for assessing the processes documented in the TIPA Process Models. The method is documented in the published TIPA handbook [25];
- Toolbox: templates, checklists, rating sheets,... supporting each step of the assessment process;
- Assessor & Lead Assessor training courses and the associate professional certification scheme.

The figure 3 shows the TIPA framework with the four artifacts instantiated to IT service management based on the ITIL best practices standard.

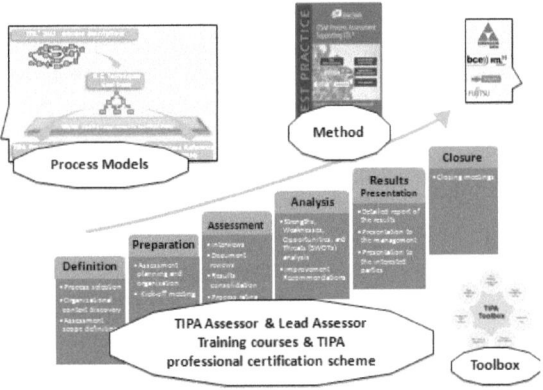

Fig. 2. TIPA's framework artifacts

In 2009, we analysed the emerging TIPA framework from the Sustainable Service Innovation Process (S2IP) point of view when two iterations had been performed throughout the innovation chain [5]. Several years later, we can deepen the analysis from a Design Science Research perspective and retroactively apply the S3IP according to the DSRM set of activities underlying S3IP presented in the previous section.

3.1 Service Value - Problem Identification and Motivation

Today, the professional best practices de facto standard ITIL exists regarding IT Service Management (ITSM). ITIL is the most widely accepted approach to IT service management in the world and provides a cohesive set of best practices. ITSM is driven both by technology and organizational environments in which it operates. Best practices are both current and practical, combining the latest thinking with sound, common sense guidance.

However a challenge for large and small companies is about how to translate these requirements and practices into a set of processes that they can deploy for demonstrating compliance and/or to measure their level of maturity regarding the performance of these processes.

In the Design Science context, the identified problem was "**how to improve ITSM processes?**". Thus with the need for improving ITSM processes, there was a lack of an objective and repeatable approach for assessing processes in order to be able to know "where we are" and a lack of a very structured improvement path in order to target "where to go". Moreover, similar approaches combining the improvement of software development processes and ITSM ones were missing [22]. Consequently, we have developed the TIPA framework to assess and improve IT service management processes based on the ITIL *de facto* standard quoted above.

Regarding the first iterations of the S3IP, the business model was weak. Nevertheless, it has been strengthened, and everything was studied in order to cover all relevant topics such as the value proposition, the benefits of TIPAs, the branding, Intellectual Property Rights, ITIL trademark and ISO standards use... In order to transfer TIPA RDI results on the market and after some business prospection and negotiations, a first company was candidate for publishing the method (TIPA handbook) [25] and a second one for commercializing the TIPA framework: a research contribution partnership contract was signed in 2010 with ITpreneurs [26] who is selling TIPA Assessor and Lead Assessor training courses, with the associated professional certification scheme. A mechanism of paying licenses had been set up. This is contributing to the Key Performance Indicators (KPI) of Tudor's Performance Contract regarding Luxembourg government.

3.2 Service Design - Define the Objectives for a Solution

The objective of the TIPA framework is to provide the key factors for determining an improvement path for ITSM processes. With the TIPA for ITIL application of the framework, we claim that the TIPA framework is a unique solution regarding ITIL. The objectives of the TIPA solution were considered in order to define what was possible and feasible. The TIPA service features were determined as follows to ensure the quality and consistency of the whole TIPA framework: 1) ISO/IEC 15504-2 conformance; 2) Process models quality; 3) Process assessability; 4) Assessment approach effectiveness; and 5) Quality of assessment results, with a particular attention paid to the Process models and the Process assessment method.

From the first drafts of the TIPA process models and the method, as well as the characterization of the TIPA training courses for Assessor and Lead Assessors, the properties of the training courses and certification scheme were defined in factsheets that are reflecting the method content.

From the State-of-the-Art of Scientific and Technological Knowledge, we can argue that the ISO/IEC 15504 standard series requirements and guidelines have been followed for building the maturity assessment model associated with TIPA as well as for the assessment method, the Assessor and Lead Assessor training courses and the certification scheme for TIPA Assessors and Lead Assessors. Goal-oriented requirements engineering techniques have been applied for the systematic organization and traceability of requirements into the process models [27, 28]. This is the main research contribution for the TIPA framework.

3.3 Service Engineering - Artifact(s) Creation Development and Demonstration of Its (their) Use

The TIPA framework has been progressively defined and experimented through its application in collaboration with two kinds of experts: ITIL ones and ISO/IEC 15504 ones. The co-design of the process description in the **process models** was performed and its usage was confirmed throughout process assessment projects with various Luxembourg (Dimension Data, Sogeti, and BCE RTL) and international companies (Dimension Data, Fujitsu Oy [29], Critical Software…) as well as with international experts in the ITIL and/or ISO/IEC 15504 communities. Several releases of the process models have been delivered, in alignment with new releases of the ITIL de facto standard. These process models releases have been formally validated by experts of the domains.

Regarding the TIPA **method**, it has been recently enhanced with the concepts of classes of assessment in order to better address the needs coming from the market for a sizeable assessment method. Moreover, at the same period, the ISO/IEC 15504 standard, on which the TIPA Process Assessment Method was previously based, had started to be progressively replaced by the ISO/IEC 33000 series. In order to propose this gradual approach for TIPA assessment services, the method modifications have been done for updating the **training courseware.** The TIPA handbook should also be updated in a near future and published in a version 2. All these changes will allow companies to use the TIPA framework with more flexibility according to their constraints: regulatory, service procurement, risk management, costs…

For the TIPA **toolbox**, updates have been performed in parallel with the various process models releases and the classes of assessment modifications in the method and training courseware.

3.4 Service Exposition - Communication

The TIPA artifacts have been used by early adopters (Qualium, DimensionData, Fujitsu Oy [29], Sogeti, and BCE RTL) and since the commercialization of TIPA via ITpreneurs, by consultants and end-users in various companies worldwide. A community of Grandfathers intervened as experts for using, supporting and promoting the framework.

TIPA trademark has been registered and a dedicated web site has been developed by our industrial partner [30]. TIPA's competitors have been identified and some works were performed and still need to be strengthened in terms of TIPA's positioning on the market and TIPA for ITIL's framework adoption curve. Some marketing efforts have been performed in order to spread the adoption of TIPA, in particular with our industrial partner, with marketing campaigns, the TIPA online website upgrade, and dissemination activities via professional and scientific events (importance of the networking efforts).

Since the beginning of the TIPA initiative, Tudor has been very active in standardization at the ISO level [23, 31, 32, 33], for national as well as for international committees. Tudor was also committed for editorship, in particular for the ISO/IEC 20000-4 (IT Service management process reference model) [32]. More recently, Tudor has carefully participated in the ISO/IEC 15504 revision for developing the new ISO/IEC 33000 series [33] on Process assessment, in order to anticipate updates to apply to the TIPA framework and also to enable the international ISO committee to take profit from the TIPA framework experience.

Last but not least, an international working group has been set in November 2013 in order to develop a new architecture and ontology on service management: this is the "Taking service Forward" initiative. The vision of "Taking Service Forward" is to provide the service community with an Adaptive Service Model. A member of the TIPA team is participating and can use some items of TIPA artifacts (including intermediate deliverables) for contributing to the discussions and developments. The "Taking Service Forward" initiative sees the need for a basis for co-creation and crowd-sourcing of future service management best practices. The initiative may give birth to the structures supporting that vision.

3.5 Service Operation - Evaluation

As previously mentioned the TIPA artifacts have been used by early adopters and experimented through living lab missions. It means that the first uses of a new release of process models have been analyzed at the end of each mission, as well as the toolbox, in order to apply an improvement loop on the artifacts..

The TIPA adoption curve is increasing regularly. Today there are 163 TIPA Assessors or Lead Assessors from 24 countries that were trained and certified in 2 ½ years all over the world [30]. The satisfaction of trainers, consultants and end-users is collected via ITpreneurs and other channels are used to collect feedback for improving the TIPA framework and its various artifacts: blogs, social networks, LinkedIn groups, TIPA training courses, TIPA process assessment missions…

3.6 Service Monitoring - Communicate the Problem and Its Importance

Tudor is responsible for the functional evolutions of the TIPA process models, method and toolbox, as well as its consequences on the training courseware. There is a maintenance agreement with our industrial partner in order to update the training courseware and certification scheme if needed as well as ensuring some support as a Subject Matter Expert. From interactions with stakeholders, we collected a set of requirements for new features such as the classes of assessment (cf. § 3.3).

The impact of TIPA's innovation still needs to be completed, even if some activities have already been performed such as publications [34] and postdoctoral research [35]. Thus, the National Fund for Research (FNR) in Luxembourg supported a postdoctoral research project entitled **"Impact Analysis of Process Assessment**

and Process Improvement on IT Service Management". The research questions were twofold: (1) What is the impact of process assessment on the success of process improvement? (2) What is the impact of process improvement on IT service quality? These postdoctoral studies were based on IT service management and process improvement – both domains being much applied and having very immature knowledge base in research. Thus the research questions came from the industry need for increasing quality and productivity in organizations and services. The research focus was on process assessment impact on process improvement and on process improvement impact on IT service quality. After the first one was completed, the second question was tackled and took us to realize that there are no common practices regarding IT service quality measurement and no thoughts for proposing an innovative artifact for measuring IT service quality. This is an open perspective in terms of research.

4 Conclusions and Perspectives

This paper presents how an innovative framework for process improvement has been designed in a design science research context of our RTO, namely Tudor. After presenting key activities of a Design Science Research Method, we explained how it is underlying a Science-based Sustainable Service Innovation Process (S3IP) model in a service system environment. The TIPA for ITIL case illustrated the whole path throughout the innovation chain.

In 2009, a first analysis of deployment of the TIPA for ITIL framework had been performed. It has shown that the innovation processes maturity level was uneven. After the TIPA for ITIL transfer on the market, we can see that it is still the case today but with the enrichment of the S3IP model with DSRM aspects, the Science-based dimension is enhanced as well as the problem-solving one for the innovative services that are developed. In the TIPA for ITIL illustration, we have seen the incremental innovations of the TIPA service system in terms of improvements and optimizations of the services throughout the artifacts evolution. We have also seen that the impact and degree of appropriation of the TIPA for ITIL services still need to be carefully analyzed and improved. The uniqueness of the ITIL-based proposed solution and the qualities of the TIPA for ITIL services for assessing and improving ITSM processes have to be strengthened. In this context, the S3IP model refinements and IT service quality research perspectives represent future works and perspectives.

References

1. Luxembourg Government, Programme gouvernemental 2013 (2013), http://www.gouvernement.lu/3322796/Programme-gouvernemental.pdf
2. Spohrer, J., Maglio, P.P., Bailey, J., Gruhl, D.: Steps toward a science of service sytems. IEEE Computer 40, 71–77 (2007)

3. Dubois, E., Rousseau, A.: Service science: A service system design science research method? In: Falcão e Cunha, J., Snene, M., Nóvoa, H. (eds.) IESS 2013. LNBIP, vol. 143, pp. 100–113. Springer, Heidelberg (2013)
4. Peffers, K., Tuunanen, T., Rothenberger, M., Chatterjee, S.: A design science research methodology for information systems research. Journal of Management Information Systems 24(3) (2008)
5. Barafort, B., Rousseau, A.: Sustainable Service Innovation Model: A Standardized IT Service Management Process Assessment Framework. In: O'Connor, R.V., Baddoo, N., Cuadrago Gallego, J., Rejas Muslera, R., Smolander, K., Messnarz, R. (eds.) EuroSPI 2009. CCIS, vol. 42, pp. 69–80. Springer, Heidelberg (2009)
6. Kubicki, S., Dubois, E., Halin, G., Guerriero, A.: Towards a Sustainable Services Innovation in the Construction Sector. In: van Eck, P., Gordijn, J., Wieringa, R. (eds.) CAiSE 2009. LNCS, vol. 5565, pp. 319–333. Springer, Heidelberg (2009)
7. Fuller, R., McHale, J.: World Design Science Decade, 1965-1975. World Resources Inventory (1965)
8. Gregory, S.A.: The Design Method. Butterworths (1966)
9. Denning, P.J.: A New Social Contract for Research. Communications of the ACM 40(2), 132–134 (1997)
10. March, S., Smith, G.: Design and natural science research on information technology. Decision Support Systems 15(4), 251–266 (1995)
11. Romme, G.: Making a difference: Organization as design. Organization Science 14, 558–573 (2003)
12. Van Aken, J.E.: Management research based on the paradigm of the design science: The quest for field-tested and grounded technological rules. Journal of Management Studies 41(2), 219–246 (2004)
13. Hevner, A.R., March, S.T., Park, J.: Design research in information systems research. MIS Quarterly 28(1), 75–105 (2004)
14. Tuunanen, T.: Critical success chains method. Technical Report LTT-Tutkimus oy, Elektronisen Kaupan Instituutti, Helsinki (2001)
15. Herstatt C., Verworn B.: The "Fuzzy Front End" of Innovation, Working paper n°4, Department for Technology and Innovation Management, Technical University of Hamburg (2001)
16. Bitran, G.R., Lojo, M.: A Framework for Analyzing Service Operations. European Management Journal 11(3), 271–282 (1993)
17. de Jong, J.P.J., Bruins, A., Dolfsma, W., Meijaard, J.: Innovation in service firms explored: What, how and why? Literature review, Strategic Study B200205. EIM Business and Policy Research, Zoetermeer (2003)
18. Gallouj, F.: Innovation in services and the attendant old and new myths. Journal of Socio-Economics 31, 137–154 (2002)
19. Miles, I.: Innovation in services. In: Fagerberg, J., Mowery, D.C., Nelson, R.A. (eds.) The Oxford Handbook of Innovation. Oxford University Press, Oxford (2004)
20. Khurana, A., Rosenthal, S.R.: Towards holistic "front ends" in new product development. The Journal of Product Innovation Management 15(1), 57–74 (1998)
21. Lim, D., Bouchard, C.: Iterative process of design and evaluation of icons for menu structure interface of interactive TV services. Behaviour & Information Technology 25(6), 511–519 (2006)
22. Barafort, B., Di Renzo, B., Merlan, O.: Benefits resulting from the combined use of ISO/IEC 15504 with the Information Technology Infrastructure Library (ITIL). In: Oivo,

M., Komi-Sirviö, S. (eds.) PROFES 2002. LNCS, vol. 2559, pp. 314–325. Springer, Heidelberg (2002)
23. ISO, ISO/IEC 15504-2: Information technology - Software Process Assessment - Part 2: Performing an assessment (2003)
24. The Cabinet Office, IT Infrastructure Library - Service Strategy - Service Design - Service Transition - Service Operation - Continual Service Improvement, The Stationery Office Edition (2011)
25. Barafort, B., Betry, V., Cortina, S., Picard, M., St-Jean, M., Renault, A., Valdés, O.: ITSM Process Assessment supporting ITIL® - Using TIPA to Assess and Improve your Processes with ISO 15504 and Prepare for ISO 20000 Certification. Van Haren Publishing, The Netherlands (2009), ISBN 9789087535643
26. ITpreneurs (2014), http://www.itpreneurs.com/
27. Rifaut, A., Dubois, E.: Using Goal-Oriented Requirements Engineering for Improving the Quality of ISO/IEC 15504 based Compliance Assessment Frameworks. In: Proc. IEEE Int'l Requirements Engineering Conference (RE 2008). IEEE CS Press (2008)
28. Barafort, B., Renault, A., Picard, M., Cortina, S.: A transformation process for building PRMs and PAMs based on a collection of requirements – Example with ISO/IEC 20000. In: Proceedings of the International Conference SPICE 2008, Nuremberg, Germany (2008)
29. Jokela, J.: Long Term Utilisation of SPICE in an IT Service Company. In: SPICE 2009, Turku, Finland, pp. 117–122 (2009)
30. TIPAonline, http://www.tipaonline.org
31. ISO, ISO/IEC 20000-1: Information technology – Service management – Part 1: service management system requirements (2011)
32. ISO, ISO/IEC 20000-4: Information technology – Service management – Part 5: Process reference model (2010)
33. ISO/IEC 33001: Information technology – Process assessment – Concepts and terminology (2014)
34. St-Jean, M., Mention, A-L.: How to evaluate benefits of Tudor's ITSM Process Assessment. In: Proceedings of the SPICE 2009 Conference, Turku, Finland (2009)
35. Lepmets, M., McBride, T., Ras, E.: Goal Alignment in Process Improvement. Journal of Systems and Software 85(6), 1440–1452 (2012)

A Framework for Systematic Change Management

Hannu Jaakkola[1] and Bernhard Thalheim[2]

[1] Tampere University of Technology,
Software Engineering
P.O. Box 300, FI-28101 Pori, Finland
hannu.jaakkola@tut.fi
http://www.pori.tut.fi/~hj

[2] Christian-Albrechts-University Kiel, Computer Science Institute, 24098 Kiel, Germany
thalheim@is.informatik.uni-kiel.de
http://www.is.informatik.uni-kiel.de/~thalheim

Abstract. Change management is an essential part of the whole software life cycle. A systematic treatment for changes is still an open issue. In order to overcome this situation we develop a framework for change management of software systems that covers the entire lifecycle and allows to focus change management within a software development process to individual steps. This framework is based on problem description, on categorisation of problems, on elicitation of causes, and solutions to these problems. We show how the framework may be extended for special systems such as database systems.

1 Change Management for Software Systems

1.1 Characteristics of Software System Development

Software systems are change-sensitive. This feature is built-in to the basic characteristics of them. Information systems typically are built for long time use and in variety of environments by the different users. Changes in software systems are most commonly related to the front-end engineering processes (requirements elicitation and analysis, design). Requirements are tended to change, because the customers do not exactly understand and know their needs. The needs are also changing in time, as well as the importance of them. In addition, new requirements appear as well as the importance of earlier detected ones is lost.

Boehm [5] separates two different approaches to software engineering (SE): *Plan driven* refers to the traditional way of software development. Engineering phases are following each other in sequence and the baseline of every phase is frozen to avoid changes to it. In this sequential development following the water-fall model the requirements baseline acts as a basis for design, design baseline for construction, construction baseline for testing. Even the incremental and iterative modifications of this process implement the same principle - frozen specifications related to every iteration / increment. Plan driven software development can also be called "contract based" - all is agreed in written contracts and assessed against the project documentation. *Agile software* development has become popular because reactivity in continuing changes (in requirements) is built-in into the development processes itself. It is based on small increments, short (time) iteration cycles, immediate integration of modules and proximity (active role) of the client during the whole development process. Attitude to documentation also differs from plan-driven culture - only such documentation is produced that is really important for the development work itself.

Boehm's article [5] does not provide Plan driven and Agile culture as alternatives to each other. In his article [4] Boehm points out five factors indicating suitability of development cultures in development situations: criticality of software, skill level of the personnel, dynamism of the application (requirement changes per time unit), organisation culture and size of development team. To simplify his characterisation, critical software having static requirements is developed by large teams having non-experienced members and the organisation itself has used to work according to predefined rules indicates plan driven culture; the opposite values (non-critical, highly skilled and experienced personnel, dynamics in requirements, work organised in small teams used to chaos) on behalf indicate the suitability of Agile culture.

One important factor is not considered in the analysis of Boehm - the expected lifespan of information systems. Long lifespan makes software systems susceptible to changes having their origin in the environment (original requirements, platforms, external connections, new interest groups, etc.).

1.2 Change Management - Specifications and Discussion

Change management is an essential part of every development step and it relates both in the product itself and the process (Fig. 1).

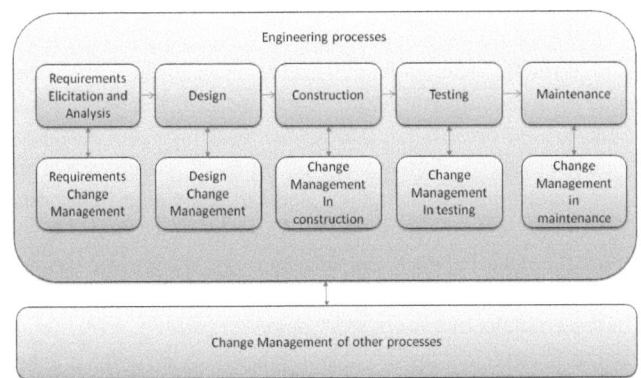

Fig. 1. The role of change management in software development

Figure 1 illustrates a development path of software pointing out some of the development steps in a process oriented way. The process structure related to software engineering is specified by ISO [1] in its "Software Life Cycle Standard". This standard introduces seven process groups and altogether 43 processes related to software life cycle. Figure 1 simplifies and completes this structure in two ways to fill better the needs of this paper: we have pointed out the main processes of software development itself (engineering processes), separated the related change management tasks (not included in the standard, as discussed later) and dispelled the other processes of the process standard (not relevant to this paper) on the background (see Figure 1).

To find the answer in question "What is change management" we have analyzed the process assessment standards ISO 12207 [1] and ISO 15504-5 [6]. The CMMI for Development Version 1.3 [11] was used to augment the analysis with additional aspects having their root in CMMI community. In addition we used SWEBOK - Software Engineering Body of Knowledge [2] document to find how change management should be taken into account in SE education.

The process standard [1] includes only two minor notifications related to change management. The first one refers to *contract change control mechanism*.
- p. 21: *"The contract change control mechanism should address the change management roles and responsibilities, level of formality of the proposed change requests and contract renegotiation, and communication to the affected stakeholders."*
- p 111: *"The purpose of the Contract Change Management Process is to develop the new contract contents as agreed by both the acquirer and the supplier when a change request affecting the agreed contract contents is proposed. This process begins with a proposal of the change request by either the acquirer or the supplier and ends with the conclusion acceptable for both parties: withdrawal or overall/partial approval of the change request."*

The process assessment standard ISO 15504-5 ([6], p. 57) recognises the need of change request as an artifact to manage. A process (SUP.10) is included in the Supporting Processes Group and its purpose is specified: *"The purpose of the Change Request Management Process is to ensure that change requests are managed, tracked and controlled."* As a result of successful implementation of it the standard lists the following outcomes: (1) a change management strategy is developed; (2) requests for changes are recorded and identified; (3) dependencies and relationships to other change requests are identified; (4) criteria for confirming implementation of change requests are defined; (5) requests for change are prioritized, and resource requirements estimated; (6) changes are approved on the basis of priority and availability of resources; (7) approved changes are implemented and tracked to closure; and (8) the status of all change requests is known. These outcomes are implemented by nine base practices (BP). In addition, the standard defines the need for *Problem and Change Management System* as a generic resource for the Process Deployment Attribute PA3.2 (p. 91). The standard also gives guidelines for the contents of *Change Management Plan* (p. 143). To conclude, the detailed guidelines related to change management are in the hands of the organisation and individual developers.

The first reference to change management in CMMI [11] is connected to General Goals and General Practices section (p. 85) as a training topic related to Organizational Process Focus (OPF) and Organizational Process Management (OPM) process areas among the list of training topics. The next references are related to Configuration Management (p. 137). Baselines are stable basis for the continuing evolution of configuration items; change management in this context relates to the changes of baselines as further defined by SG 1.2 (Establish Baseline; p. 140-142) and its SP 1.2 (Establish a Configuration and Change Management System for controlling work products). In this context change management system includes the storage media, procedures, and tools for recording and accessing change requests. The change management is further discussed in SG2 (Track and Control Changes) in its SP 2.1 (Track Change Requests). The very analogical approach is included in the Requirements Development section (p. 328). Its SG2 (Develop Product Requirements) includes SP2.1 (Establish Product and Product Component Requirements), which points out the need to traceability of requirements as a part of change management.

The SWEBOK report [2] is developed to give common guidelines on SE education. It points out the importance of requirements' changes as a part of *Software Requirements Subarea* (Chapter 2 in the document), which is seen to *span the whole software life cycle*. It includes change management and maintaining the requirements in a state that accurately mirrors the software to be, or that has been built. The document also notices the importance or recognition the inevitability of change and adopting measures to mitigate the effects of change. Change has to be managed by applying careful requirement tracing, impact analysis and *version management*.

In addition to the Software Requirements Subarea, change management is included as an essential part of *Software Configuration Control* (Chapter 7). It is concerned with managing changes during the software life cycle. It covers the process for determining what changes to make, the authority for approving certain changes, support for the implementation of those changes, and the concept of formal deviations from project requirements, as well as waivers of them. Information derived from these activities is useful in measuring change traffic and breakage, and aspects of rework. The change control process is defined in detail (p. 7-7). It has the incoming *Software Change Request (SCR)* as a starting point of the flow, which is controlled by the *Configuration Control Board (CCB)*. *Version management* is mentioned also in this context with reference to the implementation of the change.

A main conclusion of the review is that the role of change management is tightly bounded to requirements management along the life cycle of software and focused especially in configuration management. All changes are seen to have their origin in requirements changes. However, there would be need to change the architecture of software without having special request related to requirements (functional or non-functional), as well as to make changes in the coding practices having its origin in organizing the work. ISO 15504-5 [6] and CMMI [11] also point out management of process changes related to software process capability improvement. To conclude, detailed and focused discussion covering change management as a part of individual processes (Figure 1) is missing. Our approach provides a systematic conceptual approach to change management in general level; handling this topic only as a part of configuration management or process capability improvement we see too limited.

1.3 The Motivation and Structure of This Paper

As discussed above, change management is not handled in a systematic way by the important reference manuals used as guidelines to specify and develop software engineering processes. However, change management is an important area related to the whole life cycle of software. In the development time it is closely related to product management - in the form of version and configuration management. In deployment phase it is closely related to the acceptance tests of the product - as reactions to the faults detected. After deployment the software life cycle turns into "use and maintain" phase, to post-detection of faults. Van Vliet [13] lists four types of maintenance activities: corrective (correcting errors discovered), adaptive (adapting the software in the changes in its environment), perfective (improving software from some quality criteria point of view), and preventive (correcting errors that are not fired yet). This approach differs from ours: in maintenance it is more or less question on the change process, whereas our approach explicitly considers the sources of problems causing the need for maintenance; the causes are context independent and may be the same in different maintenance tasks.

The Category-Cause-Solution (CCS) Model is a systematic framework to increase understanding of the complex phenomenon of change management. The focus in our model is in the cause - source of the factor causing the need for change. The framework provides a conceptual structure for systematic handling of the complexity related to change management. Our framework consists of five steps: 1. recognising the reasons for changes (organisational, IT, business); 2. analysing the cause of the change (within the system, observations and symptoms); 3. categorising the causes in the selected categories; 4. applying the cause-solution pattern to solve the problem; 5. understanding and deployment of the solution. The aim of our framework is to remain simple. Because of that we have listed only five change categories. For every category we have given some typical example solutions, that solve the problems in a systematic way - independently on the context of the problem. The model provides means for similar solutions for similar problems and also gives a list guiding a developer to find a continuum from a problem to the cause of it and opportunity to apply a ready cause-solution template to solve it. The framework is aimed to be incremental. The user may expand the amount of categories as needed, and to add new cause-solution pairs to the patterns.

The rest of the paper is organised in the following way. The paper starts with conceptualization of change management. The basic framework introduced in Section 2 allows a systematic development of solutions for problems related to the change management of software systems. The framework is cause driven. Causes are classified in categories and solutions are given in the form of solution patterns. A pattern [6] describes a commonly-recurring structure of elements that solve a general problem is a particular context. The basic framework can be extended to fill the needs of a specific application area, e.g. database maintenance (Section 3). . This application area is selected because of two reasons: first it is a typical part of almost any information system, secondly it is an example of a complex change management problem. The beginning of the Section 3 covers problem description and the latter part gives step-by-step solution to it. The paper ends with concluding remarks self-assessment of our framework.

2 The Category-Cause-Solution Framework to Change Management

2.1 Some Problems Causing Changes of Software Systems

We can classify and manage changes based on distinction of their causes. The fault in a system indicates and error, which is the simplest and most obvious cause requiring a change (Figure 2).

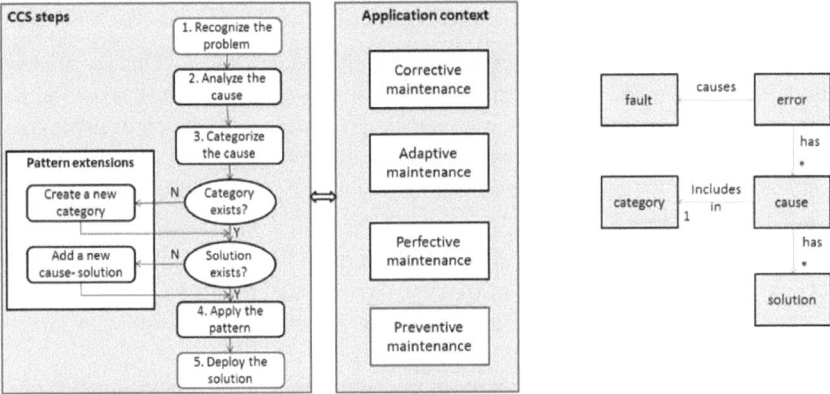

Fig. 2. The CCS framework and its conceptual model

The five step CCS framework is introduced on the left hand side of the figure. The framework implements the conceptual model on the right hand side of the figure: The error encountered has to be analyzed to find the cause for it. The source of it may be related to design, operation or organisation, and they can occur during application domain description, requirements prescription, software specification as well as during coding. The key element of our framework ist the cause-solution pattern, which provides means for solution knowledge in the form of cause-solution pairs, measures and other remarkable notifications worth of understanding in connection with solving the problem. However, there is no simple treatment for solving the problem. To simplify the problem solving the framework provides the concept of cause categories. In our basic model five main kinds of changes can be distinguished:

- The first cause requiring a change is *incompleteness* (A). A software system operates in an environment (or context), which, following McCarthy [9], we denote by (w, t), where w is a slice of the world at time t. Unfortunately it is rarely possible to determine in advance all the components of w that are relevant, and how the relevant components are expected to evolve over time. It is impossible to determine in advance the effect of these components on a computation, which means that changes due to incompleteness require human intervention.
- The second cause requiring a change is based on *insufficiency* (B) to represent the current knowledge about the application, about technology on hand or other issues such as organisational, social and strategic background. Insufficiency typically leads to so-called workarounds that partially patch or repair a situation. This approach causes another stream of changes.
- The third and fourth type corresponds to *deviation from normality*. Users, system developers, and implementers are biased by the 'normal' case and do not keep in mind that states different from the normal ones may occur. The system thus operates well in 80% of operating time and suddenly stops normal operating or suddenly behaves in a way that has not been anticipated.
    - Changes are caused when *lifespan changes* (C) are not foreseen.

- Another kind of change is caused by overestimation of the normal case. *Hidden cases* (D) are overlooked but important.
- The fifth cause requiring a change is *context dependence* (E). Systems are not operating on their own. They share resources with other systems, are used in a combined fashion by users, have different maintenance regimes, have different deployment conditions and thus must be considered to be context dependent. This kind of dependence on the system is observed for all engineering disciplines but not properly handled for software systems.

As indicated in Figure 2 we have tried to keep the model simple by allowing only one category for each cause, but in spite of that we allow several solutions for it. The model is also extendable: new categories may be defined, as well as new cause solution pairs in the patterns.

Architectures of modern computer systems, solutions to application domain tasks, and code developed under these assumptions and environments are interdependent. Change problems are typically observed at the runtime but must be directly tracked back to the systems development and deployment decisions. For instance, the *change category 'space'* with the *problem 'out of space conditions (storage structures)'* can be tracked back to *change causes* in the DBMS Oracle *'poorly forecasted data volumes in physical design'*, *'tablespace fragmentation'*, *'invalid settings for either object space sizes or tablespace object settings'*, or *'not using locally-managed tablespaces'*.

This characterisation of problems by **Category-Cause** pairs is the basis for our framework. It is combined with the characterisation by content, motivation, examples, fit criterion, measurements, and considerations.

2.2 Some Patterns for Change Management

We may now develop a framework to change handling based on the five categories and the causes of problems that require changes in a system. A number of solutions can be developed for each category-cause pair. The following list demonstrates our approach.

(A) *Incompleteness* of specifications as "modelling gap" [12]:

Cause of problem	Potential solution
incomplete knowledge	add neglected specification
incomplete coverage	develop robust specifications
macrodata modelling	redesign to microdata
library integration	complete knowledge on libraries, minimise libraries
inability to represent	apply explicit replacement specifications
missing background data	link explicitly to background

Acceptance criteria: We may apply procedures for measuring incompleteness of specification, implementation etc. Typical ones are:

completeness of schema $\frac{\#represented\ concepts}{\#application\ world\ concepts}$,

capability $\frac{\#conflict-free\ types\ among\ application\ world\ concepts}{\#types\ among\ application\ world\ concepts}$,

changes of various types (e.g. correctness),
incompleteness of the type or constructor system,
incompleteness of structuring, and
incompleteness of static semantics.

Notes: One of the most difficult incompleteness problems is the current intensive use of libraries. If a library changes then the corresponding code behaviour might change. This has already been a nightmare at PL/1 programming age [7] but it is still valid in the case of Java. It is more severe for current deployment of unknown, partially known or intentionally hidden libraries.

(B) *Insufficiency* to represent the current knowledge in the application domain:

Cause of problem	Potential solution
implementation restrictions	*extend by theories and languages*
conceptual language restrictions	*apply novel theories, advanced logics*
restricted attention of developers	*extend scope of reference models*
non-axiomatisability	*change logics*
locality of reasoning	*use interference reasoning*
partial change of objects	*separate stable and transient parts*
bundled complex objects	*separate objects according to inner life*

Acceptance criteria: Insufficiency is difficult to measure. We may however use criteria such as:
  occurrence of work around code,
  interdependent objects with complex coexistence constraints, and
  unnatural database dictionary structures that cannot be easily described.

An approach that might be used in future research is the introduction of robust schema parts based on tolerance and distance to error measures, e.g. metrics:
  correctness of schema $\frac{\#correct\ types}{\#types}$.

Notes: Insufficiency is treated through concurrent actions and overcoming locality, e.g., mapping to atomic constraint cases. Specific default values can be deployed for problematic cases in domains (e.g., dates misspelled, wrong, not according rules, or doubtful data). Often database types integrate stabile - almost not changing - properties of objects (e.g., ISBN for a book) and transient - often changing - properties of objects (e.g. shelf for storing a book). Objects are however taken as a whole.

(C) *Lifespan changes* over time due to evolution of system context:

Cause of problem	Potential solution
change-sensitive normalisation	*change of normal form*
time overload and mingling	*separate kinds of time*
non-temporal types	*use temporal types*
too restrictive models	*gain flexibility*
instability of schema	*develop dynamic schemata*
temporary runtime error	*solve similar to 9 kinds of nulls* [10]

Acceptance criteria: Lifespan changes can be characterised through statistics which are supported by measures, e.g.
  ratio of objects that are updates against the number of updates in the reality,
  subschema complexity for real world conceptions,
  evolution ratio within a database dictionary and complexity of changes, and
  ratio of types that must be supported by transactions for data modification.

In some cases we also apply criteria such as existence of an inner structuring within the value domain types, e.g. for representation of different facets of time and metadata.

Notes: Database applications as a part of software systems are often assuming certain normal forms. We can however weaken such requirements. For instance, the schema can be separated into a robust sub-schema and an evolving sub-schema. Separation of strong and soft constraints and introduction of "almost valid" constraints supports flexible constraint maintenance. Other facilitation solutions are explicit introduction of time domains and separation of time into its kinds (e.g., transaction, user, validity time). We may introduce temporal types, i.e., explicit volatile types (temporary tables) and explicit virtual types. Flexibility can be achieved through robust schemata. Dynamic schemata can use the explicit introduction of explicit semantics states. In this case, we use state management similar to classical transaction management.

(D) *Hidden cases* due to limiting the consideration to the "normal case" and neglecting the complexity of the application world:

Cause of problem	Potential solution
pragmatic assumptions	*apply explicit modelling*
hidden assumptions	*use iterative testing*
self-restrictions during development	*detect reasons*
restricted scope of users	*extend education, sharpening*
overlooked cases	*use analysis, verification*

Acceptance criteria: Hidden cases often result in a larger set of "exceptions" which are handling all cases beyond the normal ones. We may thus use criteria, e.g.
existence of exceptions or specific values as defaults,
unspecific value domain types that are restricted by constraints,
value domain types that are used as "proxy" types (e.g. string values), and
overly complex structuring for real world entities.

Notes: Assumptions must be made explicit. They can also be based on the development and programming culture within a community (e.g., dialects of the ER model (Chen, Merise, SERM, HERM styles)). It is necessary to make restrictions explicit. Developers have their own preferences and styles.

Iterative modelling can increase robustness. Explicit change and version management allows to track hidden or folklore assumptions. We need to detect reasons for self-restrictions often made by programmers. Another good practice is to broaden the scope of developers with techniques of abstract programming.

Techniques that need further research are: control and correction of completeness problems; development of completeness criteria; analysis and verification tools; and predictability of correctness and changes.

(E) *Context dependence* is rather difficult to handle since it depends on the environment. Context-aware programming is rather novel. For instance, compilers optimise expressions in their way without taking into account the order a programmer had in mind while writing the expression.

Cause of problem	Potential solution
hidden environment	*use context-aware programming*
automatic optimisation	*develop directives for the optimiser*
operational freedom	*apply dynamic hints for execution*
change from test to operational mode	*analyse defects from test environment*
consolidation and integration	*start re-engineering and redesign*

Acceptance criteria: Context dependence occurs in many facets. It seems to be impossible to measure such. We may however use observations and characteristics for context dependence, e.g.

>unexpected behaviour of the system,
>sudden behavioural picks and performance bottlenecks, and
>changes of behaviour due to other concurrent systems.

Notes: For instance, database systems rely on automatic optimisation of queries, requests and of maintenance. This optimisation is poly-dimensional and can be directed by directives. Dynamic hints are used for restricting the optimisers' freedom to choose any query plan. Software is often tested in the testing environment. Later – e.g. for performance reasons – the testing environment is switched off; the system is newly compiled and runs now differently after compilation.

The list of category-cause-solution pattern is never complete. We show however how a number of solutions can be developed for each singleton case. The list also shows that the cure of each cause problem is thus different. Therefore, self-curation of systems is not feasible for the general case..

The solution pattern cannot be developed in a general way. We may however specify these patten in dependence on the kind of knowledge. Let us consider database systems as one case. For instance, incomplete knowledge is not only caused by incomplete models but also by non-separation of three parts of the the application:

(1) the part of the application that is currently covered by the specification and the model,
(2) the part of the application that might be of interest in the future but is not yet covered, and
(3) the part of the application that is never be of interest.

It is often assumed that only the first and the third part must be considered. But then the second part strikes through and enforces changes that cannot be easily handled. Migration and evolution projects into which we have been incorporated is showed however that a systematic treatment of the second case would have given a chance to avoid evolution problems.

2.3 Validation of the Framework to Database System Changes

Database modelling does not start from scratch anymore. Typically, modellers reuse, extend, refine, adapt, integrate, or modify solutions that have already been developed. Change management is not applied systematically yet. Development of database structures can rely on the experiences of several decades of database realisation.[1]. The body of knowledge for changes in real practice is very large. It needs, however, a systematisation, categorisation, and generalisation.

We analysed the life evolution of more than 100 database application in our library. The selected applications have undergone several dozens of deep changes. Simple changes such as the addition of an attribute have been neglected. Constraint changes often resulted in a deep revision of the system. Severe changes are also observed due to platform changes, to integration and merge with other systems, to strategy and organisation in an enterprise, to performance requests, to consolidation of systems, to extension of the system for wider use, to extensions of view sets, to migration of systems, to modernisation of the information system, to integration into data warehouses, etc. Some of these systems became already legacy (better saying heritage) systems since they have been operating already since the early 90ies until now.

In order to systematise our observations we used the following frame:
Problem: explicit statement based on the database dictionary;
Category-Cause-Solution: explicit and refined statement together with the scope;
Criteria and measures: for scheduling and triggering the change;
Controller: monitor deviations from expected behaviour and evaluate;
Tradeoff: evaluation of the solution after change;
Change pattern: applied pattern with database transformation;
Data change functions: explicit functions for database renovation;
Function/view/support change mechanics: changes to the entire interface system.
This frame extends our framework. We chose a dozen among the applications and traced all changes made in the system. All these changes can be specified in our framework. The changes themselves have been specified in a three-step procedure [8] (as an extension of the transformation in [3]): (i) initialisation, (ii) intermediate database change with time constraints for observational period, and (iii) finalisation or rejection of the change.

3 Conclusion

The paper has pointed out that change management is not widely handled by the handbooks, standards and guidelines used to develop software engineering processes.

---

[1] Due to our involvement into the development and the service for the CASE workbenchs $(DB)^2$ and ID^2, we have collected a large number of real life applications. Some of them have been really large or very large, i.e., consisting of more than 1.000 attribute, entity and relationship types. The largest schema in our database schema library contains of more than 19.000 entity and relationship types and more than 60.000 attribute types that need to be considered as different. Another large database schema is the SAP R/3 schema. It has been analysed in 1999 by a SAP group headed by the last author during his sabbatical at SAP. At that time, the R/3 database used more than 16.500 relation types, more than 35.000 views and more than 150.000 functions. The number of attributes has been estimated by 40.000. Meanwhile, more than 21.000 relation types are used. The schema has a large number of redundant types which redundancy is only partially maintained. The SAP R/3 is a very typical example of a poorly documented system. Most of the design decisions are now forgotten. The high type redundancy is mainly caused by the incomplete knowledge on the schema that has been developed in different departments of SAP.

Because of that there is a need for systematic approach applicable to structurise the complex phenomenon related to the implementation of changes in information systems. The Category-Cause-Solution (CCS) framework introduced in this paper starts from the problem encountered and defines the five step process for solving the problem. The solution applies the cause-solution pattern, which is and incremental base of knowledge giving solution alternatives for problem causes classified in selected categories. Our basic framework introduces five common categories, but the structure is modifiable. In addition to the modifications in the structure the framework may be also extended to fill the needs of specific application area. The extended framework is based on the principles of the basic one, uses the solutions listed in there, but covers extra features important to know and understand in this specific application area. We do not claim that our list of causes and categories is complete. It is, however, an aim to develop a framework for systematic change management.

The CCS framework fills the requirements of good methodology, i.e.

systematic: it provides a systematic approach to a complex common problem;
simplicity: it structurizes the complexity and is straightforward to apply;
reusability: it provides means for documenting the solutions found and acts as a base for reusable knowledge;
similarity: it standardizes the solutions providing opportunity to apply similar solution in similar problems and it transfers good practices inside and between organisations;
modifiability: it is incremental, extendable and can extended to be used in complex application contexts.

The purpose of this paper is not to solve all problems related to change management, but provide a simple approach applicable for different purposes. The basic model is context independent, valid in different application areas and sufficient in most cases. The (example) extended model takes into account the special requirements of the selected application area.

Acknowledgment. We would like to thank the Academy of Finland and the German Academic Exchange Service (DAAD) for the support of this research.

References

1. ISO/IEC/IEEE Standard for Systems and Software Engineering - Software Life Cycle Processes. IEEE STD 12207-2008, pp. 1–138 (2008)
2. Abran, A., Moore, J.W., Bourque, P., Dupuis, R., Tripp, L.L.: Guide to the Software Engineering Body of Knowledge (SWEBOK). IEEE (2004)
3. Ambler, S.W., Sadalage, P.J.: Refactoring databases - Evolutionary database design. Addison-Wesley (2006)
4. Boehm, B.: Some future trends and implications for systems and software engineering processes. Systems Engineering 9(1), 1–19 (2006)
5. Boehm, B.: A view of 20th and 21st century software engineering. In: International Conference on Software Engineering, pp. 12–29 (2006)
6. ISO IEC. ISO/IEC 15504-5, information technology – process assessment – Part 5: An exemplar process assessment model. Assessment, 1–206 (2006)

7. Jones, C.B. (ed.): Programming Languages and their Definition. LNCS, vol. 177. Springer, Heidelberg (1984)
8. Klettke, M., Thalheim, B.: Evolution and migration of information systems. In: The Handbook of Conceptual Modeling: Its Usage and Its Challenges, ch. 12, pp. 381–420. Springer, Berlin (2011)
9. McCarthy, J.: Notes on formalizing context. In: 13th Internat. Joint Conf. Artificial Intelligence, pp. 555–560 (1993)
10. Schewe, K.-D., Thalheim, B.: NULL value algebras and logics. In: Information Modelling and Knowledge Bases, vol. XXII, pp. 354–367. IOS Press (2011)
11. CMMI Product Team. CMMI for development, version 1.3. Improving processes for developing better products and services. Technical Report ESC-TR-2010-033, CMU/SEI (2010)
12. Thalheim, B.: Towards a theory of conceptual modelling. Journal of Universal Computer Science 16(20), 3102–3137 (2010),
  http://www.jucs.org/jucs_16_20/towards_a_theory_of
13. van Vliet, J.C.: Software Engineering: Principles and Practice. Wiley & Sons (2008)

Engineering Process Improvement in Heterogeneous Multi-disciplinary Environments with Defect Causal Analysis

Olga Kovalenko[1], Dietmar Winkler[1], Marcos Kalinowski[2], Estefania Serral[3], and Stefan Biffl[1]

[1] Institute of Software Technology and Interactive Systems, CDL-Flex,
Vienna University of Technology
Favoritenstrasse 9/188, 1040 Vienna, Austria
firstname.lastname@tuwien.ac.at
[2] Federal University of Juiz de Fora
NEnC, Rua José Kelmer s/n
36036-330 Juiz de Fora, Brazil
kalinowski@ice.ufjf.br
[3] Department of Decision Sciences and Information Management, KU Leuven
Naamsestraat 69, B-3000 Leuven, Belgium
estefania.serralasensio@kuleuven.be

Abstract. Multi-disciplinary engineering environments, e.g., in automation systems engineering, typically involve different stakeholder groups and engineering disciplines using a variety of specific tools and data models. Defects in individual disciplines can have a major impact on product and process quality in terms of additional cost and effort for defect repair and can lead to project delays. Early defects detection and avoidance in future projects are key challenges for project and quality managers to improve the product and process quality. In this paper we present an adaptation of the defect causal analysis (DCA) approach, which has been found effective and efficient to improve product quality in software engineering contexts. Applying DCA in multi-disciplinary engineering environments enables a systematic analysis of defects and candidate root causes, and can help providing countermeasures for product and process quality. The feasibility study of the adapted DCA has shown that the adaptation is useful and enables improving defect detection and prevention in multi-disciplinary engineering projects and fosters engineering process improvement.

Keywords: defect causal analysis, automation systems, multi-disciplinary project, product improvement, product quality, process improvement.

1 Introduction

Multi-disciplinary engineering (ME) projects (e.g., building a power plant and corresponding control systems) represent complex heterogeneous environments, where participants coming from different disciplines (e.g., mechanical, electrical, and software engineering), have to collaborate efficiently in order to satisfy quality and time constraints [18]. Loosely coupled tools and data models with limited interaction and data exchange capabilities might lead to deviations and defects that are hard to identify and costly to repair [17].

Ensuring consistency and correctness of project data is crucial, as the cost for defect detection and repair can be very high. A defect can have a strong negative impact on data of several disciplines; therefore, detecting defects in primary data sources will result in required corrections in related disciplines. For instance, if a wrong sensor type was specified in the physical topology (mechanical engineering) of the automation system, wrong information could be inserted in the corresponding electrical plan (electrical engineering) and wrong value ranges could be specified for control variables (software engineering). These interrelations between artifacts of different disciplines are often not explicitly documented, which makes defect detection and correcting time and efforts consuming, increasing the risks of ME projects [2]. Thus, efficient and effective defect detection methods and the ability to learn from past defects to avoid them in the future become key factors for successful projects.

In this paper we present an adapted method based on defect causal analysis (DCA) for systematically analyzing defects and their root causes [4] to (a) enable early defect detection and (b) prevent similar (maybe systematic) defects in future projects. Main challenges focus on the main characteristics of ME projects: (a) different disciplines involved in the engineering process; (b) large number of heterogeneous engineering artifacts; and (c) inter-disciplinary dependencies in project data. As an efficient DCA implementation requires an appropriate defect classification (DC) scheme (e.g., based on [10]), we built a DC scheme reflecting specifics of the ME domain based on existing DC schemes in software engineering. We also present an application scenario of the adapted DCA in an ME project context of our industry partner. The results of the initial feasibility study show that the adapted DCA approach provides a solid foundation for improving engineering processes and product quality in ME projects.

The remainder of this paper is structured as follows: Section 2 describes related work. Section 3 highlights the research issues. Section 4 presents the adaptation of the DCA in the context of ME environments. Section 5 provides an example on how adapted DCA method can be applied in a ME project of our industry partner. Finally, Section 6 discusses the results, concludes and lists future work.

2 Related Work

This section summarizes related work on engineering processes in multi-disciplinary engineering (ME) environments, introduces defect classification approaches, and the DCA method successfully applied in software engineering.

2.1 Engineering Process in Multi-disciplinary Environments

ME projects, e.g., in the automation systems engineering (ASE) domain, typically follow a rather sequential engineering process (see Figure 1 for an example of a high-level process). However, in industry practice different stakeholders typically work concurrently because of tight time schedules and project constraints. Different phases of the engineering process involve various stakeholders who have to collaborate and exchange data. Thus, ME projects include additional potential risks coming from the heterogeneity of data models and concurrent engineering [2][17]. Defects – especially if detected in later project stages – can have a major impact on product and process quality [7]. Therefore, a key challenge is enabling efficient and effective mechanisms for early defect detection, repair, and prevention.

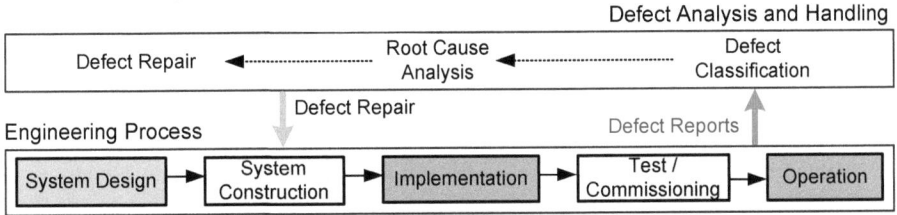

Fig. 1. Observed Sequential Engineering Process in ASE Projects, acc. to [17]

To enable high product quality in ME projects, artifacts – derived from different disciplines – have to be synchronized frequently to (a) propagate changes across discipline boundaries and (b) identify defects early. See Figure 2 for an example of a data synchronization process with defect detections mechanisms.

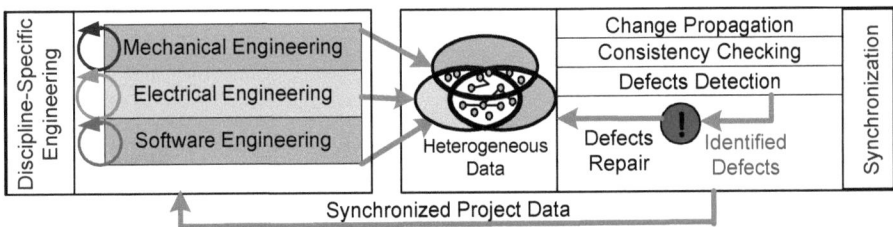

Fig. 2. Synchronization Process in Multi-Disciplinary Engineering Projects

Basically two important types of defects affect engineering processes (a) *intra-disciplinary defects* (affect data within one discipline) and (b) *inter-disciplinary defects* (affect data in more than one discipline), e.g., changing a sensor (mechanical engineering) might have an effect on the related software component (software engineering) and might lead to defects if not addressed properly. While intra-disciplinary defects are usually covered by discipline-specific tools, inter-disciplinary defects are discovered and fixed mainly during the synchronization. To better address such defects the DCA method can be applied during the synchronization process to enhance defect detection and defect prevention methods.

2.2 Defect Classification Schemes in Software Engineering

In software engineering several defect classification (DC) schemes are available for a range of software artifacts. For instance, the IBM's Orthogonal Defect Classification proposes defect classes that cover a set of different dimensions [6]: *Activity*, *Trigger* and *Impact*, which can be collected when the defect is detected; and *Target*, *Defect Type*, *Qualifier*, *Age* and *Source*, which can be collected when the defect is fixed [6]. Another DC scheme has been designed by Hewlett-Packard [8][9]. It considers three dimensions: *Origin*, i.e. the source of the defect; *Type*, i.e. the description of what is wrong; and *Mode* that can be one of missing, unclear, or wrong [8]. The latest version of the IEEE standard for classifying software anomalies [10] considers – in addition to *source*, *type* and *mode* – attributes like *defect severity*, *priority*, *status* as well as *defect insertion* and *detection activities*. Finally, another DC scheme, used mainly in the context of software inspections, has been proposed by Shull [15], who distinguishes a set of defects classes: *omission, ambiguity, inconsistent information, extraneous information* and *incorrect facts* [15].

Although these DC schemes are rather mature and there have been numerous attempts reported to apply them in software engineering projects for different purposes, none of them are commonly used in practice [16]. On the contrary, general classifications are difficult to apply in practice and need to be adapted to a specific discipline, domain, or organization [16]. Also, all these DC schemes are designed to mainly deal with the defects in selected software artifacts. The variety of different engineering artifacts that are used during the project and product life-cycle in ME projects requires adjusting the DC scheme. In addition, the presence of several different engineering disciplines that cooperate concurrently within the project must be reflected in the desired DC scheme for ME projects.

2.3 Defect Causal Analysis

In literature and industry practice many process improvement approaches (e.g., Six Sigma [14] or FMEA [3]) incorporate causal analysis activities [12]. Defect Causal Analysis (DCA) [4] is a prominent and well-established method in software engineering to analyze and classify defects and to identify root causes as important driver for improvement actions. In addition the DCA enables learning from defects to improve processes and products – an important benefit in context of continuous improvement strategies [5]. Thus, applying DCA in ME projects might increase project, product, and process quality. Card [4] proposed six basic steps of the DCA process that must be performed during the DCA session, e.g., in a workshop (see Figure 3).

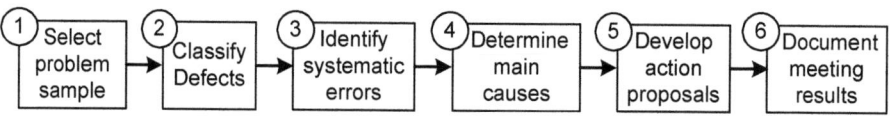

Fig. 3. Defect Causal Analysis Approach, according to [5]

The individual steps of the DCA process include:

1. *Selecting a defect sample* with focus on defects to be analyzed during the DCA.
2. *Classifying selected defects* according to a defined classification scheme.

3. *Identifying systematic errors.* A systematic error is an error that results in similar defects repeated in different occasions. To support identifying relevant systematic errors within the defect data, a common practice is to use (a) filtering on specific attribute(s) of the defect classification (DC) scheme and (b) applying Pareto charts on one (or several) other attributes from the DC scheme [12] in order to identify most common defect classes. This strategy is based on the assumption that relevant systematic errors are more likely to occur in the defect classes that contain most defects [4]; defects of those classes are read and analyzed to identify the systematic errors causing them.
4. *Determining the main causes.* Experts identify the main causes responsible for each systematic error. To support their reasoning they can use a cause-effect diagram [11], which typically graphically represents problems related to people, input, process/methods, tools, or the organization structure itself [12].
5. *Developing action proposals.* Action proposals aim to avoid similar defects in future. Objectively comparing the outcomes in future projects (number of severe defects) is important to measure the overall benefits of the DCA session.
6. *Documenting session results.* This step reinforces the importance of documenting identified defect classes, systematic errors, root causes and action proposals.

Based on the experiences in software engineering, the application of DCA in ME projects seems to be promising to improve quality of engineering processes.

3   Research Issues

ME projects require effective and efficient methods for defect detection, repair, and prevention. Thus, analyzing defects and identifying their root causes are success critical issues in order to improve process and product quality. Therefore, we identified two main research issues.

RI.1. How to adapt the DCA process to the context of ME projects? DCA has been successfully applied in software engineering [13], also in industrial settings. However, the question is to which extent the DCA is applicable (or have to be adapted) in ME environments involving distributed and heterogeneous tools and data sources. Basically, we believe that similar steps – proposed by Card [5] – are applicable. However, some adjustments regarding the defect classification scheme and DCA process are required to address requirements and needs of ME projects. Thus, the first research issue focuses on how to adapt DCA process for application in ME domains.

RI.2. How to adapt a defect classification (DC) scheme to the context of ME projects? The challenge is to identify and encode the characteristics of the heterogeneous ME environments into the desired DC scheme. The important questions are (a) how to address defects in various artifacts along the ME project life-cycle; (b) how to consider different disciplines; and (c) how to capture relationships and dependencies between different disciplines. Thus, the second research issue focuses on how to design and adapt the DC scheme for the ME domain.

4 DCA in Multi-disciplinary Engineering Environments

In this section we propose a defect classification (DC) scheme for multi-disciplinary engineering (ME) environments as an extension of existing software engineering best-practices (i.e., based on the IEEE standard [10]) and present an adapted DCA process approach with focus on ME characteristics, i.e., (a) involvement of different disciplines; (b) large number of heterogeneous engineering artifacts; and (c) inter-disciplinary dependencies in project data.

4.1 Adapting Defect Classification Scheme to the ME Environments

The minimal information captured by the DC scheme to be suitable for the DCA must cover: (a) *defect insertion* (to identify the cause of a defect); (b) *defect detection* (to understand how the defect detection methods can be improved); and (c) *defect type* (explains the nature of defect, which is useful both for identifying the possible causes and actions for process improvement) [12]. In order to build a DC scheme that is suitable for DCA in ME contexts, we base on the established IEEE standard [10]. This DC scheme already covers defect insertion and detection activities, which is important for DCA. Also, IEEE DC scheme is a good compromise between brevity and having all necessary information to describe the nature of defect, i.e., such information as type, mode, status and effect of a defect is already included. The adapted DC scheme consists of seven attributes that are described in details below.

Information about insertion and detection is represented by **Insertion Context** and **Detection Context** that both take into account the presence of different disciplines and the heterogeneity of engineering artifacts in ME projects. *Insertion Context* includes several sub-attributes, which are *Discipline*, i.e., the engineering discipline on which side a defect was inserted; *Artifact Type*, e.g., specifications, PLC code, or electrical plans; *Artifact*, i.e., specific engineering artifacts, in which a defect was inserted; *Activity* during which a defect was inserted; and project *Phase* during which the defect was inserted. *Detection Context* has similar structure and consists of *Discipline, Artifact Type, Artifact, Activity* and *Phase* sub-attributes, but related to defect detection.

Importance of inter-disciplinary relations between engineering artifacts and estimation of how a certain defect affects data in ME project are represented by 2 attributes: **Impact** and **Rating**. *Impact* describes other engineering artifacts which are affected by the original defect. These artifacts can come from the same discipline or from other disciplines involved in a project. *Rating* consists of *Priority* and *Severity*. *Priority* specifies how urgent a defect has to be fixed and *Severity* describes the potential project risk resulting from the defect. A specific value of *Severity* is assigned based on the impact that a certain defect has on data of other disciplines, i.e., a defect that influences many artifacts in other disciplines might gets a higher risk level than defects that affect only artifacts of the same discipline.

Further information related to defect nature and candidate defect causes is captured by **Current Status**, **Type** and **Mode** attributes. *Current Status* describes current defect status within the defect life-cycle. *Type* characterizes a high-level artifact type where the defect is located, i.e., in specification documents, data, interface, or logic. *Mode* represents the nature of a defect. To specify values for this attribute we adopted the classification of Shull [15], who distinguishes between *omission*, *ambiguity*, *inconsistent information*, *extraneous information* and *incorrect fact*.

4.2 Adapting DCA Process to the ME Environments

Although the general DCA process flow proposed by Card [5] remains unchanged, most of the process steps must be adapted according to the characteristics of the ME domain. Figure 4 presents the general DCA process, including the required adaptations with focus on ME characteristics: (A) refers to different engineering disciplines; (B) focuses on heterogeneous engineering artifacts and data; and (C) identifies changes related to inter-disciplinary dependencies in project data.

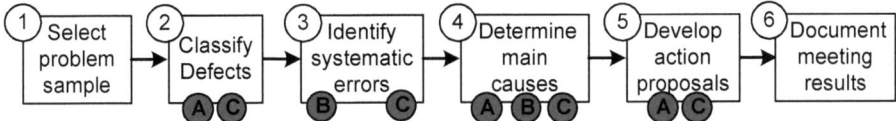

Fig. 4. Adaptation of the DCA steps in ME Environments based on Card [5]

DCA is typically executed in an expert workshop, where related disciplines have to participate in order to analyze defects and identify root causes and counter measures for defect detection and prevention. In general it is important that at least one representative from each discipline participates in a DCA meeting. This enables appropriate defect classifying and identifying credible candidate root causes (from perspective of all disciplines). It is also desirable that sample defects for a specific DCA meeting are taken from the defect data of one individual discipline. This helps to (a) narrowing the range and decreasing diversity of candidate root causes and (b) allowing a better focus of meeting participants. In addition, DCA should focus mainly on inter-disciplinary defects, as intra-disciplinary defects are usually covered by discipline-specific defect detection tools before synchronization steps (see Figure 2).

The *Defect Classification* process step is based on the adapted defect classification (DC) scheme (described in Section 4.1). Inter-disciplinary dependencies between engineering artifacts are covered by *Impact* attribute and partially by *Priority* and *Severity* attributes that reflect how many inter-disciplinary dependencies a specific defect has. Links to specific engineering disciplines are provided by the *Discipline* sub-attribute of *Insertion Context* and *Detection Context*. This information helps understanding in which discipline (a) something wrong happened and (b) which methods, tools and/or processes should be improved to avoid similar defects in the future.

Identifying systematic errors. In this step we suggest using filtering on *Impact* or/and *Rating* attributes, which will ensure that analysis focuses on defects that have the strongest impact on artifacts of other disciplines and are the most risky for the ME project. Additionally, applying Pareto charts on defect *Mode* and *Type* could be helpful to decrease the variety of engineering artifacts that must be considered during the DCA analysis and, thus, to reduce the complexity of the DCA process.

Determining main causes. Based on identified systematic errors and defects, DCA participants identify possible root causes in all related disciplines. We propose adding one extra dimension to a standard cause effect diagram [11] that will represent individual disciplines and a separate first level arrow for representing causes related to communication and exchange problems between the disciplines (e.g., defects in the change propagation tool between two disciplines). Each discipline dimension considers five standard root causes related to *people, input, process/methods, tools* and *organization*. Figure 5 shows the adapted cause-defect diagram including additional dimensions related to different disciplines and communication mechanisms in a typical ME project.

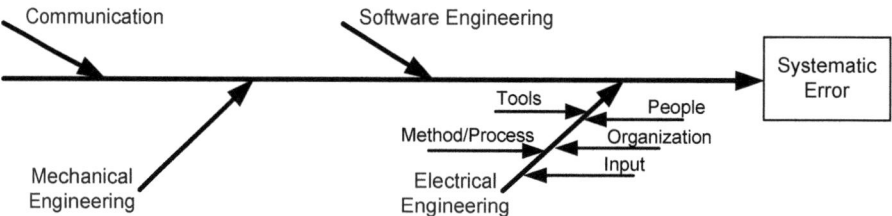

Fig. 5. Adapted Cause-Effect Diagram applicable for ME projects

Developing action proposals. Actions proposals focus on engineering processes of involved disciplines, communication, and data exchange mechanisms to enable defect correction and prevention in future ME projects.

5 Feasibility Study and Improvement Results

This section presents a typical scenario in ME project environments, observed at our industry partner, a large-scale automation systems integrator, and reports on four steps of an improvement strategy based on DCA applications. Following a pragmatic approach (see Figure 6), the authors started with a context analysis and definition (step 1), followed by an initial DCA application in ME (step 2) and the implementation of improvement actions (step 3). Finally, a second DCA session is performed to analyze if identified defect types have been addressed properly (step 4).

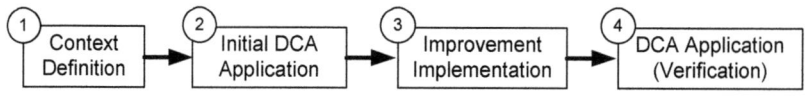

Fig. 6. Improvement Strategy based on two DCA Applications

5.1 Use Case Scenario in Multi-disciplinary Engineering Projects

As use case scenario we consider a typically ME project at a large-scale power plants systems integrator. Figure 7 (upper part, yellow) presents the initial starting point, i.e., three different disciplines involved in the ME project (i.e., mechanical, electrical, and software engineering). Every discipline applies individual and specific tools and data models with limited capabilities for collaboration and data exchange. Because of limited resources parallel engineering activities of individual disciplines is required. Thus, individual disciplines data have to be synchronized manually, which include a notable effort by experts (see Figure 7a). Note that in the observed project, a set of 20k data objects are available which makes the manual synchronization process error-prone and risky. Based on this initial setting we applied the adapted DCA process approach (see Section 4.2) to derive improvement options for engineering processes. Note that Figure 7b (i.e., lower part, green) illustrates the improved engineering process after implementing improvement actions (see Section 5.3 for details).

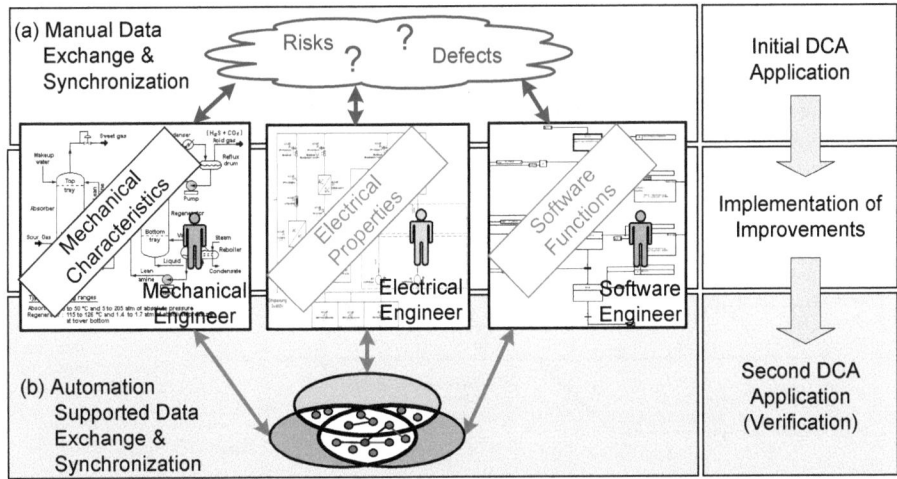

Fig. 7. Collaboration Challenges and Solution Approach in ME projects

5.2 Applying the DCA Process to Find Improvement Options

A typical check during the synchronization is the so-called end-to-end test [17] including the overall tool chain from hardware sensors (mechanical engineering) to wiring inputs and outputs (electrical engineering) and further to software variables in the Programmable Logic Controller (PLC) code (software engineering).

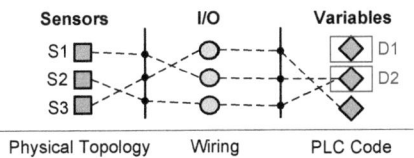

Fig. 8. End-to-End Test in ME Projects across Disciplines and Domain Data [17]

Figure 8 illustrates the related engineering objects and their connection points. Sample candidate defects are: D1 – no link from variable to the electrical wiring I/O interfaces; and D2 – variable is linked to multiple sensors. The DCA aims at finding the root causes of these types of defects.

The initial DCA meeting aims at addressing software engineering defects with a main focus on inter-disciplinary defects. We assume that the sample defect data was obtained from end-to-end test (e.g., based on Figure 8). After classifying all defects according to adapted classification scheme (see Section 4.1), systematic errors can be identified. As the main focus is on defects that have the highest impact on data across discipline borders, participants apply filtering on the *Impact* followed by a Pareto chart on *Type* and *Mode*. Result of this step includes 3-4 most common defects types, which are analyzed to identify the systematic errors. From industry partners we learned that one of the most common defect types is *"inconsistent variable data in PLC code"*. One of the systematic errors defined for this defect type is that the type of variable (e.g., integer or float) differs from the type of corresponding sensor (e.g., digital or analog). Figure 9 presents the cause effect diagram with candidate root causes for this systematic error. Basically the root causes focus on issues related to data exchange and communication, people and a lack of tool support.

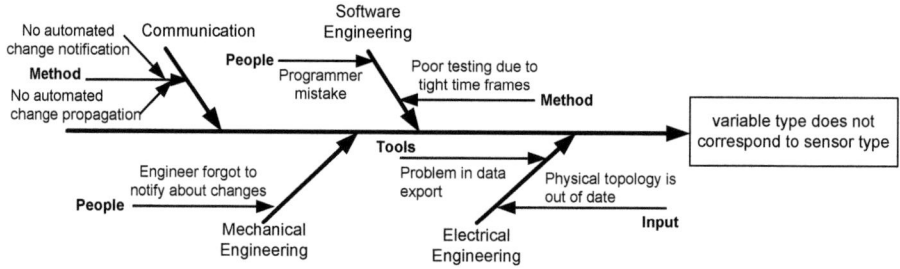

Fig. 9. Sample Defect Causal Diagram for finding Root Causes

The last step is proposing actions for process improvement based on identified root causes. Possible actions can go towards improving the exchange and notification mechanisms between the disciplines in an automated way. A specific example of such action will be the application of a common concept approach [1]. Common concepts refer to a systematic mapping of different and heterogeneous disciplines based on commonly applied information sets to support data exchange. For instance, signals in the automation systems domain [18] are used to identify individual devices (e.g., within the physical topology of the system), wires in the electrical domain to identify the voltage level of a signal, and software variables to control the systems behavior.

5.3 Improved Engineering Process Based on Action Proposals

The DCA results have shown improvement options for (a) data exchange between different data models in heterogeneous environments; (b) communication issues (changes are not propagated sufficiently to affected disciplines); and (c) people that have to overcome these technical limitations manually (including high work effort and cost). Based on the results we recommended the application of common concepts and an automation-supported synchronization [18]. The main contribution of this solution is to overcome the technical gap between different tools and the semantic gap between data models by introducing common concepts. The application of the collaboration platform (ASB) [1] enables experts to focus on changes (propagated from individual disciplines) and defects (deviations of data models linked by the common concepts). Thus, applying common concepts aims at mitigating risks from process and human related aspects to software and system related issues (see [18] for details and the pilot application at the industry partner. Figure 7b (i.e., lower part, green) illustrates the contribution of the common concepts in ME projects. Due to the automation supported communication and data exchange mechanisms, provided by the ASB, identified root causes, i.e., data exchange and communication issues (the ASB provides a link between heterogeneous sources), people (experts can focus on the most relevant parts, i.e., changes and deviations in related data models), and tool support (for the synchronization process) have been addressed.

In terms of continuous improvement strategies we repeated the adapted DCA method on the ASB solution and identified two important findings: (a) the originally identified root causes have been solved sufficiently and (b) one new root cause came up. In case of (systematic) errors in the common concepts, i.e., if the mapping between the heterogeneous data sources and the common concepts are incorrect (either missing information and/or wrongly configured mapping table), an automation supported synchronization will lead to systematic errors that have to be fixed again. Nevertheless, these defects are easier to find and to repair by experts.

6 Discussion, Limitations and Future Work

In heterogeneous and multi-disciplinary engineering (ME) environments, where stakeholders coming from different disciplines have to collaborate, defects play a crucial role. If related engineering tools are loosely connected and data models are not compatible, engineering process is error-prone and risky. Manual effort has to be invested to synchronize data in ME environments. Methods for analyzing defects and identifying their root causes, e.g., the Defect Causal Analysis (DCA) might help to mitigate related risks. However, although DCA has successfully applied in software engineering [13] there is little experience on how to apply it in ME projects.

In this paper we presented an adapted DCA approach for ME projects and applied this approach in context of a project at our industry partner in order to identify root causes of defects and to prevent them in future. Main results of this paper were that the basic DCA steps [4] are quite similar; however, individual adaptations (RQ.1) are required in individual steps of the process (see Section 4.2). Compared to defect classification schemes in Software Engineering, adaptations are required (RQ.2) to address special characteristics of ME projects (see Section 4.1).

The feasibility study, carried out at our industry partner, a large-scale system integrator in the hydro power plant domain, showed, that the application of the adapted

DCA approach can help identifying defects and root causes as well as identifying and mitigating risks in ME projects. In this context we identified three main root causes for defects (e.g., inconsistencies and errors) based on human errors (because they have to handle a large amount of data), loosely coupled tools (limited interoperability of tools), and incompatible data models (semantic heterogeneity). To overcome these limitations we introduced an automation supported synchronization process that helps experts and engineers to overcome these limitations. However, based on a second application of the modified DCA approach, we identified a new root cause that can cause a systematic error and – as a consequence – incorporates additional risks which have to be mitigated in a next step. As a result, we learned that in context of a continuous improvement process, a series of DCA can help to improve projects, processes, and products.

Limitations. Regarding the limitations of the presented approach, additional time and manpower will be required to implement DCA in ME projects. First of all, engineers (in an ideal case at least one representative from each involved discipline) must participate in a DCA meeting. Secondly, if there are no established techniques applied in a project to collect and trace necessary defect data, such techniques must be included in order to provide required input for the DCA. Finally, additional efforts are required from the engineers (possibly on the side of all involved disciplines) to implement the action proposals for process improvement.

Future work. As future work, we plan to (a) investigate the possibility for providing automated support during the execution of adapted DCA, e.g., using a knowledge base to store defect types and corresponding root causes, in order to reduce the added cost for its application; and (b) perform an experiment on the data from a ME project of an industry partner involving domain experts from different disciplines in a DCA meeting.

References

[1] Biffl, S., Schatten, A., Zoitl, A.: Integration of Heterogeneous Engineering Environments for the Automation Systems Lifecycle. In: Proc. of Industrial Informatics (Indin) (2009)
[2] Biffl, S., Moser, T., Winkler, D.: Risk Assessment in Multi-Disciplinary (Software+) Engineering Projects. International Journal of Software Engineering and Knowledge Engineering (IJSEKE), Special Session on Risk Assessment 21(2), 211–236 (2011)
[3] Campos, J.: Risk management and failure mode and effect analysis for product development. Rapid Innovation LLC (2012)
[4] Card, D.N.: Defect-causal analysis drives down error rates. IEEE Software 10(4), 98–99 (1993)
[5] Card, D.N.: Defect Analysis: Basic Techniques for Management and Learning. In: Zelkowitz, M. (ed.) Advances in Computers, vol. 65, pp. 259–295. Elsevier (2005)
[6] Chillarege, R.: Orthogonal Defect Classification. In: Lyu, M.R. (ed.) Handbook of Software Reliability Engineering. IEEE (1991)
[7] Chemuturi, M.: Mastering Software Quality Assurance: Best Practices, Tools and Techniques for Software Developers. J. Ross Publication Inc. (2010) ISBN: 978-1604270327
[8] Grady, R.B.: Software Failure Analysis for High-Return Process Improvement Decisions. Hewlett Packard Journal 47, 15–24 (1996)

[9] Huber, J.T.: A comparison of IBM's orthogonal defect classification to Hewlett Packards defect origins, types, and modes. In: Proc. Conf. on Appl. of SW Measurement, pp. 1–17 (2000)
[10] IEEE: Classification for software anomalies, IEEE Std. 1044-2009 (2010)
[11] Ishikawa, K.: Guide to Quality Control. Asian Productivity Organization Press (1986)
[12] Kalinowski, M., Card, D.N., Travassos, G.H.: Evidence-based guidelines to defect causal analysis. IEEE Software 29(4), 16–18 (2012)
[13] Kalinowski, M., Mendes, E., Travassos, G.H.: An Industry Ready Defect Causal Analysis approach exploring Bayesian Networks. In: Proc. 6th SW Quality Days, pp. 12–33 (2014)
[14] Kwak, Y.H., Anbari, F.T.: Benefits, obstacles, and future of six sigma approach. Technovation 26(5), 708–715 (2006)
[15] Shull, F.J.: Developing Techniques for using Software Documents: a Series of Empirical Studies. PhD Thesis, University of Maryland (1998)
[16] Wagner, S.: Defect classification and defect types revisited. In: Proc. of the 2008 Workshop on Defects in Large Software Systems, pp. 39–40. ACM (2008)
[17] Winkler, D., Biffl, S.: Improving Quality Assurance in Automation Systems Development Projects. In: Quality Assurance and Management, pp. 379–398. INTEC (2012)
[18] Winkler, D., Moser, T., Mordinyi, R., Sunindyo, W.D., Biffl, S.: Engineering Object Change Management Process Observation in Distributed Automation Systems Projects. In: Proc. of the 18th EuroSPI Conference, Roskilde, Denmark (2011)

Information Sources and Their Importance to Prioritize Test Cases in the Heterogeneous Systems Context

Ahmad Nauman Ghazi[1], Jesper Andersson[2], Richard Torkar[3], Kai Petersen[1], and Jürgen Börstler[1]

[1] Blekinge Institute of Technology, Karlskrona, Sweden
[2] Linnaeus University, Växjö, Sweden
[3] Chalmers University of Technology, Gothenburg, Sweden
{nauman.ghazi,kai.petersen,jurgen.borstler}@bth.se,
jesper.andersson@lnu.se, richard.torkar@chalmers.se

Abstract Context: Testing techniques proposed in the literature rely on various sources of information for test case selection (e.g., requirements, source code, system structure, etc.). The challenge of test selection is amplified in the context of heterogeneous systems, where it is unknown which information/data sources are most important.

Contribution: (1) Achieve in-depth understanding of test processes in heterogeneous systems; (2) Elicit information sources for test selection in the context of heterogeneous systems. (3) Capture the relative importance of the identified information sources.

Method: Case study research is used for the elicitation and understanding of which information sources are relevant for test case privatization, followed by an exploratory survey capturing the relative importance of information sources for testing heterogeneous systems.

Results: We classified different information sources that play a vital role in the test selection process, and found that their importance differs largely for the different test levels observed in heterogeneous testing. However, overall all sources were considered essential in test selection for heterogeneous systems.

Conclusion: Heterogeneous system testing requires solutions that take all information sources into account when suggesting test cases for selection. Such approaches need to be developed and compared with existing solutions.

1 Introduction

With the technological advancement in the software industry, more and more heterogeneous systems are introduced in the market. A heterogeneous system is comprised of multiple subsystems. A review of literature on the topic conducted by us did not reveal a commonly agreed definition of what a heterogeneous system is. Though, literature provides examples, such as, heterogeneity in this context can refer to that systems are implemented on different platforms, being developed using different processes, be of different size, etc.

A subsystem can exhibit heterogeneity in terms of both hardware and software. It does not limit itself to these aspects, though. Heterogeneity can also occur at different levels within the software development process. Heterogeneous systems are inherently complex and pose certain challenges to the verification and validation activities, such as specification, selection and execution of tests.

Testing of heterogeneous systems has received vast attention in recent years. In large heterogeneous systems it was observed that regression test suites grow, and hence require too much time to execute. In response, there is a need to prioritize and select test cases [1]. The challenge of test selection has been thoroughly investigated in previous research (e.g., in systematic reviews [4, 10]), but there still is a need to understand which information needs and sources are of relevance to guide practitioners of heterogeneous systems in selecting tests.

In this research, we identify the information sources required by practitioners involved in developing heterogeneous systems to prioritize test cases. This is done in a two step process. In the first step an industrial case study is conducted to understand how heterogeneous systems are tested and to elicit information sources, followed by an exploratory survey. The findings are compared with the literature investigating test selection independently of heterogeneous systems. The information gathered could be used in organizations to assure that the required information is available to testers to support them during the selection process. From an industrial perspective, identification of these information sources will further help to develop a framework to initiate a search space for automating test selection in different stages of development using search-based software testing techniques.

The remainder of the paper is structured as follows: Section 2 presents the related work. Section 3 outlines the research method, followed by the results in Section 4. Section 5 concludes the study by presenting a discussion of observations from the results.

2 Related Work

Heterogeneous Systems: Testing a heterogeneous system implies that several possible configurations must be tested. Reuse of artifacts is one way to speed up such repetitive activities considerably [6]. Otani et al. propose a framework that depends heavily on UML artifacts, which are used to automate independent verification and validation practices using generative technologies. These reusable artifacts are stored as XML data and reusable for other activities as well as other testing projects [5]. Otani et al. extend this work further [6] and introduce goal-driven reuse of artifacts in the context of heterogeneous systems. Changing configurations pose challenges to combinatorial testing techniques. To that end, Cohen et al. [3] conducted an empirical study to quantify the effectiveness of test suites. The study shows that there is an exponential growth of test cases when configurations change and subsets of test suites are used, similar to what is common in regression testing. Vega et al. [11] propose a TTCN-3 based framework to test HL7 health-care applications. The technique supported by the framework is generic and does not need customization every time a configuration changes. Brahim et al. [2] provide a technique to specify test cases in globally distributed environments. This framework uses the UML 2 testing profile and TTCN-3 for test specification and generation. The authors claim that the use of TTCN-3 in combination with other languages and test notations ensures transparency and cost benefits. Overall, testing of heterogeneous systems involves testing multiple configurations and dealing with complex systems accross a variety of platforms.

Test Case Selection: We identified two recent secondary studies on test case prioritization and selection (cf. [4, 10]). Singh et al. [10] conducted a systematic literature review on test case prioritization in the context of regression testing. The authors implicitly mentioned some information sources while categorizing the techniques for test case specification and prioritization. Singh et al. categorized techniques, which implicitly point to the following information sources: requirements, source code structure, historical information (with respect to changes made to the system or execution history), fault-driven approaches (e.g., fault proneness), as well as cost. Furthermore, combinations of approaches have been evaluated. Engström et al. [4] identified code-based techniques as the most commonly investigated in the literature.

3 Research Method

We first conducted a case study [9] to gain an in-depth understanding of information sources and their relevance for heterogeneous system testing. Thereafter, based on the case study results, a survey is conducted to explore the importance of the identified information sources in a more broader perspective.

3.1 Case Study Design

Objectives. The case study took place in close collaboration with industry. The long-term expectation of our industrial partner from this research is to optimize their overall test methodology and practices for the organization's software product line. The overall long-term objectives of our research are to understand the state of practice in testing heterogeneous systems, and how this relates to a system's heterogeneity characteristics. In the long-term perspective a process for optional test selection should be defined. Identifying the relevant sources for test selection is the first step towards that overall goal. The goal of this study is formulated by following the Goal-Question-Metric approach: To gain an in-depth understanding of the test process and relevance of information sources (Purpose) for test selection (Issue) in the context of heterogeneous systems (Object) from an industrial point of view (Viewpoint).

Research Questions. In this exploratory case study we intend to answer the following research questions:

- RQ1: How are complex heterogeneous systems tested in practice from a process perspective?
- RQ2: What are the different information sources used in test selection?
- RQ3: Which information sources are most relevant in selecting and prioritizing test cases for testing complex heterogeneous systems in that process?

Case and Context: Petersen and Wohlin [8] suggest a checklist to report context in relation to an object of study. The test process and related information sources for test case selection are the object of study in this research. Table 1 provides an overview of context information for the test process studied, derived from process documentation and the interviews conducted.

Table 1. Context

Context	Description
Product	*System type:* System of systems (multiple subsystems developed autonomously) with a total of 22 subsystems
	Domain: Telecommunication systems
	Customization: Highly customizable based on individual customer needs
	Programming language: Java
	Quality: The most highly prioritized quality attributes driving tests are: (1) scalability, (2) usability, (3) performance, (4) robustness and recoverability, (5) throughput, (6) stability, (7) variability, and (8) maintainability of a total of 33 attributes prioritized.
People	See Table 2
Organization	ISO 9001:2000 Certified
Size	More than 5000 employees
Market	Market-driven development (high number of potential customers)
Process	Agile software development

Data Collection: Multiple methods of data collection are used in this case study. However, the main source of data collection in this study are semi-structured *interviews* with selected practitioners from the case company. These interviews mainly resulted in identifying different dimensions of heterogeneity, the test selection process, identification of multiple key information sources that lay the foundations for the test specification process, important quality criteria, weaknesses in the test process and factors that influence test case selection.

Although the interviewed practitioners have diverse roles, the information regarding different information sources for test selection, test prioritization based on quality attributes, and challenges in the test process converged after the third interview. Table 2 provides a brief profile of the interviewed practitioners.

Interview questions were structured into six themes, namely: (1) Experience and current role of the interviewee, (2) verification model, (3) levels of heterogeneity in product and test process, (4) test prioritization based on quality attributes, (5) test selection process, and (6) tester's perspective on weaknesses in test process. These interview themes are formulated to answer the research questions as well as to gain a better understanding of the current test activities at the organization which is the case under study and the context of each activity. The interviews were semi-structured and included open-ended questions. Each interview took approximately 60 minutes.

Table 2. Practitioners' profile

ID	Description
1	The interviewee is currently the head of functional node test team responsible for test activities within a subsystem, and has been working as a functional tester in this company since 2005.
2	The interviewee has worked in this company for 16 years overall. For the first 10 years worked as a requirement engineer and currently working as functional tester for last 6 years.
3	The interviewee is working as a system developer at the company and is exposed to design, development and test activities at the company. The interviewee has also worked in development of legacy system which is to be replaced with the current system.
4	The interviewee is part of the core test team and therefore is responsible for design decisions. The interviewee has responsibility for overall development and test strategy.

Documentation is also used as a data collection method for triangulation in this case study. Process and design documents of the product were obtained to capture the development and test processes at the company. These documents provided the researchers with a better understanding of different test levels and the strategy of the company.

Data Analysis: Interviews were recorded with the consent of the interviewees and later transcribed. For data extraction from these transcribed interviews, we used color coding, where unique colors were assigned to key areas important to answer the research questions. We identified and color-coded the following key areas:

- Test activities including test selection process as well as test execution
- Information sources for test selection
- Different levels of heterogeneity exhibited by the case under study
- Quality attributes that play an important role in test selection
- Weaknesses and challenges in the current test process

The *documentation* was analyzed using the same coding scheme.

Threats to Validity: A discussion of validity threats for software engineering is provided in [7].

Objectivity: An important threat is if the questions asked during the interviews are misunderstood. However, this threat was reduced by explaining the context to the interviewees, cross referencing the information gathered with the product documentation, and through member checking. Another threat to objectivity is that the interviewees may provide the information from a single perspective depending on their roles. This threat is minimized by carefully choosing the interviewees from different testing teams and development teams.

Theoretical Validity: Theoretical validity is concerned with not being able to capture what we intend to capture. In this case, we intend to prioritize the information sources used for test selection in the context of heterogeneous systems. To reduce this threat to theoretical validity, we first captured the information sources for test selection using both documentation and the interviews. We contacted further practitioners from other organizations involved in development of heterogeneous systems. These practitioners were asked to prioritize the list of information sources extracted from the documents and interviews to strengthen our findings.

Generalizability: The exploratory nature of the case study does not allow to generalize the results for all heterogeneous systems and all types of organizations. However, the results can be generalized to large scale telecommunication organizations involved in the development of system of systems that exhibit heterogeneity. Furthermore, even though not statistically generalizable, the results from the survey allowed to make qualitative reflections on the information gathered.

Interpretive Validity: Interpretive validity is concerned with researcher bias when drawing conclusions. Since the involved researchers have no particular preference for any of the solutions presented in the case study based on previous research, this threat can be considered low in this study.

3.2 Survey

Objective: The survey captured the relative importance of information sources in relation to test case selection, leading to research question $RQ3$.

Survey Distribution and Sample: A convenience sampling strategy was followed targeting practitioners that work with heterogeneous systems. We utilized personal contacts as well as communities (e.g., LinkedIn and Yahoo Groups) to acquire additional answers. Overall we obtained 42 answers of which 27 were complete and could be used for analysis.

Instrument: The survey[1] was capturing information about respondents, the characteristics of their organization and products, as well as test coverage goals and importance of the information sources for test selection and prioritization.

Analysis: For the analysis descriptive statistics are utilized.

Validity Threats: The same types of validity threats as for the case study.

Objectivity: To avoid possible misunderstandings of the survey questions, it was pre-tested and revised based on the feedback received. Furthermore, the survey was tested for duration to take at most 15 minutes to complete to avoid maturation.

Theoretical validity: One threat to inference is the number of participants. The present results are not statistically generalizable to a whole population. However, for the given context information gathered about the participants, some interesting qualitative observations can be made.

Generalizability: The surveyed companies have specific context characteristics that limit generalizability. The majority of respondents is related to consultancy (35.7%), followed by computer industry (28.9%) and communications (25.0%); other industries are under-represented. Agile and hybrid processes have the highest representations. Another possible bias is that only persons with a specific interest may have answered the survey.

Interpretive validity: Given that only quantitative data is studied in the survey part, the risk of bias is reduced.

---

[1] The supplementary information about interview and survey can be found at http://www.bth.se/tek/aps/kps.nsf/pages/sources-for-test-case-selection

4 Results

4.1 Test Process for Testing Heterogeneous Systems (RQ1)

Heterogeneity in the System under Test: The system of systems approach [1] used in the development of software products at the case company leads to heterogeneity. We identified three different dimensions of heterogeneity: (1) hardware heterogeneity, (2) software heterogeneity, and (3) process heterogeneity. These dimensions of heterogeneity are important to consider in an overall strategy to minimize the challenges they pose to the overall system(s).

During the interviews with the practitioners, we found that third-party open-source components are also used throughout the development of subsystems of the case company's next generation billing system. As the next generation billing system is developed to replace an existing telecom billing system that is used by a large number of globally distributed customers, there exist some legacy software components that are reused in the new system. Although, the complete product is developed using Java, due to legacy software there exist heterogeneity on the platform level.

It is also important to note, that the company recommends the use of certified hardware, but does not limit the customers to use the recommended hardware, which leads to hardware heterogeneity. Another factor that leads to hardware heterogeneity is the notion of variability. The next generation billing system is shipped to customers as part of different commercial offerings customized as per customer requirements. Therefore, this system can be used on multiple clusters configured to function as a single entity.

We also found, that due to multiple test levels, the practitioners perceive the underlying heterogeneity as an important factor while designing the test strategy. Heterogeneity at the verification level at telecom grade systems is very important to be considered. Otherwise, it may lead to the challenge of dealing with a huge number of tests to be executed to reach a thorough test coverage.

Test Levels and Selection Process: The case company is involved in the development of a large system of systems that exhibits heterogeneity at multiple levels, therefore optimal test selection is an important challenge. The case under study involves a test strategy with four different test levels: (1) software component test, (2) application component test, (3) subsystem component test, and (4) offering test. Each test level involves different test activities to ensure software verification.

Software component test: Test activities at this test level comprise interface and unit testing. The test tool JUnit is used for unit testing.

Application component test: This test level is targeted for testing of sub-subsystems that comprise several software components. The major challenge at this test level is the integration of software components to form functionally independent sub-subsystems. Integration testing at this level is performed using Pax-Exam, which is a test tool specialized for integration testing of OSGi components.

Subsystem component test: To test a functionally independent subsystem comprising several sub-subsystems, this test level includes multiple test activities. These test activities are functional testing, unit testing, tests for installation, testing upgrades, integration testing and tests for stability. A virtual test environment is set up for the continuous subsystem component integration testing. This environment consists of subsystems that comprise more components. Each subsystem team owns the component and is thus responsible for its delivery, update and installation.

Offering test: Once a subsystem component is verified, it is moved into the next integration environment for commercial offering validation. At this test level, in the integration environment different configurations and end-to-end communication are tested. This test level also validates the deployability on commercial offering environments. The deployment environment consists of delivered subsystem components as per the requirement of commercial offering. Each subsystem component is evaluated upon deployability on certified hardware.

Test case selection is performed for each of the test levels mentioned above. A core test team is responsible for developing the overall test strategy for the complete product. We also found that, apart from the core test team, there are dedicated test teams for each test level that are responsible for both test selection and execution. Test prioritization at each level is also done by these dedicated teams.

For test case selection and test prioritization, an in-house software is developed. This software, based on features, tags the test cases with certain labels by analyzing the keywords in each of the test cases. These test cases are further categorized into various groups to test certain features of the system. This software also assigns weights to different feature categories taking in consideration the system's requirements to prioritize the categories to be tested more frequently under constraints. However, under the time constraints, functional system testing is given the highest priority for verification of a commercial offering.

Every software component undergoes the unit test and application test, separately. Once these components are integrated to form an independently functional subsystem, functional node testing is done to identify possible defects in the system. Sub-net testing and network integration testing are later carried out, when all subsystems are integrated in the final product.

For different test activities and levels, the case company uses different testing tools. JUnit is used for unit testing of software components and Pax-Exam is used for the purpose of integration testing. However, there are other in-house testing tools used for functional testing of the functionally independent subsystems, as well as for system testing. Other than functional testing, non-functional testing for performance is also carried out at different levels.

Weaknesses in the Process for Test Case Selection: From the interviews we found the main weakness in the current test process to be a large regression test base. There are many test levels and each test level generates a huge number of test cases. The heterogeneous nature of the system also poses a huge challenge to the testing of the complete system.

To maximize the test coverage, functional test cases to cover every subsystem, sub-subsystem and its components are developed. These test cases are most of the time overlapping with the unit tests, therefore a good test selection process is required to avoid this overlapping of functional test cases and the unit test cases. The maximum test coverage is an important test objective stated by the practitioners. However, it also leads to a combinatorial explosion and in this case a robust test selection process that can help avoid executing the same test cases again and again.

It is also a challenge that each commercial offering has a different configuration and testers are required to test all possible configurations. Therefore, a process for efficient system configuration is needed. However, this challenge is more related to the design and the development process but it affects the overall test process. There shall be a procedure to facilitate functional testing to be self contained so they can be installed and configured automatically for each customizable commercial offering.

4.2 Information Sources (RQ2)

We identified a number of information/data sources that are of vital importance for the test selection process. The information sources comprise important information sources needed for optimal selection and prioritization of test cases. Other than the information sources, different roles that are vital for test selection are included in the list of data sources. The information sources mentioned later in this section are extracted from the documentation provided by the company and further validated during the interviews with the practitioners. Practitioners are also asked to list additional information sources, which they perceive as important for test selection.

Functional and *non-functional requirements* serve as the foundation of the complete development process that also encompasses the testing. The *System model* of the complete product provides a detailed overview of the system and its constituent subsystems. This model also identifies the data flow between the subsystems as well as sub-subsystems and software components. *Configurations* are important, as the system we studied has multiple telecom operators as its target customer base. The system is developed to be customizable for different customer needs. Various system configurations need to be tested for each commercial offering. *Test objectives* are the reason or purpose that drive the design and execution of a test case. These test objectives are used to derive an effective test strategy for different test levels and also serve as an important data source for test selection under resource constraints. *Environment descriptions* and *high-level analyses*, based on tester's input, are also found to be data sources that shall be used in the test selection process.

From the interviews, we found that in *software component test*, an important data source for unit and integration test activities is the *tester's input*. However, the importance of *requirements* and *test objectives* as information sources, for test selection at this test level, can not be overlooked. All data sources mentioned for *software component test* are also valid for *application component test*. Functional testing on the basis of *requirements* and *test objectives* is carried out at this test level. *Subsystem component test* comprises mainly integration and verification activities. Hence, *environment description, test objective* and *tester's input* serve as the prime data sources at this test level. As for the *offering test*, other than all data sources mentioned for preceding test levels, *configurations* play an important role. For testing of each commercial offering, specific configurations are pushed to the system to customize it according to the requirements. These configurations must be considered for test selection at this level to avoid execution of unrelated tests in the context of specific offerings and customer requirements.

4.3 Relative Importance of Information Sources (RQ3)

Demographics: With respect to the roles of subjects, mostly technically oriented roles answered the survey, in particular developers (22.2%), software architects (18.5%), software verification and validation (18.5%), and quality control/management (14.8%). Other roles were only represented by less than 10% of the respondents (system analysts, project managers, product managers, and software process engineers). With respect to experience in software engineering the average experience was 10.55 years. The average experience in testing heterogeneous systems was 4.63 years. Companies of various sizes participated: less than 50 employees (18.5%), 50 to 249 employees (29.6%), 250 to 4499 employees (29.6%), and 4500 and more (22.6%). The most common system type was data dominant software (63.0%), followed by control-dominant software (25.9), computation-dominant software (25.9%), and systems software (22.2%). Other systems were represented by 14.8%. The most common development models were agile (29.6%) and hybrid processes dominated by agile practices (29.6%). Other processes were represented by 11% or less (e.g., waterfall, V-model, spiral model).

Coverage and Information Sources Prioritization: We analyzed the importance of coverage criteria (see Figure 1), and found that specification-based criteria are considered most important, followed by fault-based coverage. All coverages are considered overall important.

We also analyzed how practitioners prioritize different information sources (see Figure 2), and found that most practitioners consider functional requirements as the most important information source followed by test objectives and system model. Each identified information source is considered important to a significant number of practitioners and therefore cannot be neglected. One respondent mentioned that they are utilizing 37 different information sources, but did not specify which these are.

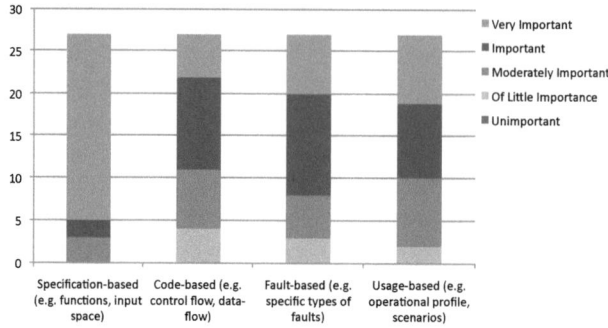

Fig. 1. Importance of test objectives

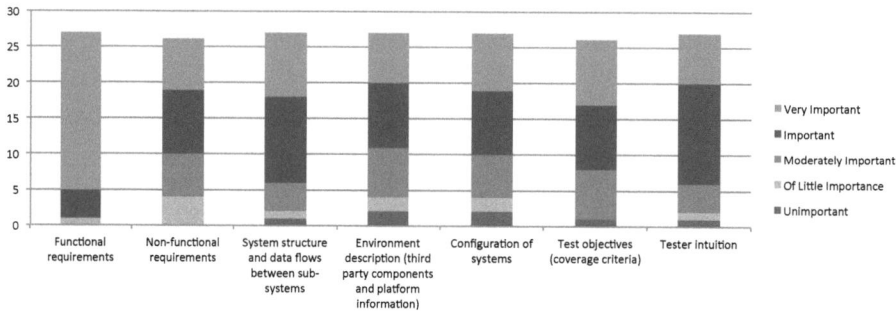

Fig. 2. Importance of data sources in test specification

5 Discussion and Conclusion

In this study, we investigated a heterogeneous testing process to understand how complex heterogeneous systems are tested. The main focus of this research was to identify information sources for test case selection. The literature as well as the results of our case study indicate that it is essential to reduce the size of continuously growing test suites.

We conducted a case study to gain an in-depth understanding of test selection in heterogeneous systems, followed by a survey to understand the relative importance of information sources. The following summarized our findings with respect to our research questions:

Test Process (RQ1): Multiple hierarchies of test levels have been identified that are relevant to test selection. Overall, the test levels map well to test levels one would expect from the V-model. Functional testing was given the highest priority, though at the same time quality characteristics were prioritized highly. The complexity of the overall system led to having several testing teams focusing on their specific test levels. Overall, a situation of overlapping tests occurred. Furthermore, core challenges were growing regression test suites and a high number of configurations to be tested when combining different (sub-)systems. The lessons learned regarding RQ1 are: First, a systematic investigation is needed to understand responsibilities of different test levels to avoid overlapping test cases. That is, one has to clearly determine which value each test level adds in terms of the kind of quality that is assured with it. Having a good understanding of this could potentially reduce the size of test suites significantly. Second, solutions from software product-line testing might be applicable to the testing of heterogeneous systems, since product-line testing faces similar challenges: when different (sub-)systems/features are combined, the number of configurations to be tested increases.

Information Sources for Test Selection and their Priorities (RQ2/3): In the research we identified multiple sources of information. Comparing with the literature, non-functional requirements and environment description are highlighted in the heterogeneous systems context. Generally, all sources were rated as either very important or important by the majority of respondents. But, the most important source of information were functional requirements. Looking at the existing techniques proposed for selection and prioritization, those techniques combining different information sources for prioritization are hence of particular interest, given that all sources appear to be of relevance when selecting tests in this context. Figure 3 shows that, given the high priority of information sources, they all have to be considered in the selection process. The selection process utilizes approaches to search for a set of good solutions for the next regression test run, taking the information sources into account.

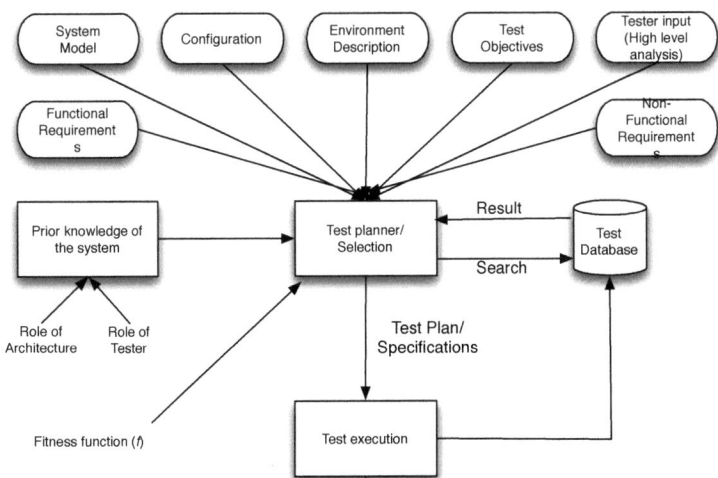

Fig. 3. Information Sources in the Test Process

In future work, we propose to focus on identifying and evaluating test selection approaches that are able to utilize all data sources for test selection, and comparing them with existing solutions on real systems.

References

1. Ali, N.B., Petersen, K., Mäntylä, M.: Testing highly complex system of systems: an industrial case study. In: ESEM, pp. 211–220 (2012)
2. Andaloussi, B., Braun, A.: A Test Specification Method for Software Interoperability Tests in Offshore Scenarios: A Case Study. In: ICGSE, pp. 169–178 (2006)
3. Cohen, M.B., Snyder, J., Rothermel, G.: Testing Across Configurations: Implications for Combinatorial Testing. Sof. Eng. Notes 31(6), 1–9 (2006)
4. Engström, E., Runeson, P., Skoglund, M.: A systematic review on regression test selection techniques. Inf. & Soft. Tech. 52(1), 14–30 (2010)
5. Otani, T.W., Michael, J.B., Shing, M.-T.: Software Reuse in the IV&V of System of Systems, May 30-June 3, pp. 1–5 (2009)
6. Otani, T.W., Michael, J.B., Shing, M.-T.: Goal-Driven Software Reuse in the IV & V of System of Systems, pp. 1–6 (June 2010)
7. Petersen, K., Gencel, C.: Worldviews, research methods, and their relationship to validity in empirical software engineering research. Mensura (2013)
8. Petersen, K., Wohlin, C.: Context in industrial software engineering research. In: ESEM, pp. 401–404 (2009)
9. Runeson, P., Höst, M.: Guidelines for conducting and reporting case study research in software engineering. Emp. Soft. Eng. 14(2), 131–164 (2009)
10. Singh, Y., Kaur, A., Suri, B., Singhal, S.: Systematic literature review on regression test prioritization techniques. Informatica 36(4), 379–408 (2012)
11. Vega, D.E.: Towards an Automated and Dynamically Adaptable Test System for Testing Healthcare Information Systems. In: ICST, pp. 331–334 (2010)

Software Process Assessment Validation and Improvement Prioritization

Sven Richter and David Escorial Rico

ESA-ESTEC,
Keplerlaan 1, 2200 AG Noordwijk ZH, The Netherlands
{sven.richter,david.escorial.rico}@esa.int
http://www.esa.int

Abstract. After a software process assessment is performed there are two main problems decision-makers face. First, how reliable are the assessment results presented. Though assessments are often performed by an independent competent third party, it is still important to be able to judge the validity of the determined capability profile and to assure that a faithful picture of the organisation has been captured. Second, in consideration of the results, identify what are the process-related risks for the organisation so they can guide the establishment of the priorities for a process improvement. This paper presents a method based on the dependencies between processes in order to support the validation of the assessment results and the identification of business critical processes for improvement.

Keywords: Space domain, ISO 15504, SPICE for Space, Risk identification, Assessment Validation, Improvement Prioritization.

1 Introduction

Process assessments provide means of characterizing an organizational unit in terms of the capability of selected processes and allow to identify strengths, weaknesses and risks related to the assessed processes. Target process profiles for these assessments are for example driven by customers who use process assessments as an input for supplier selection ("supplier capability determination") or by the criticality of the software to be developed. Often assessments are performed by a competent assessor on behalf of a so-called assessment sponsor and it is of utmost importance to the sponsor that the assessments will be performed with the required rigour allowing him to verify that the results are sound and consistent.

When the results of an assessment are evaluated, risks for ongoing and future projects can be identified and measures can be put in place to mitigate them. A common way to act on the results is to start a planned and structured process improvement initiative. However, it is usually difficult for organisations to establish a long-term roadmap for strategic process improvement. Even short-term improvement plans can be hard to define as organisations have to determine what processes they should improve first as most likely they cannot improve all at the same time, due to resource limitations. Improvement is an initial investment and requires the commitment of a company's management. If the managers do not understand clearly what can probably go wrong in future projects they are less likely to commit any resources for mitigating these risks. Without a proper approach they may not select the most business-critical processes as priority for improvement.

Voelcker et al. [11] tackled the issue of identifying critical processes for improvement and developed a method called R4S Risk Analysis with SPiCE for SPACE (S4S). S4S is an ISO 15504 (SPiCE) [7] conformant method for the evaluation of software processes in the space domain and has been developed by and for the European space industry and has been in use for more than 10 years [2]. R4S is based on four core elements: 1) a risk model which sets the generic correlation between risks and S4S processes; 2) an algorithm for risk likelihood calculation; 3) guidelines for risk severity estimation and 4) a scoring scheme for risk magnitude determination. Potential risks are identified from the risk model by using the process capability gap, i.e. the mismatch between target and achieved capability level. This capability gap is used to calculate the likelihood. The severity of the risks are determined by experts who gather in a workshop and finally establish the list of risks and their ranking based on the likelihood and severity. A similar but more straight forward approach was included in ISO 15504, Part 4, Annex A [7], as a way of analysing process-related risks.

In 2004 ISO/IEC 15504 was updated and in 2010 the European Space Agency (ESA) published its Software process assessment and improvement handbook ECSS-Q-HB-80-02 [4,5], based on the original SPiCE for SPACE. However, the approach of integrating risk management [3] into process assessment and improvement was not reflected in the handbook at the time of its publication.

A review of the R4S method revealed a number of possibilities for enhancements. R4S considers the gap analysis (achieved versus target) only at process level but not at the level of Work Products or Base Practices. This can be considered in some cases too coarse-grained for risk identification as for example for partially performed processes it is not clear which Base Practices are performed or which Work Products are produced. Additionally and more importantly, S4S and by extension R4S, as well as most of the assessment methods, consider all processes individually and do not fully take into account the interrelationship between processes. For example if one process P_1 does not produce a Work Product which is an input to another process P_2 it is likely that P_2 will be exposed to some risk not achieving its purpose. Assessment methods consider the determination of the "sequence and interaction" with other processes (see ISO15504-2, Process Attribute 3.1), although each process is assessed individually and its Process Attributes are rated independently.

2 Assumptions

This paper takes the assumption that processes in a software assessment framework are interrelated: the performance of a process has an influence on the performance of other processes to different degrees. These relationships have been shown in some studies, for example in the case of Medi SPICE [6] and CMMI [9]. However, these studies only perform an analysis within the framework models of the relationships and cross-references between processes. We propose to go one step further and assume that actual processes, evaluated in particular assessments, also influence each other's performance. Moreover, this interdependency which is supported by the process architecture specific to each organisation can be used for validating process assessments and prioritizing process improvement activities.

The method assumes that the target profiles in the assessments have been defined using techniques such as the ones described in Part 9 of ISO15504 [7]. The same standard identifies a set of generic consequences as a result of the process-related risks. We consider that these final consequences are also valid for the method presented.

This paper presents the first results of an on-going research about the creation of a method which identifies risks based on the outcome of a process assessment, taking into account the above mentioned assumptions.

3 The SCANNER Method

The developed method has been named SCANNER (**S**oftware pro**C**ess **A**ssessment validatio**N** a**N**d improvem**E**nt p**R**ioritization) as it "scans" performed process assessments in order to validate them and find priorities for improvement actions based on identified risks. The method is based on three steps. The first preparatory step can be executed once in order to create the necessary infrastructure to apply the method. The second step aims at collecting the necessary information from the assessment reports, while the last step objective is to perform the dependency analysis and visualise the results.

3.1 Preparation

Creating the Logical Reference Model. The central item of any process assessment is the Process Assessment Model (PAM) and there are a number of ISO 15504 conformant PAMs available. Most prominent examples are the exemplar software life cycle PAM as defined in ISO-15504 [7] or Automotive SPICE [1]. With many different instances of ISO 15504 conformant models it is important to ensure that the selected PAM is in itself sound and does not contain major inconsistencies.

ISO 15504 describes a process by:

- an identifier,
- a name,
- a purpose,
- several outcomes,
- several base practices, and
- several work products.

Base Practices and work products are contributing to the achievements of the outcomes.

As a first preparatory step of the research, the generic process model as defined in ISO 15504 has been converted into a logical model (see e.g. [12] pp. 7-32). Having a logical representation allows to detect inconsistencies in any PAM. Some of the consistency checks verify that a process does not expect an undefined Work Product as an input or output, or that all Base Practices of a processes support an Outcome.

Figure 1 gives a graphical presentation of the logical model as an Entity Relationship Diagram:

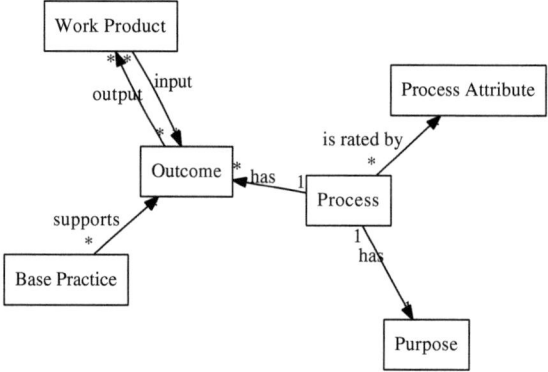

Fig. 1. Logical model of a PAM

Furthermore, having a logical representation of a PAM allows to query it using standardised languages like the Structured Query Language (SQL) and subsequently evaluate process models in an automated way.

In a second step the logical model as shown in Figure 1 has been instantiated by inserting the data from the PAM as defined in ECSS-Q-HB-80-02 Part 2A. From the population of the logical model the following was obtained:

- 6 capability levels (CL), which is a 6 point ordinal scale (0 to 5) representing an increasing capability of the performed process.
- 9 process attributes (PA), which indicate whether a process has reached a given capability. They are denoted as PA[CL].[id], e.g. PA2.2 (Work product management).
- 52 processes (P), denoted as [Class].[No], e.g. ENG.1 for the Engineering process one (Requirements Elicitation),
- 282 outcomes (O) which are observable results of the successful implementation of a process,
- 364 base practices (BP) which are activities addressing 446 outcomes (a BP can be linked to more outcomes), e.g. ENG.1.BP.1 for the first BP of ENG.1,

- 223 work products (WP) which are used for the verification of the 1.505 outcomes (a WP can be linked to more outcomes) and the performance of the BPs. They are named WPxx-xx where xx are numbers uniquely identifying the work product, e.g. WP11-05 Software Unit.

Definition of Risk Patterns. A risk is characterized by reference to potential events and consequences, or a combination of these. ISO 31000 [8] defines an event as an "occurrence or change of a particular set of circumstances". Thus, applied to our model, risk events could be defined as a violation of a relationship of the entities, e.g. a BP is not performed or a WP is not created.

These risk events can further be linked to the achievement of process attributes where defined. Considering the complexity above Capability Level 3, CL4 and CL5 are disregarded and will be addressed at a later stage.

The following list shows the identified risk events grouped by entities of the model.

Process risk events:

- P <process>is not performed, i.e. does not achieve its purpose (PA 1.1)
- P <process>takes more resources than expected
- P <process>is not managed (PA 2.1)
- P <process>is not based on a standardized process P_S (PA 3.1)
- P <process>is not properly tailored from a standardized process P_S (PA 3.2)

Outcome risk events:

- O <outcome>is not achieved
- O <outcome>loses BP <base practice>
- O <outcome>loses WP <work product>

WP risk events:

- WP <work product>is not developed (PA 1.1)
- WP <work product>is not managed (PA 2.2)
- WP <work product>is not based on a standardized work product WP_S (PA 3.1)
- WP <work product>is not properly tailored from a standardized work product WP_S (PA 3.2)

Base Practice risk event:

- BP <base practice>is not performed (PA 1.1)

In order to model the dependency between processes, we incorporated the idea of the risk of unwanted effects in our model. This means a risk event in one process generates an unwanted effect (propagation of risk) in another. Subsequently, we can define risk patterns as a combination of risk events following the logic (see also [10]):

If <Event 1>occurs <Event 2>might occur later in another process <P>.

After performing a full combination of the 12 risk events as defined above 144 (i.e. 12*12) risk identification patterns were derived.

Model and Risk Pattern Validation. During the population of the model as described at the beginning of this chapter several inconsistencies of ECSS-Q-HB-80-02 Part 2A were detected, for example a base practice was related to an outcome which was not defined for this process. Another example was that a base practice had no outcomes defined.

The 144 identified risk patterns were analysed by an expert committee. This review excluded several patterns as they were not perceived to make sense, for example "if P <process>is not performed then P <process>is not managed". Below are two examples of many generic risk identification patters which were judged to be valuable:

If	WP <work product>	is not developed
then	O <outcome>	loses WP <work product>.

'Loses' in this case means that a missing work product endangers the achievement of an outcome either of the same process or of another process which uses this WP as an input.

If	BP <base practice>	is not performed
then	WP <work product>	is not developed.

Since BPs are not directly related to WPs in the logical model of a PAM, this pattern is created by combining the relationships between BPs and Outcomes and between Outcomes and WPs. The following list shows an extract for the instantiated risk patterns for a particular process, namely ENG.6, Software construction.

If	WP06-01 (Customer Manual)	is not developed
then	outcome 3 of ENG.8	loses WP06-01 (Customer Manual).

This means that outcome 3 ("test results are recorded") of ENG.8 (Software testing) is endangered.

If	WP15-10 (Test Incident Report)	is not developed
then	outcome 2 and 3 of SUP.2	loses WP15-10 (Test Incident Report).

This means that outcome 2 ("criteria for verification of all required software work products is identified") and 3 ("required verification activities are performed") of SUP.2 (Verification) are endangered.

3.2 Collecting Information from Assessments

After an assessment is performed the results are typically captured in a so-called Process Assessment Report. Such a report gives an overview of the results as shown in Table 1 and also contains all the findings in detail.

Table 1. Process attribute rating achievement following the original target profile in the assessment plan. **Note:** The characters N, P, F and L denote the ratings: **N**ot achieved (0%-15%), **P**artially achieved(16%-50%), **L**argely achieved(51%-85%) and **F**ully achieved (86%-100%). The white boxes correspond to not in scope attributes for that process.

Process	PA1.1	PA2.1	PA2.2	PA3.1	PA3.2
SPL.2 Product Release	F	N	P		
ENG.1: Requirements Elicitation	F	N	N	N	N
ENG.4: Software Requirements Analysis	L	P	P	N	N
ENG.5: Software Design	P	N	P	N	N
ENG.6: Software Construction	P	P	P		
ENG.8: Software Testing	F	P	P	N	N
ENG.12: Software and System Maintenance	P	N	N	N	N
SUP.8: Configuration Management	L	N	N	P	N
SUP.9: Problem Resolution Management	L	N	N		

All the findings as captured in an assessment report were added to the model following these four steps:

1. Instantiate the model with only the processes assessed (see e.g. the 9 processes of Table 1)
2. For every entity add available information from the assessment report. For simplicity this has been done in a binary way only, e.g. achieved/not achieved, produced/not produced, etc. Examples are not produced work products, not achieved outcomes and not performed base practices.
3. Generate a number of risks from the model by combining the instantiated patterns as outlined in chapter 3.1 with the information added in the previous step for example by transforming the pattern

    If   WP is not developed then outcome O of P is endangered. into
    As   WP is not developed   outcome O of P is endangered.

    in the case that WP was not developed.
4. Assess the generated risks and rank them.

It is noted that sometimes Process Assessment Reports do not contain sufficient justification for particular ratings especially when a Process Attribute was only Partially or Largely achieved. This implies that assessors should be instructed, via the assessment procedure for example, to collect this additional information. Note also that use of existing assessment tools can support the automatic collection not only of the rating of Process Attributes, but also regarding the more detailed information on WPs, Outcomes and BPs.

3.3 Analysis of the Collected Data

Once all the assessment information is added to the model and the list of risks is generated the results have to be evaluated.

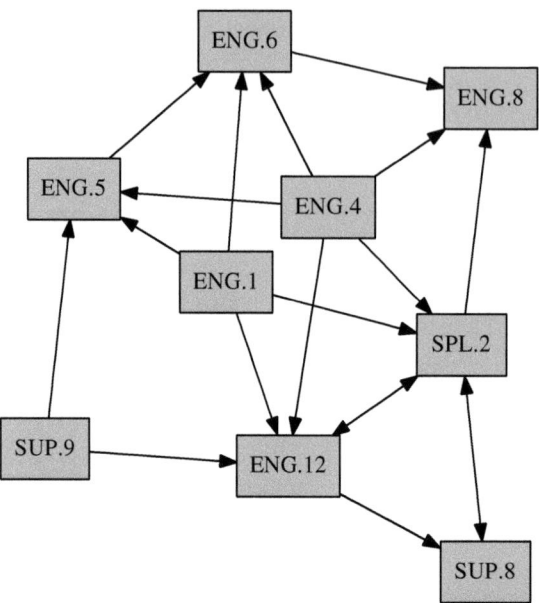

Fig. 2. Example of connected processes via work products

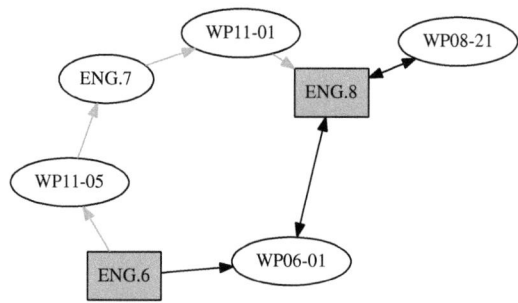

Fig. 3. Example how two processes are connected via work products

Data Visualization. In order to facilitate the understanding of the results, it was decided to generate high level views of the evaluated processes showing how the processes are connected via the work products. For the example given in Table 1 the graph which was generated is shown in Figure 2.

This graphical representation gives a high level idea about the interconnectivity. Furthermore, with the logical model at hand it is also straightforward to visualise the work product interactions between processes as shown in the next graphic for ENG.6 (Software Construction) and ENG.8 (Software Testing).

As seen in Figure 3 the two processes are directly connected via WP06-01 (Customer manual) and indirectly via ENG.7 (Software Integration) which transforms WP11-05 (Software unit) into WP 11.01 (Software product).

Some process also influence the Process Attributes of other processes (see ECSS-Q-HB-80-02 Part 2A). In the example of Figure 2 one could assume that SUP.8 (Configuration Management) and SUP.9 (Problem Resolution Management) have only little influence on the other processes. Looking at Figure 4 however shows, that these process have a high influence on the level 2 of all other processes.

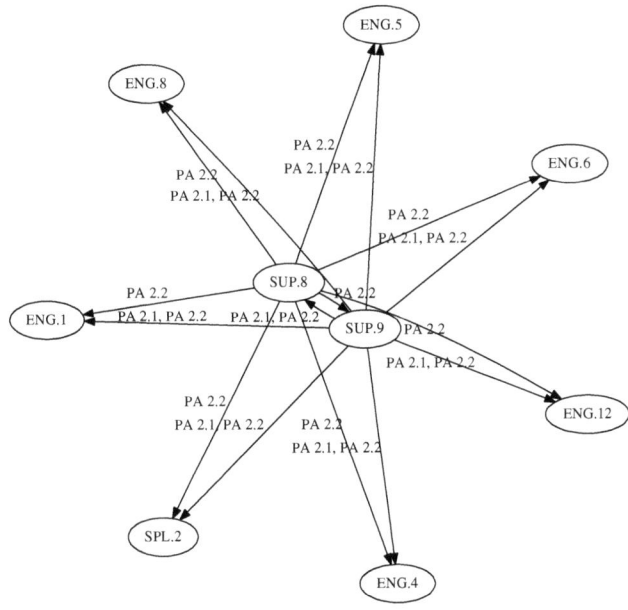

Fig. 4. Supported process attributes by certain processes

Data Interpretation. As outlined in chapter 3.2, after all the data for a certain process assessment is added to the logical model, graphs are generated and analysed.

In a first step the results are validated. In order to do that the graph as shown in Figure 2 needs to be tested: if a process P_1 depends on the outputs from other processes $P_2 ... P_n$ and $P_2 ... P_n$ do not produce all the required work products P_1 cannot be fully achieved and reach capability level 1.

As an example by looking at Table 1 and comparing it to Figure 2 immediately the question arises how ENG.8 (Software Testing) can be fully achieved on CL 1 if one of its input processes, namely ENG.6 (Software construction) is only partially achieved. In order to further analyse this the work products by which these two processes are connected were visualised (Figure 3) and it became apparent that the only direct connection is via the WP06-01 (customer manual) and an indirect connection through a not assessed process (in grey) by the software unit/product (WP11-01/05). When analysing this further it became clear that

ENG.6 produced the software, however, no unit tests were performed and as these are a big part of ENG.6 the process scored low. However, all the other products were fully created and thus this was a "false positive".

When assessing the generated risks for this assessment as described in chapter 3.2 it could be seen that indeed no risks attached to ENG.6 for level 1 were created. The patterns as shown at the end of chapter 3.1 for example were eliminated and not converted into risks as WP06-01 (Customer Manual) was created and though WP15-10 (Test Incident Report) was not created it only imposed a risk on SUP.2 which was not in scope of the assessment.

A solution to eliminate false positives earlier is to include the risks as determined into the validation right at the beginning (see chapter 5). Furthermore, this example already showed that determining risks at the level of processes is too coarse-grained in some circumstances.

The graph analysis further included the identification of processes that did not depend on any other process or the identification processes which provided inputs to many other processes and might therefore be business-critical. From Figure 2 for example it became apparent that ENG.4 (Software Requirements Analysis) influences a high number (5) of other processes directly by its output work products while ENG.8 (Software Testing) has no influence on any other process. Combining this with the generated risks as described under chapter 3.2 allows to determine which processes should be improved first. For example ENG.4 was only Largely achieved because the output work product WP17-11 (Software Requirements) was not properly developed. The risk elicitation flagged this and indicated that this work product is used by 4 of the 5 processes which depend on ENG.4. Below are the created risks for this example:

As WP17-11 is not developed
- outcome 1 of ENG.5 is endangered,
- outcome 4 of ENG.5 is endangered,
- outcome 1 of ENG.6 is endangered,
- outcome 3 of ENG.6 is endangered,
- outcome 1 of ENG.8 is endangered,
- outcome 4 of ENG.8 is endangered, and
- outcome 1 of ENG.12 is endangered.

This did not only help understand that it is critical to improve ENG.4, but it also showed which work product is crucial for improvement.

4 Evaluation of the Method

At this point the evaluation of the method was performed based on trials with the results of three assessments of different organizational size: small (less than 20 employees), medium (between 20 and 400 employees) and large (more than 400 hundred). The assessment results were fed into the method and were used for its verification, however, no quantitative data was collected, since the evaluation of the trials was based on the perceived usefulness and reliability of the method.

5 Future Work

The presented method currently relies to a great extent on manual analysis. The graph analysis for example was perceived as a valuable improvement as compared to analysing text from the evaluation of performed assessments. However, this analysis could be further automated as all the required data is present in the model. Additionally, in order to reduce false positives, the identified risks should be taken into account when the validity of the graphs is assessed.

The risk ranking is also still a manual exercise and it could be further automated taking the existing approach from the R4S method into account. Along the same line, the role of target profiles to identify business critical processes and gaps should be included. Right now, the method looks to a great extent only at the interdependency of processes which is established via work products.

The synthesis of results should be improved as well. The graphs currently visualise the processes and work products in the same way which makes it difficult to determine the ranking or even the degree of dependency of processes. Also, a method to trace the justification of the decisions on priorities for improvement has to be added, as for example backwards reasoning.

The method will be fully validated with panels of experts performing the analysis with the same assessment reports, contrasting the divergences and the justifications for the different conclusions. This can help tune the method, identifying new risks and dependencies between processes.

6 Conclusion

In this paper we present the current status of an ongoing research trying to validate the outcomes of a process assessment and to use the interconnectivity of processes to establish a prioritization of processes for improvement based on the identified process-related risks.

The conversion of the Process Assessment Model to be applied into a logical model proves to be a valuable way to detect inconsistencies.

The presented SCANNER method complements the existing R4S method as it approaches the risk problem from a different perspective. In a first step it can be used to assess the validity of a performed assessment. However, it is perceived that it generates a number of 'false positives', i.e. it indicates possible problems where there are none. This should be addressed in the future (see chapter 5).

Using graphs to visualise assessments proves to be useful for the identification of which processes to improve first. Using the interconnectivity of processes together with the elicited process-related risks gives similar results. This provides a good indication that the interconnectivity of processes and the analysis of the process-related risk propagation are valuable inputs to support the prioritization of processes for improvement.

References

1. Automotive SIG: Automotive SPICE Process Reference Model, Manchester (2007), http://www.automotivespice.com
2. Devic, M.-O., Escorial Rico, D., Richter, S.: Reflecting on ten years of Software Process Assessment and Improvement initiatives by the European Space Agency. In: 18th EuroSPI Conference Industrial Proceedings (2011)
3. European Cooperation for Space Standardization: Space project management, Risk Management, ECSS-M-ST-80C, Noordwijk (2008)
4. European Cooperation for Space Standardization: Space product assurance, Software process assessment and improvement – Part 1: Framework, ECSS-Q-HB-80-02 Part 1 A, Noordwijk (2010)
5. European Cooperation for Space Standardization: Space product assurance, Software process assessment and improvement – Part 2: Assessor instrument, ECSS-Q-HB-80-02 Part 2 A, Noordwijk (2010)
6. Flood, D., McCaffery, F., Casey, V.: Understanding the Relationships Within the Medi SPICE Framework. In: The Seventh International Conference on Software Engineering Advances (ICSEA 2012), Lisbon, Portugal, pp. 254–259 (2012)
7. ISO 15504, Information technology – Process assessment, Geneva (2003-2012)
8. ISO 31000, Risk management – Principles and guidelines, Geneva (2009)
9. Kelemen, Z.D., Kusters, R., Trienekens, J., Balla, K.: Towards Complexity Analysis of Software Process Improvement Frameworks, Technical Report TR201301, Budapest (2013)
10. Miler, J., Gorski, J.: Risk-driven Software Process Improvement - a Case Study. In: Proc. of. 11th European Software Process Improvement Conference, EuroSPI 2004, Trondheim (2004)
11. Voelcker, C., Ouared, R., Stienen, H.: R4S – Risk Reduction with SPiCE for SPACE. TN7 Part C of ESA study contract No 10662/93/NL/NB WO6-CCN5, Noordwijk (2001)
12. Wholey, J.S., Hatry, H.P., Newcomer, K.E.: Handbook of practical program evaluation, San Francisco, vol. 19 (2010)

An Exploration of Individual Personality Types in Software Development

Murat Yilmaz[1], Rory V. O'Connor[2,3], and Paul Clarke[4,3]

[1] Çankaya University, Turkey
myilmaz@cankaya.edu.tr
[2] Dublin City University, Ireland
[3] Lero, the Irish Software Engineering Research Center
roconnor@computing.dcu.ie
[4] Regulated Software Research Centre, Dundalk Institute of Technology, Ireland
paul.clarke@dkit.ie

Abstract. Previous research - using conventional psychometric questionnaires - has highlighted the importance of aligning compatible personality types in software development teams. However, there does not exist a dedicated, robust questionnaire instrument for revealing the pertinent personality types for software development practitioners. This study analyzes the validity and reliability of a 70-item (context dependent) personality-profiling questionnaire particularly developed to assess personality types of software practitioners. A systematic process of validation, using an iterative approach to questionnaire development, was employed. The questions were developed both with a qualitative analysis of interview data, and based on the opinions of expert reviewers who revised the items through a set of examination. To investigate how stable the questions and reproducible the results, we measured test-retest reliability of the instrument, yielding satisfactory results. The present study provided evidence for the construct validity of the instrument. Ultimately, an initial comparison of the results delivered by the instrument demonstrated positive correlations with the findings acquired with well-known personality assessment instrument, i.e. the big five personality questionnaire.

Keywords: Software Developers Personalities, Personality Profiling, Myers-Briggs Type Indicator (MBTI) , Questionnaire Validation.

1 Introduction

Software projects face several challenges in their dynamically changing organizational environments [1]. These challenges form perceived productivity differences among software practitioners who have a number of distinctive personality types. Considering software development as a socio-technical practice, members of a software team should interact and follow a software development process [2]. One of the key components of success in a software development organization is selection of the right employee or a team for the right tasks [3]. Indeed, compatibility of practitioners' personalities becomes an important concern for the team success [4]. It is therefore not surprising to discover that several researchers in the field of software engineering have focused on the effects of personality types on the software development process and organizational performance [5–7].

In today's software engineering landscapes, technical skills of the individuals should certainly match with the required talents and experience. In addition, to place the individuals in the right groups or jobs, the social aspects such as individuals' compatibility within a team has emerged as a research interest. This requires a new way of understanding the personality differences with a focus on personality types over structural configurations [8]. The notion of MBTI classifies personality types via four dichotomous dimensions; extroversion-introversion (E-I), which shows the methods for an individual to draw energy (outer word versus inner word of ideas), sensing-intuitive (S-N), which refers the methods of individuals to process data (facts versus possibilities), thinking-feeling (T-F), which is related with people's decision making (objective versus subjective), and judging-perceiving (J-P) identifies whether an individual has a structural or an adaptable style to deal with the word. Although the Myers-Briggs Type Indicator (MBTI) is the most well known and widely used self report instrument in the software industry, some critics argue that individuals may have problems in distinguishing their true preferences from socially desirable type of responses. In fact, some researchers hold the view that the MBTI test results may not reflect the true personality types of individuals [9, 10]. As it is a self-report measure, thus, some may fake their answers. To deal with such a problem, we envision that such a test should be conducted as an interactive face-to-face assessment where the context of the questions on such a dichotomous personality scale should be based on real situations and events extracted from software development industry. In support, Kaluzniacky argues that a personality instrumental specific to IT should be based on a IT-related content while being parallel with the original MBTI [11].

In light of these remarks, we propose a personality-profiling questionnaire, which was tested on practitioners both from academia and industry. The purpose of the present study is to investigate the developed personality-profiling tool for software practitioners and explore its reliability and validity. To evaluate its validity and internal consistency, we carried out a validation process where we assessed the aspects of content validity, and performed a factor analysis for the hypothesized 4-factor personality model. To compare the results of the assessment with other instruments, we conducted well known and a comprehensive psychometric questionnaire (i.e. Big Five questionnaire [12]) on a selected group of participants. Based on a five-factor model, the big five personality inventory is a measurement device, which is used to assess the personality traits.

2 Method

This study was conducted in six main steps. Although, it was conducted with both academia and industry in different steps of the work, the main part of the was performed within a middle-sized software company. During all industrial assessments, interviewees were selected by the managerial team of the software development organization. In the assessments conducted in academia, we used individuals, who were novice developers with at least a year of industrial experience. These individuals were picked by the criterion of either whether either they have worked together as a team for some projects or they are the individuals who worked in the same environment at least for sometime.

An illustration of all the steps used in the present study is shown in Figure 1

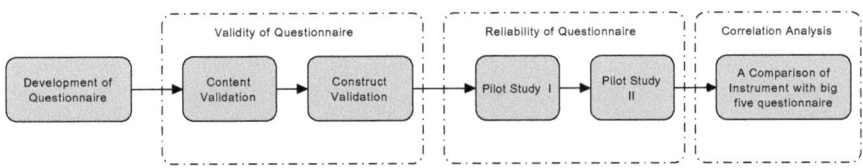

Fig. 1. The steps of the study

The first step is the question development process where a 70-item questionnaire was constructed based on a number of interviews with twenty software practitioners and selected experts from the company. In the second step, we critically reviewed the content of the questionnaire with a group of experts from the managerial team of the company to validate its content. For the third step, we investigated the assessment validity, which is based on the analysis of the correlations among the proposed questions using confirmatory factor analysis with 213 participants from the middle-sized software company. In the fourth and fifth step, to assess the reliability, a pilot study was conducted with a group of novice developers twice (six weeks after the first round of data collection) in a university environment.

Lastly, using 15 participants we conducted an alternative big five personality assessment, and the two assessment scores were compared using correlation analysis. The descriptions of all those involved are shown in Table 1.

Table 1. Research steps and number of participants

Step	Number of participants	Type of Assessment
1st	20 (12 males, 8 females)	Interviews
2nd	10 (8 Males, 2 females)	Experts Reviewers
3rd	213 (165 Male, 48 Female)	Questionnaire Validation
4th	15 (9 males, 6 females)	Reliability Study I
5th	15 (9 males, 6 females)	Reliability Study II
6th	15 (9 males, 6 females)	Comparison Study

2.1 Development of Questionnaire

In the first part of our approach, we carefully investigated the 70 questions of Keirsey's temperament sorter [13], which encompasses all four personality types of the MBTI scale as an initial template. Using 10 academics from a psychology department and 10 highly experienced software practitioners, we assessed the personality types of participants with Keirsey's sorter. Next, we conducted a total number of 30 semi structured interviews where we first asked 5 selected individuals a number of questions that were asked verbally such as *"What do you think about a content specific personality type assessment?"*, *"What kind of events or situations have you observed in software development landscapes that can be useful for an new kind of assessment?"*. Using the acquired information, we built a new set of questions and asked 10 other participants *"What about this situation; do you think about it may be able to reflect the characteristics of a software practitioner?"*, *"How would you react such a question?"*. After performing a rigorous analysis of collected data, we formed 70 questions regarding software engineering context and conducted 15 more follow-up discussions with the participants, and asked them each question *"How do you find the tone of such a question?"*, *"Do you think that question sound right?"*. Lastly, the final form of the personality-profiling questionnaire was discharged to 6 participants who had previously completed the earlier version of the questionnaire - and the results of both engagements were compared.

Table 2 outlines the profile of the 20 participants including their roles (titles), age, years of experience and level of education.

Table 2. Participants' Information

Title	Age	Years of Experience	Education
IT Specialist	33	6	MSc.
Project Manager	47	7	PhD.
Software Architect	37	12	BSc.
Software Developer	31	6	BSc.
Software Developer	33	7	BSc.
R&D Team Lead	39	14	PhD..
Software Tester	32	4	MA.
System Analysis	34	9	BA.
R&D Team Member	32	7	MSc.
R&D Team Member	31	5	MSc.
Organizational Psychologist	49	17	PhD..
Clinical Psychologist	57	20	PhD.
Student Psychologist	24	1	BA.
Student Psychologist	22	1	BA.
Novice Psychologist	26	2	BA.
Novice Psychologist	26	2	BA.
Student Psychologist	24	1	BA.
Student Psychologist	23	1	BA.
Student Psychologist	25	1	BA.
Industrial Psychologist	54	14	MA.

2.2 Content Validation

As a second step, we worked directly with 10 experts for validating the content of the questionnaire. The selection of expert reviewers was mainly based on their experience on the field and scientific qualifications. The candidates were proposed to the middle-sized software company and the selection process was executed by the management team. At this point, we conducted several expert review sessions and two panel discussions where all questions were investigated independently by experts with view to identifying problematic items. The participants were required to rate the content for clarity, readability, relevance, etc. on a 4-point Likert scale (1=not clear, 4=very clear).

Table 3 shows the profile of the 10 expert reviewers including their roles (job titles), age, years of experience and level of education.

Table 3. Expert Reviewers' Information

Expert ID	Title	Age	Years of Experience	Education
E1	Software Manager	46	20	PhD.
E2	UX Designer	36	7	MSc.
E3	Graphical Designer	30	4	BA.
E4	Software Practitioner	31	6	BSc.
E5	Clinical Psychologist	43	16	PhD.
E6	Organizational Psychologist	39	11	PhD.
E7	Instructional Designer	38	9	MA.
E8	Assist. Prof. Dr. (Researcher)	40	14	PhD.
E9	Assoc. Prof Dr. (Researcher)	45	17	PhD.
E10	Prof. Dr. (Researcher)	58	25	PhD.

Next, we quantified the extent of agreement among the participants. Based on the experts' ratings, the content validity index (CVI) was calculated as follows:

$$CVI = \frac{number\ of\ raters\ giving\ a\ rating\ of\ 3\ or\ 4}{Total\ number\ of\ raters} \qquad (1)$$

where CVI is a coefficient when calculated as 0 indicates that there is a total lack of agreement among participants, and a value 1 shows a total agreement among the experts [14]. After having a discussion with the experts, we had an agreement that items should be accepted when CVI is higher than 80%. A value between 70% and 79% was considered questionable whereas all items below that threshold were considered as unacceptable for validity of its content. Among the 70 questions, 48 questions were rated as accepted. In addition, 12 questions were found questionable (between 70% and 79%) where 8 items were found below the threshold. All questionable items were revised and all unacceptable items were completely changed regarding the reviews and further sent back to experts for rating. Finally, the finished questionnaire was discussed with experts from the software engineering field.

2.3 Assessing Construct Validity

This part of the paper investigates the construct validity with respect to personality characteristics similar to Myers-Brigs approach where four dichotomies were assumed to be the identifiable by the questions, which were asked during the assessment. To assess the validity of the developed questionnaire, the test scores were interpreted with respect to the understanding of participants and the researcher. To analyze the correlation among the questions of the instrument, personality assessment was conducted on 213 software practitioners (Cronbachs alpha was .86). We used factor analysis method where we identified four clusters of questions compatible with the personality constructs all of which were highly correlated. For example, a question regarding social interactions was found to be correlated with extroversion-introversion.

To investigate the hypothesized four factors of personality using the questionnaire, LISREL [15] is used to perform confirmatory factor analysis of the measurement items, and test the five factor model. The hypothesized model had statistically significant values of all of the factor loadings that were between .51 and .80 ($p < .05$). The independence model was clearly rejectable where the χ^2 for independence model with 170 degrees of freedom was 922.319. The proposed model yielded a good-fit[1], where $\chi^2(186, N = 192) = 242.505, p < 0.001$, and the fit indices for the proposed model were satisfactory; $RMSEA = .0615, GFI = .87, AGFI = .82, CFI = .896, NNFI = .88$). Furthermore, a χ^2 difference test was conducted, $\Delta\chi^2(24, N = 192) = 679.814, p < 0.001$).

Overall, the hypothesized factor-based model for personality, which was proposed based on the questionnaire items: EI (10 items), SN (20 items), TF (20 items) and JP (20 items) were assessed using empirical data.

Table 4 illustrates the number of items with highest loading values for the four factor design extracted in this study. For this model, loading on the first factor was the EI scale, which has all of its items. Although some items were found to be loading a few items in other scales, the offending items were essentially evenly distributed on the other scales. The four factor model approach seems to fit with the data where questions were found to be correlated with the constructs that they were suppose to measure. Overall, the analysis suggested that the structure of the questionnaire showed evidence of satisfactory item-to-scale structure.

Table 4. Number of Factors with the highest values of loading in 4-Factor Design

	Factor 1	Factor 2	Factor 3	Factor 4
EI	10	0	0	0
SN	3	17	0	0
TF	3	1	16	0
JP	0	0	2	18

---

[1] RMSEA = root mean square error of approximation; NNFI = nonnormed fit index; CFI = comparative fit index; AIC = Akaike information criterion.

2.4 Assessing Reliability

To investigate the reliability of the questionnaire, we assessed 15 novice software practitioners who were studying at a university. The participants who were selected had to satisfy the following criteria: They have all either worked as a team member previously or collaborated in a software project. Biemer suggests that the test-retest method for a questionnaire is one of the most common methods for investigation especially to identify errors of measurement [16]. In support, Presser et al. [17] indicate that parallel measurements conducted to replicated the original assessment is a useful method for assessing the quality of a survey, which can highlight problematic questions.

To assess the reliability of the instrument, the developed questionnaire was conducted twice with the same participants over a six weeks period. Without changing any environmental conditions, the reliability of responses was investigated with the replication study where same questions were asked to the same set of participants. At this point, the goal of the study was to observe *"the measurement error variance associated with the original survey response"* [16, pp. 298]. Using such a re-measurement approach, we analyzed the response of the participants for each question in the questionnaire to calculate "the ratio of question-level measure of response variance to the total response variances" for a given question termed as *index of inconsistency* (I) [18] whereas the reliability ratio $(1 - I = \kappa)$ is also known as Cohen's measurement of reliability [19]. (I) can be represented as

$$I = \frac{g}{p_1 q_2 + p_2 q_1} \qquad (2)$$

where total sample size is $n = a + b + c + d$ where a indicates the individuals who select the first option in both interviews, d shows the participants who select the second option in both runs. The number of participants who chose the first option in the first run and second option in the second run is denoted as c. Lastly, b is the number of individuals who select the second option in the first run and first option in the second run. Furthermore, $g = (b+c)/n$ is considered as the rate of disagreement, the ratio $p_1 = (a+c)/n$ shows the first answer in the first run, where for the second run the ratio is shown as $p_2 = (a+b)/n$.

To check the reliability of each question, κ values were obtained where κ ranges are shown in Table 5. During the analysis, we observed that these values are too sensitive, i.e. even one different answer could change the course of results very significantly. After discussing the sensitivity with an expert, we decided to chose 30% as a cut-off range for the question, and therefore the questions Q4, Q21, Q22, Q24, Q26, Q27, and Q31 were found below the expected value.

Further analysis showed that one question type from extroversion-introversion, and two question from other types were found to unreliable. By revisiting several experts once again, we discussed the possible updates and alterations for the identified questions. Later, the questions were readjusted. Additionally, we conducted the assessment on 15 software practitioners on a middle-sized software company. Once again, the test was replicated after six weeks to measure the

Table 5. The Range of κ numbers found for the academic pilot study

κ % Range	Number of Questions
0 - .30	7
.31 - .45	9
.46 - .60	10
.61 - .75	14
.76 - .90	30

reliability of each question. The results obtained from the analysis of κ values for the questionnaire are presented in Table 6.

Table 6. The Range of κ numbers found for the pilot study

κ % Range	Number of Questions
0 - .30	1
.31 - .45	9
.46 - .60	12
.61 - .75	18
.76 - .90	30

Data from Table 5 can be compared with the data in Table 6, which shows that two questions from 30% range has moved to 60% range, whereas four questions were moved to 75% range, hence we were able to improve the reliability of six more questions after having various iterations for fine-tuning the questionnaire.

From this data, we can see that this part of the study yielded relevant results where only 7 of 70 questions were found problematic (one question from (E/I) trait, and two questions from each (S/N), (T/F), (J/P) traits were out of range). Therefore, we performed our calculations by dropping these questions, and the ultimate results are shown in Table 7.

What is interesting in this analysis is that extroversion was observed as a dominant dichotomy during the pilot study, which is compatible with the recent findings in MBTI research in the field of software engineering (see e.g. [20]).

Table 7. Personality Types found in the Pilot Study

MBTI Type	Number of Participants	% in Sample Population
ENFJ	2	13
ENTJ	2	13
ESFJ	3	20
ESFP	3	20
ESTP	1	7
INTP	1	7
ISFJ	2	13
ISFP	1	7
Total	15	100

To reinterpret our work in terms of the five factor model, using a randomly selected subset of software practitioners, we correlated the results of the assessment device and the Big Five personality constructs. To this end, among the participants, 15 of them were assessed with the Big Five Inventory (BFI-44 item scale) [12]. Next, the results acquired from the two scales were compared using correlation analysis (see Table 8).

Correlations between the results of the proposed scale, and BFI scale are shown in Table 8. It can be seen from the table that EI was highly correlated with the extroversion, and SN scale was correlated with openness. There were also significant relations between SN versus agreeableness, and JP versus conscientiousness. However, there were no significant relationships were found between any subscales with neuroticism ($N = 15$, $p < 0.01$). The findings of the current study are consistent with those of McCrae and Costa who observed significant correlations between MBTI scale and big five personality characteristics [21].

Table 8. Pearson correlations between proposed instrument and BFI

	Extraversion	Openness	Agreeableness	Conscientiousness	Neuroticism
EI	**0.82**	0.02	-0.01	-0.15	0.10
SN	0.11	**0.58**	0.03	-0.08	0.01
TF	0.17	0.02	**0.49**	-0.10	0.03
JP	0.13	0.29	-0.03	**-0.37**	0.18

3 Discussion

One of the identified problems in the software engineering community is the improper use of personality tests or wrongly selected assessments where many tests in the field are not conducted appropriately [22]. To cope with such issues, we created a questionnaire with situation-oriented questions based on the content of software engineering context. The goal of the assessment device (i.e. questionnaire with 70-items), which was designed for software practitioners, was to measure their personality characteristics on a newly formed MBTI compatible scale. Consequently, the developed questionnaire was tested over different groups of practitioners including expert reviewers, a pilot group of university students, a large sample of software practitioners, etc.

There were several reasons that the proposed instrument was found to have acceptable levels of the content validity, reliability and construct validity. First, internal consistency reliability coefficient (as measured by Cronbach's alpha) found satisfactory for the entire questionnaire with different sample sets. Secondly, factor analysis indicated that the four-factor model has high item-scale correlations, which was found to be strong evidence for construct validity. Thirdly, to improve the content validity, problematic questions were analyzed, identified, and revised by expert reviews. After having a number of iterations, the high values obtained for CVIs were considered for evidence of content validity. Lastly, the correlative results from 15 participants for both the proposed scale and BFI was investigated. Hence, further studies should aim to compare two scales. Ultimately, future research with more participants should therefore concentrate on the investigation of the assessment scale and other personality inventories.

3.1 Threats to Validity

This section details some potential threats to validity and the methods we used to address them. To deal with internal validity problems, during the time between the two pilot studies, there was no outside event that might affect participants; therefore, we confirmed that there were no observable change that may potentially affect the results. Secondly, participants were exposed to the same questions, therefore we did not observe a testing that might potentially affect or threaten the internal validity. In other words, during the experiments, we did not change our survey instrument (i.e. measuring device), which could potentiality be a threat to validity.

In the sixth step of the work, for different personality assessments, we built *within-participants design* in which we used the participants from the same group to take measures for the two attempts. One advantage of this work is that when the same participants contribute to the same conditions, it increases the chance of having statistical significance [23].

Finally, the construct validity shows the ability of an instrument to measure the operational form of a construct (e.g. extroversion, introversion), which it was built to measure. To investigate this phenomenon, initially construct validity of the questionnaire was comprehensively discussed by using experts from several fields (see Table 3). Secondly, we corroborated with a selected group of participants to review their personality traits (i.e. how accurate their traits were described), and latter several discussions were conducted with experts to systematically investigate the validity of the measurement scale. Notwithstanding the great care that has been taken to raise the reliability and utility of our work to date, future valuable research should focus on further evaluations of the effectiveness of the instrument.

4 Conclusions and Future Work

This study set out to determine the personality profiles of software practitioners by using a context dependent questionnaire. The questionnaire is based on the concept of situational context cards [24], which relies on the notion of personality that is a product of personal choices, thoughts, and opinions. Although personality measurements could show a spectrum, which are not rigid and may consist a wider margin of variance, personality profiling is still a useful technique to understand practitioners strengths and weaknesses against particular situations [25]. However, traditional MBTI-based psychometric tests are not context oriented [11]. To deal with this issue, in this research, we formulate a context dependent approach to reveal the personality type of individuals.

This paper has shown that it is now possible to construct a context specific MBTI assessment. It potentially improves the participants engagement encouraging individuals to reveal their personality types.. The empirical findings in this study provide a new understanding of the personality profiling process, which is more context specific, tangible, and therefore obtain more concrete results from the participants. Most importantly, however, our approach explores the fabric between the actions of individuals and social landscapes of software development teams. It should therefore be possible to establish some structural improvements for a software team, based on the fact that the quality of organizational production relies on the structure of the organization [26].

The vision of this novel approach and its implementation in software development organizations can provide a way to explore the effects of personality types on team compositions where this information can be used to investigate effective team configurations. Our next goal is to dynamically portray the personality traits of an individual for designing an optimal team structure using an extended implementation of the assessment model. Such an approach should be designed to illustrate the social structure of software teams as a whole based on job roles [27], and its members' personality types.

Acknowledgments. This work is supported, in part, by Science Foundation Ireland grant number 03/CE2/I303_1 to Lero, the Irish Software Engineering Research Centre (www.lero.ie).

References

1. Stellman, A., Greene, J.: Applied software project management. O'Reilly Media (2005)
2. Acuna, S.T., Juristo, N., Moreno, A.M., Mon, A.: A Software Process Model Handbook for Incorporating People's Capabilities. Springer (2005)
3. Schwalbe, K.: Information Technology: Project Management. Cengage Learning (2010)
4. Lui, K.M., Chan, K.C.C.: Software Development Rhythms. John Wiley & Sons (2008)
5. Mazni, O., Syed-Abdullah, S., Hussin, N.: Analyzing personality types to predict team performance. In: 2010 International Conference on Science and Social Research (CSSR), pp. 624–628. IEEE (2010)
6. Lewis, T., Smith, W.: Building software engineering teams that work: The impact of dominance on group conflict and performance outcomes. In: 38th Annual Frontiers in Education Conference, FIE 2008, pp. S3H–1. IEEE (2008)
7. Su-li, Z., Ke-fan, X.: Research on entrepreneurial team members' personality traits influence on group risk decision-making. In: 2010 International Conference on Management Science and Engineering (ICMSE), pp. 937–942. IEEE (2010)
8. Capretz, L., Ahmed, F.: Making sense of software development and personality types. IT Professional 12, 6–13 (2010)
9. Kerth, N., Coplien, J., Weinberg, J.: Call for the rational use of personality indicators. Computer 31, 146–147 (1998)
10. Kline, P.: The handbook of psychological testing. Psychology Press (2000)
11. Kaluzniacky, E.: Managing psychological factors in information systems work: An orientation to emotional intelligence. Information Science Publishing (2004)
12. John, O.P., Donahue, E.M., Kentle, R.L.: The big five inventory-versions 4a and 54. University of California, Institute of Personality and Social Research, Berkeley (1991)
13. Keirsey, D., Bates, M.: Please understand me: Character & temperament types. Prometheus Nemesis Michigan (1984)

14. Lenz, E.R.: Measurement in nursing and health research. Springer Publishing Company (2010)
15. Joreskog, K., Sorbom, D.: LISREL 8: user's reference guide. Scientific Software International Inc., Lincolnwood (2001)
16. Biemer, P., Lyberg, L., Wiley, J.: Introduction to survey quality. Wiley Series in Survey Methodology. Wiley (2003)
17. Presser, S.: Methods for Testing and Evaluating Survey Questionnaires. Wiley Series in Survey Methodology. Wiley-Interscience (2004)
18. Hansen, M., Hurwitz, W., Pritzker, L.: Uinted State Bureau of the Census: The estimation and interpretation of gross differences and the simple response variance. Bureau of the Census (1963)
19. Cohen, J.: A coefficient of agreement for nominal scales. Educational and Psychological Measurement 20, 37–46 (1960)
20. Varona, D., Capretz, L., Piñero, Y.: Personality types of cuban software developers. Global Journal of Engineering Education 13 (2011)
21. McCrae, R.R., Costa, P.T.: Reinterpreting the myers-briggs type indicator from the perspective of the five-factor model of personality. Journal of Personality 57, 17–40 (1989)
22. McDonald, S., Edwards, H.: Who should test whom? Communications of the ACM 50, 66–71 (2007)
23. Jackson, S.: Research methods and statistics: A critical thinking approach. Wadsworth Publishing Company (2011)
24. Yilmaz, M., O'Connor, R.V.: A software process engineering approach to improving software team productivity using socioeconomic mechanism design. ACM SIGSOFT Software Engineering Notes 36, 1–5 (2011)
25. Yilmaz, M., O'Connor, R.V: Towards the understanding and classification of the personality traits of software development practitioners: Situational context cards approach. In: 2012 38th EUROMICRO Conference on Software Engineering and Advanced Applications (SEAA), pp. 400–405. IEEE (2012)
26. Yilmaz, M., O'Connor, R.V., Collins, J.: Improving software development process through economic mechanism design. In: Riel, A., O'Connor, R., Tichkiewitch, S., Messnarz, R. (eds.) EuroSPI 2010. CCIS, vol. 99, pp. 177–188. Springer, Heidelberg (2010)
27. Yilmaz, M., O'Connor, R.V., Clarke, P.: A systematic approach to the comparison of roles in the software development processes. In: Mas, A., Mesquida, A., Rout, T., O'Connor, R.V., Dorling, A. (eds.) SPICE 2012. CCIS, vol. 290, pp. 198–209. Springer, Heidelberg (2012)

Covering the Human Perspective in Software Process Improvement

Mirna Muñoz[1], Jezreel Mejia[1], Gloria Piedad Gasca-Hurtado[2], Claudia Valtierra[1], and Brenda Duron[1]

[1] Centro de Investigación en Matemáticas
Av. Universidad no 222, 98068 Zacatecas, México
{mirna.munoz,jmejia,claudia.valtierra,brenda.duron}@cimat.mx
[2] Facultad de Ingeniería, Universidad de Medellín
Medellín, Colombia
gpgasca@udem.edu.co

Abstract. Most of the approaches to improve software process focus on formal process descriptions based on models and standards of best practices. However, the human factor has not been covered, as a result, an important gap arises between processes description and process execution. This gap takes special value in Small and Medium Enterprises (SMEs) because most of them do not have enough resources (time, budget and human) to implement a software process improvement (SPI) without a guarantee of any result due to the investment it represents for them. In order to help SMEs in the implementation of SPI initiatives, this paper presents a set of identified needs that SMEs must face in the implementation of SPI since the human perspective. Moreover, the needs are compared with the results of a local study perform at SMEs of Zacatecas. Besides, the paper includes a proposal focusing on two factors which aims to help them covering the set of needs. Finally, the paper shows the relation of these two factors and the SPI manifesto.

Keywords: Human factor, Software Process Improvement, SPI, SME's, small and medium enterprises, SPI manifesto.

1 Introduction

Nowadays it is necessary that software development organizations have the skills to create strategic advantages with respect to its competitors [1-3] especially SMEs. Since the point of view that software quality is directly related to the quality of process used to develop it [4], improving the organizational processes offer a key opportunity for organizations to become more efficient and competitive [5].

Unfortunately, even when many authors have recognized the importance of implementing SPI as mechanism to launch the competitiveness and efficiency in software industry, it has been path full of obstacles for most organizations [6].

To help organizations in the implementation of SPI, a set of models and standards such as CMMI [7], ISO 15504[8] and Moprosoft [9], has been arising in the last 10 years. These are focused on providing a framework of best practices that serve as reference in the implementation of SPI, but they do not have the power to create competitive advantages by themselves [10].

In this context, the human factor is highlighted because it is the main source of commitment and responsibility needed to achieve effective, efficient and quality processes as strategy advantage [10].

Authors such as O'Connor and Basri [11] and Janh and Nielsen [12] have identified the involvement of stakeholders in the implementation of improvements as key aspect for achieving this successfully. Therefore, processes are nothing without being performed by people [10].

This research work arises focusing on that processes entirely depend on the organization work culture and the motivation of people to evolve processes. Then, a set of needs that SMEs must face in the implementation of SPI are identified since the point of view of the human perspective. Besides, we present a proposal as solution to covering and supporting the set of identified needs.

This paper is structured as follows: section 2 presents a characterization of a set of SPI needs covering the human perspective; section 3 shows the mapping between the identified set of SPI needs focusing on human factors and the results of an analysis done at SMEs from Zacatecas Region; section 4 describes a proposal to address the human perspective in SPI; and finally, section 5 presents the conclusions.

2 Characterizing SPI Needs in SMEs Covering the Human Perspective

To achieve the identification of a set of SPI needs, we focus on analyzing three main sources of information: 1) organization main limitations; 2) organization's experience in the implementation of SPI and 3) an analysis of models, methods and frameworks used by organizations to implement improvements. After analyzing these sources the identified SPI needs are listed.

2.1 Main limitations

This section analyzes the main limitations that an organization faces when implementing SPI from the human perspective. To have a better understanding of these, the set of identified limitations have been classified in 5 groups as follows:

- **Organization**: there is a high dependency with immature customers, and a lack of knowledge of the importance between development processes and product quality.
- **Human Resources**: lack of personnel (usually the number of their employees is minimum); lack of roles definition (employees perform several functions) and employees lack of knowledge about process improvement methods.
- **Processes**: lack of defined processes, therefore, the software is developing as a craft. Besides, implementing and providing SPI results represent a high economical investment. Finally, SMEs implement processes most of the time because it is a customer's requirement.

- **Projects**: works with very small size projects, therefore, the projects are developed in a short period of time.
- **Models and standards**: few or any experience in the adoption of SPI models and standards. Therefore, the SME is adapted to the selected model or standard to be applied; this is the reason why it is very difficult to adopt it and to achieve the SMEs' goals and vision.

2.2 Organization's Experience in the Implementation of SPI

This section analyzes the experience of organizations in the implementation of SPI. The analysis is focused on human perspective, so that manager's needs, problems and some lesson learned are highlighted:

- **Manager's needs**: studies such as [13-15] show that 67% of the managers seek for guidance on how to implement improvement initiatives, instead of what activities to implement.
- **Problems**: common problems identified when organizations implement SPI initiatives are that they: 1) do not have clear SPI objectives; 2) do not pay enough attention to the factors that promote or inhibit organizational process improvements and; 3) do not take into account the human resource, therefore, senior management tend to have an unexpected or undesirable performance of human behavior [13].
- **Lesson Learned**: 1) the business goals and SPI should be successfully combined; 2) an explicit definition of SPI goals help stakeholders to have a good information of operational tasks and monitoring; 3) providing and using interviews in early stages of SPI help stakeholders to feel important part of the SPI, making easily to understand the organization's key knowledge and specific problems; 4) using automated tools, metrics and organization' data reduce the learning curve; 5) persistence and patience is needed to face internal resistance of implementing new processes and standards; and finally 6) people needs to know the benefits involved in the SPI to reduce the resistance of implementing it [13].

2.3 Models, Methods and Frameworks Used to Implement SPI

This section analyzes the methods, models and frameworks currently used in the implementation of improvements focused on human perspective. To achieve this, a set of features was established as follows: a) it provides an improvement implementation integrated framework, b) it analyzes the organization needs, and c) it has a support tool. Table 1 shows the analysis performed.

Table 1. Analysis of methods, models and frameworks

Method/ Model /Framework	a	b	c
SPI implementation maturity model [16]	✓		
iFLAP [17]	✓	✓	
Karlstrom D. et all [18]	✓	✓	
Asato, R et all [19]	✓	✓	
iSPA framework [20]			✓
METvalCOMPETISOFT [21]			✓
Galinac Tihana et all [22]	✓	✓	
Knowledge driven model (KDM) [23]	✓	✓	
MPS model [24]	✓		✓
SPI Framework: OWPL [25]	✓	✓	
Organizational-level SPI Model (O-SPI) [26]			✓
MIGME-RCC [27]	✓	✓	

As Table 1 shows, the methods, models and frameworks analyzed do not make a completely coverage of the established features related to human factor in SPI.

2.4 Characterization of SMEs Needs in the Implementation of SPI from Human Perspective

This section shows the needs that SMEs must to face in the implementation of a SPI initiative.

a) *Define SPI based on SME´s mission, vision and values.*
b) *Use a model or standard tailored this to SMEs needs.*
c) *Find a customizable guide that addresses the organization for best way to implement SPI according to its specific needs and environment.*
d) *Provide rules adapted to the SMEs size and level of maturity in the implementation of the SPI.*
e) *Reduce the learning curve in the implementation of SPI*
f) *Support to develop skills and abilities in the implementation of SPI.*
g) *Observe tangible results in short period of time.*

These needs most of the time represent both 1) a motivation to improve and 2) an important barrier to implement SPI in SMEs. Therefore, providing a support to these needs can cover the human factor in SPI.

3 Mapping the SPI Needs to those Identified at SMEs from Zacatecas Region

An analysis of SMEs at Zacatecas-Mexico was performed to identify the SPI needs based on human factor and map them with those found in literature. It is important to highlight that the analysis included both organizations without any experience in the implementation of SPI and with any kind of experience.

3.1 SMEs' Description

The interviews were conducted at 7 SMEs, for confidentiality reasons they are named as SME1, SME2, SME3, SME4, SME5, SME6 and SME7.

SME1 is a company dedicated to develop products and services with high impact in the education of children and teenagers. Currently, it does not have staff, but it hires external staff to develop a project.

SME2 is a company dedicated to develop software and web products; support and marketing. Currently, it has a staff of 4 people, including developers and marketing.

SME3 is a company dedicated to IT consulting, marketing, digital media and web development. Currently, it has a staff of 37 employees, including developers, graphic designers, maintenance personnel and executives.

SME4 is a company dedicated to develop organizational software for educational institution. Currently, it has a staff of 13 employees, including developers, project leaders and managers.

SME5 is a company dedicated to develop high quality software. Currently, it has a staff of 8 employees, distributed in the state of Zacatecas and Mexico City.

SME6 is a company dedicated to IT consulting and training, they have Personal Software Process (PSP) and Team Software Process (TSP) couches. Currently, it has a staff of 2 people.

SME7 is a company dedicated to develop software and web development, support and security. Currently, it has a staff of 16 people, including developers and marketing.

3.2 Analysis of SMEs

Findings after analyzing the interviews performed in SMEs were identified as follows, in organizations without experience in SPI: 1) a poor understanding of using process approach to develop software product and services, as consequence, organizations perceive the implementation of software engineering practices contained in models and standards as unnecessary; 2) organizations do not match their reality with the use of models and standards; and 3) organizations do not have enough budget for performing improvement activities, being their main limitations: (a) lack of enough budget to invest in process improvement; (b) high dependence on external budget and support to implement SPI; (c) lack of knowledge and skills needed to implement SPI; (d) lack of knowledge or a guide of how to implement improvements; and (e) lack of experience in the implementation of SPI.

In organizations with any kind of experience some practices, which have helped them in the implementation of a successfully SPI, were identified: 1) setting goals since the beginning help the organization to understand the need of implementing process improvement; 2) providing a guide for addressing improvements implementation achieve better results than without any support; 3) highlighting the benefits derived from the implementation of the improvement to reduce resistance to change of stakeholders; and 4) betting on the intellectual capital of the company to achieve better results.

3.3 Mapping

The results of the interviews at SMEs from Zacatecas and the identified needs in literature were mapping in order to reinforce the actual needs of SMEs in the implementation of SPI focused on human factor. Table 2 shows the mapping between them.

Table 2. Mapping between needs focused on human factor from literature and real needs found at SMEs of Zacatecas Region

SPI needs focusing on human factor from literature	Mentioned by Zacatecas SMEs without experience	Mentioned by Zacatecas SMEs with experience
Define SPI based on SME´s mission, vision and values	Lack of experience in the implementation of SPI	Setting goals since the beginning help the organization to understand the need of the implementation of process improvement
A model tailored to SMEs needs	Lack of knowledge about the way to follow in the implementation of improvements	Providing a guide for implementing improvements achieve better results than without support
Guide for addressing the organization in the best way for implementing a SPI according to its specific environment	Lack of knowledge about the way to follow in the implementation of improvements	Providing a guide for implementing improvements achieve better results than without support
Provide rules adapted to the SMEs size and level of maturity in the implementation of SPI	Lack of knowledge about the way to follow in the implementation of improvements	Providing a guide for implementation achieve better results than without its support
Reduce the learning curve when an organization implement SPI	Lack of knowledge and skills needed to implement SPI	Betting on the intellectual capital of the company to achieve better results
Support to develop skills and abilities in the implementation of SPI	Lack of experience in the implementation of SPI	Betting on the intellectual capital of the company to achieve better results
Obtain tangible results in short period of time	Lack of experience in the implementation of SPI	Highlighting the benefits derived to the implementation of the improvement

As Table 2 shows, the needs from literature can be mapped with the needs obtained from the study of Zacatecas SMEs with experience and without experience in the implementation on SPI.

4 Proposals to Cover the SPI Needs Focused on Human Perspective

This section aims to show a proposal related to two factors: *(a) to characterize SMEs according to their SPI needs, so that, a way to address the SPI can be provided; and (b) to create and select implementation strategies* focused on helping organizations to address the human factors in SPI.

4.1 Proposal One: Characterization of Software Development SMEs' According to Their Needs for Implementing a SPI

This proposal aims to identify and define process improvements patterns, which enable an organization to identify its current scenario and to provide the best way to start a SPI according to its specific features. Therefore, this proposal is focused on providing a set of process patterns as a solution to the problem that SMEs should face in selecting a right way to implement a SPI initiative.

According to [28] process patterns are reusable building blocks that organizations adapt or implement to achieve mature software process. As Figure 1 shows in order to define processes patterns this proposal takes into account three key aspects:

1. *Pattern elements*: elements that should be included in the definition of a pattern. This research takes the elements proposed in [29, 30]: name, context, problem, forces, solution, resulting context, related patterns and known;
2. *Characterization*: features that help to characterize an organization environment. This research uses a characterization previously performed focused on characterizing software processes improvement needs in SME's [31];
3. *Contextual aspects:* a selection of contextual aspects that are considered key aspect in the implementation of SPI. This research uses the contextual aspects proposed in [32]: product, process, practices, tools, techniques, people, organization and finally market.

Besides, a software tool is proposed to use the patterns. The software tool aims to guide SME's in the selection of the optimal path to start a SPI initiative adapted to its business goals, current environment, features and specific needs.

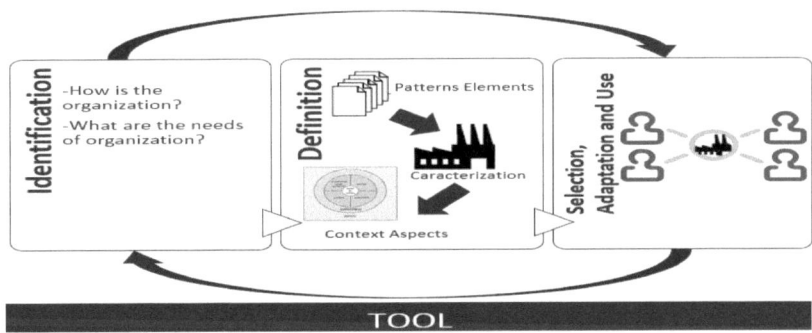

Fig. 1. Diagram of the first proposal

4.2 Proposal Two: Selection of Strategies for Implementing the Process Improvements

This proposal is focused on helping organizations to select the right strategy to implement process improvements in an appropriate way according to the specific context and organizational work culture.

According to [32], the software development process should be in harmony with the context in which the software is developed and delivered. This is the reason why even when some strategies have reported some benefits, these do not guarantee they are suitable for all organizations [33]. In other words, there is no single rule that ensure success.

Then, in order to establish if a specific strategy is suitable for an organization, should be analyzed the context and work culture of the organization in which the improvement will be implemented.

As Figure 2 shows, the proposal starts using a checklist that analyzes the organization environment such as *work culture, business goals and the process improvement goal*. Then, the organization identifies its environment according to a set of categories. After, the strategy that suits the organization' needs is provided.

It is important to highlight that to create the strategies are used the six contextual aspects proposed in [32]. Then, the process improvements are implemented following the strategy. Finally, the improvement implementation strategy is monitored to evaluate the improvement performance and to identify lessons learned.

Besides, a software tool is proposed to use facilitate organizations the selection of a strategy. The software tool aims to guide SME's in the selection of the optimal strategy to implement the improvements at a pace supported by the organization according to its current environment, features, needs and the way they work.

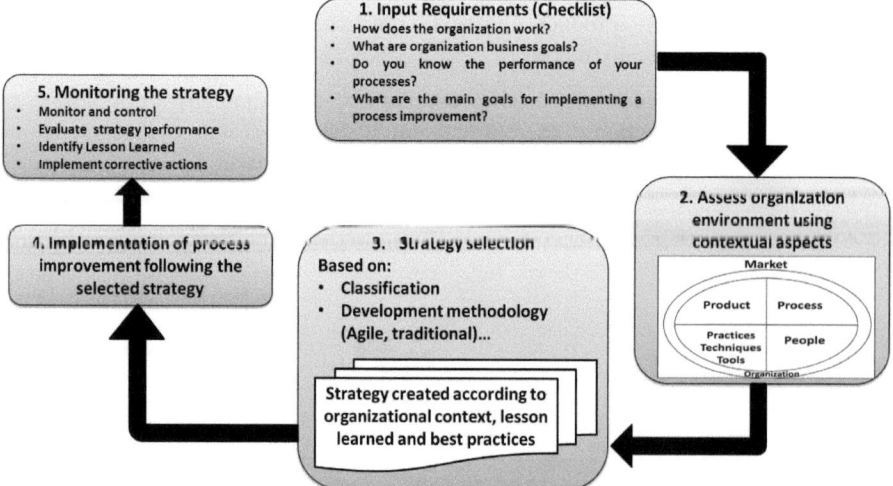

Fig. 2. Diagram of the second proposal

4.3 Mapping the Proposals with the SPI Manifesto

This section shows the analysis between the proposals and the values included in the SPI manifesto.

The SPI manifesto is a document which contains a set of values and the consequent principles. It was established in 2009 for a group of experts in SPI which aims to provide an expression of the state-of-art knowledge on SPI based on hundreds of person-years of experience and practice from organizations around the world [34]. To perform this analysis we analyse the SPI manifesto principles and our proposals. Next, Table 3 shows the analysis performed.

Table 3. Mapping between SPI manifesto and the two proposal

SPI manifesto	Proposal one	Proposal two
Know the culture and focus on needs	Provides patterns that organization can select based on its culture and current needs	Creates a strategy work culture and current needs
Motive all people involved	The improvement is addressed so that people identify the way they work	Addresses the improvement so that people identify the way they work
Base improvement on experience and measures	Analyzes and characterize the organization	Analyzes and characterizes the organization
Create learning organization	Provides the pattern that best fit with the organization or create it. Therefore, a path or way to improve is provided	Creates a strategy for implementing improvements, so that, the organization learns the suitable way to implement improvements and to identify lesson learned of using the strategy
Support the organization's vision and business objectives	Takes into account business goals to provide the optimal way to follow in the improvement implementation	Analyzes business goals to create the implementation strategy accorded to organization needs and prioritize
Use dynamic and adaptable models as needed	Provides specific models and standards or the multi-model environment as reference according to the organization specific needs	Provides strategies as the organizations evolves and their needs and business goals change
Apply risk management		
Manage the organizational change in your improvement effort	Provides a way taking into account the contextual aspects that helps to address the improvement effort	Creates a strategy taking into account the pace of change supported by the organization
Ensure all parties understand and agree on process		
Do not lose focus	Takes into account business goals to provide the optimal way to follow in the improvement implementation	Analyzes the prioritize of business goals providing the optimal way to monitor the implementation using the strategy

As Table 3 shows 8 of 10 principles are covered by our proposals. This result gives us a validation of coverage of human perspective for the proposals presented in this research work. Then, both proposals have a good coverage of the human perspective in software process improvement. Referring to the 2 principles not covered by the proposals: (1) *apply risk management*, we are going to include the identification of risk management associated to the proposals and (2) *ensure all parties understand and agree on process*, this factor will be analyzed using the software tools.

5 Conclusions

Since the point of view that quality of software product and services has a directly dependence of the quality of processes used to develop them. The implementation of SPI enables organizations to create strategic advantages with respect to its competitors. However, not all organizations obtain the same results when implementing improvements in their processes. Two main problems are associated with: 1) models and standards to be used as reference and; 2) a process definition without taking into account the human perspective.

This paper presented two proposals derived from two factors that aim to address the SPI since the human perspective. On the one way, the characterization of software development SMEs' needs for implementing a SPI aims to help organizations in selecting an optimal way to follow when starting an implementation of SPI according to its actual environment and specific needs.

On the other way, the selection of strategies provides a guide for organization in the implementation of process improvements according to the way the organization works, its culture, its organizational environment and the pace of change supported by it.

Acknowledgements. This work is sponsored by Research Center of Mathematics (CIMAT).

References

1. Gupta, J., Sharma, S., Hsu, J.: An overview of knowledge management, ch. 1. Idea Group Inc. (2004)
2. Molina, J.L., Marsal, M.: La gestión del conocimiento en las organizaciones. Ch. VII Herramientas de la Gestión del Conocimiento; IX Gestión del cambio, pp. 60–68, 87–94 (2002)
3. Turban, E., Aronson Jay, E., Liang, T.-P.: Knowledge Management. In: Decision Support Systems and Intelligent Systems, ch. 9, p. 487. Prentice Hall, Pearson, Uppers Saddle River, NJ (2005)
4. Soto-Acosta, P., Martínez-Conesa, I., Colomo-Palacios, R.: An empirical analysis of the relationship between IT training sources and IT value. Information Systems Management 27, 274–283 (2010)
5. Mishra, D., Mishra, A.: Software process improvement in SMEs: A comparative view. Comput. Sci. Inf. Syst. 6, 111–140 (2009)
6. Muñoz, M., Mejia, J., Calvo-Manzano, J.A., Cuevas, G., San Feliu, T., de Amescua, A.: Expected Requirements in Support Tools for Software Process Improvement in SMEs. In: IEEE Ninth Electron. Robot. Automot. Mech. Conf., pp. 135–140 (2012)

7. SEI CMMI Production Team, S.: CMMI for Development v1.3. Software Engineering Institute (January 2011)
8. International Organization for Standardization: ISO/IEC 15504: 2004 Information technology – Process assessment (2004)
9. Oktaba, H., Esquivel, C.A., Ramos, A.S., Martínez, A.M., Osorio, G.Q., López, M.R., Hinojo, F.L.L.: Modelo de Procesos para la Industria de Software (MoProSoft) V1.3 Agosto (2005)
10. Korsaa, M., Johansen, J., Schweigert, T., Vohwinkel, D., Messnarz, R., Nevalainen, R., Biro, M.: The people aspects in modern process improvement management approaches. Journal of Software: Evolution and Process 25, 381–391 (2013)
11. O'Connor, R., Basri, S.: The Effect of Team Dynamics on Software Development Process Improvement. International Journal of Human Capital and Information Technology Professionals 3, 13–26 (2012)
12. Jahn, K., Nielsen, P.A.: A Vertical Approach to Knowledge Management: Codification and Personalization in Software Processes. International Journal of Human Capital and Information Technology Professionals 2, 26–36 (2011)
13. Duron, B., Muñoz, M., Mejia, J.: Estado actual de la implementación de mejoras de procesos en las organizaciones software. In: 8ª Conferencia Ibérica de Sistemas y Tecnologías de Información, vol. II, pp. 856–862 (2013) ISBN: 978-989-96247-9-5
14. Mahmood, N., Wilson, D., Zowghi, D.: A maturity model for the implementation of software process improvement: an empirical study. Special Issue: The New Context for Software Engineering Education and Training 74, 155–172 (2005)
15. Goldenson, D., Herbsleb, J.: After the Appraisal: A systematic Survey of Process Improvement, its Benefits, and Factors that Influence Success. Tech. Rep. TR CMU/SEI-95-TR-009 ESC-TR-95-009 (1995)
16. Mahmood, N., Wilson, D., Zowghi, D.: A maturity model for the implementation of software process improvement: an empirical study. Special Issue: The New Context for Software Engineering Education and Training 74, 155–172 (2005)
17. Pettersson, F., Ivarsson, M., Gorschek, T., Öhman, P.: A practitioner's guide to light weight software process assessment and improvement planning. Journal of Systems and Software 81, 972–995 (2008)
18. Karlstrom, D., Runeson, P., Wohlin, C.: Aggregating viewpoints for strategic software process improvement-a method and a case study. IEE Proceedings Software 149, 143–152 (2002)
19. Asato, R., de Mesquita Spinola, M., Costa, I., de Farias Silva, W.H.: Alignment between the business strategy and the software processes improvement: A roadmap for the implementation. In: Portland International Conference on Management of Engineering & Technology, PICMET 2009, pp. 1066–1071 (2009)
20. Ali, R.Z.R.M., Ibrahim, S.: An application tool to support the implementation of integrated software process improvement for Malaysia's SME, pp. 177–182 (2011)
21. Khokhar, M.N., Zeshan, K., Aamir, J.: Literature review on the software process improvement factors in the small organizations. In: 4th International Conference on New Trends in Information Science and Service Science (NISS), pp. 592–598 (2010)
22. Galinac, T.: Empirical evaluation of selected best practices in implementation of software process improvement. Journal of Information and Software Technology 51, 1351–1364 (2009)
23. Alagarsamy, K., Justus, S., Lyakutti, K.: Implementation specification for software process improvement supportive knowledge management tool. IET Software 2, 123–133 (2008)

24. Montoni, M., Santos, G., Rocha, A.R., Weber, K.C., de Araujo, E.E.: MPS Model and TABA Workstation: Implementing Software Process Improvement Initiatives in Small Settings. In: Fifth International Workshop on Software Quality, WoSQ 2007: ICSE Workshops 2007, p. 4 (2007)
25. Alexandre, S., Renault, A., Habra, N.: OWPL: A Gradual Approach for Software Process Improvement in SMEs. In: 32nd EUROMICRO Conference on Software Engineering and Advanced Applications, SEAA 2006, pp. 328–335 (2006)
26. Yan, X., Wang, X., Luo, L., Chen, Z.: Research on Organizational-Level Software Process Improvement Model and Its Implementation. In: International Symposium on Computer Science and Computational Technology, ISCSCT 2008, pp. 285–289 (2008)
27. Calvo-Manzano, J.A., Cuevas, G., Gómez, G., Mejia, J., Muñoz, M., San Feliu, T.: Methodology for process improvement through basic components and focusing on the resistance to change. Journal of Software Evolution and Process 24(5), 511–523 (2010)
28. Ambler Scott, W.: An Introduction to Process Patterns. An AmbySoft Inc., White Paper (1998)
29. Coplien, J.O.: A development process generative pattern language. In: Pattern languages, Proceedings of PLoP 1994, pp. 183–237 (1994)
30. Appleton, B.: Patterns for Conducting Process Improvement. In: PLoP 1997 Conference, pp. 1–19 (1997)
31. Valtierra, C., Muñoz, M., Mejia, J.: Characterization of Software Processes Improvement Needs in Sme's. In: International Conference on Mechatronics, Electronics and Automotive Engineering (ICMEAE 2013), pp. 223–228 (2013) ISBN: 978-1-4799-2253-6
32. Petersen, K., Wohlin, C.: Context in Industrial Software Engineering Research. In: Third International Symposium on Empirical Software Engineering and Measurement, pp. 401–404 (2009)
33. Jeners, S., Clarke, P., O'Connor, R.V., Buglione, L., Lepmets, M.: Harmonizing Software Development Processes with Software Development Settings – A Systematic Approach. In: McCaffery, F., O'Connor, R.V., Messnarz, R. (eds.) EuroSPI 2013. CCIS, vol. 364, pp. 167–178. Springer, Heidelberg (2013)
34. Pries-Heje, J., Jonhansen, J., et al.: SPI Manifesto. Web Publishing (2010), http://www.spimanifesto.org

Assessing the Value of an Agile Coach in Agile Method Adoption

Rory V. O'Connor[1,2] and Natalia Duchonova[2]

[1] Lero, the Irish Software Engineering Research Centre, Ireland
[2] Dublin City University, Dublin, Ireland
`Rory.OConnor@computing.dcu.ie`

Abstract. This paper explores the value of Agile Coaching for companies adopting agile methods.in order to assist those who are adopting agile methods to decide on using or not using an Agile Coach by examining the value they can bring to companies adopting agile methods. In our research we surveyed three distinct groups: companies that used an Agile Coach for agile adoption, companies that adopted agile on their own and Agile Coaches themselves without the help of an Agile Coach. The data collected indicates that Agile Coaches can bring numerous benefits to companies, which in fact exceed the financial costs of using an Agile Coach. Therefore we suggest that there is financial value in using an Agile Coach for agile adoption, which is represented by faster return on investment (ROI) on the change.

Keywords: Agile Methods, Agile Coach, SPI.

1 Introduction

Since the introduction of Agile Manifesto in 2001, many companies engaging in software development have replaced the traditional methodologies by agile methods [1]. To help companies adopt agile methods smoothly, a new field of Agile Coaching has been introduced and is constantly gaining in popularity. Conferences are being held on Agile Coaching where experienced practitioners share their ideas, and some of them even started to offer Agile Coaching courses in order to teach others how to become a qualified Agile Coach [2]. In addition, some organizations developed Agile Coaching certification programs to standardize the qualification process. As a consequence, the agile community grows, however, there is evidence from numerous sources indicating a lack of qualified and well-experienced coaches to support the demand [3] [4].

The goal of this research is to assist companies who are adopting agile methods decide on using or not using an Agile Coach. This is achieved by examining the value Agile Coaches can bring to companies adopting agile methods, as so far there has been no supporting research evidence about the value they can bring to companies and whether the benefits brought exceed the financial costs. This objective is accomplished by an investigation involving Agile Coaches, companies that adopted agile methods with the help of an Agile Coach, as well as companies that adopted agile methods on their own. The value can be then identified by analyzing and comparing responses from all parties in order to get an objective point of view. Moreover, the value of different types of Agile Coaches should be understood and compared. The research should be beneficial for companies planning to adopt agile methods, but hesitating on whether to utilize an Agile Coach or not. In addition, once the company decides to use Agile Coaching for agile adoption, the research should help them identify the right type of an Agile Coach based on the company's characteristics, as well as to choose the right candidate by providing a baseline profile of an Agile Coach. Last, but not least, the dissertation will investigate how to best facilitate an Agile Coach in terms of authority given, in order to create a productive coaching environment within a company.

1.1 Agile Adoption

Agile Adoption is a term used to describe a process of adopting and implementing agile practices, processes and values in software development. The practices to be implemented may either correspond to just one agile method or to a combination of multiple agile methods. According to numerous surveys [5, 6, 7], the most popular combination of agile methods is Scrum with XP. In addition, organizations or development teams often do not implement all practices of the chosen agile method(s), but select only the ones that are compatible with the organization and/or the team. Such an adoption is called 'a la carte' agile adoption [8]. To conclude, some even customize the agile practices to suit the company's development environment [9]. Typically, the agile adoption process contains the following steps [10]:

- Set business goals (e.g. reduce time to market)
- Choose a pilot project
- Analyze company's and project's characteristics (size, criticality, etc.) and current practices
- Choose the method(s) to adopt
- Choose the practices to adopt (in case of an 'a la carte' agile adoption)
- Train the development team and the management
- Start applying the chosen practices

An interesting point to note is that despite the fact that most agile practices are considered to be very straightforward, the adoption of agile methods is not easy. The reason for that is that agile adoption represents an organizational change that will affect the company's organizational structure, processes, as well as people's behavior, and therefore it requires a carefully thought-out preparation [11]. In relation to this, a 2010 survey by Version One incorporating 4770 participants from 91 countries revealed the following list of leading causes of the failed agile projects [6]:

- Lack of experience with agile methods (14% of respondents)
- Company philosophy/culture at odds with core agile values (11%)
- External pressure to follow traditional waterfall practices (10 %)

- Reason not known (11%)
- Lack of management support (7%)
- Lack of cultural transition (8%)
- Insufficient training (5%)

In addition to this, the agile adoption process is even more difficult within large organizations, as they usually have many formalized processes, have to conform to numerous norms and standards and consist of many teams often geographically dispersed with time differences between the locations of these teams. All of this causes even bigger problems when trying to implement agile methods, therefore it is not a surprise that some companies either fail completely and reject the agile adoption for years, or they adopt an 'Agile-But', meaning that they drop the key practices and as a result the adoption may not bring the company any noticeable improvements.

One way how companies can reduce the risk of failure when adopting agile methods is to use an Agile Coach. This role has evolved naturally to provide coaching and mentoring to agile teams, and is relatively new and little researched. Therefore our aim is to find out whether Agile Coaching is really beneficial for companies adopting agile and what value it can bring them.

1.2 Agile Coach Value

The literature provides many definitions of value based on the field the value is being defined in. In marketing for example, value is defined as a difference between the price and the worth of a product, or in other words, the difference between what a customer receives and has to give in return. In coaching, value can be defined as the difference between the costs of hiring/using a coach and the benefits brought by the coach to the company in question. The value (benefits minus costs) provided by the coach can be also categorized as financial and non-financial. For evidence, a 2006 survey incorporating 30 companies revealed that coaching can bring numerous non-financial benefits (e.g. acquiring a new skill, increased motivation) as well as financial benefits (increased sales and revenue), however the financial benefits were secondary and not measurable [12].

Building upon this, value in Agile Coaching can be determined as the difference between the costs of hiring/using an Agile Coach and the benefits brought by the Agile Coach to the company in question. Despite the fact that the value of Agile Coaching is not yet researched, deriving from the previous comments about coaching it is reasonable to state that Agile Coaching may also provide financial and non-financial costs and benefits. However, these and the differences between them (i.e. financial and non-financial value) are not known and thus will be researched as part of this dissertation, with the primary focus on the non-financial value. Therefore for the purposes of this dissertation by the value in Agile Coaching we mean the non-financial value unless stated otherwise.

1.3 Research Problem

The goal of this research is to assist companies adopting agile methods decide on using or not using an Agile Coach. The motivation for this research comes from an identified gap in the literature. It is apparent that there is little published research on the area of Agile Coaching, and no published research on the value that Agile Coaches can bring to companies adopting agile methods. Moreover, there is no integrated research on what companies can benefit/not benefit from the use of an Agile Coach, and what type of an Agile Coach is most suitable for what type of companies.

On this basis, the main objective of this dissertation is to provide an answer to the following three related questions:

- RQ1: What non-financial value can Agile Coaches bring to companies adopting agile methods?
- RQ2: What factors determine whether a company should use/not use an Agile Coach for agile adoption?
- RQ3: What type of an Agile Coach is most suitable for what type of companies?

The answers to these research questions should help companies decide whether to use an Agile Coach for agile adoption and if so, what type of Agile Coach to use. To conclude, the findings of this dissertation should be beneficial from a practical point of view, and thus used in real world scenarios.

2 Agile Coaching

Agile Coaching is a subfield of coaching whose focus is to "help teams or individuals adopt and improve agile methods and practice" and "rethink and change the way they go about development" [13]. In the following sections we will look at the origins of Agile Coaching, the roles, activities, skills, competencies as well as different types of Agile Coaches. Since Agile Coaching is primarily based on the knowledge from the field of coaching, the discipline of coaching will be explained first.

Coaching has been used in many areas where guidance and advice from a more experienced person is needed, including sports, professional life and business. Despite that coaching is still a young discipline that is constantly developing. In practice, coaching is used as a technique for helping teams or individuals learn in order to improve their performance, or to develop and grow [14]. By providing the guidance of an expert the teams or individuals receive valuable information that speed up the learning process and reduce the error rate.

Since agile software development is based on teamwork and the team's performance is critical for the success of the software development project, it is not surprising that coaching has been also applied to the area of agile methods. Coaching in the context of agile methods (i.e. Agile Coaching) is intended to help software development teams learn agile practices and then to use them in an effective and efficient way, which would ultimately improve their performance [15].

Since there are numerous agile methods, an Agile Coach can specialize in one of the agile methods primarily. Therefore based on the type of agile method promoted we recognize a Scrum coach, DSDM coach, Lean coach, etc. Depending on the coach's mission, i.e. whether his/her objective is to manage the agile adoption of a team that is transferring to agile or to improve the performance of a team that has already started using agile and is struggling with it, we can identify adoption coaches and after-adoption coaches. As already stated, the focus of this dissertation is primarily on adoption coaches. Another classification is based on whether the Agile Coach is a member of the organization that is using the coach. In this case we recognize two types of Agile Coaches - external Agile Coaches and internal Agile Coaches. This classification seems to be the most commonly used one [15]. Depending on whether the Agile Coach stays with the team full-time and thus is coaching only one team at a time, or whether the coach stays with the team part-time and thus can coach multiple teams at once, we can classify the coach either as a full-time Agile Coach or a part-time Agile Coach [16].

3   Research Study

As stated above, the main purpose of this dissertation is to provide an answer to the following three related research questions stated in section 2. Furthermore our analysis of the Agile Coaching literature has led to more questions, which are related to the research questions above. Some of the additional research questions that were raised by the preliminary investigation were as follows. It is important to note that a lot more questions were initially raised, but I have chosen to ask the following set of additional questions from not only time constraints imposed on this research, but also from conceptual reason (i.e. the questions seemed to be conceptually related):

- RQ4: How do companies decide about whether to use an Agile Coach for agile adoption?
- RQ5: How do companies perceive the role of an Agile Coach?
- RQ6: What are the common adoption problems that companies cannot solve without the help of an Agile Coach?
- RQ7: Is there a financial value in using an Agile Coach for agile adoption?
- RQ8: What is the difference in value provided to companies by different types of Agile Coaches?
- RQ9: What profile should companies look for in an Agile Coach?
- RQ10: How much authority does an Agile Coach need in order to do his/her job properly?
- RQ11: When do Agile Coaches withdraw from the team?

The answers to these questions should help companies decide whether to use an Agile coach for agile adoption and if so, what type of Agile Coach to use in order to maximize the value received. Nevertheless, we acknowledge that the selected research questions are quite broad in a way that the time scope of this research does not allow us to perform a detailed analysis when attempting to answer these questions, but as already stated, the goal of this research is to do a preliminary analysis that would represent an incremental step on the way towards understanding these issues more deeply in the future.

3.1 Data Collection

This investigation involving three different groups of research participants:

1. Agile Coaches
2. Companies that used an Agile Coach for agile adoption
3. Companies that adopted agile without the help of an Agile Coach

The research participants consisted of a mixture of individuals known second-hand to the researchers and direct emails were sent to well-known Agile Coaches that contributed to the area of Agile Coaching in form of literature or online articles. In total 8 Agile Coaches participated, who had between 2 and 15 years experience (average 6) in coaching and coached companies in adopting Scrum XP, Lean, Kanban, DSDM and FDD. A total of 5 companies that used an Agile Coach for agile adoption participated via persons with key job titles of CTO and development manager. These companies varied in size from 22 to 100 persons and were involved in a range of software domains from Internet systems development to Middleware systems. Finally, 5 Companies that adopted agile without the help of an Agile Coach participated via persons with key job titles of development manager, project manager and CTO. The companies varied in size from size 10 to 40 persons and represented a range of business domains including: telecommunications, payment solutions and financial services software.

Prior to undertaking the study three interview guides for the three groups of respondents was developed. The interview guide for Agile Coaches involved 56 questions that were divided into 5 categories:

1. Agile Coach's details
2. Adoption strategy
3. Agile Coaching qualities
4. The value of Agile Coaching
5. Additional information

The interview questions for companies that adopted agile with the help of an Agile Coach (31 in total) were divided into 4 categories:

1. Company details
2. Adoption details
3. Agile Coaching qualities
4. The value of Agile Coaching

Finally, the interview guide for companies that adopted agile on their own consisted of 24 questions, which again were grouped into 3 categories:

1. Company details
2. Adoption details
3. The value of Agile Coaching

3.2 Data Analysis

The responses from each group of participants were copied into response tables to make the comparison of responses easier and more structured. Response table is a data analysis technique that allows to "view the responses of all the respondents for each of the selected questions in a survey" [17]. This technique is commonly used not only in survey-based research fields, such as marketing, but also in more technical fields such as physics to compare the achieved results under different factors. A typical response table used in a survey-based research consists of table rows that contain the survey questions and table columns that contain the names of the respondents. In total three response tables were created - one with responses from Agile Coaches, the second response table with responses from companies with an Agile Coach and the third table with responses from companies without an Agile Coach by copying the responses from the questionnaires and interview response forms.

Subsequently, common questions were identified in the three response tables, and these were then extracted together with the corresponding responses into one summary response table, which represents the selected approach to the research. Then a data pattern was looked for in the responses from each group. By a sought data pattern we mean a clear repetition of data within the responses for a particular survey question. It should be noted that some questions, however, could not be given to all three groups from logical reasons (e.g. there is no point asking respondents from companies that had not used an Agile Coach how much authority an Agile Coach needs to do his job properly). In such case, i.e. a case when a particular question did not involve all three groups of participants, the provisional hypothesis was formulated based on a clear repetition of data from within one or two response tables only.

4 Findings

A rich set of data was collected and analyzed as part of this study. Space limitations prevent a complete description of the findings this paper however, the major themes will be presented in this section.

4.1 Making the decision to use an Agile Coach

To address RQ4: How do companies decide about whether to use an Agile Coach for agile adoption? according to the Agile Coaches, companies' decision about whether to use /not to use an Agile Coach for agile adoption is based on the following factors:
- scale of the change
- ability to figure it on their own
- success (failure) of a pilot project
- ability to learn from pilot's failure
- costs of using an Agile Coach   references   about   successful implementations with/out the help of an Agile Coach in other companies
- type of company's industry

In fact, the costs were mentioned as a decision factor in the majority of responses. The following extract from Agile Coach 3 is a typical response: *"Coaches are expenses and it requires a strong commitment and buy-in from management. Therefore companies may opt for figuring it out themselves first"*.

To address RQ5: How do companies perceive the role of an Agile Coach? The Agile Coaches reported that organizations have the following perceptions about Agile Coaching:

- There is not enough awareness about the service.
- Companies perceive an Agile Coach as a savior or miracle worker.
- Agile Coaching is perceived to be expensive.
- Agile Coaching is becoming very popular.

On the contrary, companies have the following perceptions:

- Agile Coach is an expensive consultant.
- Agile Coach is a guarantee of a successful agile transition.
- Hiring an Agile Coach is an option of how to improve agile knowledge internally.

The response from Agile Coach 1 best captures the companies' current perceptions of Agile Coaching: *"Most people do not know about this service and even if they do, they think it is too expensive"*.

4.2 What Companies Should Use an Agile Coach?

In order to determine which companies should use an Agile Coach for agile adoption, the respondents from the group of Agile Coaches were asked to provide an objective view on this topic. Based on the responses a list of factors was assembled. The factors that determine whether a company should use/not use an Agile Coach for agile adoption are:

- existing agile expertise within the company
- the size/structure of a company (if a small company with a few departments, no need to use an Agile Coach)
- complexity of company processes (if simple, then no need to use an Agile Coach)
- nature of the company industry (if not a common industry, use an Agile Coach)
- impact of the agile adoption failure on a company (if critical, use an Agile Coach)
- distribution of teams (if geographically dispersed, adoption is more difficult, therefore use an Agile Coach)
- presence of continuous improvement and collaborative culture within the company (e.g. Kaizen culture) (if present, then no need to use an Agile Coach)

4.3 Common Adoption Problems Requiring an Agile Coach

When asked about the common agile adoption problems that teams cannot solve without the help of an Agile Coach, Agile Coach 3 stated: "There are tons of practicalities that the coach will help with". The Agile Coaches gave the following examples:

- how to do agile requirement management
- how to get rid of the documentation
- how to apply agile to a legacy code
- how to keep the quality of code high
- how to do incremental design
- how to track progress of an agile project
- how to get testing done within a short iteration
- what are the things that should happen before items hit the backlog

Other coaches mentioned the following adoption problems that can be avoided by using an Agile Coach for agile adoption:

- struggling with industry related agile challenges
- NIH (Not-Invented-Here) syndrome, i.e. adopting an original version of agile methodology
- how to align other (non-development) processes with the change
- still doing a lot of useless things (such as documentation) despite claiming to be 'agile'.

4.4 Financial Perceptions of Using an Agile Coach

The financial and non-financial benefits and drawbacks of Agile Coaching stated by all three groups of respondents were looked at and the financial and non-financial value of Agile Coaching was assessed. Finally, the overall value of Agile Coaching in agile adoption was examined by comparing the overall responses from companies that used an Agile Coach and from companies that did not use an Agile Coach in order to determine whether Agile Coaching is really beneficial or not.

The companies that used an Agile Coach consider the adoption to be a success and they would all use an Agile Coach again. They would also recommend other companies to use an Agile Coach for agile adoption, however, Company 1 "*would not recommend using a full-time Agile Coach if that was their only skill*".

On the other hand, companies that adopted agile without the help of an Agile Coach all claim the adoption was a success. However, as a drawback of this approach they mention a significant learning curve. When asked whether they would hire an Agile Coach if they had to undergo the agile transition again, only one company (Company 1) would do it, but "*lack of money is a real issue*". This company would also recommend using an Agile Coach to all companies that can afford it. Other companies on the other would send everyone to training. In fact, Company 3 had everyone sent to training, nevertheless, " ... *if we didn't have somebody with experience of using Agile in another company, then hiring an Agile Coach would have been essential"*. In addition, none of the companies knew other companies that would completely fail by using a similar do-it-yourself approach.

4.5 Agile Coach Profile

Agile Coaches were asked to rate the qualities on a scale based on the criticality. They rated the following qualities as critical:

- expertise in multiple agile methods
- long experience
- numerous references
- numerous IT skills
- soft skills
- knowledge on team work and team dynamics
- knowledge on change management

Two qualities were considered as not critical for an Agile Coach:

- Agile Coaching certification
- professional coaching certification

On the other hand, companies that used an Agile Coach were asked what profile they looked for when choosing an Agile Coach. They stated the following qualities:

- experience with agile implementations in companies of a similar size and complexity
- proven good track record
- strong knowledge of agile
- good cultural fit
- ability to deliver the message to senior management
- great interpersonal skills
- software development background

5 Discussion

The primary research data was collected from 8 Agile Coaches and 10 companies - 5 companies that used an Agile Coach and 5 companies that adopted agile without the help of an Agile Coach. The Agile Coaches and companies were geographically dispersed as so provided a general view on Agile Coaching. The research results can be summarized as follows:

- Half of the respondents believe that Agile Coaches are perceived as expensive consultants.
- Numerous factors determine whether a company should use an Agile Coach, such as the size of the company, complexity of its processes, the nature of its industry and company culture.

- Agile Coaches can provide both financial and non-financial benefits for companies adopting agile methods.
- According to the respondents, the benefits brought by an Agile Coach exceeded the financial costs.
- The value Agile Coaches provide is that they significantly reduce the risk of failure of agile adoption and speed up the adoption process.
- Other benefits of using an Agile Coach are tailoring of agile practices to company's needs, highlighting dysfunctions and waste in processes, sorting out industry related agile adoption challenges, etc.
- There are many practicalities Agile Coaches can help companies with, such as how to do incremental design among many others.
- All respondents from companies that used an Agile Coach for agile adoption would recommend it to other companies.
- There is difference in value provided by different types of Agile Coaches.
- External Agile Coaches can provide impartial view on the company and diverse experience, whereas internal Agile Coaches have a good understanding of the company's business and processes.
- Half of the respondents believe that non-directive coaches provide higher value than directive coaches because they teach coaches how to be self-coaching.
- Certified Agile Coaches do not necessarily provide higher value than non-certified coaches as experience matters, but they are more credible.
- Numerous factors influence companies' decision to use an Agile Coach, the major ones being existing/missing agile experience in company and the costs of hiring an Agile Coach.

5.1 Limitations and Future Work

The main limitation of this study comes from the fact that a vast majority of respondents preferred questionnaires to interviews because of geographical and time constraints. The disadvantage of using questionnaires for a qualitative research is a lack of interactivity and immediate feedback.

Further work on this study could involve running another iteration of the research process. Given longer time scale, more data would be collected on areas where provisional hypotheses did not manage to develop further and new hypotheses would be formulated and tested for validity. Possible work by other researchers may involve carrying out case studies or focus groups within organizations that adopted agile with the help of an Agile Coach. In addition it may be appropriate to broaden the scope of this study to include situational factors [18] that affect the choice of a particular agile method and how these may impact upon the adoption decision and the ultimate success [19] of the software process.

To conclude, while the research results are positive and show promise, more work should be undertaken by other researchers in order to have fully generalizable results.

References

1. Ambler, S.W.: Has Agile Peaked?, http://drdobbs.com/architecture-and-design/207600615?cid=Ambysoft
2. Agile Coach Training, http://www.training-classes.com/programs/00/90/9001_agile_coach_training.php
3. Silva, K., Doss, C.: The Growth of an Agile Coach Community at a Fortune 200 Company. In: Proceedings of the Agile, USA (2007)
4. Chung, M.W., Drummond, B.: Agile @ yahoo! from the trenches. Paper Presented at the Agile Conference, AGILE 2009, Chicago, IL, pp. 113–118 (2009)
5. VersionOne, State of Agile Development 2009, http://trailridgeconsulting.com/surveys/state-of-agile-development-survey-2009.pdf
6. VersionOne, State of Agile Development 2010, http://www.versionone.com/state_of_agile_development_survey/10/page3.asp
7. VersionOne, Agile Methodologies, http://www.versionone.com/Agile101/Methodologies.asp
8. Hovorka, D.S., Larsen, K.R.: Enabling agile adoption practices through network organizations. European Journal of Information Systems 15(2) (2006)
9. Fitzgerald, B., Hartnett, G., Conboy, K.: Customising agile methods to software practices at Intel Shannon. European Journal of Information Systems 15(2) (2006)
10. Sidky, A., Arthur, J., Bohner, S.: A disciplined approach to adopting agile practices: the agile adoption framework. In: Proceedings of Innovations in Systems and Software Engineering, vol. 3(3) (2007)
11. Nerur, S., Mahapatra, R., Mangalaraj, G.: Challenges of Migrating to Agile Methodologies. Magazine Communications of the ACM - Adaptive Complex Enterprises 48(5) (May 2005)
12. Marber, R.: Survey: What are the benefits of coaching, http://www.coachfederation.org/includes/docs/037WhatarethebenefitsofcoachingSummaryFeb07.pdf
13. The Role of an Agile Coach, http://www.agilejournal.com/articles/columns/column-articles/1917-the-role-of-the-agile-coach
14. History of Coaching, http://www.performancecoachinginternational.com/resources/articles/historyofcoaching.asp
15. Davies, R.: Adapting Your Agile Coaching Style, http://agilecoach.typepad.com/agile-coaching/2010/10/agile-coaching-zone.html
16. Certified Scrum Coach (CSC) Application, http://www.o-act.com/index.php/component/content/article/39-ed-willis/59-certified-scrum-coaching-application-ed-willis.html
17. Response Table, http://www.zarca.com/Online-Surveys-Product/RM/response-table.html
18. Clarke, P., O'Connor, R.V.: The situational factors that affect the software development process: Towards a comprehensive reference framework. Journal of Information and Software Technology 54(5), 433–447 (2012)
19. Clarke, P., O'Connor, R.V.: The influence of SPI on business success in software SMEs: An empirical study. Journal of Systems and Software 85(10), 2356–2367 (2012)

The Influence of Management on Software Product Quality: An Empirical Study in Software Developing Companies

Frank Philip Seth, Erja Mustonen-Ollila, and Ossi Taipale

Department of Software Engineering and Information Management
Lappeenranta University of Technology
Lappeenranta, Finland
{frank.seth,erja.mustonen-ollila,ossi.taipale}@lut.fi

Abstract. This study employed grounded theory, and presents six findings describing managerial issues in the software developing companies: first, managers' technical skills, experience, and knowledge in software and domain influence the developers' productivity; second, top-down decisions deprive transparency and affect the efficiency of requirements prioritization; third, the communication between managers and customers, and realistic estimation of resources sustains good customer relationship, and have positive effect to the product quality; fourth, the aim of managers' decisions on resources is not to reduce expenditure but to achieve long-term goals for both organization and customers; fifth, the managers' choice and decisions on people affect other resources and the quality of the product, and sixth, organizational structures have influence on the teams and product quality. The findings of this study may be used to enhance managerial activities in software developing companies for better product quality.

1 Introduction

The modern software development context is characterized by high volatility of products driven by rapid growth of technology, globalization of the economy, business complexities, increase of information technology (IT) knowledge and user demand [1]. Software developing companies particularly face the challenge because of the nature and complexity of the problems in the business side. The goal of software development is to solve these complex business problems. Business and domain problems demand knowledge some of which are outside the IT realms [2] hence causing more complexity in managing software developing projects.

In the past, management focused on managing resources, processes and customer requirements [3]. In the current era of rapid growth of science and technology, the knowledge-intensive and technology-focused managers are highly needed to overcome the challenges to understand and solve complex business problems [1, 4]. Suominen and Mäkinen [4] argue that software is designed to solve problems in a complex socio-technical environment. So, the success of the projects depends on the management of the processes and software design that is domain specific and at the business level.

This empirical study inquires into practical experience of software developing companies and focuses on the managerial activities at the project level. Companies have different names applied for managers' role. However, this study considers a manager as anyone who plays the role of decision making over the software development life cycle (SDLC) activities. Münch et al. [5] argue that, despite of the advancement of software process management and the state of software process research, the field is quite immature. Empirical study is required to understand the unsolved problems in the process management for the purpose of improving processes and product engineering, value creation for customers, and fulfillment of quality requirements. The objective of this study is to understand the management issues that influence efforts towards software quality construction. The research question is: *What are the management issues that influence efforts towards software quality construction?*

The rest of the paper is organized as follows: Section two presents related literature, Section three presents research methodology and data analysis, Section four presents results and finally, Section five presents discussion and conclusions of the study.

2 Related Research

In general, the managers' role pertains to the responsibility to manage resources towards achieving common goals [3]. In the software companies as applied to others, the goals include meeting both customers and company goals. In the current era of technology, IT companies face stiff competition in the IT market that necessitate managers to be equipped with skills and experience but also the knowledge [6, 7] of their customers, business environment and domain for the purpose of making sound decisions on the products they develop. Developing high quality products is costly. However, the product should meet the customers' requirements at the affordable and competitive price. In the pursuit of both customers and company goals, managers need to make reasonable compromises and prioritization [8] for the purpose of minimizing production cost, yet to get the job done, and achieve the objectives.

Principally, managers take part in every step of an organization process, giving direction to the people and aligning resources in order to achieve goals [3]. Several studies suggest that in the software development, the quality of the product depends on resources [9, 10] and processes [11, 12], and other organizational factors such as working environment and organizational culture [6, 13]. Fujimura and Moore [14] argue that a group of talented developers, motivated and hardworking software engineers may produce low quality software because of lack of schedule management and quality management. This study relates the performance of individuals in an organization with the management [14], which implies that failure of managers to perform their duties has a negative impact on the quality of products they develop.

Building quality into a product requires both information beyond those related to IT such as economics, human psychology and technical skills [6, 7]. Lack of multi-skilled and informed managers impedes success of projects. On the other hand, deprivation of information and lack of transparency within the organization lead to failure to meet desired quality of products despite of technical skills, tools and applied processes [5]. Organizational structures and the management within the organizations may be one of such factors that inhibit the transparency and communication among the teams [15].

3 Research Methodology

The objective of this study is to understand the management issues that influence efforts towards software quality construction. This qualitative empirical study was conducted in thirteen software-developing companies. The data collected was analyzed using the grounded theory approach [16]. The study covers management activities observed while studying the general software development and testing activities.

3.1 Grounded Theory

Grounded theory (GT) [16] method is a pragmatic approach for conducting social sciences research but also applicable to other fields of study such as software engineering [17]. Several versions of GT exist. This study follows the Strauss and Corbin version of the GT [16]. We chose the GT because of its systematic approach in data analysis and the ability to use data without limiting its formats. GT approach uses three levels of coding: open, axial and selective coding. In the open coding, researcher constantly compares and contrasts the concepts to establish similarities and differences. Similar concept are collected into categories and labeled. In the axial coding, the categories are studied and analyzed to establish interdependencies and relationship among them. The purpose of the selective coding is to establish the core category. Core category is the one of the developed categories that is broad enough to describe all other categories. If the core category is not found among the existing categories, a new conceptual category will be created to describe other categories. Finally, in the selective coding the core category is used to induce a theory grounded on data [16].

3.2 Research Strategy and Sample

A team of four researchers developed the interview guidelines and questions. Three researchers conducted semi-structured interviews in thirteen software-developing companies. The interviewees included software developers (5), testers (6), designers (3), managers (7), R&D and quality assurance personnel (3), and requirements engineers (1). The sample was selected using polar type criteria [19] to cover different types and sizes of organizations developing software for different domains, see Table 1. The sampling was theoretical [18]. The goal of theoretical sampling is not the same as quantitative sampling. The theoretical sampling allows a researcher to gain deeper understanding of the analyzed cases and draw inferences without limitation of quantity of representation.

This study covered three interview rounds. The interview questions were sent to the interviewees beforehand and each interview took about 60 minutes. The total amount of interviews was 40. The interview questions of the three interview rounds are available at the link[1] below. Table 1 below represents the thirteen cases companies labeled A to M, business domain, rounds of interviews, company size and the role of interviewees.

Table 1. Business domain, interview rounds and number of interviewees, company size and role of the interviewees

CASE	Business domain	1st Round interviews	2nd Round interviews	3rd Round interviews	Company size	Role of the interviewees
A	Inventory management systems.	1			Small	R&D and quality assurance manager (1).
B	Banking and insurance.	4	5		Large	Test analysts (1), test designer (2), Designer and developer (2).
C	Space satellite.	1	1	1	Small	Designer and developer (2) and Project manager (1).
D	Web applications.	1			Small	Tester and developer (1).
E	Embedded software.	4	4	2	Large	Tester (1), developer (2) and requirement management (1).
F	Quality and testing consultancy	1		2	Medium	Quality manager (1), developer (1) and consulting tester (1).
G	Various software developers.	1	1		Large	Quality manager (1) and tester (1).
H	Cloud computing Web applications.	1			Small	CEO, developer, tester and designer (1).
I	Fleet management systems.	2	1		Large	Test consultant (1) and test manager (1).
J	Cloud computing services and consultancy.	1			Small	CEO (1).
K	Banking, energy, health, etc.	1	1	1	Large	Quality assurance and tester (1).
L	Development and testing consultants.		2		Small	Consultant tester (1) and developer (1).
M	Various software developers.			1	Large	Project manager (1).
13		18	15	7	40	

---

[1] http://www2.it.lut.fi/project/STX/material.html

During the interviews, the interviewees were let to answer questions without further guidance so that they could give as much information as possible. All the interviews were conducted face-to-face in the interviewees' company premises. In some occasions, one interviewee assumed more than one role. For example, in some cases the same person worked as tester and designer at the same time; this phenomenon was common in small companies. The interviews were tape-recorded and transcribed by a specialized company. Some companies had more interviews than the others because new and interesting concepts and leads emerged during the interview. The researcher followed the leads to the next interview until the same phenomena and concepts seemed to repeat. This stage is called saturation point. Some companies just needed one interview because no new leads or concepts emerged or observations were similar with the other cases. The leads collected during the first round were used to modify the interview questions for the second round.

Second round interviews included fewer companies because of following the leads observed during the first round. The companies where no new leads or concepts emerged were left out. The few leads collected from the second round were then used to modify the interview question for the third round. Concepts collected from each round were analyzed and new leads were studied. The interviews continued until no new leads or concepts emerged. During the second round, we decided to find an additional company for the purpose of complementing leads and findings observed during the first round. The same process was repeated for the third round of data collection.

4 Results

The data analysis followed GT [16] with the help of the analysis tool ATLAS.ti [20]. The study focused on managerial issues that are directly related to software development activities. In the open coding similar concept were identified from the data, coded and categorized. Concepts that did not describe the issues related to the managers or the research goals were left out. The open coding produced 150 codes.

4.1 Categories

The open and axial coding took place in parallel. Data analysis also considered the Seaman [17] approach that allows the seed categories from research question, study objectives and predefined variables of interest. For example, to support the study we used the ISO definition of software quality [21] and the six roles of managers (i.e. planning, staffing, organizing, directing, leading and controlling) [3] as seed categories in our categorization of concepts. ISO/IEC 25010 [21] defines software product quality as the degree to which the software product satisfies stated and implied needs when used under specified conditions. In the definition of quality [21], we looked at the underlying meaning that focuses on the goals of the software development. The goals include solving business problems and satisfying the end-users of the software. When the software meets the customer requirements we say that the quality goals have been reached, and when a company makes profit out of the software we say that company's goals are met.

In the axial coding we further developed categories and their relationships. So, we kept our focus on the concepts and their relationships related to the activities of managers in software developing companies. The categorization process resulted into six categories with subcategories that describe the influence of managers on the process of software quality construction during the software development activities. Table 2 presents the seed categories, subcategories and categories.

Table 2. Categorization of the managers' activities in the software development companies

Seed categories	Subcategories	Categories
1. Planning 2. Organizing 3. Directing	i). Skills and experience, ii). Administration of standards and good practices, iii). Selection of the best teams.	1. Quality championship.
4. Controlling 5. Staffing 6. Leading	i). Requirements documentation ii). Requirements analysis and prioritization.	2. Requirements management.
	i). Customer involvement in the development process, ii). Collection of end-user feedback.	3. Customer relationships.
Software quality: satisfaction of customer requirement when the software is used in specifies condition (business, etc.)	i). Company goals, ii). Customer goals.	4. Achievement of business goals.
	i). Developers, ii). Time, iii). Finances, iv.) Tools.	5. Resources.
	i). Organizational structure, ii). Process improvement.	6. Software developing companies.

Finally, in the selective coding, the purpose is to develop core category [16]. None of the six categories was broad enough to describe the other categories so we developed a new conceptual category and named it as *the influence of managers on software quality construction*.

Table 3. Categories and their descriptions

Category	Description
Quality championship	This category refers to the capabilities and activities the managers do towards managing the technical teams (designers, developers, testers).
Requirements management	This category refers to the tasks the managers do during requirement analysis and prioritization.
Customer relationships	This category refers to the activities the managers do pertaining to the interactions with customers.
Achievement of business goals	This category refers to the activities the managers do to achieve both company and customer goals.
Resources	This category refers to the activities the managers do to manage resources towards achieving company and customer goals.
Software developing companies	This category refers to the internal systems such as organization structure and processes and how the position of the manager affects the system.

Thus, the analysis resulted into six categories: Quality championship, requirements management, customer relationships, business goals resources, and the software developing companies. The six categories and their descriptions are shown in Table 3 above.

4.2 Findings

Based on the six categories and their relationships we present the findings that explain the management activities towards software quality construction.

1. Quality Championship

Quality championship requires both good managerial and technical skills in the area the manager is working. The core role of managers is to manage people and resources for the purpose to achieve defined goals [3]. There is an advantage if the manager has technical skills on the area he/she is managing. *"So this is maybe the biggest issue for me. Flowing on information is not smooth because the product manager is not in my field."* - Case E, Development engineer.

Experience of the previous projects was noted to count on the success of the similar future projects. *"Project manager takes mostly care of the estimation work. The estimation comes very much from the experience and knowledge of earlier similar kind of projects and it is not based on any pattern or methodology."* – Case B, test manager.

The managers who do not have skills and experience on the software industry led to failure of some software projects. They might be good in hardware or other part of IT but it is important to have some skills and knowledge related to software development. *"We experienced failure because company X was a hardware company. When they started to develop software, the management didn't understand software. It is very important that companies have people with software background in the management teams. If you don't have software managers in management teams, it will be a failure."* – Case F, senior consultant.

Thus, based on the observations of the *'quality championship'* category we formulate our first finding: **Managers' technical skills, experience, and knowledge in software and domain, influence the developers' productivity.**

2. Requirements Management

Management roles emerged differently in different companies in requirements analysis and prioritization. In some companies the managers made the final decision about the requirements without involving technical teams. These companies exercised the 'top-down decisions'. On the other hand, some organizations involved technical teams and agreed on the final requirements. These companies exercised 'horizontal decisions' where all members of the teams were part of the decisions. *"We have product managers who are responsible for taking care of all the customer's requirements. It's not that easy but the product manager's task is to translate the customer's needs to us in the development teams. We have to try to think and understand in a correct way."* - Case C, Development engineer.

The 'horizontal decision' and prioritization of requirements varied between the organizations. Some organizations involved technical teams to sort the final requirements while other companies had regular meetings and specific teams' representatives who were dedicated for the requirements. *"We made sort of this team so that we have one person for each kind of product family who handles the requirements. And they collect all the needs and requirements and then they have regular meetings with the product managers where they set priorities."* Case E, Development engineer.

Thus, based on the observations of the *'requirements management'* category we formulate our second finding: **Top-down decisions deprive transparency and affect the efficiency of requirements prioritization.**

3. Customer Relationships

The category *'customer relationships'* is vital in quality construction. Customer involvement in the development process is a challenging process [22]. However, managers should establish the link between developers and costumers for the purpose of understanding requirements and achieving quality goals of the software in the development process. *"First the customer wanted just to have a quality manager. Then when I made a quality assurance plan, customer eye opened. They did not have any professional testers. So they requested testing services. We have been happy because the customer understood the importance of the quality and testing."* - Case I, consultant.

Managers play an important role in building good customer relationship and manage the trade-offs and disputes for the purpose of satisfying the customer. *"I think that cost and schedule are main drivers. If we come up with a problem, something unexpected, we have to communicate it to the customers and discuss how to handle the problem. Usually, it's about trade-offs."* - Case C, Project manager.

In most of the studied companies, developers did not have direct feedback from the customers but though their managers. *"I suppose it is up to the managers of each project to get feedback from customers and then try to evaluate any needs for change."* -Case C, Project Manager.

Thus, based on the observations of the *'customer relationships'* category we formulate our third finding; **The efficiency of communication between managers and customers, and realistic estimation of resources sustains good customer relationship, and have a positive effect to the product quality.**

4. Achievement of Business Goals

Achievement of business goals includes both company goals and customer goals. Training for developers was noted to have positive impact to both companies and the customers. Training contributes to quality of the products and revenue to the companies. *"Some complain that courses are very expensive and wonder if it worth it. You invest money but you get your money back in terms of productivity and managers have to make a wise choice on training not based on cost only."* – Case B, Security specialist.

The consultant in the case 'I' reveals that there is a relationship between improvement of organizational systems and productivity. Achieving organizational goals for improvement enables achieving goals for customers as well. *"Little by little happens some improvement of so system and our organization works better."* - Case I, consultant.

Thus, based on the observations of the *'achievement of business goals'* category we formulate our fourth finding: **The aim of managers' decisions on resources is not to reduce expenditure but to achieve long-term goals for both organization and customers.**

5. Resources

Resources included developers, time, finances and tools. We observed that developers are the resource that brings meaning to other resources. But it was also observed that the productivity of the developers depends on the managers in the team. The way the managers treat the developers has an impact to the product as well. *"The tool is not better than the user of the tool. For example, if the manager doesn't yells, he just gives a task and the developer is a nice guy, he does every good work. A tool might be very good but it might not be used at all so it no use."* - Case E, development engineer.

The observation on Case E above suggests that quality of the product depends on the quality of the people developing it. Therefore a project manager is responsible to know the capabilities of the developers. For example in Case F below we observed that few developers would cause big problems in the software and few good developers would do the best job. Managers should identify the few developers who cause problem and remove them from development work. *"Let's say 20 percent of software developers cause 80 percent of the issues. Normally it's 20/80. If I get a team of ten developers, normally there are two guys who are not competent enough. It is manager's responsibility to make sure that those two people, the losers, don't code anything."* - Case F, senior consultant.

Thus, based on the observations of the *'resources'* category we formulate our fifth finding: **The managers' choice and decisions on people affect other areas of resources and the quality of the product.**

6. Software Developing Companies

The organizational structure of the *software development companies* varied. There was observed a problem of communication in the "vertical organizational structure" especially when there was a task shared across several departments and managers of the departments do not have collective decisions. *"There are several departments in this organization and in each of those software development is taking place. I don't have full visibility in the whole picture of the company what is happening because the organizational structure is vertical."*- Case K, Testing director.

'Horizontal organizational structure' seemed to favor communication, transparency among the teams and smooth running of activities. *"We have a really 'flat organization' and that is a big help. We have two levels of organizations, maybe three if you count project managers. So, I would say that in our organization structure. People trust each other's work, it is very transparent."* - Case C, Project manager.

Mode of operation and organizational structure of some companies caused communication problems among the teams and resulted difficulties in performance. *"We are rather separate organizations and we don't have a good co-operation. Communication goes through some channels, which are not quite free".* - Case I, consultant. Thus, based on the observations of the *'software developing companies'* category we formulate our sixth finding: **Organizational structures and channels of communications within the organization, have influence on the cooperation among the teams, and have impact on the quality of the products.**

5 Discussion and Conclusions

The results of this qualitative empirical study consist of six findings that describe the influence of management on the quality of software products in the studied software developing companies. We state in our study that managers play the role of championship in quality construction. Technical skills, experience and knowledge of the managers in software and domain influence the developers' productivity and hence influence the ability to deliver quality products. Our finding is in line with Münch et al. [5] study that reveals that despite of advancement of technology, methods, processes and high skilled developers, still there are unsolved problems in the management that affect the software quality.

The managers play an intermediary role between customers and the company. In pursuit of this role, managers make decisions and use of available resources to meet the expectations of the customers and the company goals at the same time [3]. We observed that the efficiency of communication between managers and customers and realistic estimation of resources sustains good customer relationship and have positive effect to the products. This finding is similar to Colomo-Palacios et al. study [7]. Furthermore, we observed that the involvement of customers and developers differed between organizations. There was a communication problem on requirements prioritization that led us to conclude that top-down decisions deprive transparency and affect the efficiency of requirements prioritization. This problem emanated from the organizational structures and communication channels, which also led us to conclude that the organizational structures and channels of communications within the organization influence the co-operation among the teams and have impact on the quality of the products. This finding is in line with Siaka and Georgiadou's finding [13]. Furthermore, the decisions made by the managers on resources determine the efficiency and output of such resources. It was observed that the managers' choice and decisions on people to undertake particular tasks affect other areas of resources and the quality of the products. Cockburn and Highsmith [9] present similar results, which suggest that the quality product is the result of selecting right people. Cockburn and Highsmith [9] further argue that if the people in a software development project are good enough, they can use almost any process to successfully accomplish their assignments. If they are not good enough, no process or tool will compensate fully for their inadequacy.

In the role of managing resources, the ultimate goal of the managers is not to reduce expenditures but to use the money efficiently to achieve long-term goals. We observed that the managers recommended expensive training for developers which later paid-off in terms of the improvement of the products. This observation led us to a conclusion that managers' decisions and choices of training, resources and process improvement influence both organization and customer goals. A similar result is discussed in [10, 12].

In spite of these findings, however, there are several threats to the validity of this study [23]. The Grounded Theory approach [16] allows a researcher to build a theory grounding on the data collected from the field. However, more data and deeper insight into the object may reveal more findings that influence the initial theory of the same object. With this respect, the theories are dynamic and not static [16]. Klein and Myers [24] discuss treats to the validity in the principle of interaction between the researchers and the subjects. Our study involved a team of researchers who prepared the interview questions and collected the data in the natural environment at the studied companies. Interviewees were allowed to express themselves without limitation so that they could reveal as much information as possible regarding the interview themes. Interviews were tape-recorded for transcription and data analysis. We believe the threats of biases were addressed and minimized. However, there could be some expressions or language limitations that were not captured in the interviews or transcriptions. This study concludes that the managers in the project level influence the quality of the products. However, the managers' efficiency is also influenced by organizational structure, technical skills in software, domain knowledge and the ability to communicate. The future study may include investigation of challenges in software quality construction emanating from organizational structures and business models.

References

1. Edison, H., bin Ali, N., Torkara, R.: Towards innovation measurement in the software industry. Journal of Systems and Software 86(5), 1390–1407 (2013)
2. Balla, K., Bemelmans, T., Kusters, R., Trienekens, J.: Quality through Managed Improvement and Measurement (QMIM): Towards a Phased Development and Implementation of a Quality Management System for a Software Company. Software Quality Journal 9(3), 177–193 (2001)
3. Boundless, https://www.boundless.com/management/organizational-structure-2/defining-organization/management-role-in-organization/ (accessed on February 10, 2014)
4. Suominen, M., Mäkinen, T.: On the Applicability of Capability Models for Small Software Organizations: Does the Use of Standard Processes lead to a Better Achievement of Business Goals? Software Quality Journal (2013), doi: 10.1007/s11219-013-9201-7
5. Münch, J., Armbrust, O., Kowalczyk, M., Soto, M.: Software Process Definition and Management. The Fraunhofer IESE Series on Software and Systems Engineering. Springer, Heidelberg (2012)

6. Boehm, B.W., Ross, R.: Theory-W software project management principles and examples. IEEE Transactions on Software Engineering 15(7), 902–916 (1989)
7. Colomo-Palacios, R., Casado-Lumbreras, C., Soto-Acosta, P., José, F., Peñalvo, G., Tovar, E.: Project managers in global software development teams: a study of the effects on productivity and performance. Software Quality Journal (2013), doi: 10.1007/s11219-012-9191-x
8. Elbaum, S., Rothermel, G., Kanduri, S., Malishevsky, A.G.: Selecting a Cost-Effective Test Case Prioritization Technique. Software Quality Journal 12(3) (2004)
9. Cockburn, A., Highsmith, J.: Agile software development: The people factor. Computer 34(11), 131–133 (2001)
10. Bakır, A., Turhan, B., Bener, A.B.: A new perspective on data homogeneity in software cost estimation: a study in the embedded systems domain. Software Quality Journal 18(1), 57–80 (2010)
11. Ahmed, F., Capretz, L.F.: An organizational maturity model of software product line engineering. Software Quality Journal 18(2), 195–225 (2010)
12. Subramanian, G.H., Jiang, J.J., Klein, G.: Software quality and IS project performance improvements from software development process maturity and IS implementation strategies. Journal of Systems and Software 80(4), 616–627 (2007)
13. Siaka, K.V., Georgiadou, E.: Empirical Measurement of the Effects of Cultural Diversity on Software Quality Management. Software Quality Journal 10(2), 169–180 (2002)
14. Fujimura, A., Moore, F.: Quality on Time. Software Quality Journal 7(2) (1997)
15. Park, C., Pattipati, K.R., An, W., Kleinman, D.L.: Quantifying the Impact of Information and Organizational Structures via Distributed Auction Algorithm: Point-to-Point Communication Structure. IEEE Transactions on Systems, Man and Cybernetics, Part A: Systems and Humans 42(1), 68–86 (2012)
16. Strauss, A.L., Corbin, J.: Basics of Qualitative Research: Grounded Theory Procedures and Applications. Sage Publication, Newbury Park (1990)
17. Seaman, C.B.: Qualitative Methods in Empirical Studies of Software Engineering. IEEE Transactions on Software Engineering 25, 557–572 (1999)
18. Pare, G., Elam, J.J.: Using Case Study Research to Build Theories of IT Implementation. In: Proceedings of The IFIP TC8 WG 8.2 Conference on Information Systems and Qualitative Research, Philadelphia, Pennsylvania, pp. 542–569 (1997)
19. Eisenhardt, K.M.: Building Theories from Case Study Research. Academy of Management Review 14, 532–550 (1989)
20. ATLAS.ti.: The knowledge workbench. Scientific Software Development (2005)
21. ISO/IEC-25010: Software Engineering – Software Product Requirements and Evaluation, (SQuaRE)-Measurement reference model and guide (2007)
22. Lagrosen, S.: Customer involvement in new product development. A relationship marketing perspective. European Journal of Innovation Management 8(4) (2005)
23. Onwuegbuzie, A.J., Leech, N.L.: Validity and qualitative research: An oxymoron? Quality and Quantity 41(2), 233–249 (2007)
24. Klein, H.K., Myers, M.D.: A set of principles for conducting and evaluating interpretive field studies in information systems. MIS Quarterly 23(1), 67–94 (1999)

Software Development Methods and Quality Assurance: Special Focus on South Korea

Jesse Yli-Huumo, Ossi Taipale, and Kari Smolander

Lappeenranta University of Technology, Finland
{jesse.yli-huumo,ossi.taipale,kari.smolander}@lut.fi

Abstract. South Korea is well-known for big global hardware companies and now software companies are ready to follow. The purpose of this study was to explore software development methods and quality assurance practices used by South Korean software industry. Empirical data was collected by conducting a survey that focused on three main parts: software life cycle models and methods, software quality assurance including quality standards, the strengths and weaknesses of South Korean software industry. The results of the completed survey showed that the use of agile methods is slightly surpassing the use of traditional software development methods. Also the use of so called hybrid methods that include aspects from both development methods is popular. The survey also revealed an interesting result that almost half of the South Korean companies do not use any software quality assurance plan in their projects. For the state of South Korean software industry large number of the respondents thought that despite of the weakness, the status of software development in South Korea will improve in the future.

Keywords: software development methods, software testing, quality assurance, agile methods, South Korean software industry.

1 Introduction

"All software should be produced using some kind of methodology"; when large and small pieces of software are developed with methodology in mind, it can improve development [1]. Software quality is the result of project management and software engineering. With the use of quality assurance it is possible to make the infrastructure to support software engineering methods, project management, and quality control actions [2].

The wired and wireless telecommunication is the most important sector of industry in today's knowledge based society of South Korea. About 30 to 40% of South Korea's total gross domestic product (GDP) growth is contributed by the ICT industry. The market focus has started to move from hardware to services and solutions and the share of the IT market for software is expected to rise to 39% by 2015 [3]. This makes software the fastest-growing sector of the IT market in South Korea [3]. South Korea is also putting a lot of effort to the future of software industry with the IT Future Vision 2020 plan. According to eGov Innovation [4] "South Korea's Ministry of Strategy and Finance said the government is expanding financial assistance for new growth engines from 3.4 trillion won in 2011 to 3.9 trillion won in 2012, focusing primarily on strengthening of the software industry".

The objective of this study is to understand software life cycle models and methods and quality assurance in South Korea. We explore which software life cycle models and methods are being used in South Korea and especially how the use of agile methods affects software projects. In software quality assurance the focus is on quality standards and software testing. The rest of the study describes South Korean software industry, focusing on its current state and future and also its strengths and weaknesses.

This study was conducted in South Korea and all the empirical data is gathered from companies located in South Korea. People who took part in this study worked in software development units in South Korea. The study included an online survey, which was sent out to the companies. The survey is available at: http://www2.it.lut.fi/project/STX/Material/Public/SouthKoreanSoftwareIndustrySurvey.pdf. The sample of the study consists of 34 South Korean software companies. The research questions of the survey include:

- What software development methods and quality assurance plans are South Korean companies using during the software development life cycle?
- How does the use of agile methods affect the development software life cycle?
- What are the strengths and weaknesses of South Korean software industry?

The paper is structured as follows. First, we introduce related research about the topic. Secondly the research methodology and data collection method are described at in Section 3. Then the survey results are presented in Section 4. Finally, discussion and conclusion are given in Section 5.

2 Related Research

Agile software development methods are gaining popularity among software developers. Schindler [5] interviewed a total of 61 Austrian developers and found out that agile methods were adopted by 44.3% of the participants. Rodriguez et al. [6] collected a total of 408 responses from 200 software intensive organizations. The results revealed that 58% of the respondents' organizational units are using agile and/or lean methods. Garousi & Zhi [7] interviewed a total of 246 practitioners from Canada. Out of 246 practitioners 44.7% selected option "agile" whereas only 22% referred themselves using traditional methods. The rest of the respondents did not distinguish their methodology as any explicit type.

When the use of agile software development methods is getting more popular, it is important to study what is their influence. Shine Technologies [8] conducted a global survey with a total of 131 answers. The results showed that an overwhelming number of the respondents thought that productivity, quality and customer satisfaction were better after the use of agile software development methods. Laanti et al. [9] gathered over 1000 respondents from seven different countries located in Europe, North America and Asia. The results revealed that most of the respondents agree on the benefits of agile software development methods that include higher satisfaction and quality. Other similar studies have been conducted by French Scrum User Group [10] and

Garousi & Zhi [7] which also both indicate that use of agile software development methods have a positive impact on the software development life cycle.

The software development life cycle also includes quality assurance that can be performed with different quality standards available. Awad [11] surveyed the use of quality assurance standards (ISO/IEC, CMMI, and SPICE). The results revealed that a large proportion of the respondents apply some quality assurance standard.

3 Research Process

This chapter presents the research process of this study. The selected research method for this study was the quantitative survey method. According to Rajasekar et al. [12] research is a logical and systematic search for new and useful information on a particular topic. It is an investigation of finding solutions to scientific and social problems through objective and systematic analysis [12]. The basic and applied studies can be quantitative, qualitative or even both [12]. Sellers [13] describes the qualitative method as an in-depth exploration of what makes people tick on a particular subject: their feelings, perceptions, decision-making processes, etc. and the quantitative method as one that employs a larger sample which is representative of the entire population being studied.

3.1 The Sample and Interviews

The sample of the study consists of 34 South Korean companies that develop software. The selection criterion for companies was probabilistic sampling [14]. The interviewees were asked the number of employees in their company and the results were divided into four different categories. The sizes of companies in the study were following: The largest segment consists of companies between 10 and 50 people (53%). The second largest segment represents companies between 50 and 500 people (27%). The last categories consist of organizations under 10 people with 13% and organizations over 500 people with 7%. The median number of employees is 25. Therefore the companies that took part in this study are mostly small and medium sized companies (SME's) [15].

3.2 Data Collection

The used data collection method was an online survey. Other possibilities included telephone or in-person interviews. Telephone interviews were not used because of the language barrier between the interviewer and potential interviewees. The Korean language skill of the interviewer was not on a high level enough for interviewing and some of the interviewees' English language level was not high enough to understand the questions correctly. Therefore, the questions in the online survey were available both in English and in Korean, which helped respondents to understand the questions more specifically.

The collection of potential and suitable respondents started by using Google as the search engine for the websites of South Korean companies. The candidates of the sample were selected based on the knowledge gained from their web pages. The websites of the companies were mainly in Korean language, which caused some problems in the beginning. Approximately 300 randomly selected emails were sent to South Korean companies, which resulted only to 8 answers (2.6% answer rate). After the disappointment of sending the survey by email, the study continued by using telephone calling. A hired person with Korean and English language proficiency called South Korean companies and acquired personal email addresses of employees related to software development division. Therefore, the selection of respondents' specific roles was random. Then, approximately 200 phone calls were made, which resulted to extra 26 answers (13% answer rate). The answer rate is really low compared to our experiences in Finland, where companies are more eager to answer to survey inquiries.

4 Results

The data collection was conducted between April and June 2013 that included both online survey and telephone calling. The persons that took part in this study worked in software development units in South Korea. From the respondents 48% were software developers, 28% project managers and 24% executive-level employees.

The empirical data analysis has been divided into three major parts, which are further divided into smaller segments. The first part includes software development life cycles and used development methods in South Korean companies. The second part discusses software quality assurance (SQA) and used standards. The last part of the data analysis examines the current and future state of the South Korean software industry.

4.1 General Information of the Industry Sector

Table 1 shows the industry sectors of the companies that responded to the survey. The majority of the companies (80%) represent the IT industry. The other industries include manufacturing (7%), communication (7%), bioinformatics (3%) and civil engineering (3%). Table 1 also shows the IT industry further divided into more accurate segments. The largest segment inside IT included companies of software development (50%), mobile games (14%), machine vision (7%), information security (3%), system integration (SI) (3%) and internet service (3%).

Table 1. Industry sectors of the companies

Industry sector	%
IT	80%
(Software development)	(50%)
(Mobile Games)	(14%)
(Machine Vision)	(7%)
(Information Security)	(3%)
(SI)	(3%)
Internet Service)	(3%)
Manufacturing	7%
Communication	7%
Bioinformatics	3%
Civil Engineering	3%

4.2 Software Life Cycle Models and Methods

The respondents were asked about the software life cycle methods they are using in projects. This revealed that the use of traditional and agile methods is almost equal. Agile methods gathered 46% and traditional methods 42% of respondents' answers. The minority applied homemade methods (12%) that were neither recognized as traditional nor agile.

Table 2 shows most popular models and methods that the interviewees were able to name. The most popular software life cycle model is waterfall (31%) and the two agile methods Scrum (17%) and Extreme Programming (14%) are the most popular methods. Other used methods and models were Feature-Driven Development (FDD) (12%), homemade methods (12%), Spiral model (6%), Rational Unified Process (RUP) (6%) and Lean software development (LSD) (2%)

Traditional methods are known for being used in bigger companies and projects with more employees, while agile methods favor in smaller work groups and projects [16]. A hybrid model is a combination of two or more methods. It can be possible, for example, to use waterfall and involve iterative aspect of Scrum in it and make it more suitable for the project at hand. Table 3 shows what kind of methods companies are using versus their company size. Companies were divided into three different categories, small companies under 50 employees, mid-size companies from 50 to 100 employees, and big company over 100 employees. The results show that in small companies the use of software development methods varies a little, 42% are using hybrid, 32% are using only traditional methods, and 26% are using only agile methods. In medium sized companies traditional methods are used by 71% of the respondents, hybrids by 29% of the respondents, while the use of agile methods is 0%. In large companies 50% are using hybrids and 50% are using agile methods.

Table 2. Popular life cycle models and software development methods

Life cycle model/Software development method	%
Traditional methods	**42%**
Waterfall	31%
RUP	6%
Spiral model	6%
Agile methods	**46%**
Scrum	17%
Extreme programming	14%
LSD	2%
FDD	12%
Homemade methods	**16%**

Table 3. Used software life cycle method according to the company size

	Traditional methods	Agile methods	Hybrid
Small company	32%	26%	42%
Midsize company	71%	0%	29%
Big company	0%	50%	50%

4.2.1 Effects of Agile Methods

Out of 34 respondents 16 stated that they use agile methods. The results about the respondents' experience with agile methods scattered almost equally. The number of respondents that have more than 2 years of experience with agile methods was 38%. The rest have an experience from 6 months to 2 years (37%) and the respondents who have experience less than 6 months (25%). Respondents were also asked about their knowledge of agile. Respondents estimated that their knowledge is average (47%) and 23% described it as low. Rest of the answers were high (18%) and very high (12%). Nobody described their knowledge as very low.

Questions also focused on how the use of agile methods affected the software life cycle. The focus was on four aspects in the software life cycle: productivity, quality, costs and customer satisfaction.

62% of respondents answered that productivity was better than before the use of agile methods, 19% thought that productivity was unchanged, 13% estimated that productivity was much better and 6% that productivity had went down a little.

The majority (81%) of the respondents thought that quality was better and 13% that quality was much better than before, 6% estimated that quality did not change.

50% of the respondents thought that costs were unchanged, 29% that costs were a little lower, 14% that costs were a little higher and 7% that costs were a lot lower.

The majority (75%) of the respondents thought that customer satisfaction was better, 13% estimated that satisfaction was much better and 12% that satisfaction has not changed.

An interesting fact is that all companies that were using agile methods are planning to use them in the future projects.

4.3 Software Quality Assurance

Respondents were asked if their software department has any quality assurance plan. The results revealed that 55% of the respondents are using some quality assurance plan during their software development. The rest of the respondents (45%) do not use any specific quality assurance plan.

Table 4 shows which software quality assurance standards the respondents are using during their software development life cycle. Most respondents used homemade standards (47%) and 32% did not use any standards. The known quality assurance standards like the ISO and the IEEE series were not popular among responding companies.

4.4 Current and Future State of South Korean Software Industry

The respondents were asked their opinion about the current and future state of the South Korean software industry. Over 80% of the respondents think that the South Korean software industry is not in a good shape. The analysis of the answers revealed three major points that the respondents are most worried about. The three main points include labor force, support of government and problems with start-up companies.

Most of the respondents thought that the biggest problem in the current South Korean software industry is the treatment of the employees. Salaries are not high enough and they are lower than in other occupations, which hinders the interest in the software engineering sector. Work hours are too long and in some cases workers are not paid for extra hours. These kinds of problems are the reason why many students are not willing to take IT courses in the university and select the software industry. Employees with a long experience may also leave the industry sector.

Table 4. Quality assurance standards

Quality assurance standard	%
ISO 9126	14%
ISO 14598	0%
ISO 25000	0%
IEEE	0%
Homemade	47%
We don't use	32%
Other	7%

This leads to the situation where the labor force must come from other countries, while the skills of South Korean software industry workers are not developing.

The second major problem in South Korean software industry is the support of government. Most of the respondents felt that South Korean government is not giving enough financing and support at the moment, because people are underestimating the importance of the software industry. A lack of support and awareness will lead to lower competition and will start to show up in the quality of the software products.

The third major problem that the respondents mentioned was with the start-up companies. South Korean software industry relies more on big companies of system integration business than on small companies with innovative solutions. Respondents felt that starting a new company is hard due to policies and restrictions of the government. Other problems that were also mentioned included the infrastructure of South Korean software industry and difficulties with the distribution of solutions. Also one of the respondents mentioned that the use of software life cycle methods is not on a good level.

Although the majority of the respondents think that the current state of South Korean software industry is on a weak level, many of the respondents are still thinking that the future of the South Korean software industry is looking good. Many respondents think that the current government is making good changes and decisions regarding policies in software industry, which will help South Korean software industry to grow and get in a better shape in the future. A mutual vision among the respondents was that if the South Korean government starts to support the software industry it will start to grow and produce better results.

4.5 Strengths and Weaknesses of South Korean Software Industry

Table 5 shows what the respondents considered as the biggest strengths of the South Korean software industry. Almost half of the respondents (45%) think that South Korean employees are the biggest strength in the industry. Many of the respondents say that South Korean workers are diligent, fast workers that have a passion for learning software development. The second major strength is the infrastructure of the South Korean software industry (26%) that is well organized and has good networking capabilities. Three smaller strengths mentioned include rapid development (8%), culture for technology in South Korea (7%), and interest in new development methods (7%). The category others (7%) included, for example, growing awareness of software and support for education.

When asking about the weaknesses of South Korean software industry (Table 5), respondents mentioned two major weaknesses. The first major weakness is the treatment of employees that was also mentioned as the reason for the current negative state of the South Korean software industry. The second major weakness included organizational problems such as old organizational cultures, bad systems and lack of long term company plans. The rest of the weaknesses included lack of cooperation between

Table 5. The biggest strengths and weaknesses of South Korean software industry

Strengths of South Korean software industry	%
Manpower	45%
Infrastructure	26%
Rapid development	8%
Culture for technology	7%
Interest on new development methods	7%
Others	7%
Weaknesses of South Korean software industry	**%**
Treatment of employees	29%
Organizational problems	26%
Globalization	9%
Market	9%
Cooperation	9%
Government support	6%
Foundation of SW	6%
Others	6%

companies (9%), small market (9%), globalization (9%), support of government (6%), funding of software in South Korea (6%) and others (6%) such as insufficient education and the immature copyright culture.

5 Discussion and Conclusions

Our first research question asked what kind of software life cycle models and methods the responding companies are using. The results of the completed survey showed that the use of agile methods is slightly surpassing the use of traditional software development methods. Also the use of so-called hybrid methods that include aspects from both development methods is really popular. This shows that South Korean companies are adopting the use of agile software development methods. We were also interested in the use of quality assurance plans and standards. The survey revealed interesting result because almost half of the South Korean companies did not use any specific software quality assurance plan in their projects. Companies were also asked if they use any software quality standards in their plans. Most of the companies are using homemade standards or no standards at all. The use of quality assurance standards such as ISO/IEC and IEEE was low.

As the second research question it was asked how the use of agile methods affects productivity, quality, customer satisfaction and costs of a software project. It was also asked if respondents are going to use agile methods in the future and what are the biggest strengths and weaknesses in using them. The results revealed that with the use of agile methods productivity, quality and customer satisfaction are considered higher than with traditional methods. Some respondents thought that costs were lower, but overall it seems that costs do not have an effect when using agile methods. These are interesting results considering that respondents did not describe their knowledge of agile methods very high. This shows that with average knowledge, agile methods could make a project more efficient. Respondents considered that the biggest strengths in agile methods include the ability to respond to changing requirements and better communication. Weaknesses include that agile methods require people with knowledge of agile methods to work. The results also revealed that every respondent who was currently using agile methods is also going to use them in the future projects.

As the last research question it was asked what the respondents think about the current and future state of the South Korean software industry, and what are the biggest strengths and weaknesses of it. The majority of the respondents thought that the current state of the South Korean software industry is not good. The biggest mentioned reason for this was the treatment of the labor force in the South Korean software industry. The respondents thought that work hours are too long and in some cases workers are not paid for extra hours. They also thought that salaries are not high enough and they are lower than in other occupations, which hinders the interest in the software engineering sector, resulting to a lack of talented people in the software industry. Another mentioned big reason for the state of the industry was the lack of government support and difficulties in starting new companies because of unsupporting policies. Although respondents think that the current state is insufficient, many feel that the future is looking brighter. South Korean software industry has a good labor force that is talented and diligent and the infrastructure has also good qualities. Also the South Korean government is starting to make changes on the support of the software industry, which will hopefully benefit the sector.

The overall conclusion is that the South Korean software industry has clear strengths and weaknesses that will affect the current and future state. The major strengths include labor force, infrastructure and diversity in software life cycle models and methods. Companies are willing to try different styles of development to find the best one for their projects. Weaknesses include the treatment of employees, lacking government support and the lack of software quality assurance planning. The South Korean government started an IT future visions 2020 plan with the purpose of strengthen the current software industry in the future. European Union has launched Horizon 2020 program to solve same kind of problems [17]. It is interesting to see what kind of effect this plan has on the South Korean software industry.

Acknowledgement. This study was supported by the STX-project (www2.it.lut.fi/projects/STX) and funded by SFS (Finnish Standard Association) and N4S project.

References

1. Munassar, N., Govardhan, A.: Comparison between Traditional Approach and Object-Oriented Approach in Software Engineering Development. International Journal of Advanced Computer Science and Applications 2(6), 70–76 (2011)
2. Pressman, R.S.: Software Engineering: A Practitioner's Approach, 6th edn. McGraw-Hill (2005)
3. OSEC: South Korea Information and Communication Industry. Swiss Business Hub Korea Seoul (August 2011), http://www.osec.ch/sites/default/files/BB_1108_E_Branchenbericht-S%C3%BCdkoreaICT.pdf (cited March 15, 2013)
4. eGov Innovation (2012), http://enterpriseinnovation.net/article/south-korea-strengthen-software-industry-launch-it-future-vision-2020-plan (cited March 15, 2013)
5. Schindler, C.: Agile Software Development Methods and Practices in Austrian IT-Industry: Results of an Empirical Study. Technology, 321–326 (2008)
6. Rodríguez, P., Markkula, J., Oivo, M., Turula, K.: Survey on agile and lean us-age in Finnish software industry. In: Proceedings of the ACM-IEEE International Symposium on Empirical Software Engineering and Measurement (ESEM 2012), pp. 139–148. ACM, New York (2011)
7. Garousi, V., Zhi, J.: A survey of software testing practices in Canada. The Journal of Systems and Software 86, 1354–1376 (2013)
8. Shine Technologies: Agile Methodologies Survey Results (2007), http://www.shinetech.com/download/attachments/98/ShineTechAgileSurvey2003-01-17.pdf (cited January 12, 2014)
9. Laanti, M., Salo, O., Abrahamsson, P.: Agile methods rapidly replacing traditional methods at Nokia: A survey of opinions on agile transformation. Information and Software Technology 53, 276–290 (2010, 2011)
10. French Scrum User Group: A National Survey on Agile Methods in France, French Scrum User Group (June 2009), http://www.frenchsug.org (cited)

11. Awad, M.: A comparison between agile and traditional software development methodologies (2005), http://pds10.egloos.com/pds/200808/13/85/A_comparision_between_Agile_and_Traditional_SW_development_methodologies.pdf (cited October 4, 2013)
12. Rajasekar, S., Philominathan, P., Chinnathambi, V.: Research methodology (2006), http://arxiv.org/pdf/physics/0601009.pdf (cited: August 5, 2013)
13. Sellers, R.: Qualitative versus quantitative research - choosing the right approach. Originally published in The NonProfit Times (March 15, 1998)
14. Pfleeger, S.L., Kitchenham, B.: Principles of Survey Research (parts 4, 5). Software Engineering Notes 27(5) (2002)
15. European Commission: The new SME definition. User guide and model declaration (2005), http://ec.europa.eu/enterprise/policies/sme/files/sme_definition/sme_user_guide_en.pdf (cited August 11, 2013)
16. Boehm, B., Turner, R.: Using Risk to Balance Agile and Plan-Driven Methods. IEEE Computer 36(6) (2003)
17. European Commission: Horizon 2020 – The EU Framework Programme for Research and Innovation (2014), http://ec.europa.eu/programmes/horizon2020/h2020-sections (cited February 26, 2014)

A Proposal for the Improvement of Project's Cost Predictability Using Earned Value Management and Quality Data – An Empirical Study

Adler Diniz de Souza, Ana Regina Cavalcanti Rocha,
Djenane Cristina, and Bruno Augusto Constantino

COPPE/UFRJ - Universidade Federal do Rio de Janeiro
Programa de Engenharia de Sistemas e Computação
Av. Horácio Macedo, 2030, Prédio do Centro de Tec., Bloco H, Sala 319,
Caixa Postal 68511 – CEP 21941-914 – Rio de Janeiro, RJ
{adlerunifei,djenanecris,bconst123}@gmail.com,
darocha@centroin.com.br

Abstract. The present study proposes an extension of the Earned Value Management (EVM) technique, through the integration of the quality historic data as a mean of improving the technique's cost predictability. The proposed technique was evaluated and compared to the traditional technique in different hypothesis tests utilizing real data of 20 projects. The proposed technique was more accurate than the traditional technique for the Cost Performance Index (CPI) and the Estimate At Completion (EAC).

Keywords: Earned Value Management, Cost Performance Index (CPI), Project Management, Measurement and Analysis.

1 Introduction

To assess whether or not a project will reach its goals of time and cost, several measures are collected during its execution, and various performance indicators are produced and periodically analyzed. When the deviations are larger than the tolerance in some performance indicators, corrective actions are undertaken in order to improve them. Among the main available techniques for the analysis of cost and time, EVM is considered the most reliable [8].

EVM is a technique that integrates scope, time and data cost to measure project performance and predict its cost and deadline. It is based on the current performance of the team. However, it does not integrate data quality project in order to predict the cost and time.

The technique earned great importance in 1967, when the United States Department of Defense (DoD) starts requiring its use as tactics to control the costs of contracted projects [14].

Particularly in Software Engineering, some models reference like CMMI-Dev [10] and ISO/IEC 12207 [5] require to gather measures and develop indicators of the most important processes responsible for achieving the business goals of the organization.

This paper proposes an improvement in the EVM, integrating quantitative information of the processes related with quality, which are more relevant for business goals, related to cost. The main objective is to use the proposed technique like a performance model to predict the final cost of software projects.

2 Earned Value Management

The EVM is based on three basic measures, which are derived to generate other measures and performance indexes. These basic measures are: i) Planned Value (PV_{Acum}) that represents the Planned Costs accumulated up to a certain date, ii) Earned Value (EV_{Acum}) that represents the Budgeted Cost of Work Performed in certain date, and iii) Actual Cost (AC_{Acum}) representing the Actual Cost of the Work Performed in certain date [1], [7].

The CPI is a measure of work performed comparing to the actual cost or progress achieved in the project. [8]. It shows how efficiently the project team is using their resources [7], and it can be calculated by the equation bellow:

$$CPI_{Acum} = \frac{EV Acum}{AC Acum} \qquad (1)$$

The CPI_{Acum} is considered the most critical EVM index because it measures the cost efficiency of the work performed, and it can be used to provide a cost projection.

As the project progresses, the project team can forecast the Estimate At Completion (EAC), which may be different from the Budget At Completion (BAC), based on project performance [8]. EAC provides the final cost estimation and it is given by the following equation (if the cost performance remains the same):

$$EAC = \frac{BAC}{CPIAcum} \qquad (2)$$

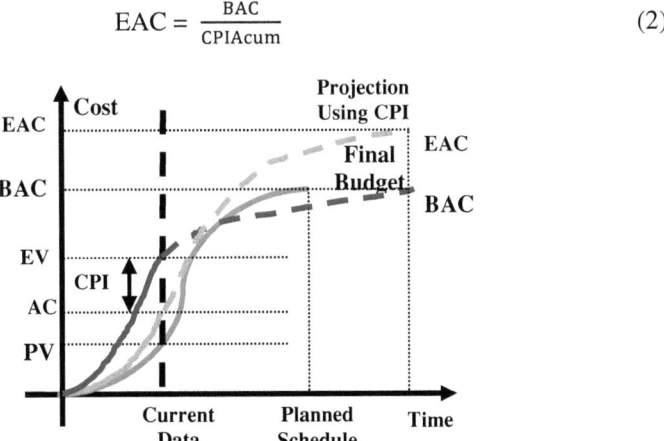

Fig. 1. EVM Performance Measures and Indicators

The fig. 1 illustrates the measures and indicators discussed, and it illustrates as well the projections that can be made from the indicators presented.

3 Problem Description

The major focus of the discussion about EVM is the CPI_{Acum} stability. According to [3], stability can be defined as a state of statistical control that provides, in a high degree of confidence, the performance prediction of some variable in an immediate future.

A study reported by [2] evaluated the CPI_{Acum} stability of several Department of Defense (DoD) projects. As result, the index was stable after 20% of project execution. This study generalized the result, concluding that any project could use the technique reliably after 20% of project execution. This information was used as a criterion in the U.S. government project. Every project with CPI_{Acum} below 0.9 after 20% of project execution was retained or cancelled, because according to the study, the index stability evidenced that a project with poor CPI was unrecoverable.

However, several other studies have questioned the generalization of these results in different contexts (projects developed outside the scope of DoD), and showed different results, i.e., they showed instability in cost performance indexes for most of the projects [4], [6] and [14].

Claiming that the CPI_{Acum} is unstable and varies widely during the execution of a project avoids making accurate projections of cost estimate at the end of the project (EAC), unless one knows or has any expectation that this variation is due to factors already known.

The proposed evolution of the earned value management technique that will be presented in the next section, suggests that the lack of quality data in the traditional earned value management technique may be one of the causes for the wide variation in the CPI and the significant drop in performance near the end of the project execution observed by [2], [4], [6].

Therefore, one of the justifications for the CPI_{Acum} instability is the occurrence of defects that have not been fixed and consequently were not considered in the calculation of performance indicators. Thus, considering the CPI_{Acum} for a given project, its deviation from the baseline should not be evaluated in isolation. This indicator should be evaluated together with another quality indicator that shows the impact of identified and expected defects in relation to project cost measures, reflecting the quality cost in the cost indicator.

The basic measurements and indicators proposed for the integration of data quality to the traditional EVM are described in section 4. The empirical-study results are shown in section 5.

4 Proposal of Quality EVM

Quality data of process are information that may impact future performance of cost performance index and are not used to make projections in the EVM. The necessary information to estimate the effort and the cost of rework to correct the defects are: (i) Estimated size of the final product, (ii) The amount of defects identified and (iii) the rework effort to correct/fix defects in some specific process.

The measure size of the estimated final product will be utilized to calculate the measure average effort to correct /fix defects in another organizational activity.

In this way, it is necessary that the company count the real size of each finalized project in a range of time that will be considered to calculate the organizational measures: defects density and the average effort to correct/fix defects.

The projects used in this activity have to use just one estimated size technique, and should have data in the same context (for example the same process version).

After identifying which process techniques will be used, it is necessary to collect the Number of Accumulate Defects Identified (DI_{Acum}) and their effort to correct the defects. Once collected this information the defects density can be calculated.

Putman [9] claim that it is possible to calculate the defect density by the unity of reviewed artifact software, collecting its encountered defects in many reviews realized, of many projects. Thereby it can use its average values to estimate the defect number that will be found in a new review of the same artifact. Thus, it measure should be generated for each process that will be used in the project, and it will be an organizational measure, generated based in historical data of several projects. It can be calculated by the following equation:

$$\textbf{Defects Density of PN} = \frac{Historical\ Defects\ of\ Process\ N}{Historical\ Size\ of\ Projects} \qquad (3)$$

- Both the **Historical Defects of Process N** measure and the **Historical Size of the Projects** measure, should be calculated through the past collected activities.

After calculating the defects density of a process, the Average Effort to Fix Defects of a process can be calculated (AEFD).

The proposal is that this measure gets available for each process context, for example projects that use the same technology and the same version of process, in other words, each process will have a specific AEFD, which can be calculated by:

$$\textbf{AEFD } PN = \frac{Historical\ Effort\ to\ Correct/Fix\ Defects\ in\ the\ N\ Process}{Historical\ Number\ of\ Defects\ in\ the\ Process\ N} \qquad (4)$$

- **Historical Effort to Correct/Fix Defects in the Process N:** represents the total effort to correct the defects related with a process. It has to consider all the projects that utilized this process;
- **Historical Number of Defects in the Process N:** represents the sum of all identified defects (it will be explained in the next session) of a given process. It has to consider all the projects that utilized this process.

This is a measure that states the average effort to correct a single defect of a given process. Thus, to get the effort to correct the identified or expected defects, just multiply them by the estimated average effort to correct the defects of this project.

Having the measures of defects density (3), it can calculate the amount of Total of Expected Defects (TED). The TED represents the expected defects for a given process used in the project. This measure will be generated considering the defects density of the software unity that will be reviewed in a given process.

According to [9] a calculation is proposed for the density average of defects in relation to the size of the software product, dividing the quantity of function points, for example. Therefore, it can be expected that the Total of Expected Defects (TED) vary in function to the size of the project implemented.

So, it can estimate the TED using the following equation:

$$\textbf{TED} = \text{Project Size} * \text{Defects Density of the Project} \qquad (5)$$

- **Project Size:** is the estimated size in the beginning of the project. It can be estimated using the function points technique, use case points or any other measure of software size, since this enterprise ALWAYS utilize historical data that utilized the same technique of the project to be estimated.

The TED represents a proposal for a baseline planning rework caused by defects.

According to [11] the failure to establish a baseline planning to the rework or the failure in accurate measurement needs the rework progress and cause loss of control in many projects.

In some moment of the project execution, the project manager can collect the Accumulated Defects Identified (ID_{Acum}) and the Accumulated Defects Expected (DE_{Acum}) to analyze the current quality performance of the process; however, it is not possible to make future projections of their behavior using these measures in an isolated way. Quality forecast could be obtained by calculating performance indicators using the measures presented.

The Quality Performance Index (QPI) is an indicator that shows how efficient the quality of a particular process is. Given a certain date, the indicator show if the number of defects is higher or lower than expected, allowing to make projections about the future quality performance through Defects Estimate to Complete (DEC), as shown in Fig. 2 – DEC projections using QPI. This index is given by the following equation:

$$\text{QPI} = \frac{ED(d)}{ID(d)} \qquad (6)$$

- ED (d): represents the total defects expected for a given date.
- ID (d) represents the total defects identified for a given date.

Values below 1 for the indicator mean that a higher number of defects than expected are being found. Values above 1 indicate that a lower number of defects than expected are being found. The purpose of the quality performance indicator is to predict the amount of future defects, given the current performance, and assess the impact of quality performance for project costs.

As the project progresses, the project team can develop a New forecast for the Defects Estimate to Complete (DEC), which may be different from Total Expected Defects (TED) based on quality performance. This new estimate should only be calculated if the trend is that the QPI remains the same, i.e., in case the TED is no longer feasible. To evaluate the TED feasibility, project progress and extent of changes that have occurred in relation to quality in a given time interval, it will be used in the

A Proposal for the Improvement of Project's Cost Predictability   175

quality baseline, or the TED measure and its projection called Defects Estimate to Complete (DEC), as illustrated in fig. 2, which can be calculated by the equation below:

$$DEC = \frac{TED}{QPI} \qquad (7)$$

The positive or negative variations in the number of defects can bring impacts on project costs. The effort and cost related to prevent, detect and fix the defects typically belong to their respective baselines, in any project. However, companies rarely consider quality information during the monitoring and controlling of cost and schedule. Thus, when quality produces different results from that expected, traditional cost performance indicator (CPI) may present wrong information. An example of this statement occurs when CPI indicates that the project is within expected budget; however, there are more identified defects than expected for the project.

Therefore, the proposed technique suggests that the DEC should be used to obtain the Defects Variations (DV) on the TED. This measure informs how different the quality is from the expected, as shown in the following equation:

$$DV = TED - DEC \qquad (8)$$

Based on DV, the cost variation should be calculated and incorporated into project Estimated At Completion (EAC). It is done through the addition of the defects cost variation to the traditional EAC. The equation is as follows:

$$EAC_{Qual} = \frac{EAC}{CPIAcum} + ECX\ (\$) \qquad (9)$$

- ECX (\$): Extra Cost Estimate to Complete, corresponds to the cost (positive or negative) of defects variation, and can be calculated by the equation as follows:

$$ECX\ (\$) = TED\ (\$) - DEC\ (\$) \qquad (10)$$

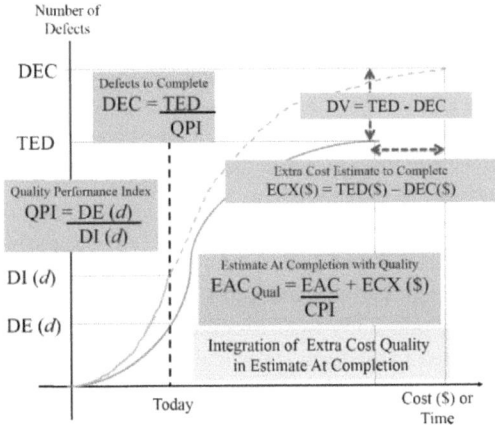

Fig. 2. Measures of Quality EVM

This study is part of a larger study using historical data to improve the predictability of project cost. Similar studies using cost historical data were conducted by the authors of this work and published in [11], [12] and [13].

This technique represents an evolution in relation to a previous technique presented in [13] and validated using simulated data of projects. Now the new version of the technique was evaluated using real data in an empirical study that will be detailed bellow in the next section.

5   Preparation

Measures from 20 software development projects were collected between March of 2009 and January of 2010.

As result, projects that were part of this study had the following characteristics:

- They had times of execution ranging from 15 days to 1 month;
- They used a single version of the above processes with 4 processes, namely: i) the Elaboration of Use Case Tests (UCT), ii) the implementation of functional requirements (IMP), iii) testing of these functional requirements (TES), using test cases produced and iv) correction of reported errors (CO);
- They were developed using the same technology (MS Visual Basic and ASP) and

The data of executed activities were collected daily in all projects considerate in this work. The main data of activities collected were: i) professional responsible to execute it, ii) estimated effort to execute it, iii) estimated cost, iv) real effort to execute it, v) real cost.

The quality-related data were always registered when defects appeared. The registered data were composed by: i) defect name, ii) defect description, iii) employee responsible to fix the defect and iv) requirement generating the defect, (v) total effort to fix the defect.

As the largest cost component in a software project is the hours required for the development of the product, all the basic measures and traditional EVM indexes were calculated based on estimated hours and actual hours, measured after the execution of activities (including activities to fix the defects).

For each activity planned in the projects, planned costs (PV) (through the estimated effort for the activity execution) and actual costs (through real effort calculated after performing the activity) were calculated.

They choose the Test process that would be used by the proposed technique.

To calculate the indicator and make EAC_{Qual} projections presented in the section 4, a database was developed, with the measures shown in Table 1.

Projects included in this study were executed on different dates. Therefore different periods were considered to perform statistical analyses using the proposed technique. During the study, in each specific period it was used the average data of the previously executed projects.

A Proposal for the Improvement of Project's Cost Predictability 177

Table 1. Project Information

Projects	Reported Defects	Estimated Effort to fix	Real Effort to Fix	Project Total Effort	Periods	
P1	11	6.0	17.7	127.3	03/11/09 a 04/01/09	
P2	6	5.1	15.2	182.5	03/16/09 a 06/04/09	
P3	8	8.5	13.0	157.03	03/23/09 a 04/16/09	
P4	1	1.0	7.05	84.45	03/26/09 a 04/17/09	
P5	1	0.4	13.7	174.2	04/20/09 a 05/19/09	P1
P6	8	12.4	22.9	83.7	04/20/09 a 05/19/09	
P7	2	4.4	7.1	98.0	04/20/09 a 06/13/09	
P8	5	5.4	11.7	135.4	04/29/09 a 05/15/09	
P9	2	0.2	9.5	107.4	04/29/09 a 05/20/09	
P10	3	5.0	10.7	121.9	05/21/09 a 06/09/09	P2
P11	2	0.8	8.0	127.2	06/15/09 a 06/30/09	P3
P12	3	2.2	5.5	77.5	06/29/09 a 07/10/09	
P13	0	0.0	4.3	55.3	07/29/09 a 08/10/09	P4
P14	5	2.7	5.0	62.1	08/11/09 a 08/20/09	
P15	2	1.8	6.2	54.1	08/21/09 a 09/04/09	P5
P16	1	3.0	7.7	87.7	09/01/09 a 09/18/09	
P17	0	0.0	6.3	75.7	09/01/09 a 09/18/09	P6
P18	6	8.6	30.7	289.5	01/04/10 a 01/20/10	
P19	0	0.0	1.9	31.2	01/19/10 a 02/03/10	P7
P20	2	1.8	16.1	208.7	01/22/10 a 02/22/10	

6 Technique Validation

The study's objective was to answer the following question: "Is the EVM traditional technique more accurate than the EVM technique with quality?". Answering that, the following hypotheses were set up to evaluate the technique accuracy:

- $H0_{Accuracy}$: the traditional EVM technique is as accurate as the EVM technique with quality.
  - $EAC_{EVM\ Error} - EAC_{Quality\ Error} = 0$
- $H1_{Accuracy}$: the traditional EVM technique is less accurate than the EVM technique with quality.
  - $EAC_{EVM\ Error} - EAC_{Quality\ Error} > 0$

Three more questions and secondary hypothesis, similar to the first one, were defined. But they were intended to answer if the proposed technique is more accurate than the traditional technique before the Test Process (capacity to estimate the cost before the Test Process). The technique was also evaluated during and after the Test Process, (capacity to projection the final cost of the project using the proposed technique indicator, integrated with EVM traditional). Then the third validation considered all project activities (in general).

The techniques presented in section 4 were evaluated through an empirical study, in which the objective was to measure accuracy of both techniques and compare them. In order to measure the technique accuracy, each CPI activity of each technique was compared with the real AC_{Acum}, which was calculated at the end of the "Correction" Process. The accuracy of the proposed technique was calculated by the equation below:

$$EAC_{QualityAccuracy} = |1 - \frac{AC\ Correction\ Process}{EAC\ Quality}| \quad (11)$$

The accuracy of the traditional technique was calculated by the equation below:

$$EAC_{TradicionalAccuracy} = |1 - \frac{AC\ Correction\ Process}{EAC\ Tradicional}| \quad (12)$$

The results of the Eq. 11 and Eq. 12 may be a positive or negative value. When the average is calculated, a positive value may compensate a negative value, and the average accuracy may be masked (i.e. the average of two errors of -20% and +20% is 0%). In this study it is a problem because it does not reflect the real error.

To avoid this problem the EAC Accuracy of the techniques was calculated using the absolute value in both equations (Eq 11 and Eq 12).

Both average of EAC Accuracy was calculated by the equation below:

$$Average\ EAC\ Accuracy = \frac{\sum_1^N EAC\ Accuracy}{N} \quad (13)$$

The project data presented in Table 1 were used to calculate the $CPI_{Quality}$ and consequently the $EAC_{Quality}$, using the equations 3 until 13. The error or accuracy of both techniques is shown in Table 2.

Table 2. Accuracy (Estimate Errors) of EAC_{Qual} and EAC_{Trad} to Correction of Process

Time	Before Test Process		During Test Process		In General		Periods
Projects	EAC_{Qual}	EAC_{Trad}	EAC_{Qual}	EAC_{Trad}	EAC_{Qual}	EAC_{Trad}	
P. 10	10.19	25.40	18.99	10.95	14.41	18.46	P2
P. 11	81.81	76.45	76.69	81.90	80.63	77.59	P3
P. 12	27.56	48.53	45.83	43.02	36.26	45.91	
P. 13	190.00	165.75	95.00	155.3	144.14	160.7	P4
P. 14	26.36	65.20	31.92	149.1	29.14	107.6	
P. 15	5.90	59.60	17.17	27.72	13.41	38.35	P5
P. 16	8.88	79.45	62.01	36.3	34.38	58.74	
P. 17	250.00	470.88	125.0	296.54	189.19	386.07	P6
P. 18	4.79	29.72	41.49	50.53	23.14	40.13	
P. 19	97.34	140.55	51.0	114.83	75.53	128.45	P7
P. 20	72.36	68.58	2.95	3.33	37.65	35.96	

The fig. 3 shows on X axis the 11 evaluated projects, and on Y axis the EAC average errors of both techniques in the "Correction Process", for each project, before the Test Process. In this moment Total Expected Defects (TED ($)) were used as $EAC_{Quality}$ of the proposed technique.

The gain of accuracy using the proposed technique was 220.88% compared to the traditional technique in project 17, and 24.25% lower than the traditional technique in project 13, both shown in fig. 3 and Table 2.

A Proposal for the Improvement of Project's Cost Predictability 179

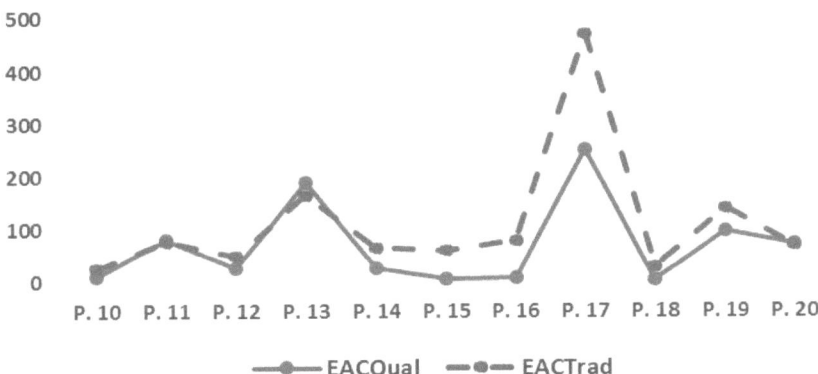

Fig. 3. Accuracy of Techniques before Test Process to Correction of Process

The fig. 4 shows the same information of the fig. 2, however, during the Test process. Now the Quality Performance Index (QPI) was used to make a projection of the Total Expected Defects (TED). The TED was integrated to the traditional EAC using the equations (3 until 13), generating the $EAC_{Quality}$.

The gain of accuracy using the proposed technique was 171.54% compared to the traditional technique in project 19 and 25.71% lower than the traditional technique in project 15 both shown in fig. 4.

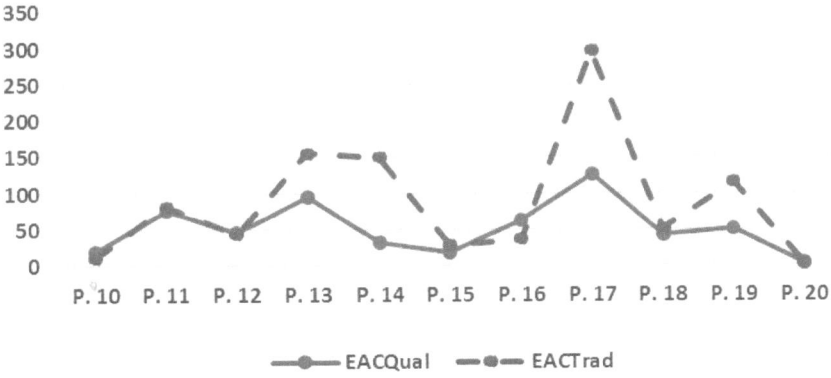

Fig. 4. Accuracy of Techniques during the Test Process

Finally the fig. 5 shows the average error between the techniques considering all project activities. Again the gain of accuracy using the proposed technique was 196.88% compared to the traditional technique in project 19 and 3.04% lower than the traditional technique in project 11 both in the fig. 5.

No errors from the 9 first projects were collected. Whereas they formed the historical data basis to carry out the projections of indexes in the second period projects, by the proposed technique.

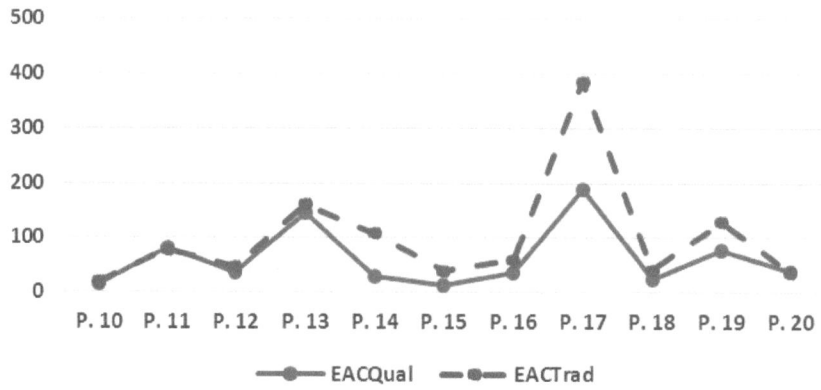

Fig. 5. Accuracy of Techniques General to Correction of Process

The "Correction" process not being executed caused the high accuracy presented in the projects 13, 17 and 19, shown in fig. 5, respectively. The correction process did not have any defects in these projects (see Table 2). Since the processes were not executed, the AC_{Final} of the projects were lower than expected, and consequently the accuracy of both techniques was poor.

The reason for better results using the traditional technique in project 13 was the CPI_{Acum} being very high in all project activities. A high CPI_{Acum} causes a lower EAC, which favors the traditional technique, in the context of this study.

In other hand, better results using the proposed technique in project 17 in the fig. 5, were caused by the TED ($) providing the cost estimate smaller than EAC.

To evaluate the hypotheses previously shown, statistical tests based in the table III (EAC_{Trad} and EAC_{Qual}) were performed to confirm that applying the proposed techniques, the difference in accuracy found, were significant. The Action tool was used to perform the hypotheses tests of T paired samples, with significance level of 90%.

Table 3. Accuracy Hypothesis Test

Hypothesis	Tests	T	P	Conclusion
H0 Accuracy Before Test Process	$Error_{EAC.Trad.} - Error_{EAC.Hist.} = 0$	2,08	0,032	Refute H0
H0 Accuracy During Test Process	$Error_{EAC.Trad.} - Error_{EAC.Hist.} = 0$	1,98	0,037	Refute H0
H0 Accuracy General	$Error_{EAC.Trad.} - Error_{EAC.Hist.} = 0$	2,184	0,026	Refute H0

The analysis of data in Table 3 allows inferring that the proposed technique provides greater accuracy in cost estimations, considering the average error of EAC.

7 Conclusion

This study described the proposal of a technique of Earned Value Management, which integrates quality data as a way to improve the predictability of project costs. The study consisted of an empirical study based on real projects with the purpose of determining whether the technique was more accurate compared to the traditional technique. The technique was also evaluated during and after the Test Process, (capacity to projection the final cost of the project using the proposed technique indicator, integrated with EVM traditional). Then the third validation considered all project activities (in general). In order to evaluate the feasibility of the proposed techniques, several hypothesis tests were performed on different research questions posed during the validation of the technique. All the tests of hypotheses showed that the results were significant at the 90% significance level.

References

1. Anbari, F.T.: Earned Value Project Management Method and Extensions. Project Management Journal 4, 12 (2003)
2. Christensen, D., Heise, S.R.: Cost Performance Index Stability. National Contract Management Journal 25, 7–15 (1993)
3. Florac, W.A., Carleton, A.D.: Measuring the Software Process: Statistical Process Control for Software Process Improvement. Addison-Wesley (1999)
4. Henderson, K., Zwikael, O.: Does Project Performance Stability Exist A Re-examination of CPI and Evaluation of SPI(t) Stability. Cross Talk (2008)
5. ISO/IEC12207, Systems and software Engineering-Software life cycle processes (2008)
6. Lipke, W., Zwikael, O., Henderson, K., Anbari, F.: Prediction of project outcome, the application of statistical methods to Earned Value Management and Earned Schedule performance indexes. International Journal of Project Management (2009)
7. PMI, Practice Standard Earned Value Management Pennsylvania, Project Management Institute (2005)
8. PMI, Project Management Body of Knowledge - PMBOK Newton Square. PMI (2013)
9. Putnam, L.H.: Five Core Metrics: The Intelligence behind Successful Software Management. Dorset House (2003)
10. SEI, S.E.I., CMMI® for Development (CMMI-DEV), V1.2, CMU/SEI-2006-TR-008. SEI (2006)
11. de Souza, A.D., Rocha, A.R.C.: A proposal for the improvement of the technique of Earned Value Management utilizing the history of performance data. In: Proceedings of the Twenty-Fourth International Conference on Software Engineering & Knowledge Engineering - SEKE, pp. 753–759 (2012)
12. de Souza, A.D., Rocha, A.R.C.: A proposal for the improvement the predictability of project cost using EVM and Historical Data of Cost. In: 35th International Conference of Software Engineering-ICSE, ACM SRC, San Francisco (2013)
13. de Souza, A.D., Rocha, A.R.C.: A Proposal for the Improvement Predictability of Cost Using Earned Value Management and Quality Data. In: McCaffery, F., O'Connor, R.V., Messnarz, R. (eds.) EuroSPI 2013. CCIS, vol. 364, pp. 190–201. Springer, Heidelberg (2013)
14. Zwikael, O., et al.: Evaluation of Models for Forecasting the Final Cost of a Project. Project Management Journal 31(1), 53–57 (2000)

Software Development Processes for Games: A Systematic Literature Review

Ann Osborne O'Hagan[1], Gerry Coleman[1], and Rory V. O'Connor[2]

[1] Dundalk Institute of Technology, Ireland
{ann.osborneohagan,Gerry.Coleman}@dkit.ie
[2] Dublin City University, Ireland
roconnor@computing.dcu.ie

Abstract. This paper describes the methodology and results from a Systematic Literature Review (SLR) of the software processes used in game development. A total of 404 papers were analyzed as part of the review and the various process models that are used in industry and academia/research are presented. Software Process Improvement (SPI) initiatives for game development are discussed. The factors that promote or deter the adoption of process models, and implementing SPI in practice are highlighted. Our findings indicate that there is no single model that serves as a best practice process model for game development and it is a matter of deciding which model is best suited for a particular game. Agile models such as Scrum and XP are suited to the knowledge intensive domain of game development where innovation and speed to market are vital. Hybrid approaches such as reuse can also be suitable for game development where the risk of the upfront investment in terms of time and cost is mitigated with a game that has stable requirements and a longer lifespan.

Keywords: Game Development, Software Process, Software Process Improvement (SPI), Software Engineering, Systematic Literature Review (SLR).

1 Introduction

Creating computer games is a complicated task that involves the expertise of many skilled professionals from various disciplines including computer science, art and media design and business. The pressure on game development to get to market as quickly as possible means that there are often schedule over runs with correspondingly poor time estimation. Classic software engineering issues associated with game development can include requirements management, configuration management, and verification and validation; these problems can be magnified by geographically distributed teams [1]. Typically the 5 phases involved in the process of creating a game are: concept; plan; design; develop and test [2]. Although best practices from traditional software development are adopted by game development [3], a fundamental difference is that game software aims to provide an experience rather than say productivity. This can cause a divergence in practices, usability testing is not always suitable for games, as game software often has the objective of providing increasingly difficult tasks that the user has to accomplish so that they feel appropriately challenged and eventually satisfied when they complete the challenge. In game development the emphasis is more on evaluating user experiences and using the feedback to drive design iterations. Callele et al.[4] identify clearly that it is necessary to extend the traditional techniques of requirement engineering to support the creative process of the electronic game development.

Developing software for the games industry is evolving rapidly and becoming ever more complex. A Systematic Literature Review (SLR) by Ampatzoglou and Stamelos [5] to assess the current state of the art on research in games development showed that research activity in game engineering is growing at a higher rate than software engineering. The aim of the present study is to assess and document the state of the art of the software processes used in game development. This could provide a foundation and direction for further research in game development processes. Section 2 outlines the research methodology used in this review. Section 3 provides an analysis of the results. Section 4 presents a conclusion of the review.

2 Research Methodology

The research process used has been taken from the guidelines set out by Kitchenham and Charters [6] for performing SLRs in software engineering, and the researcher (as a single researcher) has undertaken the '*light*' version of the review guidelines. The 3 phases of the review and the steps associated with each phase are shown in figure 1.

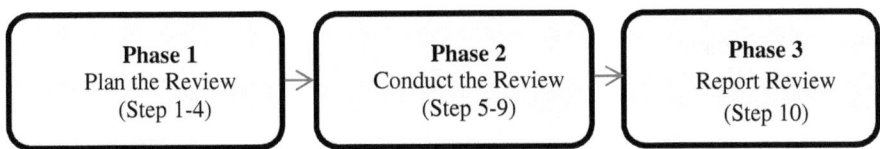

Fig. 1. Phases and Steps of SLR

Phase 1: Plan of the Review. The researcher demonstrated the need for the review (step 1) by searching the Google Scholar digital library and the Evidence Based Software Engineering (EBSE) website [7]. No such research was found by the researcher.

The PICOC (Population, Intervention, Comparison, Outcome and Context) criteria were used to help frame the research questions. Three primary research questions (RQ) were addressed by the review (step 2):

- **RQ1:** What Software Process Models are used in Game Development?
- **RQ2:** What Software Process Improvement (SPI) initiatives are in use in Game Development and to what extent is SPI used in practice?
- **RQ3:** What factors influence the adoption of Software Process Models and SPI in Game Development in practice?

A review protocol (step 3) was developed to reduce researcher bias and to ensure that the review could be replicated. The evaluation of the protocol (step 4) and the subsequent process of implementing the review iteratively improved the design of the review. The final review protocol is described in sections 2.1 to 2.5 (Steps 5-9 incl.).

2.1 Phase 2: Conduct the Review, Search Strategy (Step 5)

Creation of the search protocol consisted of a trial search similar to that performed by Unterkalmsteiner et al. [8]. A search was conducted with the keywords identified in the research questions and was compared against a known primary set of 25 papers requested from an expert in the field of process and process improvement. The keywords were iteratively improved until there was a >= 90% match rate. The terms computer, pc, mobile, software, video, online, console, serious, learning, educational, simulation, entertainment, role-playing, case study, engine, framework and interface were added to the intervention to ensure that the quota of papers were captured. The final search string captured all 25 reference papers.

A search of digital libraries was used to locate peer reviewed journal papers, conference proceedings and published books. The time period covered by the review was 2002 to 2013 (inclusive). The reference lists of primary studies were checked to find other primary studies. The search strategy showing population (P) and intervention (I) for each RQ is outlined in Table 1.

Table 1. Search Strategy

RQ1, RQ2, RQ3 (P)	RQ1 (I)	RQ2 (I)	RQ3 (I)
(game AND (development OR computer OR pc OR mobile OR software OR video* [1] OR online OR console OR serious OR learning OR educational OR simulation OR entertainment OR "role-playing" OR "case study" OR engine OR framework OR interface))	(process OR life-cycle or model OR method* OR requirement OR design OR management OR agile OR Scrum OR test*)	(innovation OR improve* OR SPI OR quality OR initiative OR strategy OR practice OR technique OR tool OR "lessons learned")	(motivation OR benefit OR advantage OR enable OR promote OR success OR barrier OR difficulty OR issue OR problem OR challenge OR disadvantage OR deter OR inhibit OR failure)

The searches revealed more than seven thousand publications and a procedure was put in place to help store, track and reference the studies in an organized and reproducible fashion. The following tools were used by the researcher: Microsoft excel was used to store search results; End note was used as a reference manager; and Atlas TI was used to store full text studies and to help with data extraction and categorization.

---

[1] * denotes a wildcard.

2.2 Primary Study Selection Criteria (Step 6)

A sample of the inclusion and exclusion criteria included peer reviewed journals, conference papers and published books showing qualitative and quantitative research relating to the development process in game development are included. The following studies were excluded: Non English texts; studies relating to Game Based Learning; Artificial Intelligence; networking; graphics algorithms; game theory; affective gaming; computational intelligence; human centered computing (HCI); user interaction; gamification; game based tools, and game based development approaches.

Study Selection Procedure. The researcher conducted a study selection pilot and a data extraction pilot to help with the problem of a single researcher applying inclusion/exclusion criteria and undertaking all the data extraction. This pilot helped ensure that the study selection criteria and the study classification were consistent between the researcher and the supervisor. There was satisfactory agreement, as illustrated by a Cohen Kappa [9] value of 0.63. Cohen's kappa coefficient is a statistical measure of inter-rater agreement for qualitative (categorical) items, and is thought to be more robust than percentage agreement as it takes agreement by chance into account. The equation for the coefficient is:

$$k = \frac{Pr(a) - Pr(e)}{1 - Pr(e)} \qquad (1)$$

The hypothetical probability of chance agreement was $Pr(e) = 0.62$ and the relative observed agreement among the raters was $Pr(a) = 0.86$. Conflicts in the results were resolved with a post mortem and this helped fine-tune the inclusion and exclusion criteria. The selection procedure started at this point. Searching the digital libraries was unlikely to find all relevant papers (see Section 2.5) and more papers were found by following up references in included papers [7], this is referred to as snowballing. A total of 7506 papers were retrieved from the searches. Duplicates and unavailable studies were excluded and each set was reduced to the full text studies of 404 papers, as illustrated in Table 2.

Table 2. Primary study selection

Digital Library	Initial number	Round 1 (Title, Keyword and abstract)	Round 2 (Full text) Duplicate[2] and unavailable removed	Final count
ACM	751	115	72	43
IEEE	2408	419	249	170
Science Direct	2204	111	42	69
Springer Link	1290	192	98	94
Wiley	232	37	17	20
IGI Global	583	30	28	2
Inderscience	38	7	1	6
Total	**7506**	**911**	**507**	**404**

---

[2] Studies that were listed in more than one digital library (duplicate) were resolved by keeping the copy that was most easily accessible to the researcher.

2.3 Study Quality Assessment (Step 7)

Study quality assessment can be used to guide the interpretation of the synthesis findings and determine the strength of the inferences according to [6]. The quality assessment performed in this review reports on reporting rather than study quality, as it is not possible to assess the authors' ability to address threats to validity [8]. Qualitative (Table 3) and quantitative (Table 4) studies had key questions answered during the data extraction.

Table 3. Quality assessment for Qualitative Studies

ID	Qualitative studies (361 Studies)	Yes	Partially	No
QA1	Clear unambiguous findings	165		196
QA2	Referenced Well	218	98	43

Table 4. Quality assessment for Quantitative Studies

ID	Quantitative studies (43 Studies)	Yes	Moderately	No
QA1	Aims clearly stated	42	N/A	1
QA2	Approach clearly explained	39	1	3
QA3	Context of research setting well described	31	10	2
QA4	Threats to validity considered	8	N/A	35

2.4 Data Extraction (Step 8) and Data Synthesis (Step 9)

The primary studies data were collected by means of a data extraction form initially; some of whose properties are shown in Table 5. The properties were extracted and tabulated to answer the research questions. The quantitative and qualitative studies were synthesized separately. The studies were classified according [8] to: Industry that refers to studies in where the research was performed in collaboration with or embedded in industry; or Non-industry that refers to studies performed in an academic setting or where the research environment is not properly described.

Table 5. Extracted Data

Property	RQ's
Identify the Software Process Models used in game development.	RQ1
Identify what SPI initiatives exist in game development.	RQ2
Identify the extent of SPI initiative being practiced in industry.	RQ2
What factors aid/deter the adoption of process models in practice?	RQ3
What factors aid/deter the adoption of SPI initiatives in practice?	RQ3

2.5 Phase 3: Report the Review, Study Report and Validation (Step 10)

The researcher identified 2 primary threats to the validity of the review: Firstly, telemetry, game metrics and data analytics would traditionally have had nothing to do with the game development process but from the research papers identified, the boundary is now shifting and this information is feeding into the development process. Secondly, there is no standard abstracting service, all the digital libraries use different interfaces, and there is a potential inconsistency in the search strategy.

3 Analysis of Results

A total of 404 primary studies were collated and analyzed as part of this review. There was an increase in publications from 2004 onwards with a peak in 2012. A total of 33 genres were recorded with serious games occurring most followed by generic/multi genre. Six types of platforms were recorded, 'mobile' occurring most often followed by the 'online' platform. There were many research methods recorded; case studies being the most frequently used. The majority (73%) of the primary studies were non-industrial (N) the balance (27%) was industrial (I).

3.1 RQ1: What Software Process Models Are Used in Game Development?

A total of 356 software processes were identified and grouped into 23 process models. The models belonged to either an agile (47%) or hybrid (mixture of traditional and agile) (53%) approach to game development. Agile and hybrid approaches differ on the expected amount and role of iteration. Development in the hybrid approach aims for a minimum number of iterations between phases, whereas development in the agile approach expects to return to the design and requirements stage, and there may be much iteration of the design and testing phase [10]. The primary studies were categorized according to quantitative (11%) and qualitative (89%) methods and each were analyzed according to development approach and context, examples are presented.

Analysis of the Quantitative Studies. There were fewer industrial (46.5%) than non-industrial studies (53.5%). In an Industrial context, agile accounted for 9% of the software processes and hybrid for 91%. In a non-industrial context, agile accounted for 41% of the software processes and hybrid for 59%.

Agile development in an Industrial context used Kanban and Scrum methodologies [11] and in a non-industrial context Rapid Application Development (RAD) [12] was used. Hybrid development in Industry used Component Based Development (CBD) [13], Modular Development [14], The Staged Delivery model (incremental) [15], and an empirical model of the game software development processes is proposed [16]. In a non-Industrial context Novak [17] proposes a generic model of the game development process.

The agile approach of XP [11] methodology and the hybrid approach of Reuse were common in both industrial and non-industrial studies. Reuse was the most commonly used software process in game development.

Analysis of Qualitative Studies. There are substantially fewer industrial studies (25%) than the non-industrial studies (75%). In an industrial context 64% of the software processes were agile and 36% were hybrid. In a non-Industrial context 41% of the software processes were agile and 59% were hybrid.

Agile development in an Industrial context used Kanban [18], XP [19], and Ad-hoc development processes [20]. Hybrid development in Industry used IEEE SS&E [1], ETVX model [21], and SDLC [20]. In a non-Industrial context Model Driven Development (MDD) [22] and RUP [23]. Agile approaches which are evident in both contexts include: Evolutionary [24]; Spiral Process [2]; and Scrum [2]. Hybrid approaches evident in both industry and non-industry studies include: Modular [25] ; Reuse [26]; and Incremental model (Waterfall with iterations) [2].

3.2　RQ2: What SPI Initiatives Are Used in Game Development? To What Extent is SPI Used in Game Development in Practice?

A total of 148 SPI initiatives across both quantitative (17%) and qualitative (83%) studies were recorded in both industrial and non-industrial studies. There were no studies reporting the extent of SPI in practice. The SPI initiatives identified were grouped into requirement, design, development, evaluation and deployment. The initiatives were analyzed in terms of context; examples of SPI initiatives are presented.

Analysis of Quantitative Studies. There were fewer Industrial (48%) than Non-Industrial (52%) studies. The industrial studies contained design (67%) and development (33%) initiatives. The non-industrial studies contained design (77%), development (8%) and evaluation (15%) initiatives.

A development approach (I) concluded that Object Oriented development should be used with great care in the development of mobile games, and that structural programming can be a very competitive alternative [13]; An evaluation strategy (I) [27], used the MIPA (Middleware Infrastructure for Predicate detection in Asynchronous) framework to perform efficient evaluations to identify more usability defects.

Analysis of Qualitative Studies. The Industrial studies (36%) are substantially lower than the Non-Industrial (64%) studies uncovered by the research. The industrial studies contained Requirement (4%), Design (33%), Development (56%), Evaluation (5%) and Deployment (2%) initiatives. The non-industrial studies contained Design (62%), Development (23%), Evaluation (14%) and Deployment (1%) initiatives. The following examples of SPI initiatives are all from industrial studies. A requirement approach [28], a design technique called a 'game jam' [29] and a deployment strategy are described [30]. A company transitioned from a "Laissez-faire" waterfall team to a simple and well-tuned Lean/Agile team by introducing agile and Kanban in [18]. Paring CMMI with IEEE CS SS&E standards in [1] is a development framework used by the US Defense Forces known as 'America's Army' gaming. A method for extracting a product line and evolving it, relying on a strategy that uses refactoring expressed in terms of simpler programming laws is described [31].

3.3　RQ3: Adoption Factors of Software Process Models and SPI in Practice

Adoption Factors of Process Models. The factors that aid or deter the adoption of the process models described earlier are taken from the industrial studies and are described according to the approach taken agile or hybrid. The following factors are all from qualitative studies with one exception [11].

Agile Adoption Factors. Functional prototypes are useful for communicating requirements to a development team and the iterative approach is useful where organizations lack knowledge of another's area of expertise [32]. Organizations can play a role by fostering a collaborative spirit and providing the physical tools needed [33]. The XP methodology is by its nature suited to Bottom Up development, where requirements are likely to change and the build is incremental. The spiral process model [24] is suited to large projects: investment in training; having the right mix of people working together such as those with functional and gaming skills; a focus on features; a loose—tight discipline throughout the project; and quality and insurance against feature creep are all important for adoption. Scrum [11] is a suitable model: when requirements are hard to pre-define and are volatile; where product innovation and first-to-market thinking are a priority; and there is a desire to improve the quality and productivity of game development. Scrum in practice can cause problems especially the use of the sprint backlog, Lean principles such as Kanban can alleviate these issues in the production stage. The Scrum project management process requires flexible timetabling between designers and other stakeholders to implement [34]; the manager needs to be ready to move at the same or faster speed as the team to be in the lead [35]; and lessons learned in GameDevCo [36] report that to support their transition efforts to Scrum, the company retained an external consultant to mentor their Scrum masters. It was detrimental to the company that the consultant left before passing on the knowledge, which led to variations in the development process. Lack of training for contract employees and the lack of an effective tool to support the rapid development cycle time has also caused adoption issues of Scrum.

Hybrid Adoption Factors. Reuse processes such as the use of Mobile Games Product Lines can be incremental and may offer moderate costs and risks [31]. On the other side of this argument is that the proactive approach to product lines may be inadequate due to prohibitively high investment and risks. The hierarchical model of software product families is argued to be primarily suitable for large organisations with long-lived products. A considerable maturity with respect to development process and management is required. Systems with relatively stable requirement sets and long lifetimes are substantially more suitable than products whose requirements change frequently and drastically, such as due to new technological possibilities. Fathammer [37] has succeeded in creating a hierarchical software product family model that suits its needs very well. The demand for artistic vision, the need for novelty and the demand for creative designs are some of the unusual features of game development that promote the adoption of ISO/IEC 29110 [38]. A deterrent to using ISO/IEC 29110 is that it needs more support for iterative development to allow easier adaptation to real-life organizations.

Adoption Factors of SPI. The factors that aid and deter the adoption of SPI in game development were analyzed under the following headings: SPI Design; SPI

Development; and SPI Evaluation. Some examples are described in this section. A Taxonomy and Visual Notation for Modeling Globally Distributed Requirements Engineering Projects helped the process [39] as there was a need for this in requirements engineering, whereas designing a video game with a proposed Game Design Document (GDD) [28] required experience and training. The lack of version control on this GDD was a deterrent to adopting this process improvement. SPI development approaches and frameworks have been adopted to improve the flexibility of a development team and help provide a sustainable iterative pace by integrating Kanban into the iterative process [21]. Having a good product owner and scrum master are critical for process improvement. Putting the required time and money into establishing these conditions is necessary for process improvement according to [40]. A paring of CMMI with IEEE CS SS&E standards in [1], helped to train staff and to improve SE practices.

4 Conclusion

The software processes identified by RQ1 were almost evenly distributed across agile and hybrid approaches, however the qualitative industrial studies reported almost double the use of agile processes, whereas the quantitative industrial studies were dominated (90%) by the use of hybrid processes.

Almost a fifth of the SPI initiatives identified by RQ2 emanated from quantitative studies, and there were a disproportionate number of industrial papers in the qualitative studies (half that of non-industrial). The qualitative studies contained a much broader range of SPI initiatives across all the development phases of the game development process such as Requirement, Design, Development, Evaluation and Deployment, compared to the quantitative studies that only reported SPI initiatives on the Design, Development and Evaluation phases. The industry quantitative studies had double the SPI Design and half the Development initiatives compared to the industry qualitative studies.

RQ3 highlighted how lightweight agile approaches such as XP, Scrum and Kanban are suitable where time to market and innovation are critical, the risk driven Spiral model is suitable for larger projects. Hybrid approaches, such as reuse, are needed when the investment in terms of time and cost are warranted by more stable requirements and products/games have longer lifespans. Good motivation and the provision of critical resources such as expert training were described as essential for SPI.

All the findings in this review are influenced by the predominance of non-industrial studies in the literature and the motivational differences between industry and research for using various process models. In academia, research rigor, rather than time-to-market, can be seen as more important, Model Driven Development (MDD) was used only in research [22]. The fact is that there are more studies available from the academic side. Many of the reports from industry exist in 'grey' literature, such as magazines, websites etc. This prompts future research to investigate what is actually happening on the ground in game development. Recommendations for future research would be the development of a best practice model for game development. A closer look at the game testing phase and how it is being conducted is also warranted.

References

1. Land, S.K., Wilson, B.: Using IEEE standards to support America's Army gaming development. Computer 39, 105–107 (2006)
2. Kanode, C.M., Haddad, H.M.: Software Engineering Challenges in Game Development. In: Sixth International Conference on Information Technology: New Generations, ITNG 2009, pp. 260–265 (2009)
3. Petrillo, B., Pimenta, M., Trindade, F., Dietrich, C.: Houston, we have a problem...: a survey of actual problems in computer games development. In: Proceedings of the 2008 ACM Symposium on Applied Computing, pp. 707–711. ACM, Fortaleza (2008)
4. Callele, D., Neufeld, E., Schneider, K.: Requirements engineering and the creative process in the video game industry. In: Proceedings of the 2005 13th IEEE International Conference on Requirements Engineering, pp. 240–250 (2005)
5. Ampatzoglou, A., Stamelos, I.: Software engineering research for computer games: A systematic review. Information and Software Technology 52, 888–901 (2010)
6. Kitchenham, B.A., Charters, S.: Guidelines for performing Systematic Literature Reviews in Software Engineering V 2.3. School of Computer Science and Mathematics Keele University, Department of Computer Science University of Durham (2007)
7. Evidence Based Software Engineering (EBSE), http://www.dur.ac.uk/ebse/
8. Unterkalmsteiner, M., Gorschek, T., Islam, A.K.M.M., Chow Kian, C., Permadi, R.B., Feldt, R.: Evaluation and Measurement of Software Process Improvement—A Systematic Literature Review. IEEE Transactions on Software Engineering 38, 398–424 (2012)
9. Emam, K.: Benchmarking Kappa: Interrater Agreement in Software Process Assessments. Empirical Software Engineering 4, 113–133 (1999)
10. Kasurinen, J., Maglyas, A., Smolander, K.: Is Requirements Engineering Useless in Game Development? In: Salinesi, C., van de Weerd, I. (eds.) REFSQ 2014. LNCS, vol. 8396, pp. 1–16. Springer, Heidelberg (2014)
11. Koutonen, J., Leppänen, M.: How Are Agile Methods and Practices Deployed in Video Game Development? A Survey into Finnish Game Studios. In: Baumeister, H., Weber, B. (eds.) XP 2013. LNBIP, vol. 149, pp. 135–149. Springer, Heidelberg (2013)
12. Birchall, J., Gatzidis, C.: The Periodic Table of Elements via an XNA-Powered Serious Game. In: Pan, Z., Cheok, A.D., Müller, W., Liarokapis, F. (eds.) Transactions on Edutainment IX. LNCS, vol. 7544, pp. 1–28. Springer, Heidelberg (2013)
13. Weishan, Z., Dong, H., Kunz, T., Hansen, K.M.: Mobile Game Development: Object-Orientation or Not. In: 31st Annual International on Computer Software and Applications Conference, COMPSAC 2007, pp. 601–608 (2007)
14. Ampatzoglou, A., Chatzigeorgiou, A.: Evaluation of object-oriented design patterns in game development. Information and Software Technology 49, 445–454 (2007)
15. Petrillo, F., Pimenta, M.: Is agility out there?: agile practices in game development. In: Proceedings of the 28th ACM International Conference on Design of Communication, pp. 9–15. ACM, Brazil (2010)
16. Seung Hun, L., Gum Hee, L., Hyun Hoon, C., Doo Heon, S., Sung-Yul, R.: An Empirical Model of the Game Software Development Processes. In: Fourth International Conference on Software Engineering Research, Management and Applications (2006)
17. Francillette, Y., Gouaich, A., Hocine, N., Pons, J.: A gameplay loops formal language. In: 2012 17th International Conference on Computer Games (CGAMES), pp. 94–101 (2012)
18. Polk, R.: Agile and Kanban in Coordination. In: Agile Conference (AGILE) (2011)
19. Musil, J., Schweda, A., Winkler, D., Biffl, S.: Improving Video Game Development: Facilitating Heterogeneous Team Collaboration through Flexible Software Processes. In: Riel,

A., O'Connor, R., Tichkiewitch, S., Messnarz, R. (eds.) EuroSPI 2010. CCIS, vol. 99, pp. 83–94. Springer, Heidelberg (2010)
20. Zaibon, S.B., Shiratuddin, N.: Towards Developing Mobile Game-Based Learning Engineering Model. In: 2009 WRI World Congress on Computer Science and Information Engineering, pp. 649–653 (2009)
21. Pa, P.S., Su, T.-P.: Quality Control of Artistic Scenes in Processes of Design and Development of Digital-Game Products. In: Yan, X.-T., Ion, W., Eynard, B. (eds.) Global Design to Gain a Competitive Edge, pp. 103–113. Springer, London (2008)
22. Cooper, K.M.L., Longstreet, C.S.: Towards model-driven game engineering for serious educational games: Tailored use cases for game requirements. In: 2012 17th International Conference on Computer Games (CGAMES), pp. 208–212 (2012)
23. Gomez-Rodriguez, A., Gonzalez-Moreno, J.C., Ramos-Valcarcel, D., Vazquez-Lopez, L.: Modeling serious games using AOSE methodologies. In: 2011 11th International Conference on Intelligent Systems Design and Applications (ISDA), pp. 53–58 (2011)
24. Walfisz, M., Zackariasson, P., Wilson, T.L.: Real-time strategy: Evolutionary game development. Business Horizons 49, 487–498 (2006)
25. Poderi, G.: Simple conversational practices in the case of free and open source software infrastructure. In: Proceedings of the 12th Participatory Design Conference: Exploratory Papers, Workshop Descriptions, Industry Cases, pp. 45–48. ACM, Roskilde (2012)
26. Wu, Y.-H., Yao, X.-X., He, J.: Design and Implementation of the Game Engine Based on Android Platform. In: Internet Technology and Applications, iTAP (2011)
27. Lee, J., Im, C.-Y.: A Study on User Centered Game Evaluation Guideline Based on the MIPA Framework. In: Kurosu, M. (ed.) HCD 2009. LNCS, vol. 5619, pp. 84–93. Springer, Heidelberg (2009)
28. Salazar, M.G., Mitre, H.A., Olalde, C.L., Sanchez, J.L.G.: Proposal of Game Design Document from software engineering requirements perspective. In: 2012 17th International Conference on Computer Games (CGAMES), pp. 81–85 (2012)
29. Musil, J., Schweda, A., Winkler, D., Biffl, S.: Synthesized essence: what game jams teach about prototyping of new software products. In: 2010 ACM/IEEE 32nd International Conference on Software Engineering, pp. 183–186 (2010)
30. Alves, V., Cardim, I., Vital, H., Sampaio, P., Damasceno, A., Borba, P., Ramalho, G.: Comparative analysis of porting strategies in J2ME games. In: Proceedings of the 21st IEEE International Conference on Software Maintenance, ICSM 2005, pp. 123–132 (2005)
31. Alves, V., Matos Jr., P., Cole, L., Borba, P., Ramalho, G.L.: Extracting and Evolving Mobile Games Product Lines. In: Obbink, H., Pohl, K. (eds.) SPLC 2005. LNCS, vol. 3714, pp. 70–81. Springer, Heidelberg (2005)
32. Taylor, A.S.A., Backlund, P., Engstrom, H., Johannesson, M., Lebram, M.: The Birth of Elinor: A Collaborative Development of a Game Based System for Stroke Rehabilitation. In: Second International Conference in Visualisation, VIZ 2009, pp. 52–60 (2009)
33. Tran, M.Q., Biddle, R.: Collaboration in serious game development: a case study. In: Proceedings of the 2008 Conference on Future Play: Research, Play, Share, pp. 49–56. ACM, Toronto (2008)
34. Pulman, A., Shufflebottom, M.: A Virtual Infection Control Simulation: The Development of a Serious Game in the Health-Care Sector. In: Petrovic, O., Brand, A. (eds.) Serious Games on the Move, pp. 43–56. Springer Vienna (2009)
35. Friis, D., Ostergaard, J., Sutherland, J.: Virtual Reality Meets Scrum: How a Senior Team Moved from Management to Leadership. In: 2011 44th Hawaii International Conference on System Sciences (HICSS), pp. 1–7 (2011)

36. Srinivasan, J., Lundqvist, K.: Organizational Enablers for Agile Adoption: Learning from GameDevCo. In: Abrahamsson, P., Marchesi, M., Maurer, F. (eds.) XP 2009. LNBIP, vol. 31, pp. 63–72. Springer, Heidelberg (2009)
37. Myllärniemi, V., Raatikainen, M., Männistö, T.: Inter-organisational Approach in Rapid Software Product Family Development — A Case Study. In: Morisio, M. (ed.) ICSR 2006. LNCS, vol. 4039, pp. 73–86. Springer, Heidelberg (2006)
38. Kasurinen, J., Laine, R., Smolander, K.: How Applicable Is ISO/IEC 29110 in Game Software Development? In: Heidrich, J., Oivo, M., Jedlitschka, A., Baldassarre, M.T. (eds.) PROFES 2013. LNCS, vol. 7983, pp. 5–19. Springer, Heidelberg (2013)
39. Laurent, P., Ma, X., der, P., Cleland-Huang, J., Steele, A.: A Taxonomy and Visual Notation for Modeling Globally Distributed Requirements Engineering Projects. In: 2010 5th IEEE International Conference on Global Software Engineering (ICGSE), pp. 35–44 (2010)
40. Kniberg, H., Farhang, R.: Bootstrapping Scrum and XP under Crisis A Story from the Trenches. In: Conference on Agile, AGILE 2008, pp. 436–444 (2008)

Software Requirements Development: A Path for Improving Software Quality

Gasca-Hurtado Gloria Piedad [1], Mirna Muñoz[2], Jezreel Mejia[2], and Calvo-Manzano Jose A.[3]

[1] Facultad de Ingeniería, Universidad de Medellín
Medellín, Colombia
gpgasca@udem.edu.co
[2] Centro de Investigación en Matemáticas
Av. Universidad no 222, 98068 Zacatecas, México
{mirna.munoz,jmejia}@cimat.mx
[3] Facultad de Informática, Universidad Politécnica de Madrid Campus de Montegancedo,
Boadilla del Monte, 28660 Madrid, Spain
joseantonio.calvomanzano@upm.es

Abstract. In this paper we propose a path to guide software development organizations, who are seeking continuous improvement, for developing high-quality software. The process improvement path was established carrying out a similarity study among models and standards related to software requirements development. This study allows us to establish similarities and to determine the most useful aspect of one or more models and standards. The similarities can support software development organizations to achieve the implementation of efficient requirements development process.

Keywords: requirements development, standards, models, similarities, software development organizations, process improvement path.

1 Introduction

Models and standards have been created for standardizing the use of software engineering practices in organizations. The standardization of these practices aims to perform processes in the same way by everyone within an organization; therefore the use of a specific model or standard provides a guide for organizations to achieve software quality and productivity [1]. In this context the CMMI model and standards such as ISO 12207, ISO 15504, and ISO 9001:2000 are a reference for organizations which are trying to achieve quality improvement, then, all of them are widely accepted and used in the software industry [2][3][4].

However, many surveys and studies such as [5-7] have confirmed that those models and standards are not easily implemented mainly because they are focused on large organizations, without addressing the needs of the small ones. The main reason of this is because small and medium enterprises (SMEs) focus on economic aspects as well as in the required effort to implement them. Therefore, they perceive the implementation of these models too expensive and too difficult because their Return of Inversion (ROI) is produced in a long-term period [8] [9].

The context above mentioned reflects the reality of Latin America because most software organizations are SMEs, which need to adapt efficiently software engineering practices but do not have the economic conditions to implement quality models and standards. Therefore, these organizations need to start adapting software initiatives according to their size and type of business in a continuous way of process improvement to achieve high maturity levels; those who are required to produce high quality software [10] [11]. These needs are the main reason for us to perform this research.

In this work we establish the similarity among the most representative models and standards related to the requirements development process, because according to [12] it is considered a key process for small organizations and should be improved for software development organizations in Latin America. Then, to perform the comparison of similarities we selected and used the *Models and Standard Similarity Study* (MSSS) method [10] because it has been proved in many studies [10][13][14][15][16] and [17] with relevant results.

This paper is structured as follows: Section 2 describes briefly the adaptation of the MSSS method to the research context; Section 3 shows the similarity study performed to the requirements development process; and finally, Section 4 presents the conclusions and future work derived from the obtained results.

2 Tailoring the MSSS Method to the Research Context

The MSSS method is used to establish the similarity among models and standards of software industry. This method consists of a sequence of steps that allows us understanding how models and standards can be complemented or reinforced respect to others.

To implement the MSSS method in this research work it must be adapted. As a result, the order of the seven steps originally proposed has been modified as follows:

1) *Select the process to be analyzed*: define the requirements development process as the focused process to perform the comparison. This process is selected because of its importance in software projects success.

2) *Select models and standards*: identify the models and standards that contain the requirements development process.

3) *Choose the base model*: identify a model to be taken as a "base or core" to perform the comparison analysis. Requirements management experts should select this model or the standard.

4) *Identify the similarity among models and standards*: the identification of similarities should be done performing a comparative analysis among all models and standards based on the core model or standard selected in the previous step. As a result of performing this step common and complementary information must be defined.

5) *Create a correspondence template*: this template should facilitate the analysis and comparison among the models and standards by storing the analyzed information. The

template is generated, first taking the information provided by the base or core model or standard. Then, adding the complementary information provided by the rest of analyzed models and standards. By doing this, it is obtained both relevant information and the identification of those models that have been excluded because they do not contain the requirements development process.

6) *Establish the detail level*: following the recommendations of MSSS method to facilitate the information analysis, in this step a glossary is built, therefore a level to perform the analysis can be established.

7) *Show the obtained results*: in this step both the obtained results and findings should be showed.

Next section shows the implementation of the MSSS method in the requirements development process.

3 Performing Similarity Study to Requirements Development Process

3.1 Select the Process to be Analyzed

The Chaos Report [18] from the Standish Group shows statistics as evidence that indicates the percentage of projects success and failure as follows: 24% of projects are cancelled prior to completion; 44 % of projects are performed late, over budget, and/or with less than the required features and functions, and just 32% are delivered on time, on budget, and with required features and functions.

These data highlight that around 68% of projects have any type of problems that most of the times are related to an immature requirements development process or the lack of it. Therefore, to develop adequately the requirements of a software project includes carrying a formal process of gathering and maintaining the requirements. Requirements Development is the process of identifying, documenting, communicating, tracking, and managing project requirements, as well as changing those requirements. It is not a single point in time occurrence, but rather it must be an ongoing process that stays in lockstep with the development process. Losing sight of requirements is often the first step on the road to failure [19]. This is the reason to focus this research study on the requirements development process to provide organizations a path of its implementation.

3.2 Select Models and Standards

The models and standards included in the analysis were selected taking into account the following criteria: 1) those that address the requirement development process, 2) those that report a significant percentage of use in Latin America, and 3) those with public and updated information.

The models and standards that covered the criteria were: CMMI-DEV v 1.3 [6], PRINCE2 [20], ISO/IEC 15504 [2], IEEE 830 [17], IEEE 1233 [4], PMBOK [21], ISO 9001:2000 [22], ISO 12207 [5], and ISO/IEC 25000[23].

3.3 Choose the Base Model

After analyzing the features of the selected models and standards, all the researchers involved in the project performed an analysis of them. The analysis consisted of making a qualitative assessment of all included models and standards taking into account a set of features and assessment criteria previously defined. As a result the model or standard to be taken as "base" of the study is selected. The set of features and assessment criteria defined in the study was:

- *Features:* (Feature 1) Model or standard focused on management of software requirements development; (Feature 2) Trends in research related to process improvement mainly in Brazil, Mexico, Peru, Ecuador, and Colombia; and (Feature 3) model or standard with available information, public and updated.
- *Assessment criteria:* It is assigned "H" to a model or standard that according to the evaluator researcher, has a complete coverage of the feature. It is assigned "M" to a model or standard that according to the evaluator researcher, has a medium coverage of the feature. And it is assigned "L" to a model or standard that according to the evaluator researcher, has a low coverage of the feature.

Table 1 shows a summary of the features after analyzing the results of all researchers involved in the project.

Table 1. Results of applying the criteria for analyzing models and standards

Model or Standard	Feature 1	Feature 2	Feature 3
CMMI-DEV v 1.3	H	H	H
PRINCE2	M	M	M
ISO/IEC 15504	H	M	M
IEEE 830	H	M	M
IEEE 1233	H	M	M
PMBOK	M	M	H
ISO 9001:2000	L	M	M
ISO 12207	M	M	M

After analyzing the obtained results, CMMI-DEV v1.3 was selected as the "base model" to perform the study because this model has covered more features than others, having a process focused on providing best practices on requirements development (RD).

3.4 Identify the Similarity among Models and Standards

Following the recommendations proposed by the MSSS method, the information of the requirements development process of the base model was analyzed, and the correspondences and complementary information of the rest of the selected models and standards were identified. To identify the correspondences among them, the structure of each model and standard were analyzed including the "base model", getting a base line for making the comparison.

The base line to determine the similarity should be set in the lowest component found in all models and standards, in this research work this level was found at specific practices. Making a comparative analysis at specific practices level allows: 1) to cover most of the structure of the base model structure and 2) to have a closest comparison respect to the base model and the others selected models and standards.

3.5 Create a Correspondence Template

A template was designed based on the CMMI-DEV v1.3 structure because it was selected as the base model to do the study. This template allows having a knowledge asset in a detailed analysis of information such as: inputs, subpractices, tools & techniques and work products contained in all models and standards. Besides, it facilitates the interpretation of the obtained results.

3.6 Establish the Detail Level

To establish a detail level three key questions were designed and applied in the analysis of each model and standard. To answer each question, the information contained in each model and standard was reviewed in a deep level of detail. The three defined questions were:

- *Question 1*. Is there any information in model "x^1" that identifies the requirement development process according to the items defined in the template? (Y/N)
- *Question 2*. What is the information? (identify the information of each model & standard)
- *Question 3*. What is the additional information provided by the "x" model that could help to carry out the requirements development process according to the items defined in the template? (analyze the identified information and select those whose should be included)

After answering the questions for each model and standard, the next steps were performed in order to fill out and refine the correspondence template: 1) reporting the information proposed by the base model; 2) reporting the information identified in the analyzed models and standards; and 3) analyzing and verifying the information. This last step allows us to verify and to refine the information storage in the template in order to adjust the possible inconsistences in the knowledge assets.

3.7 Show the Obtained Results

According to the recommendations of the MSSS method, we established a glossary named "nomenclature" in this research work. This nomenclature has been defined to facilitate the understanding of the obtained templates. As Table 2 shows, the defined nomenclature is built with the first letters of the models or standards, followed by the numbers that codify the model or standard.

---

[1] "x" model refers to the model or standard analyzed.

Table 2. Models and standards nomenclature

Nomenclature	Standard or model
C	CMMI-DEV v1.3
P	PRINCE2
IE1	ISO/IEC 15504
I8	IEEE 830
I1	IEEE 1233
IS1	ISO 12207
IS9	ISO 9000:2000
PM	PMBOK

It is important to mention that the similarity study performed in this research work has allowed us identifying two kinds of relations of any item for each model or standard: indirect and direct.

Next section presents the findings of analyzing the requirements development process.

4 Results

This section presents the findings established for each specific practice. Table 3 shows an example of the template used to perform the similarity study for each specific practice of the requirements development process. Due to the length of the paper, we decided to include in this section a summary of the most representative findings after perform the similarity study:

- *The specific practice SP 1.1 Elicit Needs of CMMI-DEV v 1.3* aims to collect customer requirements and identify additional requirements not explicitly provided by customers. This practice is the only one that presents the coincidence of 100% among models and standards.
  This is the reason why this specific practice is the best complemented with respect to the rest of the analyzed practices. Regarding to tools and techniques, it is observed that CMMI-DEV v 1.3 offers more detail and quantity of items than the others models and standards. Besides, the analysis showed that IEEE 1233 standard has more similarities with the base model that with the rest of the models and standards analyzed.
  The work products of this specific practice are focused on specifying customer requirements and the relevant complementary information that allows us having a better performance of this specific practice. Finally, the performed analysis shows that the output information of all models and standards offer different alternatives of work products.
- *The specific practice SP 1.2 Transform Stakeholders Needs of CMMI-DEV v1.3* aims to develop and prioritize customer requirements and ensure that all input information has been obtained and consolidated and all conflicts are resolved. The analysis showed that CMMI-DEV v1.3 is the only model that explicitly addresses this practice. However, the IEEE 1233 standard establishes a set of general

recommendations of requirements specification regarding to formulation of requirements terms and organization based on meaningful categories. These categories are recommended to clearly show the interpretation between the customers' needs and the technical community.

Table 3. Results of the Specific Practice SP 1.1 Elicit Needs

SG 1 Develop Customer Requirements		
SP 1.1 Elicit Needs		
Inputs	**Tools and Techniques**	**Work Products**
Customer requirements (C, P, IE1, I8, I1)	T1.1.1 Technology demonstrations (C)	Results of requirements elicitation activities (C)
Customer needs and expectations (C, P, IE1, I8, I9, IS1, I1)	T1.1.2 Interface control working groups (C)	Product planning (P)
	T1.1.3 Technical control working groups (C)	Customer requirements (IE1, I8, IS9, IS1, I1)
	T1.1.4 Interim project reviews (C)	Communication records (IE1)
Business policies (C)	T1.1.5 Questionnaires, interviews and scenarios obtained from end users (C, IE1, I1)	Change control records (IE1)
Standards (C)	T1.1.6 Operational, sustainment and development walkthroughs and end-user task analysis (C, I1)	Analysis report (IE1)
Previous architectural design, decisions and principles (C)	T1.1.7 Quality attribute elicitation workshops with stakeholders (C)	Stakeholders or stakeholders groups (I8, IS1, PM)
Business environmental requirements (C)	T1.1.8 Prototypes and models (C, IE1, I 8, I1)	Definitions, acronyms and abbreviations that require properly interpret the SRS (I8)
Technology (C)	T1.1.9 Brainstorming (C, I1)	
Legacy products or product components (C)	T1.1.10 Quality Function Deployment (C)	
	T1.1.11 Market surveys (C, I1)	References to documents mentioned in the SRS (I8)
Regulatory statutes (C)	T1.1.12 Beta testing (C)	
External products (P)	T1.1.13 Extraction from sources such as documents, standards, or specifications (C, IE1, IS1, I1)	Project Scope (I8, PM)
Possible product states (P)		Legal and regulatory requirements applied to the product (IS9)
Project constitution meeting (PM)	T1.1.14 Observation of existing products, environments, and workflow patterns (C, IE1)	Any additional requirements that the organization considered necessary (IS9)
Project Work Statement (PM)	T1.1.15 Use cases (C)	
Enterprise environmental factors (PM, I1)	T1.1.16 User stories (C)	
	T1.1.17 Delivering small incremental "vertical slices" of product functionality (C)	
Organizational processes assets (PM)	T1.1.18 Business case analysis (C)	
	T1.1.19 Reverse engineering (C, I1)	
Experience of the technical community (I1)	T1.1.20 Customer satisfaction surveys (C)	
	T1.1.21 Planning based on the products (P)	
	T1.1.22 Simulations (IE1, I1)	
	T1.1.23 Configuration management to track the requirements (IE15)	
	T1.1.24 Joint meetings with the customer or formal communications to check the status of your needs and requests (IE1, IS1)	
	T1.1.25 Expert Judgment (PM)	
	T1.1.26 Formal or contextual model (IS1)	
	T1.1.27 Structured workshops (I1)	
	T1.1.28 Assessment competitive system (I1)	
	T1.1.29 Processes and systems benchmarking (I1)	

- *The specific practice SP 2.1 Establish Product and Product Component Requirements of CMMI-DEV v1.3* aims to express the functional and quality attribute requirements in technical terms so that they can be used for design decisions.

  The analysis showed a total coincidence between the CMMI-DEV v1.3 model and the ISO/IEC 15504 standard regarding to inputs, tools & techniques, and work products. However, an indirect relationship between the standards IEEE 830 and ISO 9000:2000 was identified analyzed in more detail for input elements and work products. Moreover, the input elements and work products allow us defining requirements expressed in technical terms that can be used for design decisions.

- *The specific practice SP 2.2 Allocate Product Components Requirements of CMMI-DEV v 1.3* aims to allocate the product requirements to product components including to allocate product performance, design constraints, and fit form and function to meet requirements and facilitate production. The analysis showed that this practice does not have any explicit o direct coincidences among analyzed models and standards. However, there is an indirect relation of the ISO 12207 standard, which proposed as input the definition of system resolution constraints. This input is set-up as proper activity of the requirements identification.

- *The specific practice SP 2.3 Identify Interface Requirements of CMMI-DEV v 1.3* aims to identify and define the interface requirements between products and product components identified in the product architecture. The analysis showed coincidences between CMMI-DEV v1.3 and ISO/ IEC 15504. Besides, a general way of how inputs are complemented with the IEEE 830 standard was identified.

- *The specific practice SP 3.1 Establish Operational Concepts and Scenarios of CMMI-DEV v 1.3* aims to ensure that all events, which may occur in the development use, or sustainment of the product are taking into account to make explicit some of the functional or quality attribute needs of the stakeholders. The analysis showed that this practice had a lack of explicit or direct coincidences among the analyzed models and standards.

- *The specific practice SP 3.2 Establish a Definition of Requirement Functionality and Quality Attributes of CMMI-DEV v 1.3* aims to establish and maintain a "functional analysis" to describe what the product is intended to do. It can include actions, sequence, inputs, outputs, or other information that communicates the manner in which the product will be used, and generate as a result its functional architecture.

  The analysis showed a total coincidence between this specific practice of CMMI-DEV v1.3 and the PMBOK model regarding to inputs, tools and techniques, and work products. However, it is established in an indirect way with the PRINCE2 model, which complements inputs information contributing in the definition of the quality attributes. Besides, there was found an indirect relationship with the standard ISO/IEC 15504, which complements the techniques to delimit the quality attributes and the functionality definition.

- *The specific practice SP 3.3 Analyze Requirements of CMMI-DEV v 1.3* aims to analyze requirements to determine whether they are necessary and sufficient to meet the objectives of higher levels of the product hierarchy.

  The analysis showed coincidence among this specific practice and the standards ISO 12207 and ISO 9000:2000 regarding to input and work products, but in tools and techniques there were not coincidences found.

- *The specific practice SP 3.4 Analyze Requirements to Achieve Balance of CMMI-DEV v 1.3* aims to analyze requirements to balance stakeholders' needs and constraints in aspects such as cost, schedule, product or project performance, functionality, priorities, reusable components, maintainability, or risk.
  The analysis showed direct coincidences among this specific practice and the ISO 12207 and ISO/IEC 15504 standards regarding to inputs and work products, but there were not coincidences found in tools and techniques.
- *The specific practice SP 3.5 Validate Requirements of CMMI-DEV v 1.3* aims to validate the requirements to ensure that stakeholders' needs and expectations are included since early development stage.
  The analysis showed direct coincidences among this specific practice and the ISO 12207 and ISO/IEC 15504 standards regarding to inputs and work products, but there were not coincidences found in tools and techniques

4.1 Summary of the Path to Improve Requirement Development Process

Taking into account the findings obtained performing the similarity study of the models and standards analyzed; this section presents a proposal of a path to improve requirement development process. This path was established integrating indirect and direct relationships of practices for each model and standard analyzed. Figure 1 shows the established path.

The presented path is composed of rectangles and circles; the rectangles represent the key path of activities associated according with the recommendations of the models and standards analyzed, and the circles indicate the contribution that each model or standard can make for the implementation of activities, tools, techniques, inputs or work products.

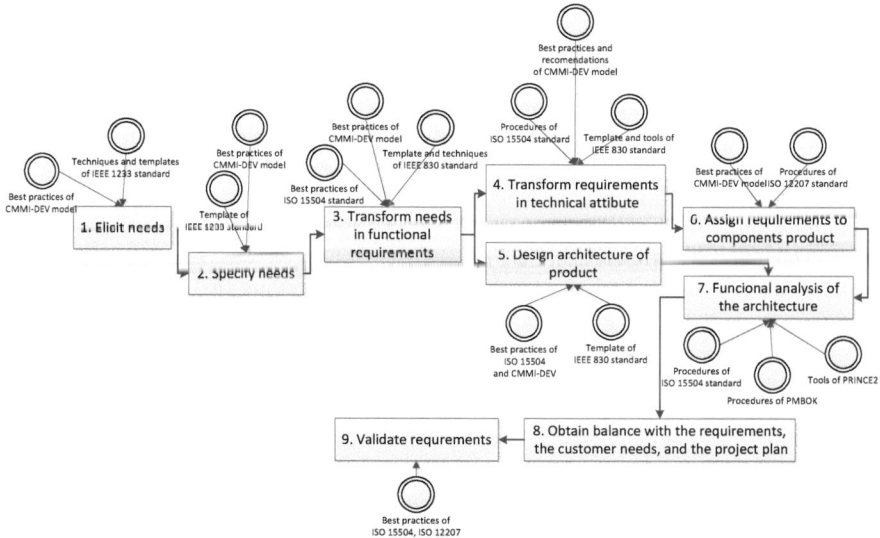

Fig. 1. Path for improve the requirements development process

5 Conclusions

The analysis showed in this research paper among models and standards such as CMMI-DEV v 1.3, PRINCE2, ISO/IEC 15504, IEEE 830, IEEE 1233, PMBOK, ISO 9000:2000 and ISO 12207, focused on software requirements development as part of the research works that are being developed and performed in Latin America in countries such as Chile, Colombia, and México.

The obtained results in this research allow us to establish the first results providing a guide to SMEs, which are looking for best practices, as a solution to issues related to the lack of customer requirements development in software development projects. Besides, the similarities and correspondences among models as well as the completeness, robustness, and detail of them were established for tailoring and implementing models and standards (see Table 4).

Table 4. Summary of explicitly similarities addressed by the models and standards

CMMI-DEV v 1.3		PRINCE2	ISO/IEC 15504	IEEE 830	IEEE 1233	PMBOK	ISO 9001:2000	ISO 12207
Specific Goal	Specific Practice							
RD SG 1	SP 1.1	Yes	Yes	Yes	Yes	Yes	Yes	Yes
	SP 1.2	No	No	No	No	No	No	No
RD SG 2	SP 2.1	No	Yes	No	No	No	No	No
	SP 2.2	No	No	No	No	No	No	No
	SP 2.3	No	Yes	No	No	No	No	No
RD SG 3	SP 3.1	No	No	No	No	No	No	No
	SP 3.2	Yes	No	No	No	Yes	No	No
	SP 3.3	No	No	No	No	No	Yes	Yes
	SP 3.4	No	Yes	No	No	No	No	Yes
	SP 3.5	No	Yes	No	No	No	No	Yes

Moreover, it is considered important to highlight tree points.

- All models and standards have a complete coincidence with the specific practice of CMMI-DEV v1.3 SP1.1 Elicit Needs.
- The CMMI-DEV v1.3 model and the ISO/IEC 15504 standard are focused on the process improvement of IT, so they offer a definition of specific practices that should be performed to implement the requirements development. Moreover, both of them present a high level of detail referring to inputs, tools, techniques and work products contained in them.
- The PRINCE2 and PMBOK are models for project management; these models focus their effort in requirements development in the phases of project scope definition and analysis, definition of functionality and quality attributes, and manage requirements changes.

Finally, the path for improving the requirements development process was defined from direct relationships identified in the similarity study of the models and standards and reinforced with the indirect relationships (represented in the circles in Figure 1) indicating the element provided and which model or standard it belongs to. Moreover, the researchers' team proposes the following recommendations: (a) software development organizations which implement best practices for developing software focused on specific practices from RD process area of the CMMI-DEV v1.3 should take into account complementary elements such as tools and techniques contained in others models and standards; (b) specific practices SP1.1 and SP 3.2 from the RD process area are considered key practices to perform this process; therefore, they must be performed following in detail the recommendations from the CMMI-DEV v1.3 model. Besides, these practices should be the first practices to be implemented in improvement of the software development process. Beginning with some of these practices helps to reduce causes of failures associated with issues such as: lack of user involvement, incomplete requirements definitions and requirements changes without an adequate handle; and (c) the specific practices SP 1.1, SP 2.2, SP 3.1, SP 3.3, SP 3.4 and SP 3.5 of the RD process area are complementary practices because not all models and standards address them in an explicit way. It is important to take into account that they are part of the process improvement but they can be implemented after the key practices.

Acknowledgements. This work is sponsored by Universidad de Medellin, Centro de Investigación en Matemáticas (CIMAT) and the Polytechnic University of Madrid through the Research Chair in Software Process Improvement for Spain and Latin American Region. This work had the technical support of the Master's student Lina María Giraldo.

References

1. Piattini, M., García, R.: Calidad En el Desarrollo y Mantenimiento del Software, Alfaomega Grupo (2003)
2. Garzás, J., Fernández, C., Piattini, M.: Una aplicación de la norma ISO/IEC 15504 para PYMES y pequeños equipos de desarrollo. In: Proc. II Conferencia Iberoamericana de Calidad del Software, Alcalá de Henares (2009)
3. IEEE. IEEE 030, Recommended Practice for Software Requirements Specifications (1998)
4. IEEE. IEEE 1233, Recommended Practice for Software Requirements Specifications (1996)
5. Hareton, L., Terence, Y.: A Process Framework for Small Projects. Software Process Improvement and Practice 83, 6:67–6:83 (2001)
6. Saiedian, H., Carr, N.: Characterizing a software process maturity model for small organizations. In: Proc. ACM SIGICE Bulletin, pp. 2–11 (1997)
7. Staples, M., Niazi, M., Jeffery, R., Abrahams, A., Byatt, P., Murphy, R.: An exploratory study of why organizations do not adopt CMMI. Proc. Journal of Systems and Software 80(6), 883–895 (2007)
8. Rico, D.: ROI of Software Process Improvement: Metrics for Project Managers and Software Engineers. J. Ross Publishing (2004)

9. García, J., Amescua, A., Velasco, M.: Top 10 de Factores que Obstaculizan la Mejora de los Procesos de Verificación y Validación en Organizaciones Intensivas en SoftwareRevista Española de Innovación, Calidad e Ingeniería de Software (REICIS), Madrid, Spain, vol. 2(2), pp. 18–29 (2006)
10. Calvo-Manzano, J., Cuevas, G., Muñoz, M., San Feliu, T.: Process Similarity Study: Case Study on Project Planning Practices Based on CMMI-DEV v1.2. In: Proc. EuroSPI 2008 (2008)
11. Fayad, M., Laitinen, M., Ward, R.: Software Engineering in the Small. Proc. Communications of the ACM 43(3), 115–118 (2000)
12. Gasca-Hurtado, G.P., Manzano, J.C., Giraldo, L.M., Arias, J.A.E.: Statistical analysis of the implementation for best practices in software development organizations. In: 8th Iberian Conference on Information Systems and Technologies, CISTI 2013 (2013)
13. Gasca, G.: Metodología de Gestión de Riesgos para la Adquisición de Software en Pequeños Entornos – MEGRIAD, Department of Languages and Computer Systems and Software Engineering, Doctor, UPM (2010)
14. Vega, V., Gasca, G., Echeverri, J.: Análisis Comparativo de Modelos de Calidad, Identificación de Mejores Prácticas para la Gestión de Calidad en Pequeños Entornos. In: Proc. Infonor (2012)
15. Muñoz, M., Cuevas, G., San Feliu, T.: Metodología Multimodelo para Implementar Mejoras de Procesos Software. Editorial Académica Española, p. 367 (2012)
16. Gasca, G., Vega, V., Calvo-Manzano, J.: Identificación de Patrones de Proyectos de Adquisición del Software mediante la aplicación del método MECT. In: Proc. 7ª Conferencia Ibérica de Sistemas y Tecnologías de Información CISTI (2006)
17. Vega, V., Calvo-Manzano, J.: Metodología para el Aseguramiento de la Calidad en la Adquisición del Software (proceso y producto) y servicios correlacionados (MACAD-PP), Departamento Department of Languages and Computer Systems and Software Engineering, Doctor, UPM (2012)
18. The CHAOS REPORT, The Standish Group International (2009)
19. The Standish Group International, CHAOS Manifesto 2011. The Standish Group International, Inc. (2011)
20. OGC. Managing Successful Projects with PRINCE2 (2005)
21. IEEE, A Guide to the Project Management Body of Knowledge, IEEE Guide Adoption of PMI Standard A Guide to the Project Management Body of Knowledge (2004)
22. NTC-ISO 9001, Norma Técnica Colombiana, Sistemas de Gestión de la Calidad (2008)
23. ISO/IEC 25000 SQuaRE, Software Product Quality Requirements and Evaluation (2005)
24. Kappelman, L., McKeeman, R., Zhang, L.: Early warning signs of IT project failure: The dominant dozen. Proc. Information Systems Management 23(4), 31–36 (2006)

A Traceability Process Assessment Model for the Medical Device Domain

Gilbert Regan, Miklos Biro, Fergal Mc Caffery, Kevin Mc Daid, and Derek Flood

{gilbert.regan,fergal.mccaffery,kevin.mcdaid,
derek.flood}@dkit.ie, Miklos.biro@sch.at

Abstract. Traceability of requirements through the software development lifecycle (including supporting processes such as risk management and change management) is a difficult and expensive task. The implementation of effective traceability allows organizations to leverage its many advantages, such as impact analysis, product verification and validation, and facilitation of code maintenance. Traceability is conducive to producing quality software.

Within the medical device domain, as in other safety critical domains, software must provide reliability, safety and security because failure to do so can lead to injury or death. However, despite its criticality most software systems don't employ explicit traceability between artefacts. Numerous barriers hamper the effective implementation of traceability such as cost, complexity of relationship between artefacts, calculating a return on investment, different stakeholder viewpoints, lack of awareness of traceability and a lack of guidance as to how to implement traceability.

To assist medical device organisations in addressing the lack of guidance on how to implement effective traceability, this paper aims to present the development of a traceability process assessment model and how traceability process assessment and maintenance could be fully automated using the Open Services for Lifecycle Collaboration (OSLC) initiative. The process assessment model will allow organisations to identify strengths and weaknesses in their existing traceability process and pinpoint areas for improvement.

Keywords: Requirements traceability, Traceability assessment, Medical device, Safety critical, Process assessment, Automation.

1 Introduction

Medical device software is considered safety critical, meaning that failure in the software can result in loss of life, significant environmental damage, or major financial loss [1], therefore medical device software must provide reliability, safety and security. Manufacturers must ensure their software is safe and establish effective software development processes that are based on recognized engineering principles appropriate for safety critical systems. At the heart of such processes, they must incorporate traceability.

Traceability is the ability to establish links (or traces) between source artefacts and target artefacts [2]. In addition to tracing requirements through each phase of the software development lifecycle (SDLC) the medical device standards and guidelines also require traceability through the supporting processes of risk management and change management. Implementing traceability through risk management helps ensure that risk control measures for identified hazards have been implemented and tested. Similarly, implementing traceability through the change management process helps ensure that changes in the software, agreed as a result of problem reports or user requests, have been implemented and tested.

Traceability is a requirement of many regulatory bodies such as the Federal Aviation Administration who specify in their DO-178C standard [3] that "software developers must be able to demonstrate traceability of designs against requirements" at each stage of the development. The Food and Drug Administration (FDA) state that documentation provided in a submission for approval should "provide traceability to link together design, implementation, testing, and risk management" [4]. The automobile safety standard ISO 26262:2011 [5] states that "safety requirements shall be traceable…to: each source of a safety requirement at the upper hierarchical level, each derived safety requirement at a lower hierarchical level, or to its realization in the design, and the specification of verification".

However despite its many benefits and regulatory requirements, most existing software systems lack explicit traceability links between artefacts [6]. Numerous reasons have been identified for reluctance in implementing traceability including cost, complexity, building a requirements trace matrix (RTM) is time consuming, arduous and error prone [7], stakeholders having differing perceptions as to the benefits of traceability [1], developers may fear that traces could be used to monitor their work [8], and difficulties with trace tools [9]. Finally almost no guidance is available for practitioners to help them establish effective traceability in their projects and as a result, practitioners are ill-informed as to how best to accomplish this task [10, 11].

To assist medical device organisations in addressing the lack of guidance on how to implement effective traceability, this paper presents the development and validation of a traceability process assessment model (PAM). To be effective, organisations need to know how well their current traceability process helps them achieve their goals. Additionally an assessment of a process will lead to an increased understanding of the actual performance and management of activities, and the potential for improvement.

The remainder of this paper is structured as follows: Section 2 outlines current assessment models' relationship to traceability and the need to automate the assessment and maintenance of traceability. Section 3 outlines current assessment of traceability in medical device standards and guidelines and assessment models such as ISO 15504 [12]. Section 4 outlines the methodology used to develop the PAM while section 5 details the structure of the developed PAM. Section 6 discusses how traceability assessment and maintenance could be automated using the Open Services for Lifecycle Collaboration (OSLC) initiative. Finally section 7 concludes the paper.

2   Related Work

A literature review was conducted to determine what other traceability assessment models were available in the general, safety critical or medical device domains. This review returned only one model on traceability compliance/ capability assessment called Med-Trace [10]. Med-trace is a lightweight traceability assessment method, completed in 8 stages, whose goal is to assist medical device organizations to improve their software development traceability process. The authors completed assessments on two medical device companies and were able to identify areas for improvement in each company's traceability process.

There are a number of process assessment models which provide common frameworks for assessing software process capability. These models include ISO 15504 SPICE , Automotive SPICE [13], SPICE 4 SPACE [14], and the Capability Maturity Model CMMI [15] among others. These frameworks assess processes such as software design process, software construction process, software testing process etc. However the frameworks do not include a dedicated traceability assessment process. The frameworks do include traceability assessment but it is spread out across a lot of processes and sometimes difficult to interpret (as detailed in section 3-1) e.g. base practice 4 of the software construction process (Eng. 6) in SPICE states;

"*Verify software units. Verify that each software unit satisfies its design requirements by executing the specified unit verification procedures and document the results*".

Explicit traceability is not required in the above statement but it may be implied. It is open to interpretation.

It is important to highlight that traceability has been considered as a key issue by the agile community as well. Scott Ambler, one of the key personalities of the agile movement, states in 1999 that "My experience shows that a mature approach to requirements traceability is often a key distinguisher between organizations that are successful at developing software and those that aren't. Choosing to succeed is often the most difficult choice you'll ever make—choosing to trace requirements on your next software project is part of choosing to succeed." [16]

The same Scott Ambler's advice in 2013 [17]:
"Think very carefully before investing in a requirements traceability matrix, or in full lifecycle traceability in general, where the traceability information is manually maintained. When does maintaining traceability information make sense?

- Automated tooling support exists
- Complex domains
- Large teams or geographically distributed teams
- Regulatory compliance"

While the above view reflects the reluctance in implementing traceability as discussed in the introduction, it also shows its importance in the case of the medical device domain being both complex and subject to regulatory compliance requirements.

Considering all of the above discussion, the need for the automation of assessing and maintaining traceability is imminent. It is this automation to which the Open Services for Lifecycle Collaboration (OSLC) initiative opens the way also as discussed in this paper.

3 Software Process Assessment

A Software process provides a framework for the key activities of software development. Good management of the process should provide for a sustained orderly improvement of the process. Software process assessment assist organizations in understanding the current state of their software process by identifying strengths and weaknesses in their process and thus providing focus on areas for improvement. In addition to assessing their own process an organization can use software process assessment to determine the state of a supplier's process.

3.1 Traceability assessment

To understand how traceability is currently assessed, four software process improvement frameworks, and the medical device standards and guidelines, have been analysed for their requirements for traceability through the SDLC.

The results of this analysis are shown overleaf in Table 1. Figure 1 is a depiction of the SDLC, with the numbered double head arrows indicating bi-directional traceability between the different phases and between the phases and test. These numbers are represented in the first column of Table 1. The assessment models and documents analysed were;

- Capability Maturity Model Integration (CMMI)
- ISO/IEC 15504-5 Process assessment model
- Automotive SPICE Process assessment model
- SPICE 4 SPACE Process assessment model
- Medical device standards and guidelines documents
    - A. IEC 62304 -   Medical device Software-Software lifecycle processes
    - B. FDA - General Principles of Software Validation (GPSV)
    - C. FDA -   Guidance for Premarket Submissions for   Software in Medical Devices
    - D. FDA   - Guidance on Off-The-Shelf Software Use in Medical Devices
    - E. ISO 13485 -   Medical devices — Quality management systems
    - F. ISO 14971 -   Application of risk management to medical devices

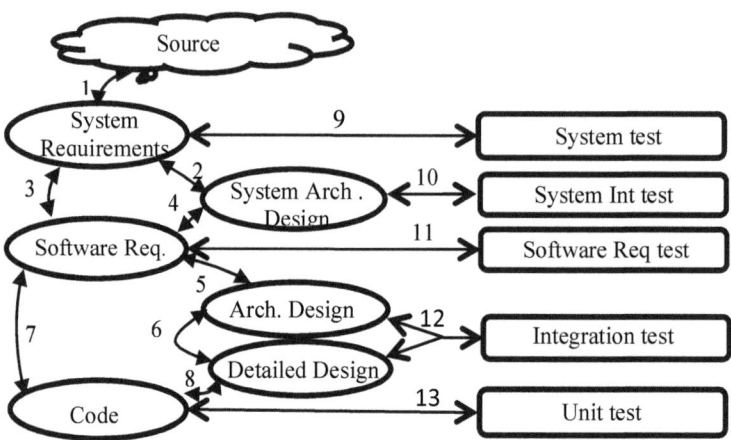

Fig. 1. SDLC and links between phases @Annex E of the Automotive SPICE® PAM

Table 1. Traceability links across different assessment models

Link	Medical Device Standards	15504 SPICE	Auto SPICE	SPICE 4 SPACE	CMMI
1	E - 7.3.2	ENG 2 BP 5	ENG 2 BP 6	ENG2 BP 5	RD – SG2
2	E - 7.1(d)	ENG 3 BP 6	ENG 3 BP 6	ENG3 BP 6	REQM - SP 1.4
3	A	ENG 4 BP 4	ENG 4 BP 6	ENG 4 BP 4	REQM - SP 1.4
4	E	ENG 9 BP 6	ENG 4 BP 7	ENG 9 BP6	REQM - SP 1.4
5	B	ENG 5 BP 5	ENG 5 BP 9	ENG 5 - BP 6	REQM - SP 1.4
6	A	ENG BP3/5	ENG 5 BP10	ENG 5 - BP 3	REQM - SP 1.4
7	C	ENG 6 BP 3	ENG 6 BP 9	ENG 6 - BP 3	REQM - SP 1.4
8	B	ENG 6 BP 3	ENG 6 BP 8	ENG 6 - BP 3	REQM - SP 1.4
9	E - 7.3.5	ENG 1 BP 1	ENG 10 BP 5	ENG 10-BP 1	REQM - SP 1.4
10	E - 7.3.5	ENG 9 BP 2	ENG 9 BP 7	ENG 9 - BP 2	REQM - SP 1.4
11	A	ENG 8 BP 1	ENG 8 BP 5	ENG 8 - BP 1	REQM - SP 1.4
12	B	ENG 7 BP 2	ENG 7 BP 7	ENG 7 - BP 2	REQM - SP 1.4
13	B	ENG 6 BP 4	ENG 6 BP10	ENG 6 - BP 4	REQM - SP 1.4

Table 1 indicates that each of the traceability links are required through an assortment of the medical device standards and guidelines and that each of the assessment models requires traceability for each link. However a difficulty arises with understanding the clarity of the requirement for traceability, with some models somewhat open to interpretation. For example Automotive SPICE is very definite and clear about the traceability links required whereas CMMI is more general. This point can be illustrated by looking at the requirement for link 4;

Base practice 4 of the Software requirements analysis process (ENG 4) in Automotive SPICE states *'Ensure consistency and bilateral traceability of system architectural design to software requirements'* whereas CMMI states *'Maintain requirements traceability from a requirement to its derived requirements and allocation to functions, interfaces, objects, people, processes, and work products'*. This CMMI statement takes some interpretation and it is the view of this study that this statement covers all links from 2 to 13.

The difficulty with understanding the requirements for traceability in the frameworks is further compounded by the fact that the traceability requirements in each of the assessment models are spread out across many processes so extracting the requirements is a time consuming task. A point of note from Table 1 is that the medical device standards' requirement for traceability is matched by the traceability requirements from the improvement frameworks, therefore it is envisaged that the assessment model developed as part of this study, with slight modifications should be easily transferable to other domains.

4 Research Methodology

The traceability process assessment model is based on the ISO 15504-2 [18]. It was decided to base the traceability assessment model on ISO/IEC 15504 as this improvement and capability determination model was derived from ISO/IEC 12207 [19] and since ANSI/AAMI/IEC 62304:2006 (Software lifecycle processes for medical device software) is derived from ISO/IEC 12207 it was determined that there was good synergy between ANSI/AAMI/IEC 62304:2006 and ISO/IEC 15504. Additionally, 15504 is used extensively in other safety critical industries such as the automotive industry (Automotive SPICE), space industry (SPICE 4 SPACE) and the medical device industry (Medi SPICE).

The first stage was to develop a traceability PRM. The PRM was developed using the requirements from traceability (taken from the medical device standards and guidelines), and ISO 15504-2 section 6.2 which sets out the requirements for a Process Reference Model. While ISO 15504-2 details the minimum requirements that a PRM and a PAM should meet, it provides no guidance on how to develop the models i.e. it does not tell you how to transform requirements into a PRM or PAM. To address this issue, this study based the development of the PAM on the Tudor IT Service Management Process Assessment (TIPA) transformation process. The TIPA transformation process complies with the requirements for PRMs and PAMs as expressed in ISO/IEC 15504-2. The transformation process contains the following steps [20];

1. Identify elementary requirements in a collection of requirements
2. Organise and structure the requirements
3. Identify common purposes upon those requirements and organize them towards domain goals
4. Identify and factorize outcomes from the common purposes and attach them to the related goals

5. Group activities together under a practice and attach it to the related outcomes
6. Allocate each practice to a specific capability level
7. Phrase outcomes and process purpose
8. Phrase the Base Practices attached to Outcomes
9. Determine Work Products among the inputs and outputs of the practices

5 Structure of Traceability PAM

The traceability assessment framework, illustrated in Figure 2, consists of 4 traceability processes which are Change Management (CM) traceability, Risk Management (RM) traceability, Software Development Lifecycle (SDLC) traceability, and Best Practice traceability.

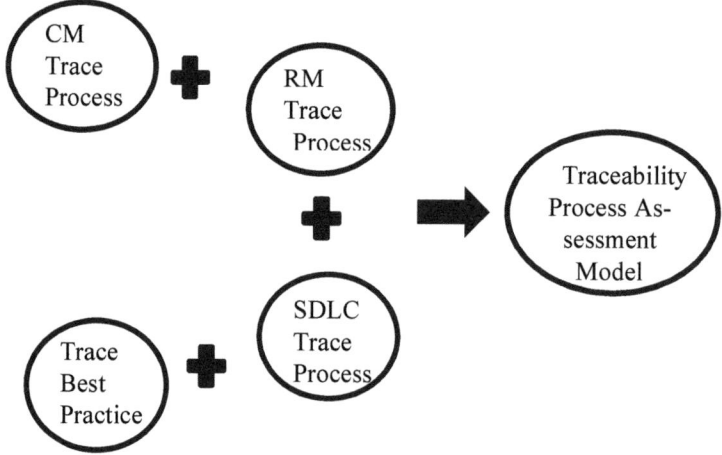

Fig. 2. Traceability Process Assessment Framework

Each of the processes contains: (i) Title; (ii) Purpose, which contains the unique functional objectives of the process when performed in a particular environment; (iii) Outcomes, which are a list of expected positive results of the process performance; (iv) Base practices, whose performance provides an indication of the extent of achievement of the process purpose and process outcomes; and (v) Work Products (WPs) are either used or produced (or both), when performing the process.

The CM Traceability Process: The purpose of this process is to ensure that traceability is adequately addressed throughout all stages of the Change management/Problem resolution process by assessing the following application of bi-directional traceability: between each Problem Report (PR) and Change Request (CR); between each CR and its analysis and evaluation; between approval of CR and identification of software modification; between each denial of CR/PR and reason for denial; between each identified software modification and its implementation and verification; and between each modification implementation and regression testing.

The RM traceability process: The purpose of this process is to ensure that traceability is adequately addressed throughout all stages of the risk management process by assessing the following application of bi-directional traceability: between analysis of risk to the identification of hazards; between hazardous situation and software item; between software item and specific software cause; between each hazard to estimation of risk of each hazard; between each risk estimation to evaluation of acceptability of the risk; between hazards and identification and implementation of risk control measures; between implementation and verification of risk control measures; and between residual risk to assessment of acceptability of those risks.

The SDLC traceability process: The purpose of the SDLC Traceability Process is to ensure that traceability is adequately addressed throughout all stages of the SDLC process by assessing the following application of bi-directional traceability: between software requirements and system requirements; between software requirement and software architectural and software detailed design; between software detailed design and source code; between software requirements and source code; and between each phase of the SDLC and test for that phase.

Traceability best practice process: The purpose of the Traceability Best Practices process is to ensure that traceability best practices are established when implementing traceability through the SDLC and the supporting processes of risk management and change management. This is achieved by assessing if a company policy and a standard operating procedure for traceability have been developed, the resources required for successful traceability implementation are made available, and the appropriate techniques for successful implementation are deployed.

6 Automation of Traceability Assessment and Maintenance: The Future of Traceability Best Practices

As discussed in section 2, there is imminent need for the automation of traceability assessment and maintenance. Considering the clear definition cited in the introduction, traceability is the ability to establish links (or traces) between source artefacts and target artefacts [2]. According to the state of the art of web technology, we have today the means to identify and to establish links between immense numbers of artifacts which can even be seamlessly traced on the basis of these links.

Our vision is that the processes defined in the Traceability Process Assessment Model of this paper could be executed using a system accessing all of the necessary artifacts which would be accessible on the web (internet or intranet). By consequent, this system would ultimately have full traceability assessment and also resulting traceability maintenance capability.

Application Lifecycle Management (ALM) tool vendors are perfectly aware of this need, and some of the tools [21] contain features supporting a given level of automation. However, current ALM tools have following inherent weaknesses:

- Traceability is basically restricted to the closed ALM system. APIs are available for providing internal data, however, no standardized open form of exchange was made possible before the below discussed OSLC initiative.
- Useful traceability reports can be generated, but they are static while requirements and identified defects are very dynamically changing artefacts, and may even originate from outside the ALM system.
- Assessors and users may be easily confused by the complexity of the set of widgets, such as buttons, text fields, tabs, and links which are provided to access and edit all properties of resources at any time.
- Assessors and users need to reach destinations such as web pages and views by clicking many links and tabs whose understanding is not essential for the assessment.

Open Services for Lifecycle Collaboration (OSLC) is the recently formed cross-industry initiative aiming to define standards for compatibility of software lifecycle tools. Its aim is to make it easy and practical to integrate software used for development, deployment, and monitoring applications. This aim seems to be too obvious and overly ambitious at the same time. However, despite its relatively short history starting in 2008, OSLC is the only potential approach to achieve these aims at a universal level, and is already widely supported by industry.

The unprecedented potential of the OSLC approach is based on its foundation on the architecture of the World Wide Web, which is unquestionably proven to be powerful and scalable, and on the generally accepted software engineering principle to always focus first on the simplest possible things that will work.

The elementary concepts and rules are defined in the OSLC Core Specification which sets out the common features that every OSLC Service is expected to support using the terminology and generally accepted approaches of the World Wide Web Consortium (W3C). One of the key approaches is Linked Data being the primary technology leading to the Semantic Web which is defined by W3C as providing a common framework that allows data to be shared and reused across application, enterprise, and community boundaries.

The OSLC Core Specification is actually the core on which all lifecycle element (domain) specifications must be built upon. Examples of already defined OSLC Specifications include:

- Architecture Management
- Asset Management
- Automation
- Change Management
- Quality Management
- Requirements Management

Let us focus for example on the Change Management Specification which is of particular interest in the Traceability PAM discussed in this paper. Its version 3.0 is under development in 2014, and builds of course on the Core, briefly mentioned above, to define the resource types, properties and operations to be supported by any OSLC Change Management (OSLC CM) provider.

Examples of possible OSLC CM Resources include defect, enhancement, task, bug, activity, and any application lifecycle management or product lifecycle management artifacts. Resource types are defined by the properties that are allowed and required in the resource.

The properties defined in the OSLC Change Management Specification describe these resource types and the relationships between them and all other resources. The relationship properties describe in most general terms for example that

- the change request affects a plan item
- the change request is affected by a reported defect
- the change request tracks the associated Requirement
- the change request implements associated Requirement
- the change request affects a Requirement

7   Conclusion

To assist medical device organizations improve their traceability, a traceability assessment model has been developed. This model, which consists of four processes, is based on the ISO 15504 structure and used the TIPA transformation process for development. By assessing for all traceability requirements from the medical device standards and guidelines and by assessing for traceability implementation best practices, this traceability assessment model will assist medical device organisations understand their actual traceability performance and management of activities, and the potential for improvement. It will also allow an organisation assess the state of a supplier's traceability process.

If our envisioned system, based on the processes defined in the Traceability Process Assessment Model of this paper, could seamlessly access the resources and their relationships using OSLC across all tools applied in the entire software development lifecycle (SDLC), then traceability process assessment and maintenance could be fully automated.

Acknowledgement. This research is supported by the Science Foundation Ireland (SFI) Stokes Lectureship Programme, grant number 07/SK/I1299, the SFI Principal Investigator Programme, grant number 08/IN.1/I2030 (the funding of this project was awarded by Science Foundation Ireland under a co-funding initiative by the Irish Government and European Regional Development Fund), and supported in part by Lero - the Irish Software Engineering Research Centre (http://www.lero.ie) grant 10/CE/I1855.

References

1. Kannenberg, A., Saiedian, D.H.: Why Software Requirements Traceability Remains a Challenge. CrossTalk the Journal of Defense Software Engineering 5 (2009)
2. Gotel, O., Mader, P.: Acquiring Tool Support for Traceability. In: Cleland-Huang, J., Gotel, O., Zisman, A. (eds.) Software and Systems Traceability. Springer, Heidelberg (2012)

3. FAA: DO-178C, Software Considerations in Airborne Systems and Equipment Certification. RTCA (2012)
4. FDA: Guidance for the Content of Premarket Submissions for Software Contained in Medical Devices. CDRH, Rockville (2005)
5. ISO: 26262: Road Vehicle. Functional Safety (2011)
6. Lucia, A.D., Marcus, A., Oliveto, R., Poshyvanyk, D.: Information Retrieval Methods for Automated Traceability Recovery. In: Cleland-Huang, J., Gotel, O., Zisman, A. (eds.) Software and Systems Traceability, pp. 88–111. Springer, Heidelberg (2012)
7. Cleland-Huang, J.: Just Enough Requirements Traceability. In: Proceedings of the 30th Annual International Computer Software and Applications Conference, vol. 01, pp. 41–42. IEEE Computer Society (2006)
8. Jarke, M.: Requirements tracing. Commun. ACM 41, 32–36 (1998)
9. Regan, G., Mc Caffery, F., Mc Daid, K., Flood, D.: The Barriers to Traceability and their Potential Solutions: Towards a Reference Framework. In: 38th Euromicro Conference on Software Engineering and Advanced Applications, pp. 319–322. IEEE, Cesme (2012)
10. McCaffery, F., Casey, V.: Med-Trace: Traceability Assessment Method for Medical Device Software Development. In: EuroSPI, Denmark, pp. 1.1–1.8 (2011)
11. Mader, P., Gotel, O., Philippow, I.: Motivation Matters in the Traceability Trenches. In: Proceedings of the 2009 17th IEEE International Requirements Engineering Conference, RE, pp. 143–148. IEEE Computer Society (2009)
12. ISO/IEC: 15504-5 : An exemplar Process Assessment Model. ISO, Switzerland (2006)
13. SIG, A.: Automotive SPICE® Process Assessment Model (2010)
14. ECCS: Space Product Assurance- Software process assessment and improvement – Part 2: Assessor instrument. ESA Requirements and Standards Division, Netherlands (2010)
15. Institute, S.E.: CMMI® for Development, Version 1.3. Improving processes for developing better products and services (2010)
16. Ambler, S.: Tracing Your Design. Dr.Dobb's Journal: The World of Software Development (1999)
17. Ambler, http://www.agilemodeling.com/essays/agileRequirementsBestPractices
18. ISO/IEC: 15504-2: Process assessment — Performing an assessment. ISO, Switzerland (2003)
19. ISO/IEC: 12207: Systems and software engineering — Software life cycle processes. ISO, Geneva, Switzerland (2008)
20. Barafort, B., Renault, A., Picard, M., Cortina, S.: A transformation process for building PRMs and PAMs based on a collection of requirements – Example with ISO/IEC 20000. SPICE, Nuremberg, Germany (2008)
21. Gartner, http://www.techostan.com/docs/quadrant.pdf

Project Valorisation through Agility and Catering for Stakeholder Expectations

Elli Georgiadou[1], Kerstin Siakas[2], and Richard Messnarz[3]

[1] Middlesex University, School of Science and Technology, and SEEQMA Ltd, UK
e.georgiadou@mdx.uk
[2] Alexander Technological Educational Institute of Thessaloniki, Greece
siaka@it.teithe.gr
[3] ISCN, Austria
rmess@iscn.com

Abstract. Project valorisation is paramount for gaining value in an increasingly competitive world. There is evidence that the majority of projects even when they are completed within budget and time fail to valorise (disseminate and exploit) their results so that they can deliver value to the organisation. Projects often have many stakeholders with different requirements and expectations. Identifying and understanding synergies, conflicts and changing requirements hold the key to project success. In this paper we discuss the challenges and failures of lack of valorisation from industry, government, academia and the European Union. Using the VALO project we demonstrate how the integration of the project plan, the quality plan and the sustainability plan started delivering value to a multiplicity of stakeholders throughout the project lifetime and beyond its completion. We propose a meta-framework for this integration taking into account the process maturity of an organisation for successful valorisation of projects.

Keywords: Valorisation, stakeholder expectations, agility.

1 Introduction

Projects and systems however small in size, nature, complexity and duration need to be planned and implemented within specified constraints of time and cost. The assumption is that the user requirements are understood fully and are satisfied at least in terms of functionality and reliability. However, most projects including those funded by the European Union (EU) suffer from lack of flexibility and adaptability to changes in requirements. The EU templates of activities and deliverables follow largely a sequential model, and although a small degree of tolerance on completion dates is allowed, there is no adaptability in terms of budget and indeed non-completion of any deliverables is subject to penalties.

Assuming that a project is completed within time and budget and it also delivers all planned functionality and outputs can we be sure that it will continue delivering value after its completion? All projects need to valorise their results i.e. disseminate and exploit their results for sustainability and maximisation of achievements after their completion. Exploitation includes transfer of results and best practices to different and broader contexts; potential tailoring to the needs of others; continuation after the funding period has finished; influences on policy and practice; serving the public good. The emphasis is on optimising the value of a project and on boosting its impact. The concept of valorisation expert training and certification is intended for training professionals to help dissemination and exploitation of knowledge that is created in all kinds of projects, including innovation, EU projects etc, in a sustainable way. By this way the benefits of investments that are made into developing new knowledge can be multiplied. The training is aiming to developing professionals for increasing their skills and competences in valorisation. In order to maintain uniform level of professionalism, certification is also created for the professionals in this area.

Valorisation needs to become a solid and integrated part of product development projects. Companies with more than one product development project targeted to the same market and same customers may need to interlink the valorisation activities between these projects and why not even create clusters of companies using common valorisation tools aiming to the same markets and customers instead of competing against each other. In the valorisation process the early identification of information of interest to potential stakeholders is important. This information then needs to be transformed into relevant format and communicated further to the potential stakeholders, who in turn receive the information, reflect on the need for the product or output of the project in their activities and business. The aims for the organisation / project that want to reach potential stakeholders are to find a way to get connected and linked into different stakeholder networks, expert clusters, and organisational strategies of leading industry to get the ideas, outcomes and project accepted, exploited and used in a broad sense. Stakeholders have different perceptions and values dependent on context (e.g. group, professional, organisational and national culture). These perceptions can also change depending on political, economical, social and technological influences. Therefore it is important to constantly monitor and send signals to suitable audience to continue their interest and to create new interest. A good valorisation strategy must find ways to disseminate and network into the industry. Contemporary business approaches include communication between product development projects and customers, called open innovation. Also social media is increasingly used to catch the opinion of the potential customer/user and to spread the information in a word-of mouth manner (Siakas et al., 2012).

2 Stakeholder Requirements and Expectations

Often stakeholder requirements are not fully understood and specified, additionally requirements change due to internal and/or external demands. Sequential and rigid process models (waterfall type) have generated their own share of failed projects that do not satisfy stakeholder requirements.

Identifying the stakeholders and understanding their requirements is paramount for a solid foundation of every project. A cyclic process model such is the Deming PDCA (Figure 1) emphasise the need to evaluate and repeat every stage of the process until the quality standards are met.

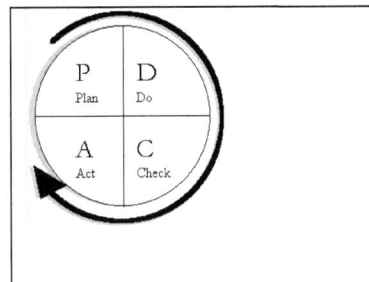

Fig. 1. The Deming Wheel

(Adapted from http://qualitysafety.bmj.com/content/early/2013/09/11/bmjqs-2013-001862/F1.large.jpg)

Gilb's Evolutionary Development and in particular his ValuePro Management Process (Figure 2) incorporates learning and stakeholder values as well as systematic quantification.

Fig. 2. Value Pro Management Process (Source: http://www.gilb.com//Site+Content+Overview)

Crossan and Apaydin (2010) provided a systematic review of frameworks for organisational innovation, and Gavenda et al. (2013) examined the ways in which innovation and entrepreneurship can be fostered with reference to VET projects. Brodie and Woodman (2010) use the terms stakeholder and stakeholder value interchangeably. They define the term 'stakeholder' as *"any group of people with an interest in the system, who can be identified by role and/or by location. An assumption is made that conflict over value within such a group is reasonably likely to be rare"*. We consider that this assumption is risky as there is evidence of potential conflict between value expectations by different stakeholders.

Thompson and Austin (2006) believe that *"Values frame our value judgements regarding courses of action and our judgements of value regarding the merits of attributes of products or services. They form value systems that are held at the individual and organisational levels. Any meaningful attempt to deliver value to multiple stakeholders involved in the same project must consider their values. Value and values are intimately linked and the action of one upon the other must be considered"*. They further developed a three-part VALiD Framework which aims to help stakeholders to:

1. understand each others' values so that compromises can be made when reaching a single solution;
2. inform project design by setting targets for value delivery in the form of benefits, sacrifices and resources; and
3. judge value delivery performance throughout the project life cycle, from inception through to obsolescence.

Sheriff and Georgiadou (2011) explored the relationship between quality and value. They identified a multiplicity of types of value, its nature and origin and they produced a taxonomy of value shown in Figure 3.

3   Cyclic Models and Agility

As shown by the cyclic models such as the PDCA, and Gilb's Value Process Model the process is repetitive just as the notion of the circle which never ends. Every repetition of the cycle demands and allows for review and improvement. However, if the project plan adheres to a linear process model such as the Waterfall necessary changes of requirements cannot be accommodated easily. For example, the standardisation of the EU template for project proposes could induce a degree of rigidity in terms of non-negotiable overall project costs. In contrast an agile approach can cater for misunderstood, missing and/or changing requirements. Milestones and interim delivery times can be adjusted as long as the overall timeframe is adhered to excepting any extenuating circumstances. Thus, funding allocations among partners and work packages can be renegotiated within the consortium provided the allowed percentage variations are within the allowed limits specified.

Risks can be identified and managed more effectively in agile processes as evidenced by their extensive and successful use in Software Projects (Sheriff & Georgiadou, 2011).

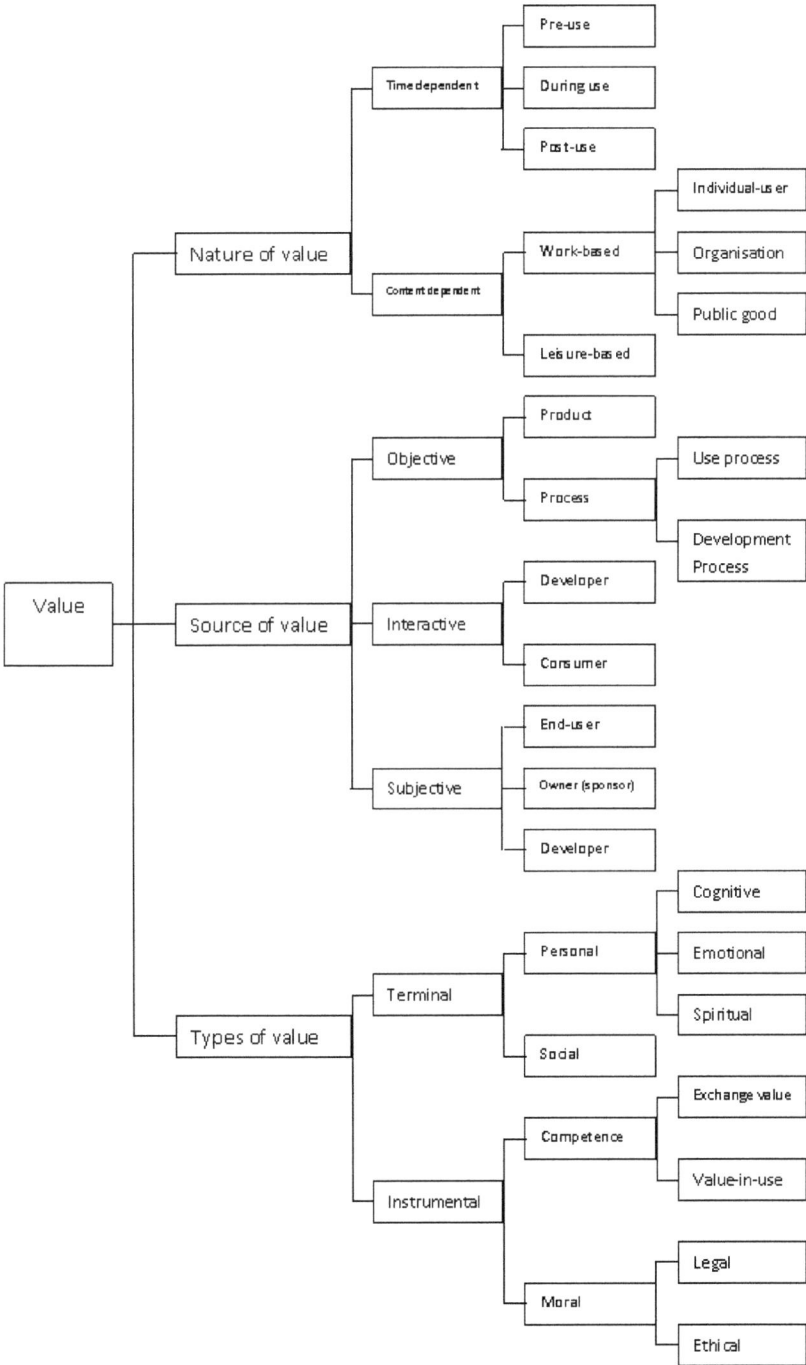

Fig. 3. Value Analysis Tree (source: Sheriff and Georgiadou (2011))

4 Building Valorisation into the Project Plan

Building on expertise and know-how the INCISIV model was developed particularly for the VALO project to help manage the Quality Assurance, Quality Monitoring and Quality Enhancement of the project. Incorporating the PDCA cycle (or Deming wheel) at every stage of the process as well as Sustainability and Evaluation the INCISIV model provides agility, adaptability and continuous improvement.

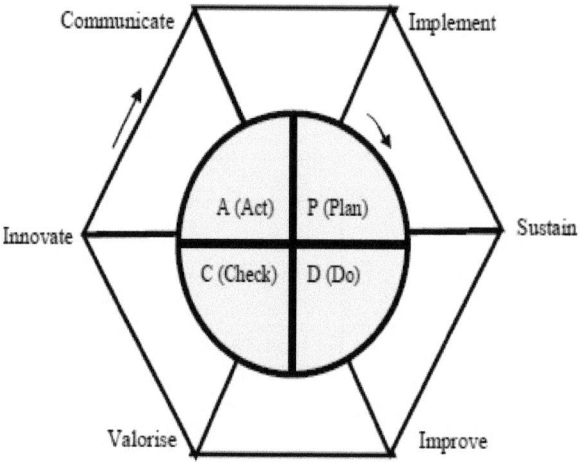

Fig. 4. InCISIV model (Siakas and Georgiadou, 2012)

Further to using INCISIV the need Siakas and Georgiadou emphasised the need to identify, pre-empt and possibly avoid tensions which could evolve into conflicts. One such potential conflict could be the lack of awareness and appreciation of cultural diversity. Teams, projects, consortia are these days increasingly multicultural. The ultimate object of innovation is to create and sustain value, preferably across various cultures.

As an evolution from InCISIV the INCUVA meta-framework (Figure 5) was proposed (Sheriff et al, 2013), which comprises the following four dimensions:

(1) defining and understanding value
(2) determining the potential value manifestations
(3) understanding the diverse cultural settings in which the innovation would be used
(4) developing and adopting effective dissemination strategies and tools to optimise the value of the innovation.

		Tensions →		
Synergies ↓		Innovation	Culture	Value
	Innovation	Innovation: Application of new ideas to the products, processes, or other aspects of the activities of a firm that lead to increased value (Greenhalgh and Rogers, 2010)	Control in decision making, control of information flow, or even perceived control in the form of reward systems Cultural clashes Culture induced stress	Non-alignment of value perceptions Temporality of value Conceived value does not always equate to Object and/Operative value Short term orientation
	Culture	Supportive structures with cooperative teams and group interaction. Clearly specified cross-cultural goals Support mechanisms such as appropriate reward and recognition schemes. Behaviour that encourages innovation (mistake handling, continuous learning culture, open communication, competitiveness, support for change, encouragement of risk taking and idea generation. Freedom and autonomy)	Culture: A set of assumptions, beliefs, attitudes and values that are shared by existing members and taught to new members of a group (e.g. organisation)	Conflicting perceptions of value. Cultural idiosyncrasies Past Orientation
	Value	Innovator's appreciation of the complexity of value Catering for the time-variant and context dependent user conceptions of value Alignment between the innovator's perception of value and that of the beneficiaries The extent to which the beneficiaries like and hence utilise the innovated object or service	Cultures characterised by collectivism, mutual aid, reciprocity, and Diversity Future Orientation Doing rather than being culture	Value: A function of utility, environmental conditions and circumstance of evaluator at the time of evaluation (Sinden and Worrell, 1979)

Fig. 5. The INCUVA Meta-Framework (Source: Sheriff et al, 2013)

Innovation is seen as the main vehicle for value creation in business organisations as well as in civic societies. Consequently, funding agencies and businesses continue to invest huge amounts of money and other resources on innovative projects with a view to creating and sustaining the desired value outcomes. However, creating value is not the same as sharing and sustaining value, especially when such value needs to be shared and sustained in a multicultural space. Sheriff et al, (2013) analysed the interaction of three key elements, namely Innovation, Culture and Value, that could facilitate or inhibit the sharing and sustenance of value created through innovative projects.

5 Case Studies

5.1 Case Study 1 – Using VALO in European Industry - New Valorisation Methods Impacting the Traditional Networking Approach

The VALO skills set also addresses a new strategy of marketing which evolves with the increasing networking capability of the society. If you nowadays can create a vision and post it into a network which automatically transports it worldwide and finds supporters then this leads to a snowball effect in a net.

For two European networks, EuroSPI and ECQA, we applied the VALO principles and elaborated a 2020 marketing strategy for the future.

The workshops consisted of 5 major phases and a number of online meetings to discuss the homework of the collaborating researchers and industry managers.

Phase 1
- Register at ECQA.ORG as Valorisation Expert
- Connect to learning portal.
- Think about how EuroSPI / ECQA could use in: Create Stakeholder value, Mainstreaming

Phase 2
- Discuss in a GotoMeeting Telko with all the exercise, elaborate a strategy proposal to implement the three topics in a EuroSPI / ECQA
- Review the uploaded materials and refine the materials

Phase 3
- Login again at ECQA.ORG as valorisation Expert
- Connect to learning portal.
- Think about how EuroSPI / ECQA could use: Exploitation Strategy, Communication to Potential Stakeholders

Phase 4
- Discuss in a GotoMeeting Telko with all the exercise, elaborate a strategy proposal to implement the three topics in a EuroSPI / ECQA
- Review the uploaded materials and refine the materials

Phase 5
- Integrate the valorisation strategy for EuroSPI
- Integrate the valorisation strategy for ECQA

The skills element stakeholder value in VALO forces companies to think about the typical customers and stakeholders, their interest profile and how you can add value for them. In the skills element mainstreaming a vision and goal set is build which could have the power to create a critical mass of your stakeholders to follow the ideas you created.

In VALO also the networking approach is explained and we used the analysed vision and goals as a basis to create a networking and social media based marketing strategy. The skills element exploitation gives guidance about what an exploitation plan should consider, and the skills element communication to stakeholders elaborates different scenarios to link the stakeholders in a continuous communication to your vision and goals.

5.1.1 Examples from Practice

In the following we illustrate some selected parts of the VALO analysis results for EuroSPI. This VALO approach can be used for any part of partner network or industry association.

Fig. 6. Contents of the VALO result elaborated by EuroSPI members

Applying the training from VALO a team of EuroSPI members created a valorisation strategy for EuroSPI, as can be seen in figure 6.

In the stakeholder analysis we used a core value analysis approach. The core values, which every group would share is in the middle and different segments of typical industry and research are surrounding the core (see Figure 7). The main difficulty in this analysis is that you identify many stakeholders with different interest profiles, but what is the core that interests all and drives the common interest to move the crowd?

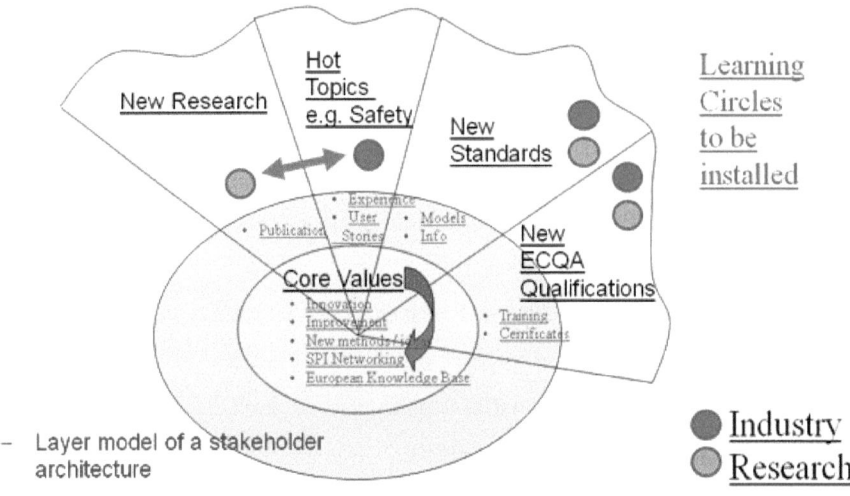

Fig. 7. Core Value Analysis Model

Once the core interests are analysed a new (element mainstreaming) vision and set of goals must be set up towards the efforts and the interest of the stakeholders will be driven (see Figure 8). This work included the creation of a new mainstreaming mission to build a EuroSPI community / crowd. In the exploitation the vision is converted into a set of concrete measures to be implemented in a continuous manner (learning cycles). Figure 9 shows examples of such measures in the EuroSPI case study.

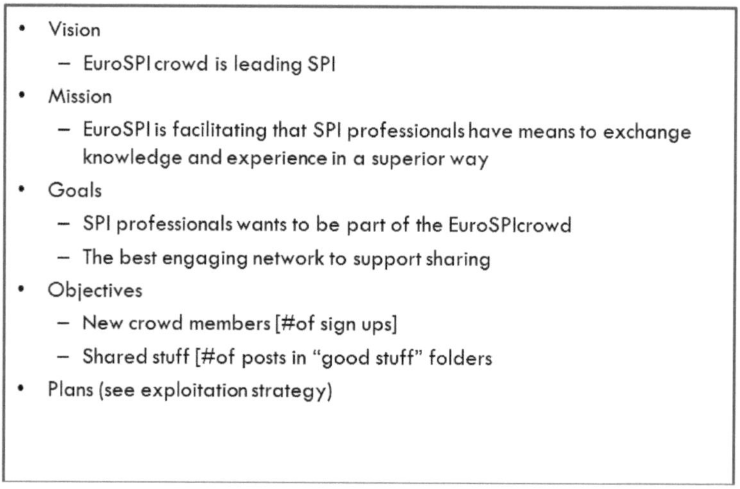

- Vision
  - EuroSPI crowd is leading SPI
- Mission
  - EuroSPI is facilitating that SPI professionals have means to exchange knowledge and experience in a superior way
- Goals
  - SPI professionals wants to be part of the EuroSPIcrowd
  - The best engaging network to support sharing
- Objectives
  - New crowd members [#of sign ups]
  - Shared stuff [#of posts in "good stuff" folders
- Plans (see exploitation strategy)

Fig. 8. An example screen shot from the material elaborated for mission building

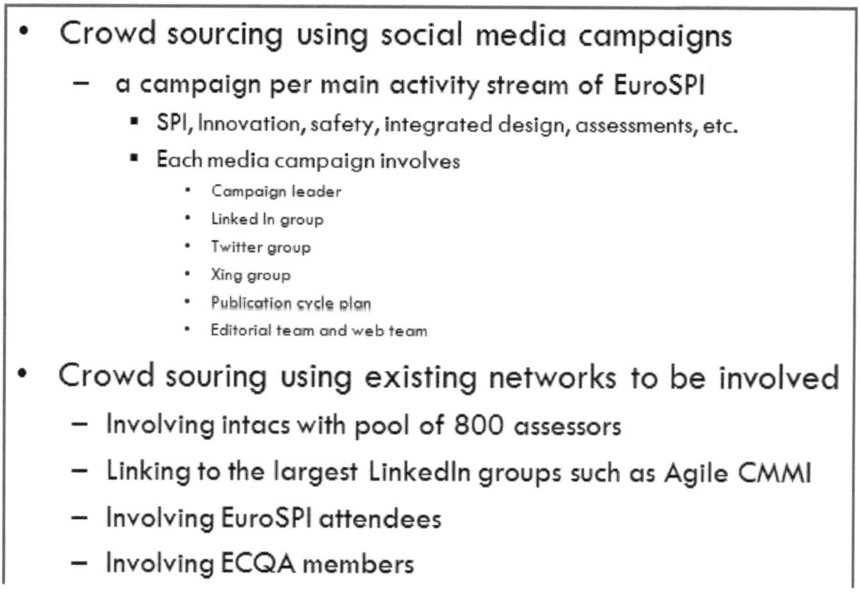

- **Crowd sourcing using social media campaigns**
  - **a campaign per main activity stream of EuroSPI**
    - SPI, Innovation, safety, integrated design, assessments, etc.
    - Each media campaign involves
      - Campaign leader
      - Linked In group
      - Twitter group
      - Xing group
      - Publication cycle plan
      - Editorial team and web team
- **Crowd souring using existing networks to be involved**
  - Involving intacs with pool of 800 assessors
  - Linking to the largest LinkedIn groups such as Agile CMMI
  - Involving EuroSPI attendees
  - Involving ECQA members

Fig. 9. An example measure for exploitation and communication with stakeholders (VALO elements)

5.1.2 Conclusions from This Case Study

The VALO approach works for networks in industry and research. It can lead to a new networking based valorisation strategy based on crowd sourcing, networking, mainstreaming and vision building.

5.2 Case 2: EU Projects – VALO

The VALO project was funded by the EU Leonardo da Vinci Transfer of Innovation (TOI) for two years until end of December 2013. The aims of the project were to develop training material for lifelong learning. The trainings are leading to certification of skills and competences in valorisation by the European Certification and Qualification Organisation (ECQA). The main purpose of the project is thus to create readiness for training and qualification of valorisation experts.

The consortium consisted of seven partners from five different countries (Austria, Ireland, Finland, Greece, UK). Since the project was submitted as a TOI project to the Greek National Agency there were three Greek partners, including the project co-ordinator, a Higher Educational Institution, a Vocational Educational Institution (VET) and a Chamber of Commerce and Industry.

Already in the kick-off meeting the need to '*practice as we preach*' was discussed and a valorisation strategy was created including local dissemination activities needed from each consortium partner to spread the information about the project to potential interested stakeholders and to mainstream to suitable decision makers. A common Web-page (www.valo.teithe.gr) was created and evaluated by all partners. Also every partner created their own local web-pages in their own languages. Social networking was utilised including social business network groups in LinkedIn and other social media networks, such as Face book, Twitter and BlogSpot. A needs analysis was carried out in the beginning of the project by asking member companies of Thessaloniki Chamber of Commerce and Industry in Greece, as well as the European industry participating in EuroSPI 2012 their opinion about the planned content (Skill Card) of the ECQA Valorisation Expert training material. The feedback was good and there was a clear indication of the need of this job-role in the market.

It was decided to develop a basic set of units and elements to cover the main issues of dissemination, exploitation and valorisation methods. However, during the pilot trainings it became clear that depending on the previous skills and experiences of the trainees the teaching method needed to be flexible and build on group dynamics for added value by all involved stakeholders. Thus industrial trainees created valorisation strategies for their own projects (companies). An essential feature of the trainings built on knowledge sharing and participant and group synergies.

Finally within the project lifetime a VALO newsletter was created and sent out to potential stakeholders. Also articles were published in the ECQA newsletter and the Thessaloniki Chamber of Commerce and Industry (TCCI) quarterly bulletin. The concept of VALO was published in six papers/articles in five Scientific Peer-reviewed International Conferences (EuroSPI 2012, 2013, INSPIRE 2012, SQM 2013, EEEE 2013) to disseminate the VALO approach in academia and industry. The scientific publications were published in the proceedings of the conferences including Springer.

In addition four presentations concerning VALO were also made in the International Conference ECQA days 2012, 2013 and the abstracts were published in the proceedings of the ECQA days' conferences.

A direct impact of the VALO project was the creation of a EuoSPI and ECQA Valorisation strategy. The EuroSPI VALO strategy was elaborated with a tool for planning Social Media campaigns; ECQA is establishing a Social Media strategy for successful valorisation. Also two Greek companies, members of the TCCI are currently implementing valorisation strategies with the consultancy of VALO trainees for increased dissemination, exploitation and sustainability.

In total 204 trainees were trained in the pilot study and 144 ECQA Valorisation Expert certifications were issued as well as 15 trainers certificates. A questionnaire was completed by all trainees regarding the training material quality. The results were analysed and improvements were made. Also a follow-up questionnaire in English was created to evaluate the usefulness of the course for the participants. This questionnaire will be translated into German Finnish and Greek and distributed about six months after project completion.

On the whole it can be said that the VALO project covered needs of improving skills and competences of the European workforce (and beyond) in valorisation matters. A Job Role committee has been created to continuously update the training material and an exploitation agreement has been created between the partners who took part in the creation of the training material to cater for further exploitation of the outcomes of the project.

The implementation of the project followed the InCISIV model and the stakeholder value aspects were handled using the INCUVA meta-model. Quality assurance, quality monitoring and enhancement as well as sustainability were incorporated into the original project plan submitted with the proposal. The philosophy was based on agile principles and on a belief that neither quality nor sustainability should be left as afterthoughts. Activities were re-scheduled as a response to availability patterns of resources both technical and human ones.

6 Maturity of Process and Valorisation

Valorisation of projects requires understanding of stakeholder expectations and process planning so that solid foundations can be laid for successful implementation and dissemination was well as sustainability planning to ensure added value is gained during and beyond the lifetime of the project.

The general process maturity level of the consortium member organisations and even of the individuals involved determines the capability of understanding the requirements of the project, the constraints and risks. It is natural that different consortium members will have reached a different level of maturity. Also different cultures are likely to have differing levels of tolerance and discipline to deadlines. Technical knowhow and expertise, as well as project management experience and overall levels of commitment affect the way in which the consortium as a whole is able to implement and valorise projects. During the VALO project implementation insights gained in the effort to plan its valorisation lead to the development of the VALO$_5$ (Georgiadou and Siakas, 2013) based largely on the architecture of CMMI. The VALO$_5$ model shown in Figure 10 represents the maturity level that characterises the valorisation process and its likelihood of success within a project team, an organisation, a group, a partnership/consortium. The circles underneath the steps (levels) depict the PDCA circle. Continuous effort, awareness and commitment are required for valorisation process improvement.

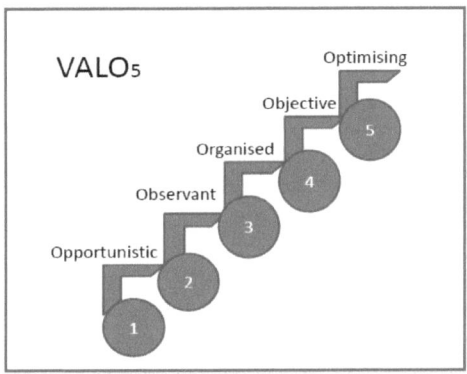

Fig. 10. The VALO$_5$- Valorisation Maturity Process (Georgiadou and Siakas, 2013)

At the objective (fourth) level measurements are in place. Data are collected, innovators are recognised and rewarded and systematically sponsored, knowledge is shared across the whole organisation. Exploitation of innovations is institutionalised. Innovations can be sustainable and successes are objectively measurable thus added value is gained (and quantified).

At the optimising level (fifth valorisation maturity level) data are collected, analysed, interpreted and knowledge is shared at all levels (teams, projects, departments, partners, stakeholders). Evaluation and feedback are institutionalised. Valorisation is planned, organised, funded and deployed across groups, departments, the whole organisation and across partnerships/consortia. Value-adding activities continue beyond the completion of projects resulting in sustained improvements.

7   Conclusion and Future Work

Integrating quality management and sustainability management in a project plan and implementing using a cyclic process model like InCISIV ensures effective monitoring and controlling of risks as well as maximisation of opportunities for effective valorisation. Understanding the requirements of all stakeholders, avoiding and minimizing the possibility of conflict and exploiting synergies provide a fertile ground for valorising project outputs and maximize impact. Quality and sustainability must not be afterthoughts but an integral part of any project.

References

1. Brodie, L., Woodman, M.: Absolute Scales to Express Stakeholder Value for Improving Support for Prioritization. ENASE 2010, pp. 48–57 (2010)
2. Crossan, M.M., Apaydin, M.: A Multi-Dimensional Framework of Organizational Innovation: A Systematic Review of the Literature. Journal of Management Studies 47(6), 1154–1191 (2010)
3. Gavenda, M., Riel, A., Azevedo, A., Pais, M., Homolová, E., Balcar, J., Antinori, A., Metitiero, G., Giorgakis, G., Photiades, P., Ekert, D., Messnarz, R., Tichkiewitch, S.: Fostering Innovation and Entrepreneurship in European VET: EU Project "From Idea to Enterprise". In: McCaffery, F., O'Connor, R.V., Messnarz, R. (eds.) EuroSPI 2013. CCIS, vol. 364, pp. 282–293. Springer, Heidelberg (2013)
4. Georgiadou, E., Siakas, K.: VALO^5 – Innovation, Maturity Growth, Quality and Valorisation. In: McCaffery, F., O'Connor, R.V., Messnarz, R. (eds.) EuroSPI 2013. CCIS, vol. 364, pp. 294–299. Springer, Heidelberg (2013)
5. Messnarz, R.: From process improvement to learning organizations. Software Process Improvement in Practice (SPIP) Journal 11(3), 287–294 (2006)
6. Sheriff, M., Georgiadou, E.: Relating Software Quality Models and Process Methods to User Value. International Journal of Human Capital and IT Professionals 4(2), 27–42 (2013)
7. Sheriff, M., Georgiadou, E., Siakas, K., Abeysinghe, G.: Towards extending the Balanced Scorecard with an explicit Value Model. In: Georgiadou, E., Ross, M., Staples, G. (eds.) Quality Comes of Age, The BCS Quality Specialist Group's Annual International 21st Software Quality Management (SQM) Conference, pp. 117–129. British Computer Society, London (2013) ISBN is 978 0 9563140 8
8. Sheriff, M., Georgiadou, E.: The effect of software quality management and risk management on user value. In: 19th International Software Quality Management (SQM) Conference, Loughborough, UK (2011)
9. Sheriff, M., Georgiadou, E., Abeysinghe, G., Siakas, K.: INCUVA: A meta-framework for sustaining the value of innovation in multi-cultural settings. In: McCaffery, F., O'Connor, R.V., Messnarz, R. (eds.) EuroSPI 2013. CCIS, vol. 364, pp. 270–281. Springer, Heidelberg (2013)
10. Siakas, K., Georgiadou, E., Siakas, E.: The Quality Assurance Process of the VALO Project. In: Georgiadou, E., Ross, M., Staples, G. (eds.) Quality Comes of Age, The BCS Quality Specialist Group's Annual International 21st Software Quality Management (SQM) Conference, 3-5 September, pp. 139–152. British Computer Society, London (2013)
11. Siakas, K., Messnarz, R., Georgiadou, E., Naaranoja, M.: Launching Innovation in the Market Requires Competences in Dissemination and Exploitation. In: Winkler, D., O'Connor, R.V., Messnarz, R. (eds.) EuroSPI 2012. CCIS, vol. 301, pp. 241–252. Springer, Heidelberg (2012)
12. Thomson, D.S., Austin, S.A.: Using VALiD to understand value from the stakeholder perspective. In: Manage Projects To Maximise Value: Proceedings of 46th SAVE International Annual Conference, Savannah, Georgia, June 4-7 (2006)

Leadership in Sustainability

Gabriela Fistis[1], Tomislav Rozman[2], Andreas Riel[3], and Richard Messnarz[4]

[1] Universitatea Politehnica Timisoara, Romania
gabriela.fistis@denkstatt.ro
[2] DOBA Faculty Maribor, Slovenia
tomislav.rozman@bicero.com
[3] EMIRAcle c/o Grenoble Institute of Technology GSCOP UMR5272, France
andreas.riel@emiracle.eu
[4] ISCN LTD/GesmbH, Austria & Ireland
rmess@iscn.com

Abstract. In the last decades the innovation in engineering has been focused on producing reliable products and services. Also the international standards for work place safety, machine directive for safety and functional safety of a product have been considered. Usually such paradigm shifts in engineering mean that you must develop functions and services in these fields to sustain your leadership on the market. A new development in the last 10 years is the growing importance of social responsibility (Messnarz, 2014) based on the new published ISO 26000 standard (ISO 26000, 2010) for social responsibility. Based on that growing social awareness of industry and society new functions, features and services are developing which will form a large part of innovation in the next decade. This paper gives some outlook into that future.

Keywords: leadership, sustainability, lifelong learning, leadsus.

1 Introduction

Sustainable development is not country dependent and has to be a concentrated and cumulative direction coming from profit oriented organizations, regardless of the company's, institution's, or even non-profit organization's types of activities; all organizations have to act in a sustainable manner in order to preserve the environment and act in a social responsible way, above their economic orientation.

In recent years, important global issues surrounding energy security, unstable fuel prices and greenhouse gas emissions, as well as sustainable procurement, the purchase of raw materials from sustainable sources, ethical trade and corporate social responsibility (CSR), has led organizations increasing their commitment to move towards in a more sustainable business model, with great improvements of their carbon food print and adopting an energy efficient model. The United Nations' Division for Sustainable Development confirms these tendencies in the report "Trends in Sustainable Development – Towards Sustainable Consumption and Production" by registering a steep increase in the number of companies certified to ISO 14001 and

ISO 26000 (the environmental management and social responsibility standards), as well as an increase in the number of social and environment concerned consumers, revenue figures from Fair-trade products having grown to € 2.9 billion despite the recent economic troubles. The same report reveals that governments are also, following the sustainability trend by highlighting sustainable procurement policies, both in developed and in developing countries (UNDESA, 2010).

Furthermore, the European Sustainable Development Network in its ESDN Quarterly Report number 25 (Pisano et al., 2012), being published soon after the United Nations Conference on Sustainable Development (that take place on 20 - 22 June 2012), provides a comprehensive overview of the actions, policies and strategies to the Rio+20 (UNCSD, 2012), together with the conference outcomes, such as: outcomes on institutional framework for sustainable development.

The outcomes on institutional framework for sustainable development strengthen the three dimensions of sustainable development; wherein capacity building is one of the means of implementation and part of the sustainable development goals. The roles of technology, of technology transfer and of the science-policy interface are also, emphasized with a special focus on the need to facilitate informed policy decision-making on sustainable development issues. In this regards, capacity building has a major status together with the importance of human resource development that includes "training, the exchange of experiences and expertise, knowledge transfer and technical assistance for capacity-building" (Pisano et al., 2012). Also, the European Union Council's stand regarding Rio+20 is similarly oriented, according to press release given by EU Council in March 2012, in the period of Rio+20 conference preparation (EC, 2012). In this context, the Council of the European Union:

"Stresses that sustainable development cannot be achieved without respecting and promoting democracy, human rights, the rule of law, good governance, education, the role of youth and gender equality,

"Stresses the importance of gender equality and the vital role that women's equal economic and political participation has for achieving sustainable development and underlines that education is essential to build skills and competences;

"Underlines the important role played by cooperation on technology, research and innovation, education and training programmes and emphasizes the need to improve mechanisms for international research cooperation and for the development of information and communications technology on major sustainable development challenges."

2 Leadership in Sustainability

2.1 What Is Leadership?

What kind of characteristics make a good leader? What differentiates a leader from the manager (or a boss)? The boss: demands, relies on authority, issues ultimatums, says "I", uses people, takes credit, places blame, says "go", thinks "my way is the only way". In contrast, a leader coaches, relies on goodwill, generates enthusiasm, says "we", gives credit, accepts blame, says "let's go" and thinks "strength in unity".

The article of authors Avolio, Wlumbwa and Weber [1] explores the literature of current theories, research and future directions of leadership. They examined for example new-genre leadership, which focuses on symbolic leader behavior; visionary, inspirational messages, emotional feelings, ideological moral values, individualized attention and intellectual stimulation. These concepts are quite different as in traditional leadership: leader-follower relationship, setting goals, providing direction, providing support on the basis of the economic cost-benefit assumptions. As we see, the definition of leadership is changing in the research literature over the years. Moreover, e-leadership is becoming common in distributed organizations. Authors Boal and Hooijberg [2] argue that the essence of strategic leadership involves *the capacity to learn, the capacity to change, and managerial wisdom*.

2.2 Leaderships in Sustainability - Can Be Taught?

When we are talking about sustainability, we are talking first about values and then about knowledge and skills. The values are driven first by the families, and then by the society here we are talking about the education systems and not the least by the environment of leaving and working. Education today is crucial for the ability of leaders and citizens to find solutions and create new paths to a better future. Education for sustainability is mainly aimed at better understanding the complex interdependence between human needs and the natural environment, including socio-economical and cultural development in a local and global context. Education should focus on skills, abilities, values and perspectives that encourage and support the public's participation in the decisions that affect their community.

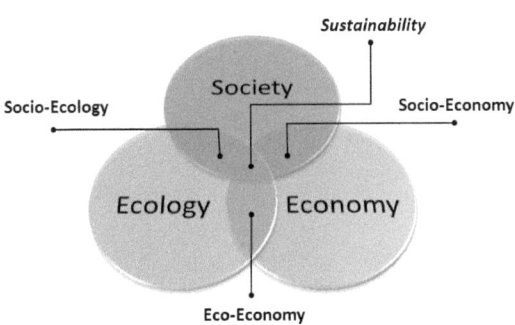

Fig. 1. What is sustainability?

2.3 What Is Sustainability?

A cross-section between managing environmental issues, economy, and society [Fig 1.]. Sustainability has become a keyword (or 'buzzword') for product development in several sectors. It is very important to note that sustainability covers three main areas, as is shown in the figure: Ecologic, economic, and social sustainability. Very often, sustainability is reduced to the ecologic factor. Really sustainable design, however, takes into account all three areas, including their overlapping regions. They make up our environment, the environment being defined as "everything which surrounds us".

Sustainability is an integrated approach to ecological, social and economic impact issues (both internal and external), which leads to long term, sustainable profit growth.

2.4 What Is Leadership in Sustainability?

"Leadership in sustainability" phrase is quite a new according to Google Trends (Fig. 1). Google Trends is a software which analyzes a percentage of Google web searches to determine how many searches have been done for the terms you've entered compared to the total number of Google searches done during that time. According to this analysis, the phrase started to interest people appear around 2011. But the first awards for leadership in sustainability were issued much earlier. For example, "Sustainability leaders award" has been around from 2006 (http://awards.edie.net/).

Fig. 2. Google trends – "Leadership in Sustainability"

What does the research of the academic literature show? M. Ferdig [3] in her article discusses the term 'sustainable leader' and his/her personal characteristics. She argues that the balance between contradictory demands for economically, socially and environmentally sustainable solutions is grounded in a personal ethics that reaches beyond self-interest. Dr. Wisser et al. [4] in his article explains the model of sustainability leadership in practice. His research is based on the interview of business leaders, which conforms the Cambridge sustainability leadership model. This model includes the following seven key characteristics of sustainability leadership: 1. systemic thinking, 2. emotional intelligence, 3. values orientation, 4. compelling vision, 5. inclusive style, 6. innovative approach and 7. long term perspective. He also offers a definition of sustainability leadership as: *"A sustainability leader is someone who inspires and supports action toward a better world"* [4]. The bottom-line of his research is that the main task of sustainable leader is survival.

2.5 Sustainability and Quality / IT Management

When we lower our perspective from the high level leadership down to the operations management within organizations and companies, ensuring its sustainability means dealing with real and everyday issues. Requirements for the sustainable business from the internal managerial, IT or Quality point of view could be defined with the following dimensions:

- **Sustainability of the organization's knowledge.** This means the knowledge of the employees should be preserved and re-used. Firstly, the knowledge how to perform operations should be preserved. One of most influential methodologies for this purpose is BPM – Business Process Management. When the organization identifies, models, documents and measures its processes, the knowledge is preserved and reused by many employees. One of such examples is the project HEI-UP, where authors identified and captured the processes in higher education institutions [5][6], which ensures their sustainability. Now, all other higher education institutions can re-use them, adapt them and become more sustainable. The next possible strategy to preserve the knowledge within the organization is establishing internal e-learning infrastructure and processes. The most knowledgeable employees should become the authors of the learning content and teachers to other employees. Some organizations are using various expert systems to preserve its knowledge. All mentioned systems act like a collective memory of the organization and ensuring its sustainability.
- **Sustainability of the information technology resources**. Information technology resources (databases, information systems, files, documents,...) are nowadays blood and flesh of the business operations. Sustainability of the data can and should be ensured on all organization's levels: from the infrastructure to the strategical and process level. On the infrastructure level, organization should ensure the redundancy of the computer equipment, which stores its data. On the organizational level, the organization should have established processes related to the business continuity (Business Continuity plan, backup and restore related processes etc.) [7]. According to several studies, the majority of companies which lose their business data, disappear within a year. Therefore we can conclude the sustainability of the organization's resources greatly influences the company's sustainability.
- **Sustainability of the resources needed for the organization operations**. The most important aspect for ensuring the sustainability of the organization is to ensure its resources (financial, human resources, materials, equipment, technology etc.), needed for the operations. This topics is so complex and huge it will not be covered within this article.

Mentioned aspects are somehow internal and not related to the organization's environment, which will be described in the following chapters. If we want to raise the awareness of the people about the sustainability, we should train them, coach them, provide them resources, case studies, good examples how sustainable thinking was implemented in similar companies. This is the main objective of the 2-year LeadSUS project, which was started on Nov. 2013.

3   About the LeadSUS Project

LeadSUS – Leadership in sustainability – Sustainability Manager is a Lifelong Learning Programme – Leonardo Da Vinci – Transfer of Innovation project, oriented to capacity building of employees in Sustainable management.

LeadSUS project's goal is to develop and provide a training program which is certified by a prestigious European organization (the European Certification and Qualification Association, ECQA, www.ecqa.org) so, that individuals (potential trainees as employees, managers of different organizations) are able to attain the broad range of experience, skills and knowledge needed to transform them into successful Leaders in Sustainability or Sustainability Managers, while also, being able to certify their competence (and get an European certificate as a recognition of their acquired professional competencies in the field). The general objective of LeadSUS project is to transfer and integrate a new skill at the level of European industry and institutions. The specific objectives are (LeadSUS, 2013):

Objective 1 - Adaptation, harmonization and refinement of existing training materials (from the existing training programs available on the ECQA e-learning platform, as: Environmental Management System, Business Process Management, Integrated Design Engineer) and their integration into a new, actual and original professional training program dedicated to employees of companies, institutions and VET organizations (European certification of the new training program and job role as "ECQA Certified Sustainability Manager", with respect to the ECQA framework and guidelines);

Objective 2 - Creation and development of the e-learning platform within the ECQA framework. This will allow trainees from different European countries to register and have access to the training materials (multimedia materials and references, case studies, exercises) in the field of sustainability management;

Objective 3 - Extension of the ECQA Capability Adviser, that is a process management software tool that has to be extended with LeadSUS formal assessment section;

Objective 4 - Testing and validation of the developed training program in two of the participating members' states (Romania and France);

Objective 5 - Building Capacity in Sustainability Management in three countries (Romania, Slovenia, France).

LeadSUS project addresses to a large target group consist of: managers (in the field of Facilities, Environmental, Occupational Health and Safety, Operational, Production, Quality, Engineering), employees with environmental responsibilities, public administration references or officers, environmental leaders, institutional environmental officers, technical employees. PhD. and master's students and generally, all employees of companies acting in different industry sectors with sustainable development responsibilities (LeadSUS, 2013).

The LeadSUS projects' objectives and activities will be developed in an international consortium consists of six partners, all VET organizations (of public or private nature), all having strong knowledge, competences and expertise in developing and implementing international projects and having complementary skills within the project. Most of them have already undertaken Lifelong Learning Program – Leonardo da Vinci projects as leaders or partners in other international consortiums. Due to their exceptionally wide spectrum of contacts in different sectors and levels of education due to their status of VET organizations, the partners will have a major impact in the dissemination process and the exploitation of the project's results (LeadSUS, 2013).

The innovative part of the project is that the consortium partners will evaluate the market needs for such skills in different countries were partners belong and will develop a complete and practical oriented training program which will match the need of public institutions employees /directors and also the employees / managers from private companies from 5 different countries.

The consortium members have a broad experience in capacity building (training development) in the area of sustainable development and is formed by: DENKSTATT Romania, UPT – Universitatea Politehnica Timisoara, Romania, Grenoble INP, BICERO Ltd., ISCN Ltd. and EMIRAcle association.

LeadSUS consortium's vision is to create a great impact of the training and European certification program in the case of organizations (companies and institutions) located in Romania, Slovenia and France. Employees (trainees of the LeadSUS program) that will follow the LeadSUS training and certification program will exploit their knowledge and new competencies in the direction of sustainable development of their organizations; leading sustainability is a key issue in companies and institutions. LeadSUS professional trainers in the field of sustainability management (trainers that will be trained during the LeadSUS project development and that will be evaluated and certified also by ECQA) will impact companies and institutions on a long term, providing capacity building for future leaders in sustainability and sustainability managers. LeadSUS project impact will be in three countries (Romania, Slovenia, and France) and four corresponding regions as: West and Bucharest Region in Romania, North-Eastern Slovenia, South – Eastern France. Long term impact of the LeadSUS project (together with its sustainability) at the European level will benefit from the support of a new ECQA certified job role in a new profession, available for EU citizens and more (LeadSUS, 2013).

3.1 Relation of the LeadSUS Project and the Process Improvement and Maturity

The partners consider that there is a close relationship between leadership in sustainability and organization capability and maturity in that the successful and sustainable deployment of sustainability issues in an organization requires organizational orientation across the entire organization hierarchy. This orientation, in turn, is only effective if it becomes an integral part of the organization's culture and strategy. This, however, is an essential property of high capability/maturity levels (according to both CMMI and SPICE).

Moreover, to ensure the company itself is sustainable, its core, management and supporting processes must be defined already at the start-up phase. We can say that well defined processes are pre-requisite for 'inner sustainability' or, ensuring the survival of the organization. To ensure this inner sustainability, many various methodologies exist: from Lean Six Sigma, BPM (Business Process Management), RECP (Resource Efficiency and Cleaner Production) etc. We can suspect that higher maturity processes achieve, more sustainable the organization is.

This kind of the sustainability must go hand-in-hand with the external sustainability (relations with the environment). Again, we can state that the processes, which have impact on the environment, should be highly mature, no matter which methodology we use to measure their maturity.

A manager which possess all mentioned skills in mind and combines them with the sense of social responsibility and emotional intelligence, is the real leader. So the main purpose of the project is to create the future leaders prepared for the challenges of tomorrow.

4 Sustainability in Engineering

Sustainability of products and services does not happen by itself; it has to be proactively taken into account in their design. In technical terms, it has to "engineered" using methods of integrated engineering design [7]. Hereby, the notion of the product/system life cycle plays a central role. In integrated design, the product/system life cycle comprises all phases that the product/system goes through from the idea to its end-of-life and revival. The principal phases that a product or system typically runs through in its life cycle are design, manufacturing, distribution, customization, and the end of life – including revival. In integrated design, we always have to take into account the closed life cycle, and thus integrated design goes beyond the often-cited notion of "from craddle to grave" to "from cradle to cradle".

Due to the importance of life cycle issues for integrated product/system design, systematic methods to take them into account have been developed. The Life Cycle Engineering (LCE) approach offers a set of methods which are able to optimize a product from an integrated technical, ecological and economic point of view. It is a Management Practice that combines all relevant information about Economy, Enrichment, Finance, and Technology in one Decision Support Tool. Its objective is to chart an optimum life cycle for a manufactured product. LCE connects different angles from which one should look at new developments and in particular, it involves technical, costing and ecological points of view. Companies using LCE are able to save money and therefore able to fulfil all demands on today's and future products and services.

There is an increasing interest in the ecological impacts of products. Complex products such as automobiles need effective methodologies and tools to evaluate their environmental impacts without neglecting the technical and cost implications, and the consequences of developing new products and services need to be analysed. Companies need to have sound methods, and powerful tools based on them. Life Cycle Engineering is also an approach to assess the environmental impacts in conjunction with economic impacts under consideration of technical boundary conditions. The scope of the assessment is usually the whole life cycle of a product consisting of production, use phase and end of life:

- The environmental impacts are assessed according to the ecological life cycle assessment (LCA).
- The economic impacts are assessed according to the life cycle costing (LCC) approach.
- Technical boundary conditions are taken into account providing some limitations on the model, thus verifying the technical feasibility.

Life Cycle Engineering increasingly aims at providing a complete system of support tools for the product/system life cycle. The economic objectives of LCE are adding value extension of business areas, reduction of fixed cost, and increase the profitability of products and services.

Life Cycle Assessment (LCA) is a technique for assessing the potential environmental aspects and potential aspects associated with a product (or service), by:

- compiling an inventory of relevant inputs and outputs,
- evaluating the potential environmental impacts associated with those inputs and outputs, and
- interpreting the results of the inventory and impact phases in relation to the objectives of the study.

When conducting an LCA, the design/development phase is usually excluded, since it is often assumed not to contribute significantly. However, one has to note that the decisions in the design/development phase highly influence the environmental impacts in the other life cycle stages. The design of a product strongly predetermines its behavior in the subsequent phases (e.g., the design of an automobile more or less determines the fuel consumption and emissions per kilometer driven in the use phase and has a high influence on the feasible recycling options in the end-of-life phase).

The figure illustrates this interdependency between design/development and the other phases of the life cycle. Therefore, if the aim of an LCA is the improvement of goods and services, one of the most important LCA applications, then the study should be carried out as early in the design process as possible and concurrently to the other design procedures. This applies analogously to the design or improvement of a process within a life cycle of a product, especially if interactions with other processes or life cycle stages can occur.

Life Cycle Costing (LCC), also called Whole Life Costing, is a technique to establish the total cost of ownership. It is a structured approach that addresses all the elements of this cost and can be used to produce a spend profile of the product or service over its anticipated life-span. The results of an LCC analysis can be used to assist management in the decision-making process where there is a choice of options. The accuracy of LCC analysis diminishes as it projects further into the future, so it is most valuable as a comparative tool when long term assumptions apply to all the options and consequently have the same impact. The life cycle cost of an item is the sum of all funds expended in support of the item from its conception and fabrication through its operation to the end of its useful life. Product Structure Assessment (ProSA) is used to assess a product's features in terms of disassembly, recycling and reuse from the viewpoint of cost optimization. It gives the inputs for calculating the end-of-life costs related to these activities.

In terms of tools that support Life Cycle Engineering (LCE), we distinguish between several general classes of IT systems in modern enterprise infrastructures:

- SCM (Supply Chain Management) – for the management of the supply chain;
- CRM (Customer Relationships Management) – the systems that store information about the history of customers' interaction with the company (business offers, purchases, services, etc.);
- PPC (Production Planning and Control) – for the management of manufacturing system (purchases, orders, production planning and scheduling);
- PLM (Product Lifecycle Management) – the class of IT systems that collect and manage the data that emerges during product lifecycle;

BPM (Business Process Management) – systems which support BPM methodology offer the fastest cycle from the conceptual process model (BPMN) to IT system. Those systems are highly customizable and can support any kind of business process.

The classes presented above are the general division from the functionality point of view. The particular system may have the functionality from the four areas (i.e., a mixture of them). This concerns especially the large IT systems from main players in the market (like SAP, IFS, etc.)

Even if the focus of engineering and innovation is originally on economic and technical criteria, modern and sustainable innovation management is also increasingly challenged by ecological and societal issues. Nowadays, no innovation can be sustainable without meeting key challenges of our modern environment, and today's society. The main consequence for the innovation management function within an organisation is that it has to understand and take into account challenges imposed by the environment, i.e., by ecology, economy, and society. As it is practically impossible that this knowledge can be concentrated in one person and job role, modern sustainable innovation management has to be built on a system rather than on individuals. This system has to integrate a large number of stakeholders inside and outside the company all along the innovation management process, each of them having different expertises and views on the complete product/system life cycle [8]. This is the major challenge of modern innovation management, also denoted as integrated innovation management.

5 The Preliminary Industry Research

5.1 The State of Leadership in Sustainability in Romania

The Romanian National Institute of Statistics' publication, entitled "Romania in numbers 2011- statistics compendium" indicates a total of 426,320 active Romanian companies for the first semester of 2010, of which 49,668 belong to the industrial sector. Related to the Romanian companies ISO 14001 certification, the 2011 International Standard Organization survey in this field (1993 - 2010), reports a number of 9,557 Romanian ISO 14001 certifications out of 106,700 total at European Union level (figures related to the end of 2010), more than doubled amount of the 3,884 certifications reported in 2008 (in Slovenia there were reported a number of 414 ISO 14001 certificates in 2010 versus 444 certificate in 2008 that demonstrate a loss in certificates). These figures demonstrate that Romanian companies have improved their policies and strategies in the field of sustainability in the last years, but there are still a lot of organizations that need to move forward for managing sustainability (implementing ISO 14000 and ISO 26000). This will need effective education and training programmes that could support employees and managers, organizational leaders to develop new skills in order to support their approach in managing sustainable development (related to products, processes and/or systems as the organizations are).

In the regulation field, the Environmental Management Systems (EMS) standard ISO 14001:2004 will be revised and adapted to the needs of the users (initiation was on Nov. 1st 2011). The amendment process is applied for three years. According to the International Standards Organization (ISO), the following subject areas shall be considered (ISO/TC 207/SC 1 Future challenges Study group N7 theme on www.tc207.org):

- EMS as part of sustainable development and corporate social responsibility;
- EMS for an improved environmental performance and therefore an assessment of environmental performance on the basis of key figures;
- EMS and the compliance of legal basis and other regulations;
- Integration of EMS into the strategic business management;
- Acceptance and application of EMS in small and medium-sized businesses;
- EMS and the environmental impacts within the value-added and procurement chain;
- EMS and the integration of clients and suppliers on the strategic level;
- Structural adaptation of EMS to superior management structures;
- EMS and external communication;
- Positioning of EMS in national/international agendas.

Taking into consideration the previously mentioned reports, communications, statistics and future changes of ISO 14001 we conclude that education is a necessity in order to ensure continual improvement towards sustainable development and market competitiveness. Statistics and reports have underlined that a lot of companies are not yet certified and they do not applying for ISO 14001, but they understand the new trends for improving environmental performance, integration into business management and reorientation towards sustainability. In the case of these companies, in order to face the new challenges and attend the environmental performance on both the national and international markets, to be competitive, responsible and sustainable, they require employees that are qualified in the field (that exploit the new knowledge in the field). In the same time, managers have to change their behavior and attitudes and get attached to leadership in sustainability, and/or sustainability managers and that suppose integrated environmental, social and business skills (also, known as green skills or competencies). Nowadays, there is an increasing demand on the labor market's for such specialists and also, for training programs in the field (Jackson et al., 2011), (Luna et al., 2012), (Fien and Guevara, 2013).

This transition towards sustainability management can also be witnessed in Romania, where based our practical experiences and observations there have been revealed that many employees, dealing with environmental management, have seen a shift in requirements from strictly technical responsibilities towards issues such as interdepartmental communication, aiding the marketing department by incorporating the company's environmental and social performance into sales materials, helping with product innovation regarding new 'green' products or finding ways to improve existing products as well as developing strategies. Thus, the role of Environmental Manager is gradually morphing into the role of Sustainability Manager. However, the problem for Romania and many other European countries (France and Slovenia, as well) is the fact that there is currently no national standard available for this field and subsequently, neither there do not exist any occupational classification codes or certified trainings.

During the project proposal development a small research in identifying the needs toward more skills in the area of sustainable development was launched in Romania.

Questioners were sent to different organizations from different field of activity such as industry (automotive, electronics, food, telecom, IT, constructions, bank) and also public institutions (hospitals, public administration, schools, Universities). A number of 100 questioners were submitted and out of these around 30 answers were gathered in-house.

The research reveals a major interest of the automotive and electronics industry as well as food industry in skills development in sustainable development in a more advance level, topics like `Sustainable development of processes`, Strategic and change management in the context of sustainable development`, ` Supply chain management`, `Environmental costing and resource management`, `Eco marketing`, `Ecodesign`, `LCA – Carbon foot printing`, `Process Life Management` and `CSR`.

Also the institutions considered the skills in sustainable management as very important even that here the basic knowledge sometime is missing, the above mentioned topics were also highly interested as a whole, with less applicability in practice but nevertheless the orientation of institutions management style toward a more comprehensive and structure way of process management is considered driven towards a sustainable development of institutions, and the questioned persons were able to express the importance of different approach in institutions which will drive for major good changes.

Interest were express also by bank and IT industry especially in the Social Responsibility field of actions and Service Sustainability, considering their activity as highly indirect impacting the society as a whole, and skills which would be needed inside these organization are definitely oriented towards a more sustainable approach of services that they are delivering, and the community engagement of these organization might help in behavior change of the citizens.

5.2 The State of Leadership in Sustainability in Germany and Austria

In Germany and Austria the LeadSUS questionnaire was distributed inside a working party of leading Automotive and IT industry companies. The working party SOQRATES was formed 2003 with the support of the Bavarian software initiative and became a German and Austria wide set of task forces where leading industry exchanges best practices in innovation topics, like safety design, testing, etc. This includes leading industry such as Continental Automotive, ZF Friedrichshafen AG, Elektrobit, HELLA, and many more. The below statements only highlight areas where the majority of the industry agreed to:

- In average they agree that competence and operations will improve using sustainability.
- They highly agree in RECP Methodology
- They highly agree in social responsibility skills
- They highly agree in stakeholder management
- and they see a very strong need in knowledge management (Messnarz, 2011)

The other factors you offered were either rated lower or did not show a clear agreement. Important to know is that this industry group wanted to add a further factor to your questionnaire: *"Different leadership cultures"*. Most of the companies who were asked had a global market with products or services sold in all European countries and continents. Their sites are distributed and many of them had sites in Romania, namely in Timisoara, Craiova, and Sibiu. This is also the reason why the working in multinational partnerships is a topic for solving the sustainability issues.

6 Outlook

For many years the leadership on the market was driven by offering more functions and services at a better price. In the last 10 years the safety was added, especially because cars, planes, trains, etc. are safety critical and many of the functions are solved by electronics and software. So it became important to have e.g. a product which is safe (a car in which we trust it will have no unwanted steering, a plane which we trust that speed sensors are accurate, etc.).

In future the world shift in social responsibility thinking will change the market behavior again and will lead to more functions and innovations and other design. E.g. using re-usable parts, using electric motor concepts, inventing new chemical procedures in production with less waste, and much more.

LeadSUS ideas will contribute to this new move, and Process Improvement and innovation will again be expanded to cover a more holistic view in the next decade.

LeadSUS will develop a training and coaching program to prepare industry partners for this new journey of innovation.

The training program will contain important elements in the area of Sustainability management, Economic sustainability, Environmental sustainability, Social Sustainability, and also Product or Service Sustainability, Product sustainability.

The training program will be developed in a very practical way, considering for all technical elements beside theoretical inputs also exercises and best practice examples. Also project development in the area of sustainability will be one of the key aspects which will be oriented to target group based on the aspects learned within the training, and the project will be developed in close collaboration and supervision of an internal coach. With this approach the trainees will gather new aspects on how sustainability concepts shall be practically implemented in the organization and how the process management and innovation approach can help their organization to step ahead to a sustainability management approach as a whole in the organization development.

With the competences reached by the trainees with different responsibilities in the organization we expect that the process improvement process will take a more sustainability oriented approach in the organization, beside the economical orientation of the management they will figure out how the interdepartmental communication, internal process management, clear objectives in social and environmental field can complete the development of the organization into a more green and competitive organization on the market.

The trainees involved in this program will learn about how they can calculate the organization carbon footprint (the environmental impact), how they can act and plan different sustainability program with relevant objectives and targets, and how such a Sustainability program can be part of the organizational strategic approaches as a whole. Also an important aspect will be the knowledge management, how the organizations can establish a better internal communication and sustainable data treatability and how the management can control and monitor the progress within the organization, in close relation with the targets achievements. Process innovation is a part of the continuous program of an organization, and the basis for innovation is the baseline established for one organization considering different sets of data, including production and consumption but nevertheless also some other dates which concerns the stakeholders.

The process of stakeholder engagement and management of an organization is a very sensitive one, but for a B2C (business to consumers) organization as example, this is essential. The trainees will learn also how they can handle and involve stakeholders in their organization life and how these can help the development of the organization and can add value by being involved in different activities.

Competitiveness of one organization is very much depending on the inside process management and of course about how the priority setting are driven, but nevertheless the most competitive organizations on the market will be those who are integrating into their business strategy also social and environmental performance indicators and they start to drive innovation within the activity considering the needs of the market.

References

1. Avolio, B.J., Walumbwa, F.O., Weber, T.J.: Leadership: current theories, research, and future directions. Annu. Rev. Psychol. 60, 421–449 (2009)
2. Boal, K.B., Hooijberg, R.: Strategic leadership research: Moving on. Leadersh. Q. 11, 515–549 (2000)
3. Ferdig, M.A.: Sustainability Leadership: Co-creating a Sustainable Future (2007)
4. Visser, W., Courtice, P.: Sustainability Leadership: Linking Theory and Practice. Leadership 14 (2011)
5. Rozman, T., Geder, M., Reiner, M., Godzik, E., Messnarz, R., Ekert, D., Blažunioniene, Silva Kumanova, T.: HEI-UP (Improvement of Business Process Management in Higher Education institutions) project proposal documentation (2011)
6. Rozman, T., Geder, M.: Procesno usmerjeno vodenje visokošolskih ustanov, http://journal.doba.si/letnik_4_2012_st__2?aid=453&m=1
7. Rozman, T.: Varna shramba digitalnega dokumentarnega gradiva v skupnem varnem prostoru: celovit pogled. Atlanti (2009)
8. Pisano, U., Endl, A., Berger, G.: European Sustainable Development Network (ESDN). In: The Rio+20 Conference 2012: Objectives, processes and outcomes, pp. 39.40 (2012)
9. Rio+20: Pathways to a Sustainable Future - Council conclusions - 3152th ENVIRONMENT Council meeting, Brussels (March 9, 2012)
10. Riel, A., Tichkiewitch, S., Messnarz, R.: Qualification and Certification for the Competitive Edge in Integrated Design. CIRP Journal of Manufacturing Science and Technology. Special Issue on Competitive Design 2(4), 279–289 (2010)
11. Hall, J., Vredenburg, H.: The Challenges of Innovating for Sustainable Development. MIT Sloan Management Review 45(1), 61–68 (2003)

Game Changing Beliefs for the Product Developing Organization

Morten Elvang

DELTA, Venlighedsvej 4, DK-2970 Hørsholm
meg@delta.dk, @mortenelvang

Abstract. How can you improve as a product developing organization? Are there principles that you as an organization can chose to believe in, which will then help change the odds of success in your favor? This paper will argue for a positive answer to this question and further attempt to suggest a useful set of such beliefs – I call them 'Game Changing Beliefs'

Keywords: Effectiveness, Success, Value based leadership, Agile, Lean Product Development.

1 The Quest for Meaning

In the years just before and following the turn of the millennium, agile software development practices gained popularity – to some degree as a rebel movement opposing the plan-driven 'waterfall models'. Enthusiastic teams, often smaller rather than larger, practicing XP, SCRUM and other schools of agile, demonstrated amazing productivity and results compared to the less motivated crowds operating under the 'dark regiments of waterfall'. Later we have learned that the contrasts are less sharp and also that schools like SCRUM became less powerful if applied in non-ideal conditions. Being close to perfect for small teams working on short application projects close to the customer, SCRUM performed less convincing for e.g. maintenance teams, HW/SW development projects or larger organizations. Under less favorable conditions the power of the ingrained rituals diminished. Sometimes the rituals worked, sometimes they didn't. Reinertsen (Reinertsen, 2009) – in its extreme form - calls this phenomenon the 'cargo cult'. When learning this I had already used the phrase 'rain dance 101' for some time. Also experienced teams became challenged – performing the SCRUM practices by the book, the question rose of what to do next. Like many, I started wondering about the meaning behind – understanding the principles behind the rituals would enable you to work with the rituals and change them in more favorable ways – understanding the meaning, would enable you to start optimizing – optimizing the flow of value.

2 How This All Started

Part of gaining experience is to develop 'tacit knowledge' – you learn to use certain practices knowing that they will work as expected. And also when not to use the 'normal' practice and instead revert to practices demanded by special conditions. For the inexperienced by-stander, observing the work of an experienced person can be puzzling and hard to understand. It all appears like rituals – sometimes they work and sometimes different rituals are required to bring about the same effect. If the same rituals are repeated by an inexperienced person, very different – and unexpected – results may occur. Perhaps, even no results at all. Or, perhaps everything just works out fine.

This is when you start wondering why? Why, why, why … why? And how does it all work? You want to know what's behind the rituals. Building and sustaining a successful organization is something that you cannot buy a fail proof recipe for. Some figures (Ries, 2011) say that only one out of twenty new startups succeeds. And even after that sustaining success is demanding. (Don't quite know how to fit this is – another point is that some successful organizations don't know or don't remember where the success is coming from – to learn more about this aspect, read 'Hunger in Paradise' by Rasmus Ankersen (Ankersen, 2014) – back to the red thread …) On the other hand, there are lots of learnings and advice of what to consider. There might even be a book out there with a title like 'How to build and sustain a successful organization'. For me, this started from a mix of personal experience and observations as well as reflections on what I picked up from others. If you aspire to build an effective and successful product development organization, then what are the things you can chose to believe in to change odds for success in your favor? Behind the rituals, what are the principles you can trust to push your luck?

3   How the Many Pieces Came Together

The famous golfer Jack Nicklaus (col.) is quoted for having said: 'The more I practice, the luckier I get'. Another famous quote goes 'Luck is where preparation meets opportunity'. Tom Gilb (col.) says: 'If you don't know, what you are doing, then don't do it on a larger scale'. Richard Branson (col.), Virgin, says: 'People, people, people', when asked what's behind his success. Abraham Lincoln (col.) said: 'The best way to predict the future is to create it'. Etc, etc, etc

Empirical results have shown that as much as half of all defects found in software can be traced back to the requirements (Vinter et.al., 1999). Wrong, missing or changed requirements are the largest culprits. One thing that is in common among successful product management models is the notion of fast and frequent feedback (col.). Today all project management approaches pays huge attention to 'stakeholder management'. It's possible to create freedom through structure (col.). Success often leads to complacency. The amount of personal stress (Groth-Brodersen, 2013) for the knowledge-worker is rocketing. Etc, etc, etc

Add to this personal experience of 'well-managed' organizations and 'chaotic' organizations and everything in between. Among other things learning the true meaning of 'integrity' and 'accountability'. And understanding the value of having a clear policy, which can guide the organization. Etc, etc, etc

Finally, there are all the publications of models and theories – capability maturity (CMMI, 2010), evolutionary delivery (Gilb, 2005), standards, life-cycle models, theory of constraints (Goldratt, 2012), lean product development (Reinertsen, 2009), etc etc. There are more books and papers written than most normal people will ever be able to read. The growth is exponential – for every research paper published, the room for at least two more is created.

All, in all, there are so many one-liners, so much empirical and tacit knowledge, so much advice from publications and so many experiences and learnings. How can you grasp the essence and how can you piece all this together to make sense? It's like a big puzzle, with an infinite number of pieces, like illustrated in the last paragraphs just above (I hope).

The only way to cope with all this complexity is to find a way to reduce it – make it simpler (there was another one ☺). Let's turn things around and look from another perspective:

> *If you should create a high-performing organization in which performing with agile would be possible, which are the principles you would chose to rely on to change your luck?*

This is how I started thinking about 'game changing beliefs'. Principles you can chose to believe in, which have high odds of changing your game favorably. Based on everything you know ... up till now ... and picking just a few ... what would they be?

4 Exercise – Before You Study My List

If you should build and sustain a successful product development organization, which are the 3-5 most powerful things you would bring into play?

Your list:

1. _____
2. _____
3. _____
4. _____
5. _____

5 The Game Changing Beliefs (version 1.18, 19-Jan-2014)

Now, it's my turn! Is there a set of principles, such that each has the potential of a game changing impact on 'operational effectiveness' and 'success' in any hi-tech product developing organization? And what might they be?

Below you find the things I chose to believe in to make a difference. The list is constantly changing. You can find the latest version published on the internet[1].

ELEVEN GAME CHANGING BELIEFS - for the product development organization

- The OPPORTUNITY SPACE is huge – There is always a better way – NEVER STOP SEARCHING
- Know who you are (IDENTITY) ... be relentless (STRATEGY/MAKE CHOICES) in what you are aiming for (VISION) (Collins, 1994)
- PEOPLE make the difference
- Your organization must enable everyone to EXPERIMENT, LEARN, DEVELOP and ACT INTELLIGENTLY (Saarinen, 2004)
- Understand what VALUE is and where it comes from (BUSINESS MODEL)
- Optimize the FLOW OF VALUE (Reinertsen, 2009)
- The worst COST is what you can't or couldn't do, because of what you did
- Accept that MOST IDEAS ARE BAD (Wedell-Wedellsborg, 2013)
- RISK and UNCERTAINTY are in everything you do – or don't do
- SMALL, FAST, SIMPLE beat large, slow, complex any day
- ENGAGE with the world – SHARE what you know and don't know; STEAL with pride

6 Conclusion

The work on perfecting the Game Changing Beliefs continues – in reality they are nothing more than condensed personal experiences – from an intractable set of sources – blended and mixed for this presentation. Based on what has been collected so far.

- The question is not whether they are right or wrong. They are!
- The question is which principles you yourself chose to believe in to favor your game!

While you work on yours, you can continue to follow my progress on: www.42ndstreetcompany.com. Any contribution is welcome!

References

Ankersen, R.: Hunger in Paradise - beat the hell out of complacency (2014)
CMMI, CMMI for Development, v1.3. Software Enginering Institute, CMU/SEI-2010-TR-033 (2010)

---

[1] See: www.42ndstreetcompany.com/game-changing-beliefs/, for the latest version of the game changing beliefs.

Collins, J.: Built to Last: Successful Habits of Visionary Companies. Harper Business Essentials (1994)

Gilb, T.: Competitive Engineering: A Handbook for Systems Engineering, Requirements Engineering, and Software Engineering Using Planguage. Butterworth-Heinemann (2005)

Goldratt, E.M.: The Goal: A Process of Ongoing Improvement. North River (2012)

Groth-Brodersen, S.: Selvledelse: Fra ledelse til selvet: En socialpsykologisk analyse af forholdet imellem selvledelse, ledelse og stress i det moderne arbejdsliv (Danish). Copenhagen Business School (2013)

Reinertsen, D.: The Principles of Product Development Flow: Second Generation Lean Product Development. Celeritas Publishing (2009)

Ries, E.: The Lean Startup: How Today's Entrepreneurs Use Continuous Innovation to Create Radically Successful Businesses. Crown Business (2011)

Saarinen, E.: Discovering a hidden competence in human action and organisational life. Helsinki University of Technology (2004)

Vinter, O., et.al.: PRIDE - A Methodology for Preventing Requirements Issues from Becoming Defects (1999), http://ottovinter.dk/engreqeng.htm

Wedell-Wedellsborg, T.: Innovation as Usual: How to Help Your People Bring Great Ideas to Life. Harvard Business Publishing (2013)

The Need for a Structured Approach towards Production Technology Roadmaps in Innovation-Driven Industries

Martina Flatscher[1], Andreas Riel[2], and Tobias Kösler[1]

[1] ZF Friedrichshafen AG, Friedrichshafen, Germany
{martina.flatscher,tobias.koesler}@zf.com
[2] EMIRAcle c/o Grenoble Institute of Technology GSCOP UMR5272, Grenoble, France
andreas.riel@grenoble-inp.fr

Abstract. As innovation cycles are becoming shorter and technological progress faster, the need for reliable decision support for product and production planning is rapidly gaining crucial importance. To this aim, strongly innovation-driven industries like automotive use roadmaps relating products and technologies to a timeline from a specific company's viewpoint. The roadmapping process, however, is typically neither systematic nor transparent. Furthermore, there is a lack of integration of product roadmaps and production technology roadmaps, although these cover complementary and mutually dependent aspects. This paper investigates the motivation and necessity for systematic and integrated roadmapping with a specific focus on production industries, and introduces a related automotive supplier industry research project that aims at designing and implementing a holistic approach to integrated technology roadmapping.

Keywords: Innovation Management, Technology Management, Technology Planning, Process Innovation, Ideation.

1 Introduction

The automotive industry is one of the most highly innovation–driven industries [1]. Actually, suppliers engineer and manufacture most of the vehicle parts for the Original Equipment Manufacturers (OEMs). In doing so, the global automotive suppliers and engineering firms will invest approximately 65 billion Euros in research and development in 2015 – far more than twice as much as the OEMs [2]. Therefore suppliers need to enhance their innovative power. In addition, the suppliers are faced with the increasing of network complexity on all levels. Thus, one of the specific challenges of the automotive sector is that the automotive suppliers are forced to be innovative in the way they develop and manufacture components that need to be integrated in a complex network of systems and subsystems linked to different networked organizations. In this context, the innovative planning of production technology (PTP) assumes a vital role as a facilitator of product and process innovations.

In the PTP process, roadmaps are established as an important means of strategic planning and decision support. Surprisingly enough, the development and evolution of such roadmaps is typically non-systematic and opaque to a large number of directly affected stakeholders inside and outside industrial organizations, which is a clear contradiction to their fundamental importance as decision-support instrument.

This article investigates this issue from the point of view of a large tier-1 automotive supplier and in the context of the wider scope of innovation management, and with a special focus on the necessity of establishing a consistent relationship between the early ideation phases of innovation with strategic roadmaps. Section 2 gives an introduction to the particular challenges of innovation management in industrial production organizations. Section 3 points out that innovation management in production is based on a lot of information assets which should all be taken into account in continuous roadmap development. Section 4 assembles a list of key research questions that are associated with the need of rendering roadmap development systematic and embedded into the innovation management process from the earliest ideation phases. Section 5 gives an outline of the methodological approach towards the related research activities that are carried out at a German tier-1 automotive supplier in collaboration with the G-SCOP laboratory of the Grenoble Alpes University. Finally, Section 6 concludes by summing up the major challenges, and giving an outlook on the next research steps.

2 Innovation Management Challenges in Industrial Production Organizations

Under the increasing innovation pressure, enterprises have established innovation processes in their organizations [3]. These processes typically attempt to give a structure to the steps leading to innovative products, services and processes in order to make the management of innovation possible. Making such innovation processes operational and improving their performance within their organizations is one of the biggest challenges that companies are facing. They are actually looking for measures allowing them to assess the way in which the various activities and communication flows are effectively rooted, and which initiatives to undertake in order to improve innovation performance.

The Institute of Technology and Process Management (ITOP) in Ulm defined a holistic process map in which innovation management is positioned with respect to the company and its environment, and its fundamental elements are made explicit [4]. As shown in Figure 1, the innovation management addresses numerous different aspects that are interlinked.

The Strategy Development is business driven and sets the strategy of technology coordinated with the corporate strategy by defining the relative technology position and considering make-or-buy decisions. The idea management is essential for competitiveness. Along the ideation process ideas are generated, collected, evaluated and organised. The Portfolio Management engages future portfolios in compiling and assessing the portfolios quantitatively. Actions are built to reach the target state. The technology management deals with the operative planning and coordination of technology development. Intrinsically the technological innovations have to be generated by an integrated approach. The IP management regulates the protection of intellectual property and generates corporate values. Development and Launch describes the process beginning by the technology development over the production development and service to launch. The Product Lifecycle Management identifies and analyses the product lifecycle regarding market requirements as an input for the TUI Strategy and the Portfolio management. The Performance Management makes the strategy operational based on business objectives measured by qualitative and quantitative governing factors and corporate management. The Intelligence and Analytics is as the idea management crucial. Information concerning the process map of technology and innovation is generated, analysed and structured. These methods of analysis are enhanced continuously [4].

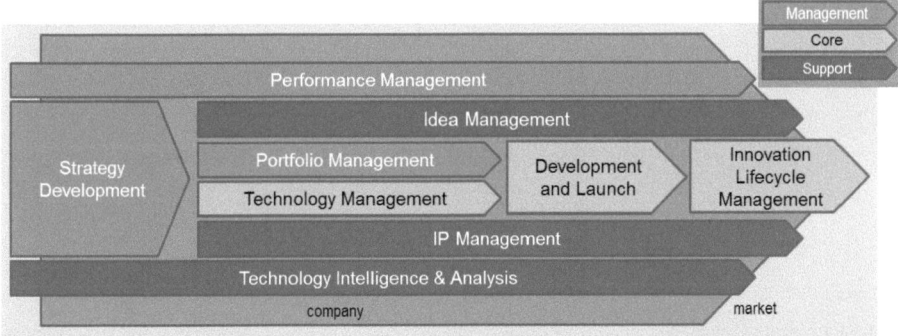

Fig. 1. The Technology and Innovation Strategy Process according to [4]

Innovations in the PTP have been classified as one type of innovation among other types. However, further classifications within the PTP have not been made so far [5]. It is desirable to adopt a holistic approach to technology and innovation management as proposed by the ITOP to the PTP with close connections to the product development and purchase.

3 Key Information Assets for Production Innovation Management

As a first step towards an actionable structured holistic approach towards PTP, one has to take into account the key information assets that the PTP has to incorporate in order to make PTP consistent with the global corporate innovation management and planning. From the point of view of challenges to the instrument innovation database, Gausemeier discusses the key information assets linked to the innovation management process as shown in Figure 2 [6]. Market segments define future challenges for products which must be realized on technological and organizational levels. Product ideas are mapped to functions which are linked to specific technologies that have to be mastered and get implemented properly within the organization. The morphological box in Figure 2 associates such technologies with the product functions. Therefore, the management of technologies is vital.

The Innovation Roadmap positions technologies as solutions for product functions on the time line. The central role of the technology roadmap emphasises it as one of the most important technology planning tool for managing PTP by its mid- and long term perspective. All the named entities are implemented using documents like project plans, analysis posters, presentations, etc. These documents have to be kept consistent and managed organization-wide by the concept of an IT solution that is most frequently implemented on the basis of an innovation database which represents the basis for targeted provision of information based on the various information assets that employees can access [6].

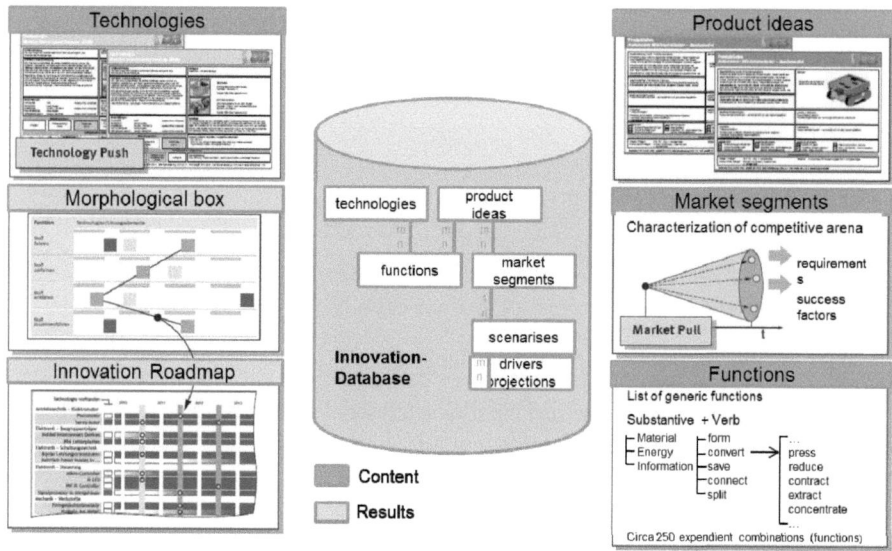

Fig. 2. Key Assets linked to Innovation Management according to [6]

The key message in the context of researching a holistic and structured approach to PTP is that the PTP has to take into account and nurture all these different entities permanently in a consistent and fully traceable manner. As roadmapping requires prospecting future developments, roadmaps are inherently dynamic and the associated processes and tools have to support the permanent dynamic learning process of the organization with respect to knowledge acquired about the prospected products and technologies.

4 Key Research Questions

As underlined previously, the technology roadmap is a crucial tool for PTP. The industrial relevance of dynamic roadmaps with an innovative methodology is a key to the industry's competitiveness and manufacturing capability. Industry can benefit from those roadmaps for business strategy and technology development [7].

Given their instrumental role in decision support, technology roadmaps have to be developed and managed in a consistent and structured way. Researches indicate that roadmaps exist in firms but every firm has its individual approach to manage roadmaps. There are only few practical guidelines offered towards building the technology roadmap. This makes it appear to have limited flexibility in terms of building a process and final outputs [8]. There is no system in developing the technology roadmap and no evidence how technology roadmaps are managed and validated. Mostly roadmaps are linked with strategy decisions but without connection to other important facets like trend analysis, long-term strategy, outside assets, internal requirements, etc. However, these links have to be considered if all inputs of the technology roadmap should be taken into account and be situated in the industrial context [9]. Moreover, the traceability of roadmap entries to decisions and the responsible stakeholders is crucial for the continuous updating and adjustment of the roadmaps, as well as their consistent deployment and follow-up. In order to investigate this subject closer, one can basically identify two major sources of inputs for production technology roadmaps, both are depicted in Figure 3 below.

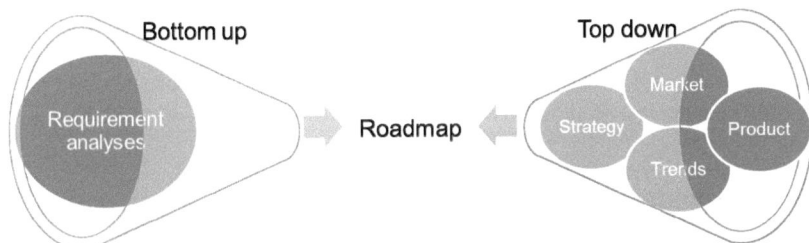

Fig. 3. Major input sources for technology roadmaps

One source groups together any kind of input based on requirements raised by the internal organization whereas the other collects inputs coming from the external environment. Given the specific nature of origins and influence paths, the former may be called "bottom-up inputs", whereas the latter can be signified as "top-down inputs". As the connecting element between the two input sources, the technology roadmap contains reactions of external and internal requirements in the form of innovation ideas positioned on a time bar.

Bottom-up inputs mainly originate in requirements regarding the product development, production and purchase. Top down inputs include trend analyses of customer needs, the supply chain, production development, trend-relevant search fields, strategy decisions and many others. In the systematic processing of top down and bottom up inputs, the technology roadmap reflects innovation.

A systematic, holistic and traceable treatment of these inputs, however, does not happen in large industrial organizations in general, as this involves dealing with a multitude of questions that are mostly linked to the early and unstructured phases of innovation.

Key questions raised in this research in industrial context are the following:
- What search fields are relevant for trend analyses?
- How to identify and process trends?
- How can the impact of trends on production technology be assessed?
- How to prioritise topics and identify the "big waves" within the trend extrapolations?
- How can strategic guidance deliver input for the technology roadmap?
- Which stakeholders should be involved in the roadmapping process, how and when?
- How can recommendations for action and measures from trend extrapolations and technology roadmaps be used to support the management?
- How to assure the traceability from roadmap topics to the stakeholders and actions that have led to the positioning of these topics?
- Which IT infrastructure is required to help keep the whole process consistent and traceable?

A structured and fully traceable innovation process approach to production technology planning on the basis of roadmaps promises answers to all these questions.

5 Methodological Research Approach

As technology and innovation planning is inherently rooted in the very early phases of the innovation management process, it is evident to start research by a systematic review of actionable concepts developed in Front-End of Innovation (FEI), Fuzzy Front-End (FFE), and New Product Development (NPD) research.

One essential element of all these concepts is the need for the systematic involvement of various stakeholders from the very beginning. Along the treatment of trends and the generation and processing of ideas, diversity can improve the extrapolation of trends and idea management by reinforcing

- the creativity,
- the workforce,
- the top management attention, and
- the innovation culture.

The precondition for such benefits through diversity, however, is an adequate management [11]. A holistic way of thinking is important for the management approach. For example, the integration of stakeholders in the areas like product development and purchase in a cooperation-based organizational culture would ensure a suitable constructive networking in the context of the PTP [9], [12].

Examining the identification and processing of trends more closely, the open way of problem solving proposed by Geschka and shown in Figure 4, can be used as fundamental process element [13]. Starting with a problem like a relevant search field of a trend, the divergent thinking step identifies trends with a very wide open angle of view. Out-of-the-box thinking is the major objective of this phase, which is then followed by a consolidation phase where methods for finding convergence are applied. Here, the major ojective is to process relevant trends in a way that topics can be prioritised and focal points can be identified [13].

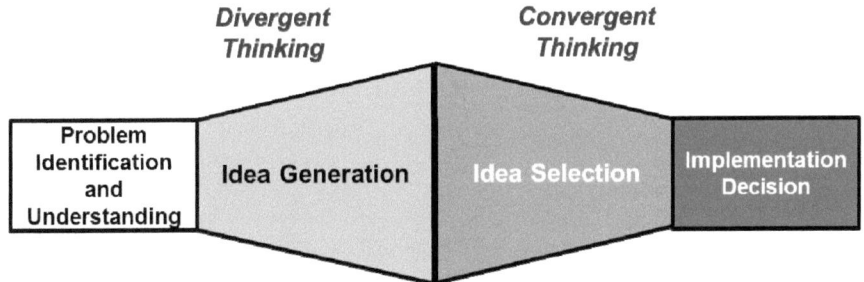

Fig. 4. Fundamental problem solving process cycle element [11]

By an efficient preparation of trend extrapolations by means of evaluation criteria and involvement of stakeholders, the management has the possibility to focus their attention on mutually valuable issues. Effective and efficient evaluation criteria have a vital role in the phase of convergence, and form the very basis for any managerial decision [14].

By actionable directives and criteria for the different sub-phases, the resulting higher managerial support for the activities in trend management and idea management avoids unwanted and unconsciously individual decision-making and filtering procedures by individuals in such an important stage. Evaluating all the various decision criteria requires a lot of different expertises and points of view, which is why multifunctional group decisions on different levels are important [15].

A very helpful guideline for the development of a systematic approach this integration for PTP roadmaps is provided by the key success factors of the FFE according to Neumann [12]. The challenge is to implement these success factors in a structured and fully traceable process centered on the consistent development of PTP roadmaps.

The current research activities focus on the implementation of such problem solving process cycle elements specifically for production technology roadmapping activities on a pilot project level. Each cycle is mainly realized by moderated ideation workshops that bring together several key stakeholders of different departments from production, product development, procurement, etc. In the next section, the authors will elaborate on the need for these specific strongly networking-focused activities.

6 The Complexity of Production Technology Planning

An approach of process improvement of the innovation management in the PTP tries to make the production fit for the future. In order to capture the numerous dependencies this process has, it makes sense to distinguish between the activity groups related to the planning of PTP, the actual content of Planning in the PTP and the specific innovation areas in the PTP, which are depicted in Figure 5 below.

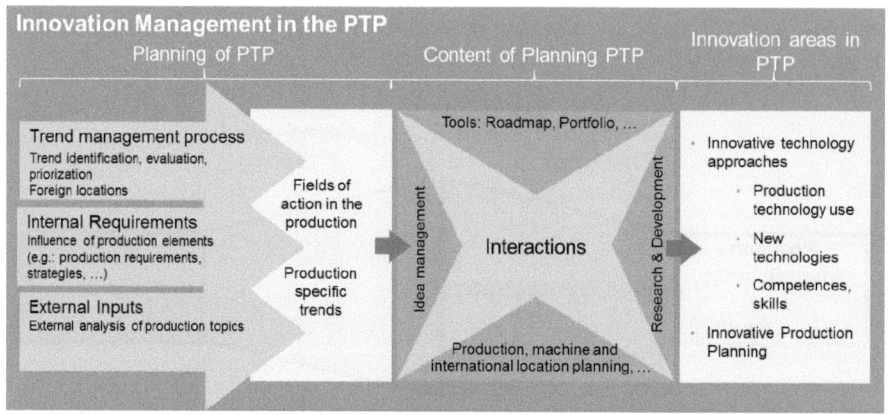

Fig. 5. Fundamental problem solving process cycle element

In the planning the PTP, many assets and activities are associated with the innovation planning of production technologies, especially the roadmap development, as indicated in Figure 2. Many external and internal inputs that influence the production have to be reflected adequately. There are aspects of the internal requirements coming from the production constraints, foreign locations, strategy, investment and so on. Moreover the proper handling of trends in the production is critical, because trends often refer only to the product without drawing conclusions about the manufacturing of these products. In addition to that, the active procurement and capitalization on external inputs (e.g. external analysis of production topics) is often not carried due to lack of resources made available to this aim. Mostly this is the consequence of poor management attention to pro-active innovation management for the production. The key research questions identified in section 4 aims precisely at guaranteeing an optimal planning of the PTP to identify fields of action in the production in the context of production specific trends.

In all the mentioned activities and especially in content of planning PTP, there is a need of interaction with many sub-systems such as machine planning, production system design, international location and layout planning. Furthermore activities regarding research, strategic operational business, development, innovation management, etc have to be agreed upon the stakeholders. As described in Section 5 in every step of PTP various stakeholders within the production and from neighboring areas have to be involved systematically, At this stage the PTP is methodologically supported by strategic considerations in different dimensions. Tools such as the portfolio tool (do we produce and assemble internally or externally?) and the roadmap (how do we produce?) can help in the strategic PTP. The technology roadmap hedges a suitable use of production technologies, e.g. to achieve the goal of an optimal degree of automation in the production and the development of skills and competences in the production whereas a production portfolio can improve the connection between foreign locations and make or buy decisions concerning production planning aspects. On the operational level an appropriate idea management with respect to an adequate trend management is important to ensure the right use of strategic tools with the right topics.

Innovations in the PTP can happen especially on the basis of the active management and implementation of new production technology ideas that are dynamically positioned in the roadmap according to a defined process and taking into account clearly defined criteria (e.g. the technology's alignment with the company strategy, its core competencies and corporate image). Considering the example of the trend topic lightweight construction, ideas have to be generated to find materials, technologies and related production methods that lead to weight reduction. This, however, also implies to think about how and when to build up methodological competences around these topics, as well as material expertise. Consequently innovation in the PTP is successful if it succeeds in getting the organization engaged in right topics with the right actions at the right points of time. In that manner the PTP ensures innovative technology approaches such as the suitable use of production technologies, dealing with new technologies, building of competences and skills, as well as an innovative production planning.

In all mentioned findings dependencies between PTP elements and tools exist and are complex. Figure 6 shows superficially the building elements of innovation management in the PTP in general terms, consisting of different inputs, networks, methods and a structured innovation process, which was described above.

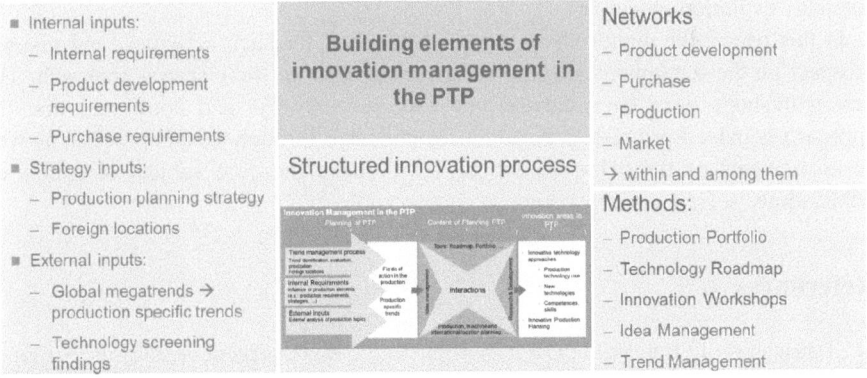

Fig. 6. Building elements of innovation management in the PTP All inputs that influence the production have to be identified and further processed. Tools support the PTP in all dimensions. Especially a systematic approach for the PTP is crucial in order to quantify the individual phases of the PTP and ensure the traceability and transparence. Regarding the coherences in between the PTP, all elements and especially the interaction with stakeholders are all strongly influences by one other and are of complex nature. Therefore, these relations must be identified and nurtured carefully by the PTP innovation management. This is why it is extremely important to network in all elements of PTP at least with product development, product line management, purchasing, production and foreign locations. There is a need to map the complex relationships on the company's specific organization in order to build the network needed to address the complicated and far-reaching questions related to the PTP.

7 Conclusion and Outlook

The numerous interdisciplinary dependencies of Production Technology Planning make the process complex. Strategic roadmapping is an important and widely used means of decision support for innovation management in the several industry sectors, most notably the automotive sector. In current practice, the roadmapping of products and product technologies is often done with only few links to the roadmapping of production and production technologies, which leads to the fact that companies perform sub-optimally with respect to the speed and timeliness of build-up of production technology, as well as with respect to production set-up times. Given the ever increasing speed of technological progress and changes, one can presume that there is a huge potential of improving competitive advantages by mastering the integration of production technology planning with product/service planning better than competitors do.

The industrial research project introduced in this paper aims at addressing this challenge by designing and experimenting a systematic approach to integrated product and production technology roadmapping on an enterprise level. At the heart of this approach is the systematic collaboration of key stakeholders from different organizational units and departments (research and development, production technology, procurement, site planning, etc.) in moderated ideation workshops. These workshops take the involved stakeholders from technological, societal, economical and ecological megatrends to their specific impact on the company from the viewpoint of production technology in relationship with products and strategic company evolution objectives.

In this paper, the authors have justified the need for such activities, and given a prospect on the fundamental methodological elements of the research approach. The first workshops have been carried out very successfully, and confirmed that the approach is indeed promising. Experiences collected throughout this process, as well as assessments of the achieved progress will make the core subject of follow-up publications.

References

1. Dannenberg, J., Burgard, J.: Car Innovation 2015 – A comprehensive study on innovation in the automotive industry, Oliver Wyman Automotive, Munich (2007), http://www.car-innovation.com (last accessed on September 29, 2013)
2. Dannenberg, J.: Große Chance für Zulieferer. In: Automobil Produktion, interviewed by Tina Rumpelt, Special Issue: Innovationen in der Automobilindustrie, pp. 18–19 (May 2008)
3. Ili, S., Albers, A., Miller, S.: Open innovation in the automotive industry. R&D Management 40(3), 246–255 (2010)
4. Stelzer, B., Brecht L.: TIM Method - Technology and Innovation Management from a Business Process Perspective. In: Huizingh, K.R.E., Torkkeli, M., Conn, S., Bitran, I. (Hg.) Proceedings of the XXI ISPIM Conference on CD-ROM, Bilbao, Spain (2010)

5. Yamamoto, Y., Bellgran, M.: Four types of manufacturing process innovation and their managerial concerns. In: Procedia CIRP, vol. 7, pp. 479–484 (2013)
6. Gausemeier, et al.: Technologieorientiertes Innovationsmanagement mit der Innovations-Datenbank. Industrie Management, Band 25, Heft Nr.1, pp. 40-44 (2009)
7. Manufuture. European Mechatronics for a new Generation of Production Systems — The Roadmap (2006)
8. Lee, S., et al.: Technology roadmapping for R&D planning: The case of the Korean parts and materials industry. Technovation 27, 433–445 (2007)
9. Khurana, A., Rosenthal, S.R.: Towards Holistic "Front Ends" in New Product Development. Journal of Product Innovation Management 15(2), 57–74 (1998)
10. Flatscher, M.: Erarbeitung eines systematischen Prozesses zur Ableitung von Technologiebedarfen aus der Produktentwicklung für die Planung der Grundlagenentwicklung: Ulm: Master Thesis, Ulm University (2012)
11. Wagner, L., Ehrenmann, S.: How Diversity Management supports the Fuzzy Front End of Innovation. In: XXI ISPIM Conference 2010, on CD-ROM
12. Neumann, M.: Ideation Reference Process Model for the Early Phase of Innovation. Grenoble: PhD Thesis, Grenoble University (2013)
13. Geschka, H.: Das Offene Problemlösungsmodell (OPM) und andere Problemlösungsstrategien. In: Preiß, L. (Hrsg.) Jahrbuch der Kreativität, Köln (JPKM), pp. 82–100 (2010)
14. Martinsou, M., Poleska, J.: Use of Evaluation Criteria and Innovation Performance in the Front End of Innovation. Journal of Product Innovation Management 28(6), 896–914 (2011)
15. Jacobi, A., Braet, J.: Improving performance in the Front-end of Innovation. In: XXIII ISPIM conference – Action for Innovation: Innovating from Experience, Barcelona, Spain, June 17-20 on CD-ROM (2012)
16. Riel, A., Neumann, M., Tichkiewitch, S.: Structuring the early fuzzy front-end to manage ideation for new product development. CIRP Annals – Manufacturing Technology 1(62), 107–110 (2013), doi:10.1016/j.cirp.2013.03.128

Empowering Entrepreneurship in Europe: Going from the Idea to Enterprise in 4 EU Countries

Eva Homolová[1], Andreas Riel[2], Marek Gavenda[1], Ana Azevedo[3], Marisa Pais[3], Jiří Balcar[1], Alessandra Antinori[4], Giuseppe Metitiero[4], Giorgos Giorgakis[5], Photis Photiades[5], Damjan Ekert[6], Richard Messnarz[6], and Serge Tichkiewitch[2]

[1] RPiC-VIP, Ostrava, Czech Republic
{gavenda,homolova,balcar}@rpic-vip.cz
[2] EMIRAcle c/o Grenoble Institute of Technology GSCOP UMR5272, Grenoble, France
{andreas.riel,serge.tichkiewitch@grenoble-inp.fr}
[3] ISQ, Lisbon, Portugal
{aiazevedo,marisa.pais}@isq.pt
[4] CIRSES, Rome, Italy
ale.antinori@cirses.it, g.metitiero@primaforma.net
[5] EUROSC, Nicosia, Cyprus
{george,photis}@eurosc.eu
[6] ISCN GmbH, Graz, Austria
{dekert,rmess}@iscn.com

Abstract. Innovation and entrepreneurship are among the top priority areas of the European Union in order to exit the economical crisis and assure sustainable and profitable growth and competitiveness on a global level. Although more and more entrepreneurship training and education programs exist in different EU countries, there is little cross-country cooperation and complementary among these activities. This paper introduces a European approach to a certified entrepreneurship training program that has been established in a consortium of several European training and education organisations. This program has been implemented around the long-term mission of empowering people to make ideas become real in the European context.

Keywords: Innovation, Entrepreneurship, Lifelong Learning.

1 Introduction

Innovation and entrepreneurship have become key topics of the EuroSPI community with the objective of building up long-term sustainable European partnerships around certified qualification programs on VET and higher education levels. The first related collaborative EU-project in the entrepreneurship area was ResEUr (ECQA Certified Researcher-Entrepreneur), which was an innovation project that has been co-financed by the European Commission from November 2009 to November 2011, and carried out by a consortium of five partners in Europe in order to propose a competence set for entrepreneurial minds, as well as a complete e-Learning based training and certification program [1][2]. These partners were EMIRAcle (BE), University Politehnica of Timisoara (RO), Grenoble INP (FR), ISCN Ltd. (IE), proHUMAN (SI), and Skills International GmbH (AT).

All these partners have a long-time experience in entrepreneurship and innovation, and are active members of the ECQA (www.ecqa.eu). With ResEUr, their target was to define a competence set that is complementary to existing training and education programs in entrepreneurship. ResEUr primarily addresses the phases before the decision of creating an enterprise is made. It aims at sensitising researchers for entrepreneurship and innovation rather than teaching them how to do business plans. This idea results from the conviction that the issue of taking into account innovation and marketing issues already during research is crucial.

"From Idea to Enterprise" (Idea2Enterprise) has been launched in October 2012 in order to transfer ResEUr to VET and secondary education on a European level, following the national priorities in many EU member states. The project partners are the following: RPIC-ViP s.r.o. (CZ), ISQ (PT), EMIRAcle (BE), ISCN (AT), EUROSUCCESS CONSULTING (CY), CIRSES (IT). This project has been introduced at EuroSPI 2013 [3] with a clear focus on the results of the needs analyses carried out by the project partners in each partner country. This article summarizes different viewpoints on dissemination and exploitation strategies in the consortium partner countries Cyprus, Czech Republic, Italy and Portugal. It thereby gives a contribution to better understanding the specific needs of theses four EU countries in the field of entrepreneurship.

Section 2 of this paper outlines the principal missions of the Idea2Enterprise qualification. Fulfilling these missions is at the basis of the consortium's dissemination nd exploitation strategy. The four subsequent sections are dedicated to dissemination and exploitation strategies in the four countries mentioned above. The paper concludes with a common view on dissemination and exploitation on consortium level, where the ECQA has a major stake.

2 Missions of the Idea2Enterprise Program

Beyond being a training program on entrepreneurship, Idea2Enterprise strives to implement the following core mission statements on a European level:

1) Empowering creative people to turn ideas into reality.
2) Networking with academia and industry for sustainable future success.
3) Becoming part of an international Innovation Community via EuroSPI and ECQA.
4) Turning passion into business.
5) Identifying talent and using it.

These missions have guided the development of the entrepreneurship training program, which is now entering the phase of pilot trainings in the four target countries Cyprus, Czech Republic, Italy, and Portugal. The need for these missions has been clearly confirmed in the extensive needs analysis that has been carried out by the project partners in each of these countries [3]. The following sections will explain the challenge of meeting needs of the different countries' target groups while following a common core set of principles relevant to the subject of entrepreneurship in the context of the missions cited above.

3 Dissemination and Exploitation in Cyprus

3.1 Key Target Audiences

In Cyprus there is no special training for people starting from pupil age until the age of 18, except for one week at the age of 16 which is called "working week", where all students have to "work" for one week in jobs of their preference. Moreover, the training that higher education students receive is more on a theoretical base and not in practical, which does not help them develop their business ideas.

The target groups in Cyprus are pupils in their last year in school and students in the last university year, as well as unemployed young graduates and VET institutions.

3.2 Key Institutions to Partner Up with

The main institutions that Eurosuccess have chosen to partner up and cooperate with are:

- European University Cyprus [4]
- University of Cyprus [5]
- Frederic University [6]
- Cyprus Chamber of Commerce and Industry [7]
- Nicosia Chamber of Commerce and Industry
- Business and Professionals women association
- Neorama Education Centre
- M.M. Knowledge and Consulting

The reason of the above selection is that the members or clients of each of the above organizations are the ones stated above in section 3.1 as the key target group. Moreover, the professionalism and the successful history of each of the above organizations, ensures the exploitation and viability of the project.

3.3 Key Events/fairs to Attend

The main events/fairs that EUROSUCCESS members will attend are the ones organized by their organization (seminars, conferences, and other projects meetings) and also the events/fairs that the above cooperating bodies will organize, like student fairs, information days, seminars and conferences.

3.4 Key Facilitators

The key facilitators that can be found in Cyprus are:
- Agricultural Research Institute (ARI),
- Cyprus Neurology / Genetics Institute (CING),
- Research Promotion Foundation (RPF).
- Cyprus Business Incubator Association
- Diogenes Business Incubator University of Cyprus
- Ermis Research and Incubator Centre – ERIC
- Helix Business Incubator LTD
- Promitheas Bussines Innovation Centre LTD

4 Dissemination and Exploitation in the Czech Republic

4.1 Key Target Audiences

Based on national priorities, the main target audience is limited to initial vocational education and training which means mainly the students of secondary schools in the Czech context. There is a lack of technically educated professionals as well as students of technical secondary schools in Moravian-Silesian region, on the other side the local economy used to be and still is oriented to technical industry. One of the biggest Technical Universities is located in Ostrava.

Based on research done in the Ostrava region, it is estimated that 25,000 additional workplaces in industry will be needed in the future eight years, more than 3,000 per year. About 2,300 graduates of professional secondary schools stay on the labour market per year (i.e., do not continue on higher level of education). This means at least 5,000 graduates of technical secondary schools will be missing [8].

Even if this seems to be a reason of motivating pupils to go to technical secondary schools, their interest is still very low for different reasons. A training to develop their entrepreneurial skills and spirits in the pre-last year of their studies is considered not only a way of providing them some complementary competencies or making their studies more attractive but also as a strategy of multiplying the number of technically oriented companies and of increasing the employability of the graduates.

Therefore RPIC-VIP decided to pilot the trainings with young people in the pre-last year of studies in professional secondary schools.

4.2 Key Institutions to Partner Up with

The Regional Consulting and Innovation Centre (RPIC) itself has a direct link to professional secondary schools in their region thanks to projects realized in recent years (e.g. [9]).

The competencies in secondary education are set on regional level in the Czech Republic. Even if we suppose easy acquisition of students because of long term cooperation with schools, the strategic partnership with Regional Authority of

Moravia-Silesia in the matter of training promotion will be initiated. The cooperation with public authority increases the sustainability of project outputs.

4.3 Key Exploitation Channels

RPIC-ViP participates in processes of development of educational system and active labour market policy in the region. The programming period 2014+ is being prepared in cooperation with local stakeholders to face the regionally specific challenges. The key facilitators of the negotiating the priorities are Regional Office and Regional Authority. The team members will attend relevant workshops, roundtables or conferences and actively discuss the topic and actions to be taken to improve the competencies of graduates for future development of Moravia-Silesia.

The importance of activities of Technical University of Ostrava in the field of promoting innovation and start-ups is still growing. Start-up shows or innovative company competition events represent very convenient audiences to use the potential of the training.

At national level, RPIC-VIP is one of the facilitators of the smart specialisation strategy focusing for 2014+ on entrepreneurial discovery process.

5 Dissemination and Exploitation in Italy

5.1 Key Target Audiences

In the Italian VET System there are not figures devoted to support boys and girls "from idea to enterprise". The training courses are in fact mainly focused on the theoretical knowledge, rather than to assist the realization of a professional project. However in some VET curricula, some experiences are carried out named "Enterprise Training Simulation" or "alternative school-work experience".

The Enterprise Training Simulation is a virtual company animated by students who make market on the net, e-commerce, with the mentoring of a real company who is the reference model for each phase of the business life cycle: from the business idea to the business plan, from the registration in the chamber of commerce and in the office registry to the commercial transactions, from the financial transactions to the tax compliance [10].

The Enterprise Training Simulation allows building the concrete working model of a real company in a "laboratory" environment and therefore appears closer to the action-oriented learning methodology. A company tutor, corresponding to a real company operating in the area, cooperates with teachers setting the simulated company and its management in order to create a link with the real Labour Market designing real roles and duties for the students.

Following the above, the primary target group for Italy is typically the profiles interested in the Enterprise Training Simulation, as well as the key stakeholders involved in this training. More specifically, CIRSES will disseminate the Idea2Enterprise training mainly to the following target groups:

- Business consultants
- Recruitment consultants
- Chambers of Commerce Consultants
- Guidance Experts
- Tutors for entrepreneurship
- Professionals accountant

5.2 Key Institutions to Partner Up with

The main institutions CIRSES have chosen to partner up and cooperate with are the following:

- Prima Forma - Progettazione Ricerca e Management per la Formazione
- Chamber of Commerce of Naples (Campania Region)
- Business Consultants - Rome
- Business Consultants – Naples
- Business Management Order – Roma
- Business Management Order – Naples
- ARLAS - Campania Region Agency for employment, education and
- training
- Cora Roma Onlus (Gender Guidance Association)
- Federimprese
- Università dei Sapori di Perugia – National Center on Training and Food Culture (Umbria Region)
- Confcommercio di Perugia
- Italia Lavoro
- ISFOL – Leonardo da Vinci National Agency/ERASMUS+

6 Dissemination and Exploitation in Portugal

6.1 Key Target Audiences

One of the goals of the Portuguese government within the scope of the New Opportunities Initiative is to increase the participation in initial VET (IVET). Therefore, the government has launched a wide media campaign known as "It pays to learn" in order to stress the importance of qualifying the Portuguese active population.

Since 2007, a total of eight campaigns were launched, specifically aimed at either young people or adults, or targeted at both audiences. The latest campaign, whose main message was to establish the completion of secondary education as a common goal to both youth and adults, was launched in September 2010 and was directed at adults who had not completed the 12th grade of secondary education and young people who at the time had started the secondary educational level.

The Portuguese participation in the Euroskills and Worldskills initiatives also intended to contribute to the growth of VET's public visibility. IVET participation is also encouraged by several economic benefits, such as training allowances.

Some measures were taken in order to assure the quality of double certification provision, particularly monitoring studies on vocational courses and their extension to the network of public schools. Vocational courses are a double certification training pathway which was previously delivered almost exclusively by private vocational schools. The target groups in Portugal to be addressed in this project are mainly VET students, either from the initial VET or the continuous VET systems.

Even if the higher education institutions, university students, universities staff members, unemployed youngsters, VET professionals and VET centres and are not part of the chosen target group, due to the topic of the project they will be important stakeholders and also main target groups of the project, respecting the dissemination project activity itself.

6.2 Key Institutions to Partner Up with

The main institutions that ISQ have chosen to partner up and cooperate with are:

- National Body for Qualification
- Portuguese Institute for Employment and VET
- Training Center for Trade Area
- Training Center for Handcraft Area
- Portuguese Foundation
- National Institute for SME's and Innovation
- Portuguese Entrepreneurial Association

The reason of the above selection is that they are partners in several networks of ISQ, and they fall into the target groups mentioned above in section 6.1. Moreover, the professionalism and the successful history of each of the above organizations, ensures the exploitation and viability of the project.

6.3 Key Events/fairs to Attend

ISQ has involved several staff members in a few events of different organizations, with the main aim of create awareness for the project objectives and future activities.

ISQ has been present in some meetings and seminars involving project stakeholders, mainly other VET centers where the project, its objectives, main activities and results were presented, in order to disseminate the project and at the same time create interest in the future phases, mainly for the project pilot training. For the future, ISQ foresees that all main events and fairs will be organized in Portugal, by several of our stakeholders in the training area. They can be seminars, conferences, and other projects meetings and also the events/fairs more oriented to students, like fairs, information days, seminars and conferences. However, ISQ intends also to have a spotlight in this project from some European and International organizations, like EVBB and SOLIDAR, two networks acting in the VET area that will gain a huge sustainability degree for the project results.

Conclusions and Outlook

This article has introduced the dissemination and exploitation aspect of a European initiative to introduce a certified training program that empowers creative minds to make their ideas become real in the form of sustainable entrepreneurship. While the first program of this initiative, ResEUr, is targeted at university students, the follow-up program Idea2Enterprise is mainly oriented towards VET and initial VET education levels. Rather than focussing on the formal process of company creation, Idea2Enterprise is focussed on the aspect of shaping ideas and successfully implementing them in entrepreneurship context. One key aspect of its uniqueness is that it integrates the visions and needs of eight EU countries, and is embedded in two other European initiatives, EuroSPI and the ECQA.

Dissemination and exploitation of Idea2Enterprise are carried out according to the framework rules of the ECQA, however with very specific strategic target groups and partners as pointed out in this article for the countries Cyprus, Czech Republic, Italy, and Portugal. The project partners are currently carrying out the initial pilot trainings, and there is opportunity for EuroSPI community members to join.

Acknowledgements. The "From Idea to Enterprise" project is financially supported by the European Commission in the Leonardo da Vinci part of the Lifelong Learning Programme under the project number CZ/12/LLP-LdV/TOI/134007. This publication reflects the views only of the authors, and the Commission cannot be held responsible for any use which may be made of the information contained therein.

References

1. ResEUr – ECQA Certified Researcher-Entrepreneur. Leonardo da Vinci project number 503021-LLP-1-2009-1-BE-LEONARDO-LMP
2. Tichkiewitch, S., Riel, A.: European Qualification and Certification for the Lifelong Learning. Keynote Paper. In: Fischer, X., Nadeau, J.-P. (eds.) Research in Interactive Design: Virtual, Interactive and Integrated Product Design and Manufacturing for Industrial Innovation, pp. 135–146. Springer (2010) ISBN 978-2817801681
3. Gavenda, M., Riel, A., Azevedo, A., Pais, M., Homolová, E., Balcar, J., Antinori, A., Metitiero, G., Giorgakis, G., Photiades, P., Ekert, D., Messnarz, R., Tichkiewitch, S.: Fostering innovation and entrepreneurship in european VET: EU project "From idea to enterprise". In: McCaffery, F., O'Connor, R.V., Messnarz, R. (eds.) EuroSPI 2013. CCIS, vol. 364, pp. 282–293. Springer, Heidelberg (2013)
4. European University, http://www.euc.ac.cy (last accessed on 07/04/2014.)
5. The University of Cyprus, http://www.ucy.ac.cy/en/ (last accessed on April 07, 2014)
6. Frederic University, http://www.frederick.ac.cy (last accessed on April 07, 2014)
7. Cyprus Chamber of Commerce and Industry, http://www.ccci.org.cy/ (last accessed on April 07, 2014)

8. Gavenda, M.: Prediction on supply and demand on labour market in Moravian-Silesian Region with focus on industry: Analysis for Joint Action Plan (2014) (last accessed on April 07, 2014)
9. Competencies for Life, http://www.kompetenceprozivot.cz/competencies-for-life/ (last accessed on April 07, 2014)
10. The Enterprise Training Simulation, http://www.ifsnetwork.it/portaleifs/index.php (last accessed on April 07, 2014)

Linguistic Analogy for Software Process Innovation

Kouichi Kishida

Software Research Associates, Inc., Tokyo, Japan
k2@sra.co.jp

Abstract. There are many useful metaphorical notions in linguistics to think about software process innovation. Continuous evolutionary change is the essential nature of any software system. Human languages also change over time. In this paper we will investigate some notions in linguistic study to apply issues of software process innovation.

Keywords: Conceptual Modelling, Language Change, Innovation Factors.

1 Conceptual Design in Software Development

American philosopher Nelson Goodman wrote in his famous book "Ways of World-making" as follows: *Countless worlds made by use of symbols. As a result, the multiplicity of worlds are given to us. A variety of components – matter, energy, waves, phenomena – are made along with the worlds. But made from what? Not from nothing, after all, but from existing other worlds. World-making as we know it always starts from worlds already on hand; the making is re-making.*

Software system development is a kind of world-making, because it is an activity to make a model of the target application world. Conceptual design in software development process is the most important phase which needs some innovative idea to make the system active. Goodman categorized following 5 logical process steps in conceptual design activities of world-making:

1. Composition and Decomposition
2. Weighting
3. Ordering
4. Deletion and Supplementation
5. Deformation

Composition and Decomposition

This is the first logical step of conceptual design. On the one hand, whole system are divided into parts and partitioning each components into sub-components, analyzing complexes into features, drawing distinctions; on the other hand, composing some components out of parts and members and subclasses, combining features into complexes, and making connections. Such composition or decomposition is normally effected or assisted or consolidated by the application of labels, names predicates, etc.

Weighting

The second logical step on conceptual design is to give weights for each component. When some relevant objects of a design are missing from another, we might perhaps better think that the two designs contain some classes sorted differently into relevant and irrelevant kinds. Some relevant objects in the one design, rather than being absent from the other, are present as irrelevant kinds; some differences among designs are not so much in entities comprised as in emphasis or accent, and these differences are no less consequential. Ratings of relevance, importance, utility, value often yield hierarchies rather than dichotomies.

Ordering

Designs not differing in entities or emphasis may differ in ordering. Ordering of a different sort pervade perception and practical cognition. The classic waterfall style ordering of software lifecycle model follows the linear logical sequence of development activities, but the spiral or iterative lifecycle model curls the straight logical line of sequential activities into a circle. Orderings alter with circumstances and objectives. As we often see in various design diagrams, the nature of shapes (icons) changes under different geometries, so do perceived patterns change under different orderings. Radical reordering of another sort occurs in building a unified and comprehensive image of a system from temporally, spatially and quantitatively heterogeneous observations and other items of information.

Deletion and Supplementation

Also, the making of one design out of another usually involves some extensive weeding out and filling – actual excision of some old and supply of some new material. According to psychology, in everyday life, we find what we are prepared to find, and we are likely to be blind to what does not help our purpose. In the painful experience of proofreading and the more joyful one of watching a skilled magician, we incurably miss something that is there and see something that is not there. Memory edits more ruthlessly. And even within what we do perceive and remember, we dismiss as illusory or negligible what cannot be fitted into the architecture of the design we are building. Perhaps the most spectacular metaphorical case of supplementation can be found in the perception of motion. There are many psychological experiment to make illusion by supplementing false objects.

Deformation

Finally some changes are reshaping or deformations that may be considered either corrections or distortions according to the designer's point of view. This process step is important because it is the final touch of design presentation rhetoric. These are ways of that designs are made. As Goodman wrote above classification is not comprehensive or clear-cut or mandatory. Often the actual processes will occur in combination or in random sequence. For example, some changes may be considered alternatively as re-weighting or reshaping or as all of these, and some deletions are all matters of differences in composition. Actual practice of conceptual design phase of software world-making activity is a random mixture of the above 5 logical steps performed upon virtual knowledge-base of already existing software systems. As

Goodman pointed out, world-making is a re-making. Our innovation is not a creating something new from nothing, but composition/decomposition, weighting, ordering, deletion/supplementation, and deformation of various components which can be found in the knowledge-base. The tool in our hand is "language": a variety of programing languages, symbolic diagrams, and natural languages.

2 Changing Nature of Language

Structural linguistics research originated by Swiss linguist Ferdinand de Saussure has many useful notions to think about various issues of software process innovation. For example, Saussure distinguished notions of *langue* and *parole*. According to him, *parole* is the specific utterance of speech, whereas *langue* refers to an abstract phenomenon that theoretically defines the systems of rules that govern a language. Applying simple analogy, *parole* is the specific activity of software development and *langue* is an abstract process model that defines the systematic rules for project management.

But situation is not so simple, rather more complicated. Looking back to the history, all languages have been changed over time. Structural linguistics has been putting focus of research on the static nature of langue and neglecting dynamic aspect of parole. So, it could not solve the difficult issue caused by the antinomie between synchrony and diachrony of langue.

The essential character of language is "Change". Software changes also. To keep its function active in the process of adapting to the change in operating environment, software must change its structure over time. Romanian linguist Eugenio Coseriu strongly advocated that linguistic study should concentrate the focus on dynamic changing nature of language. He criticized Soussure's *"langue-parole"* dichotomy and proposed a new trichotomy of *"system-norm-speech"* instead. He pointed that "language continuously change, could not perform its function without change."

In Coseriu's famous work "Sincronia, Diacronia e Historia (Synchrony, Diachrony and History)" contains many important suggestions useful when we consider about software process innovation. His notion of *"system"*, which corresponds to Soussure's *langue*, is our notion of software process model, and *"speech"*, which corresponds to Saussure's *parole*, is particular activity of software development in our daily life. Coseriu's unique notion of *"norm"* bridging the gap between *"system"* and *"speech"* seems to be an important key for process innovation.

As Jose Ortega=y=Gasset told in his last lecture "Man and People", we are not born to be a human being. When you are born, you are just an anonymous animal baby. You become a human by growing up in a human family and society. Through this growing up process, language plays a key-role for you. At first, you see a number of nameless people are walking around you. Your self-recognition is that you are also similar being like them. To live with those people, gradually you must understand the meaning of *speech,* coming out from people's mouth. That is the first close encounter with language for you.

As time flows you can distinguish some of people with specific faces and names as your family, friends, etc. Step-by-step, you learn how to use language as basic communication tool with them: meanings of various words, rules or patterns to present your feeling or thoughts in your speech. Those are the *norm* of language, which has been accumulated in the community around you. Later, in the lessons in various schools, you learn the *system* of your mother-tongue language in more complicated style as dictionary and standard grammar.

Other than communication support, we should not forget one more important feature of language: it is the fundamental recognition tool for us to understand the world by articulating things into their components. When you speak some words like "flower", "butterfly", or "process", already you have concrete images correspond to these spoken words in your mind. Such kind of word-to-matter correspondence is the common basis of our understanding of the world around us, and it also works as the *norm* of our communication via language.

But, sometime you suddenly feel an inconvenience with such a given *norm*, which are posed by the tradition, in presentation of your own unique idea or feeling. It seems necessary to modify the meaning of word or to invent new style of rhetoric in your speech or writing. That is the motivation for change.

For example, let's looking back to the change of meaning of the word "process" in our community. In 1960s, early days of computer science, optimization of "program execution process" inside computer hardware was the hottest topic of the age. Around 1970, new discipline of software engineering was born. People's concern moved out from hardware, and many new idea were proposed to solve technical or managerial problems in "software development process" outside of hardware. Then, during 1980s and 1990s, advances in micro-electrics and network technology resulted downsizing of computers and wide growth of application field. To deal with social requirement for more-and-more software development power, "technology transfer process" of training new generation of software engineers became big issue to solve. And now, we are in the Internet age, a variety of network-based social application systems were born. Those large-and-complex systems are evolving to adapt themselves for continuous change in their operating environment. We are now facing to the issue of how to deal with "system evolution process".

According to Coseriu, it is wrong to ask about the reason of language change. Because such a question is based upon belief that language is unchangeable thing. He claims that change is the essential nature of language. To ask "why?" about change of language is not a causality question. Language changes not because of some external reasons, but because of internal motivation within the mind of users of language.

We speak or write our idea by language. Speaking or writing is a kind of creative activity of human beings. Language is not imposed to us as a collection of restrictive rules. It is given as a model or tool for thinking and for communication. We create and present our own idea using our knowledge of traditional *norm* of language. When we feel some inconvenience with it, we can change it freely because it is just a tool. Language continuously evolves through such innovative process. This is the answer to the question of why language change.

Software system is also given to us as a model or tool to support our intellectual activity of information processing. It changes or evolves over time. There exist many stake-holders of software change. As Professor M.M.Lehman pointed out in his great theory of Software Evolution Dynamics, the process of change or evolution of software should be considered as a multi-level, multi-loop and multi-agent feedback system. A variety of human agents, not only developers and users but also managers and researchers of the process, are involved in this infinite loop of evolution.

Starting from the Waterfall Model (1970 by Winston Royce), many models of software evolution have been proposed so far. Most of them present some kinds of bird-eye view on the process from outside and discuss issues of process innovation. But, because everybody are involved in the evolution loop, no one can take such a bird-eye viewpoints. We need to consider how to construct an inside view of the maelstrom of software evolution process to discuss about innovation.

3 Innovation Factors in Language

In early 18th century, there lived a young philosopher in Osaka, Japan. His name was Nakamoto Tominaga, the third son of a rich merchant Hoshun Tominaga, who was a co-founder of the Kaitokudo Academy: a private school of philosophical study (mainly on Confucianism) for young people in the city. Nakamoto was a kind of genius child. During teen age, he studied almost all of contemporary Confusion philosopher's works in Japan, and after expounding many classic Chinese scriptures, he summarized his radical idea on the history of Confucianism in a book titled as "Setsu-Hei (Philosophical Obscurantism)". Publication of this book was treated as a scandal and the book was completely lost including its woodcut printing blocks. Nakamoto expelled from Kaitokudo. After this accident, he moved to another small private school and continued his research, this time careful investigation of large volumes of Buddhism scriptures.

One year before his early death as 31 years old, Nakamoto published 2 books: "Okina- no-Fumi (Testament of an Old Man)" and "Shutsu-Jou-Kou-Go (Words after Buddha's Enlightenment)". The latter book was a philological review of the history of Buddhism. He found a cardinal principle of "Ka-Jou (Transformative Accretion)" in the chronological evolution of various Buddhism sects; namely every new emerging sect adds some new idea or notion to Buddha's original sermon for the purpose of transforming it more attractive style.

Nakanoto also proposed that in doing philological analysis we should be careful about three fundamental factors of language: namely (1) who is the Person using it, (2) historical period of Time in which it is used, and (3) the Context of its use. As for the context, there are five typical Categories: Expansion, Inclination, Afloat, Limitation, and Irony. These categories work as the hidden driving forces of language change. Nakamoto wrote as follows: "My method of study emphasizes these three factors by which any human discourse can be properly understood. As long as one's approach is made through these three factors, there is no discourse that rejects clear understanding."

Nakamoto's approach was very much neutral one. But his book received strong attacks from contemporary Buddhists because the target of analysis was their sacred scriptures. As a result, his name was almost eliminated from the philosophical record of the age. It was needed 200 years of time until a famous Professor Konan Naito of Kyoto University re-discovered him and evaluated his intellectual contribution properly. Nakamoto's "3 Factors and 5 Categories" approach is useful for us to make philological analysis of various innovations in software technology. For example, as for various process models like "Waterfall", "Spiral", "Incremental", "Process Programming", "CMM", "SPICE", etc., it is interesting who proposed these models, in which period of time, and they were emerged in what kind of context. Also, as for a variety of software design methods, category analysis of each method will produce interesting result to consider new technological innovation in future.

4   Final Remark

In this paper, I've introduced three philosopher's work on conceptual modeling, change of language, and philological study approach as useful metaphors to think about issues of innovation. It seems better to stop your feet for a while and consider those philosophical background of technology evolution before jump into technical matters directly.

References

1. Goodman, N.: Ways of Worldmaking. Hacket (1978)
2. Coseriu, E.: Sincronia, Diacronia e Historia. Madrid (1973)
3. Gasset,J.O.Y.: Man and People, W.W.Norton (1966)
4. Lehman, M.M.: Programs, Lifecycles, and Law of Software Evolution. Proceedings of IEEE (1980)
5. Najita, T.: Visions of Virtue in Tokugawa Japan – The Kaitokudo, Merchant Academy of Osaka. University of Hawaii Press (1988)

Finding Threats with Hazards in the Concept Phase of Product Development

Masao Ito

Nil Software Corp., Tokyo, Japan
nil@nil.co.jp

Abstract. In this paper, we present an approach to find threats together with hazards. We've already presented the hazard identification approach in [1]. In this paper, it is elaborated and extended to identify threats too. The basic approach is the same as the previous paper and has four steps. First of all, we roughly describe the static structure and dynamic behaviour. Then using the goal-oriented approach, we depict the goal tree of a system. The top goal of the tree is the most abstract representation of a system and we will divide it repeatedly. If S is a sentence as a description of each goal, we can make the new sentence S-* by applying the *guideword* of HAZOP [2] (when we adopt the NO *guideword*, we name the new sentence S-NO, asterisk means the meta-character here). S is a desirable goal; S-* is an undesirable goal (i.e. anti-goal [3]). Using the previous static structure and dynamic behaviour, we then consider whether it is possible to create this negative situation caused by the malfunction of each node or attack to a relation between nodes. The exhaustiveness is important for finding hazards and threats. In our methods, we check them in two ways. One is the checking of the sentence of the goal description using the *guideword*; the other covers every structural and dynamic elements of a target system.

Keywords: Security, safety, hazards, threats, goal model, ISO 26262.

1 Introduction

Recently, improving security of software-intensive systems is one of the crucial issues for system / software development. Many embedded systems in the home electric appliances, cars and so on are becoming connect to the network, which may have the risk portal for the malicious people [4]. This phenomenon resembles the situation already occurred in the world of the Personal Computer.

Therefore, we need the technique for the security risk analysis. There are several techniques for analysis [5], but as for the concept phase of the system development, the number of the methods by which we can find the threats is small. The COARS [6, 7] or EVITA approach [8] is new and gives a comprehensive development process to achieve high security capability. The former is providing the systematic way for analysing the unsecure system, but gives threats after discussing in a workshop by the collective wisdom of the participants: "[We] expect from the participants" (p.130). In the latter approach, we can find threats after assigning functions to an architecture, which means that the phase to find threats is not a concept one.

We recently extend our CARDION [1] approach for the functional safety in order to capture the security threats. In the automobile, the security is not only attacking the assets[1], but also it is relating to the safety. If malicious people attack the core of the braking control, the behaviour of a car is dangerous even if there is no failure in the braking parts.

Our method has three positive features; (a) It can be applied in the concept phase of the product developments. (b) It can handle both threats for security and hazards for safety. (c) It provides clear steps to find the threats / hazards.

First we present our approach in detail (Chapter 2) and we compare it against the related works (Chapter 3). Finally we conclude them (Chapter 4).

We clarify the detailed steps in the concept phase of product development. And it makes us easy to check or assess those activities.

2 Process

Our approach has four process elements.

- Sketching a system schematically (2.1)
- Writing top-goal and decomposing it repeatedly (2.2)
- Applying *guideword* to each goal (2.3)
- Finding the candidate of threats and hazards (2.4)

The iterative execution of this process is essential. We might find the missing information from the previous loop. For example, when we decompose the goal, we might find a lacking element of an original goal and it helps us to find other candidates of threats and hazards.

2.1 Making a Rough Sketch of a System

The schematic sketch of a system that is composed of the static and dynamic part is important. The schematic description gives a clue for our intuition on finding threats and hazards and helps to assure the completeness of our checking. The representation of static structure of a system gives by the diagram, for example, class diagram of UML, internal block diagram of SysML [9] or the specification type representation of CATALYSIS approach [10]. The finite state diagram is good for indicating the system behaviour. But roughness is important because in concept phase we cannot get the detailed information of the target system.

---

[1] In the standard (ISO/IEC 27000:2012), the word asset is "[an] asset is any tangible or intangible thing or characteristic that has value to an organization. There are many types of assets. Some of these include obvious things like machines, facilities, patents, and software…"

Finding Threats with Hazards in the Concept Phase of Product Development   279

The static representation gives us the relationship between the nouns in the description of a goal. Here, we use an Adaptive Cruise Control (ACC) system as an example. The phrase, S1: "The system of a self car can recognise the forward car by the milliwave radar" can be described like this.

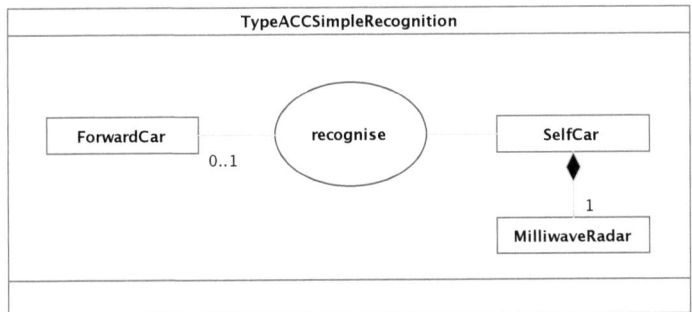

Fig. 1. A static representation (type representation of ACC)

We can find correspondences here between the nouns "self car" / "milliwave radar" / "forward car" in the S1 and the class SelfCar / MilliwaveRadar / ForwardCar in the static representation respectively. Name of behaviour (ellipse shape like use case) shows the verb of a sentence, "recognise". It is a kind of action.

This correspondence between the description of the semi-formal form and the expression in the natural language is important, and we discuss it again in the section 2.4.

Dynamic representations show the change of a system after running an action. If the 'recognise' action successfully identifies the forward car, the event 'recognised' occur and the state changes from the "StandBy" state to the "Following" state. It is depicted in the Finite State Machine (FSM) diagram (Figure 2 upper left, FSM_A). We also write the FSM of ACC switch (Figure 2 down left, FSM_B).

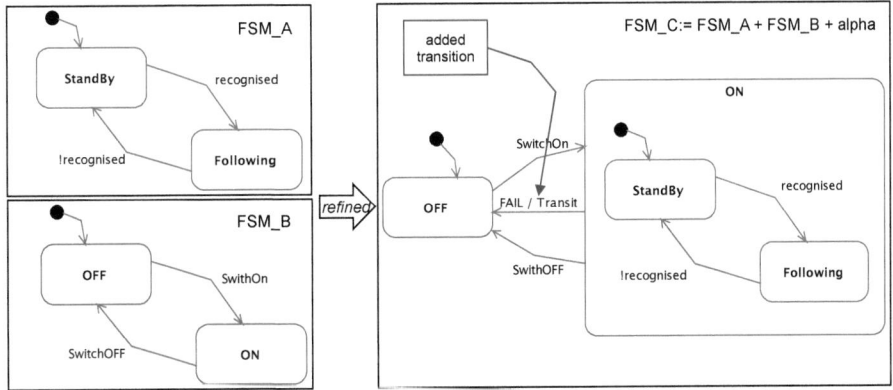

Fig. 2. Dynamic representations: first diagrams (left), refined diagram (right)

These first dynamic representations are refined by the operation of synthesis. We synthesise FSM_A and FSM_B, and can get the refined FSM_C (Figure 2 right). The important point is that this operation is not always a mechanical one. We might think exceptional cases after synthesis. In this diagram, we add the new transition for the occurrence of FAIL event.

The level of refinements is corresponding to the level of the goal decomposition (2.2). Decomposing goal needs further refinement of static and dynamic representation.

2.2 Goal Decomposition

We analyse the system using the goal model of KAOS approach [11], which is one of the most well-known goal-oriented requirements analysis methods. There are several resemblances between the requirements analyse and the process for safety and security in the concept phase; those are the process of defining the requirements, the architecture of a product is obscure, and we consider many merits and de-merits to achieve the stakeholders' goal.

The goal is decomposed by the AND/OR refinement. The AND-refinement shows the link that relates a goal to a set of sub-goals and the OR-refinement shows alternatives to satisfy the upper goal.

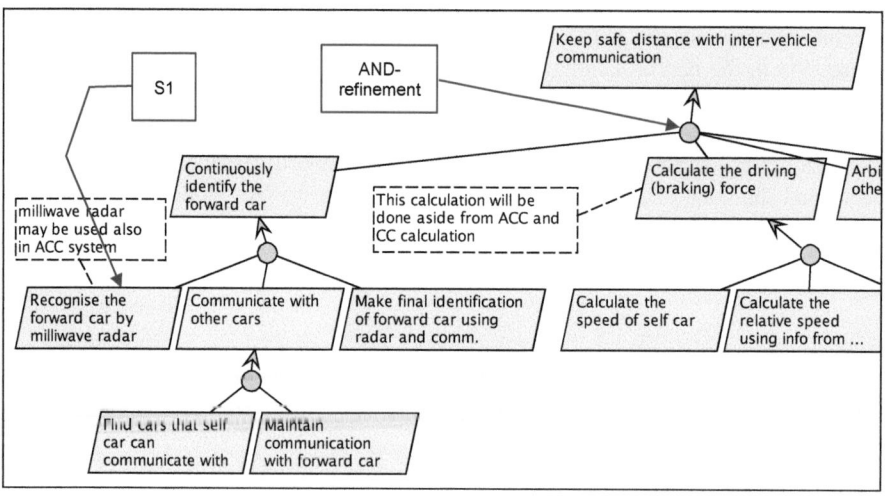

Fig. 3. A goal model

2.3 Applying Guidewords

We apply the *guidewords* of HAZOP [2, 12, 13] to the description of each goal. The *guidewords* are categorized in two types; time relating ones (Table 1) and space relating ones (Table 2).

Table 1. HAZOP guidewords of the space category

Guideword	Meaning
NO or NOT	Negation
MORE or LESS	Increases or decreases
AS WELL AS	Qualitative increase
PART OF	Qualitative decrease
REVERSE	Opposite
OTHER THAN	Substitution

Table 2. HAZOP guidewords of the time category

Guideword	Meaning
EARLY or LATE	Related to the clock time
BEFORE or AFTER	Relating to order or sequence

If a goal has a sentence S1:"the system of a self car can recognise the forward car by the milliwave radar", the new sentence S1-NOT applied NOT *guideword* is "the system of a self car can NOT recognise the forward car by the milliwave radar". This negative sentence will be the start line to find out hazards and threats in the next section.

2.4 Hazards and Threats Finding

2.4.1 Hazards

Then we can investigate this situation more deeply with the schematic expression. If we are in the "Following" state in figure 2 and the system abruptly changes to OFF mode without an operation, the car might go close into the forward car that is decelerating.

Another example comes from a static representation (figure 1). The cardinality of the forward car is zero or one, but we apply MORE *guideword*. It means that there are two or more forward cars and the system cannot distinguish them. If one of the forward cars accelerates, the system might try to follow the car and cause the crash with other forward car.

2.4.2 Threats

There is a difference between hazards and threats. The hazard comes from the failure of parts or insufficient design of a system. The threats arise by the malicious attacker.

So the interpretation of the sentence that applied a *guideword* is a little bit different, but we can find threats in a similar fashion. We think that bad situation shown in the sentence is caused by the attack. For example, S1-NOT means that the system does not recognise the forward car because of attacker's behaviour.

There are two points to find out threats from the sentence with a *guideword*. First point is the asset that should be guarded from the threat. The second is the intra-communication in a system or the inter-communication with other system. For example, the figure four shows the static representation of a Cooperative Adaptive Cruise Control (CACC) system [14]. The node, which is expressed by the class, is the candidate of an asset to be guarded. Here we choose the software-relating node; "History Data" holds the information of recognition results per calculation cycle. We can use this data for the plausible check of forward car recognition. If there is a big difference between current data and the data of previous cycle, it means the error / attack occurrence. The spoofing of this historical data is a threat because it can change the behaviour of the system. The other candidate is the communication for target recognition. The communication is easier for tampering than the node, and this action is the second candidate of the threat.

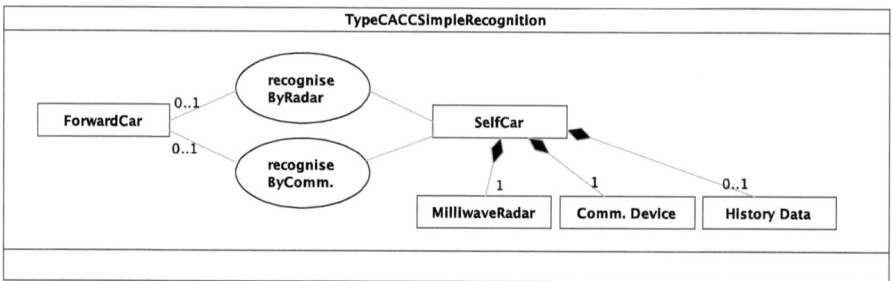

Fig. 4. CACC static representation

We can imagine other threats (e.g. modifying the content of memory, message of CAN tampering) by the later system design or hardware design phase. But those are out of scope of our paper.

3 Related Work

Though there are several researches that can handle finding threats and hazards, those don't have the detail process in the concept phase of products.

The CORAS approach [6] is the method of risk analysis, especially focused on the security risk analysis. This is a model-based approach and the central diagram is the threat diagram.

Original KAOS methods can deal with the security [3]. Using the patterns that "are associated with specializations of the SecurityGoal meta-class, namely, Confidentiality, Integrity, Availability, Privacy, Authentication and Non-repudiation goal subclasses", the anti-goal model tree will be built. This tree is good for showing the cause-effect relationship of an anti-goal. The key idea for finding threat is the application of those patterns.

The STAMP-based Process Analysis (STPA) [15] is the safety analysis method focusing on the inter-action of controller. Recently it is extended to include security analysis; STPA-Sec [16]. It, like safety, checks the vulnerability caused by the controller-interaction. This method can handle both safety and security, but it needs the system-level requirements "when the analysis process begin" ([15] p.213). So, it is not suitable for the concept phase.

As for automobile field, EVITA is a European project for "secure and trustworthy intra-vehicular communication", and it has a method for risk analysis [17, 18]. In this method, the use case is described and then the assets are defined. Candidate type for asset is the operational performance, safety, privacy or financial property. The threats are derived from the dark-side scenario "which are intended to establish ways in which the system could become a target for malicious attacks". If we could describe a system in detail, we also can write the detailed scenario and attacker tree.

4 Conclusion

To handle the security, we extend our safety analysis method, CARDION [1]. In this paper, we show concrete steps to find threats along with hazards. Our methods start from describing a system roughly with the viewpoint of static structure and dynamic behaviour. Then we discuss the functionality of a system by the goal-oriented approach. In the example, we use the goal model of KAOS approach. The goal is repeatedly subdivided into the sub-goal. We apply the *guideword* to the description of each goal and we can get the base sentence to find out hazards and threats. The rough sketch of a system of a system is very useful in this step; the node and their relation in the static structure diagram (e.g. class diagram), and the state transition in the dynamic behaviour diagram (e.g. finite state machine diagram) is the candidate of them. In [1], we show how to introduce the safety goal and safety requirements. In terms of security, we also can derive the security goal and security requirements in the same manner. Some security violations might cause the safety problem. So, it is very useful to simultaneously analyse a system from the viewpoint of safety and security.

References

1. Ito, M.: An approach to manage the concept phase of ISO 26262. In: Euro SPI 2013. DELTA, Dundalk (2013)
2. CEI/IEC, Hazard and operability studies (HAZOP studies) - Application guide, CEI/IEC 61882:2001, IEC (2001)
3. van Lamsweerde, A.: Elaborating security requirements by construction of intentional anti-models. In: Proceedings of the 26th International Conference on Software Engineering. IEEE Computer Society (2004)
4. Shi, J., et al.: A survey of cyber-physical systems. In: 2011 International Conference on Wireless Communications and Signal Processing (WCSP). IEEE (2011)
5. Kleidermacher, D., Kleidermacher, M.: Embedded systems security: practical methods for safe and secure software and systems development, 1st edn., xx, 396 p. Elsevier, Amsterdam (2012)
6. Lund, M.S., Solhaug, B., Stølen, K.: Model-driven risk analysis: the CORAS approach. Springer (2010)

7. Brændeland, G., Dahl, H.E.I., Engan, I., Stølen, K.: Using dependent CORAS diagrams to analyse mutual dependency. In: Lopez, J., Hämmerli, B.M. (eds.) CRITIS 2007. LNCS, vol. 5141, pp. 135–148. Springer, Heidelberg (2008)
8. Henniger, O., et al.: Securing vehicular on-board it systems: The evita project. In: VDI/VW Automotive Security Conference (2009)
9. OMG, OMG Systems Modeling Language (OMG SysML) V1.1, formal/2008-11-01, OMG (2008)
10. D'Souza, D.F., Wills, A.C.: Objects, Components, and Frameworks with UML: The Catalysis Approach. Addison-Wesley Professional (1998)
11. van Lamsweerde, A.: Requirements engineering: from system goals to UML models to software specifications. John Wiley & Sons Ltd. (2009)
12. Kletz, T.A.: Hazop and hazan: identifying and assessing process industry hazards, 3rd edn., viii, p. 150. Institute of Chemical Engineers. Rugby (1992)
13. Winther, R., Johnsen, O.-A., Gran, B.A.: Security assessments of safety critical systems using HAZOPs. In: Voges, U. (ed.) SAFECOMP 2001. LNCS, vol. 2187, pp. 14–24. Springer, Heidelberg (2001)
14. Van Arem, B., van Driel, C.J., Visser, R.: The impact of cooperative adaptive cruise control on traffic-flow characteristics. IEEE Transactions on Intelligent Transportation Systems 7(4), 429–436 (2006)
15. Leveson, N.: Engineering a safer world: Systems thinking applied to safety. MIT Press (2011)
16. Young, W., Leveson, N.G.: An integrated approach to safety and security based on systems theory. Commun. ACM 57(2), 31–35 (2014)
17. Kelling, E., et al.: Specification and evaluation of e-security relevant use cases. EVITA Deliverable D2.1, EVITA project (2009)
18. Ruddle, A., et al.: Security requirements for automotive on-board networks based on darkside scenarios. EVITA Deliverable D2.3, EVITA project (2009)

Integrating Functional Safety, Automotive SPICE and Six Sigma – The AQUA Knowledge Base and Integration Examples

Richard Messnarz[1], Christian Kreiner[2], Andreas Riel[3], Serge Tichkiewitch[3], Damjan Ekert[1], Michael Langgner[4], and Dick Theisens[5]

[1] ISCN LTD/GesmbH, Schieszstattgasse 4, A-8010 Graz, Ireland and Austria
rmess@iscn.com
[2] Graz University of Technology, Austria
[3] EMIRAcle c/o Grenoble Institute of Technology GSCOP UMR5272, Grenoble, France
[4] Automotive Cluster Austria, Austria
[5] Symbol BV, Netherlands

Abstract. AQUA stands for Knowledge Alliance for Training Quality and Excellence in Automotive. The AQUA project is financially supported by the European Commission in the Leonardo da Vinci part of the Lifelong Learning Programme under the project number EAC-2012-0635. This paper extends the EuroSPI 2013 publication [4] which discussed (based on the EU project AQUA) how the core elements of three complementary approaches (Automotive SPICE, Functional safety, Six Sigma) and standards can be integrated into one compact skill set with training and best practices to be applied. In this paper we describe the modular knowledge base which was elaborated and highlight some aspects where the integrated use of all three methods can be demonstrated. The results of the project are disseminated to Automotive industry in partnership with a set of European Automotive associations.

Keywords: Automotive SPICE, Functional Safety, Lean Six Sigma, Integrated Approach for Engineering, AQUA - Automotive Knowledge Alliance.

1 The AQUA Modular Knowledge Base

AQUA [4] developed an architectural concept that allows focusing on specific core areas (e.g. Product Development – Life Cycle) and to access an introduction and proposed best practices from four different views (see Fig. 1):

1. Integrated View
2. Automotive SPICE [6]
3. Functional Safety [9]
4. Six Sigma [7]

This modular strategy (in German "Baukasten") allows companies to select each method separately or also to gain an advanced insight into how these methods in fact are working together in advanced engineering companies.

While there are publications about how to integrate Automotive SPICE with Functional safety [2],[3],[4], [5], there are no materials available so far about how to integrate all three methods in an integrated engineering life cycle.

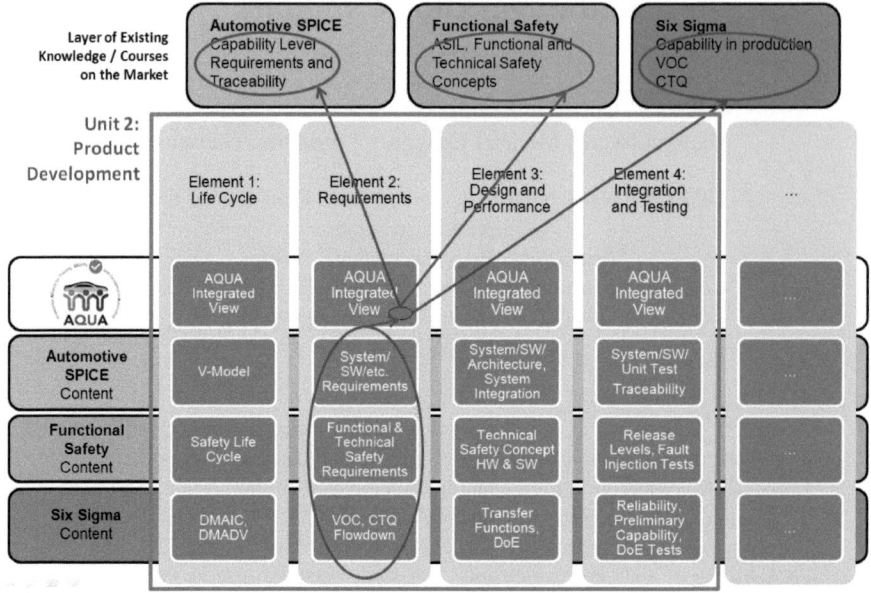

Fig. 1. The AQUA Architectural Concept

In the year 2013 the modular structure and a first baseline of the modules have been developed. Units (U1 to U4) represent main areas of knowledge and skills elements (e.g. E1) form specific knowledge areas in which an integrated view can be implemented.

UnitID	Unit Name	Element ID	Element Name
AQUA.U1	Introduction	AQUA.U1.E1	Integration view and general part
		AQUA.U1.E2	Organisational readiness
AQUA.U2	Product Development	AQUA.U2.E1	Lifecycle
		AQUA.U2.E2	Requirements
		AQUA.U2.E3	Design
		AQUA.U2.E4	Integration and Testing
AQUA.U3	Quality and Safety Management	AQUA.U3.E1	Capability
		AQUA.U3.E2	Hazard & Risk management
		AQUA.U3.E3	Assessment and audit
AQUA.U4	Measure	AQUA.U4.E1	Measurements
		AQUA.U4.E2	Reliability

Fig. 2. The AQUA Training Elements

Not in all areas of the three methods a synergy can be achieved, and the Fig. 2 illustrates the areas where the AQUA team identified synergy potentials in engineering.

For each element in Fig. 2 four types of modules exist:
1. From the integrated perspective
2. From the Automotive SPICE perspective
3. From the Functional Safety perspective
4. From the Six Sigma perspective

2   An Integrated Life Cycle Perspective at Start

AQUA decided to use the V-Model as a common known pattern to create a mapping of the 3 methods on a high level. A V-model published in a book together with Continental Automotive (Software Engineering nach Automotive SPICE) was used as an underlying framework.

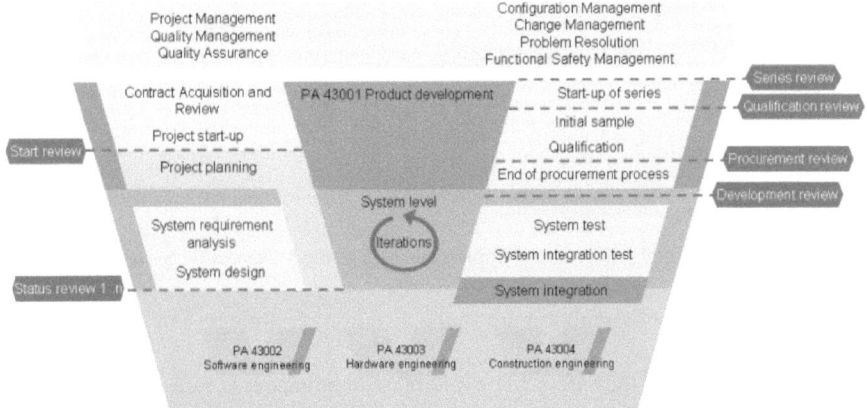

Reference: Software Engineering nach Automotive SPICE – Ein Continental Projekt auf dem Weg zu Level 3

Fig. 3. Automotive SPICE based Implementation of the V-Model on System Level

both trainers and trainees to capitalise on existing training programs in the three expert areas while providing them convenient and understandable access to the core vehicular knowledge that links them together. Figure 1 indicates the concept that the project team has implemented: based on existing established programs in the areas Automotive SPICE, Functional Safety, and Six Sigma, some specific "linking elements" have been defined. For each of these elements (e.g. life cycle, requirements, etc. in Figure 1), new training modules have been developed ("AQUA Integrated View" in Figure 1), explaining the relevance of key terms related to the respective element, and how they relate to the specific (vernacular) terms used in the three expert areas. Thanks to this modular architecture, companies can compose trainings that correspond to their specific needs in terms of building up capacities fostering the integrated treatment of quality and risk aspects in their specific organisations.

Starting from this V-Model it is straightforward to overlay the existing Automotive SPICE processes (see Fig. 3) with specific ISIO 26262 (Functional safety) related results (see Fig. 4). This was in fact discussed and published in safety management related papers at EuroSPI 2012 and EuroSPI 2013 [2], [3], [5].

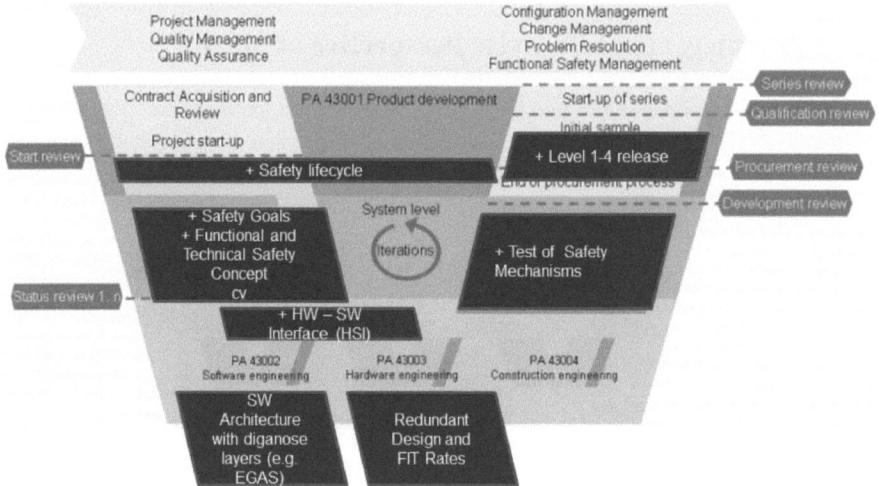

Fig. 4. Functional Safety based Implementation of the V-Model on Systems Level

Comparing Figure 3 with Figure 4 the overlaying strategy can be explained as follows:

In project planning the safety life cycle must be planned as well (adding to project planning). In system requirements the safety goals from the hazard and risk analysis and the counter measures from the FMEDA are considered and a Functional Safety Concept is created (adding to system requirements analysis). In systems design the functional safety concept is refined into a set of technical safety requirements and a technical safety concept (adding to systems design).

Usually in recent Automotive projects extra release levels 1 to 4 have been added, with 1 meaning the release for bench test, 2 meaning the release for test driver on inner circuit, 3 meaning test driver on road and 4 meaning the normal driver on the road (adding to the test levels).

However, if you have already an Automotive SPICE based traceability of requirements in place this only means additional filters for safety requirements and level releases. The main concept of traceability stays the same.

Also we asked the Six Sigma experts to position them in this framework, and the result is shown in Fig. 5.

Comparing Figure 3 with Figure 5 the overlaying strategy can be explained as follows:

In Six Sigma the management of the improvement project follows the DMAIC (Define – Measure – Analyze – Improve – Control) and DMADV (Define - Measure - Analyze - Design – Verify) cycles (adding to the management processes). Six Sigma tools like QFD (Quality Function Deployment) and VOC (Voice of the Customer) help in identifying the customer requirements which have the highest impact on success (adding in the planning of the project part). For systems design the DFMEA (Design FMEA) helps to analyze potential malfunctions and causes. It defines counter measures in turn that help to increase the product reliability (adding in the system requirements analysis and system design). A method like DOE (Design of Experiments) helps in system design to analyze the dependency of design parameters and decide about optimized design parameters which have an impact on e.g. reliability and quality (adding in the implementation phase).

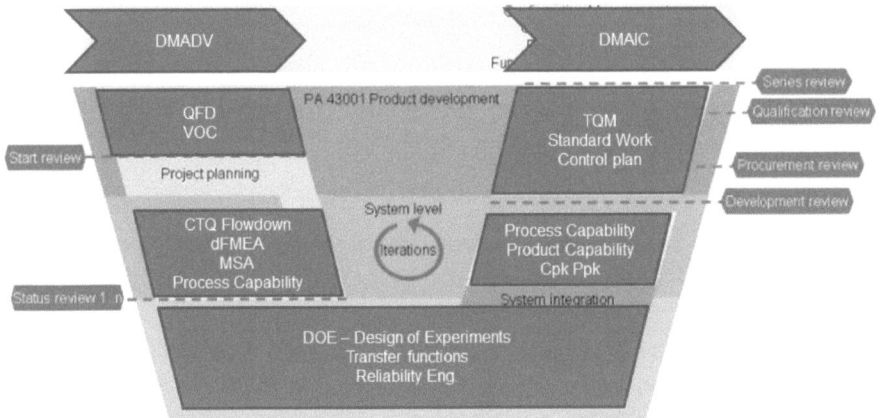

Fig. 5. Mapping of Selected Six Sigma Tools / Methods onto the V-Model on Systems Level

This integrated V-Model view leads to the conclusion that it is possible to set up an integrated engineering life cycle in which areas where the three methods overlap can identified and a more integrated automotive quality engineering approach can be used.

3   Integration Aspects on a Technical Level – Example Systems Design

Systems Design (AQUA U2.E3) is only one core element where an integrated view can be implemented. In total we created 11 such views in AQUA.

Experts from Automotive SPICE, functional safety and Six Sigma started from the integrated V-Model view and elaborated a set of best practices to be represented in a systems design which would satisfy all 3 methods.

Each of the three methods expects a specific life cycle in the design (see Fig. 6): 1 - Blue (Automotive SPICE), 2 – Green (Six Sigma), and 3 – Red (Functional Safety).

ASPICE

Iterations of the V model producing HW, SW and mechanical samples that are planned as phases and grow in functional maturity.

DfSS

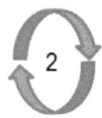
DMAIC – Define Measure Analyse Improve and Control Focussing on specific quality problems using statistical tools to reach targets within low variation

Functional Safety

Safety Life Cycle – Assuring the phases and results required by ISO 26262 to assure a product where a failure of SW or HW or electronics cannot lead to a hazard

Fig. 6. Specific Life Cycle Understanding per Method

An integrated design approach then requires:

- A function-oriented design view in all three life cycle aspects
- A consideration of the complete system in terms of
    - Software
    - Hardware (E/EE/PE)
    - ALL THE REST (mechanics, hydraulics, etc.)
- Embedded, integrated iterations of 1-blue (ASPICE) and 3-red (Functional Safety) design cycles for safety critical functions
- Embedded, integrated iterations of 2-green (DfSS – Design for Six Sigma) and 1-blue (ASPICE)/2-red (Functional Safety) design cycles on system level

Fig. 7 explains this integrated approach using the example of an electronically controlled damper system in cars.

An adaptive damping system is a safety-critical item consisting of several systems and subsystems. Special design measures have to be taken to assure a certain defined quality and reliability of the whole signal path that is related to the adaptive damping function. E.g. an architectural design decision has been taken to use a redundant analogue damping pressure signal in addition to the digital signal on the FlexRay bus is a system-level design decision that has to be integrated in the whole system-level design cycle (→ *3-red cycle embedded in the 1-blue cycle*).

The consistent and reliable choice of the pressure sensors requires DfSS methods (failure rate/FIT determination and verification), as well as a DOE to analyse the dependency of design parameters. That means, there is a 2-green cycle linked to the 3-red cycle, and therefore also influencing design decisions.

Both 1-blue (ASPICE) and 2-red (Functional Safety) cycles are integrated in a 2-green (DfSS) cycle to assure the continuous improvement of the design parameters.

Another typical example of a link between Six Sigma (2-green), Functional safety (3-red), and Automotive SPICE (1-blue) cycles is that Six Sigma delivers FMEA results which become requirements to be traced in ASPICE, and lead to implemented counter measures to avoid hazards in functional safety.

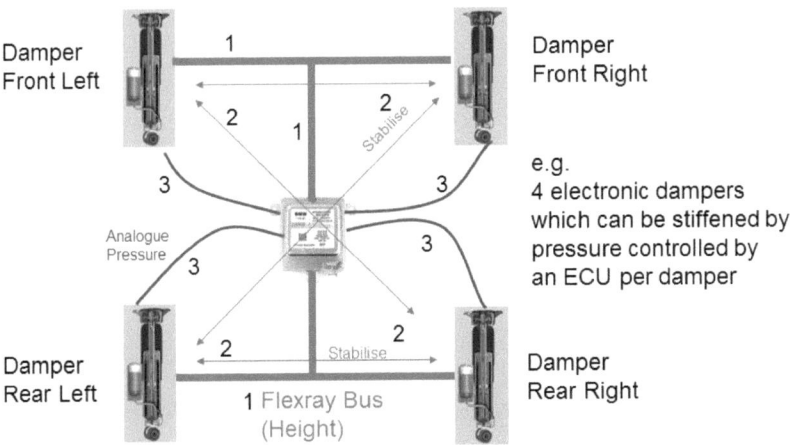

- **System Architectural Design** describes the components, their interfaces, and the system functions.

Fig. 7. Example Design Integrating Aspects of all 3 Methods

The conclusion is that in Automotive projects developing HW/SW/Mechanics it is required to integrate aspects of all three methods to assure that all functions are complete and tracked (Automotive SPICE), all functions and design measures to avoid hazards and to achieve safety are implemented (Functional safety), and that the dependency of design parameters is understood to assure a reliable product as well (Six Sigma).

4 Influencing the Future PEPs – Product Engineering Process

AQUA did not only develop examples in technical areas where all three methods are integrated. AQUA also analyzed the impact of the integrated view on the overall product engineering process life cycle.

Here we differentiate between different views again:
- Timeline View
- Components View
- Level of Detail View

Fig. 8 illustrates the timeline view and the typical scope of the methods. Automotive SPICE and Functional safety are mainly used in the development till the SPO. Six Sigma is mainly used in the production but offers many tools (DFSS, DOE, QFD, etc.) which help in the engineering process (therefore an overlapping of the phase is shown).

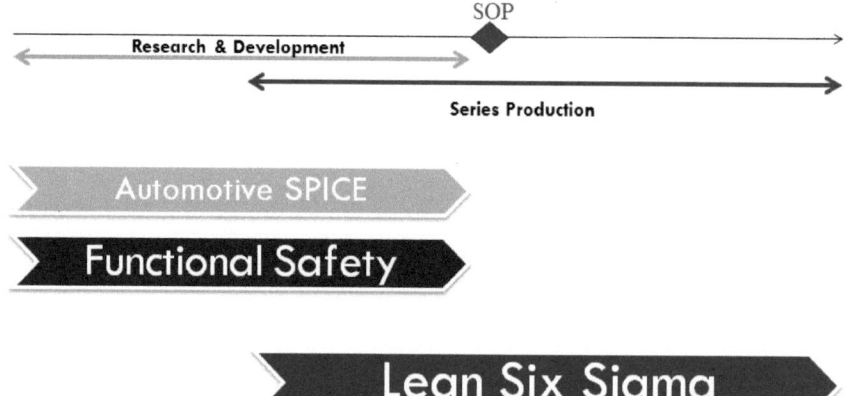

Fig. 8. Integrated Product Engineering Process (PEP) – Timeline View

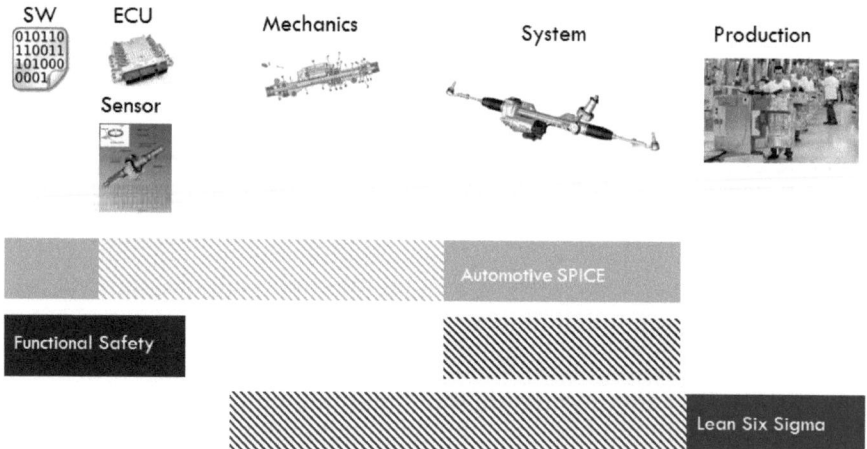

Fig. 9. Integrated Product Engineering Process (PEP) – Components View

In Fig. 9 typical components of a steering system are illustrated and which method directly influences the design of which type of component in such an integrated Automotive engineering product.

Automotive SPICE focuses on system and software requirements and their traceability. Functional safety focuses on the hardware and software components in the system. And Six Sigma focuses on the whole product and mostly mechanical parts.

Fig. 10 illustrates that in many parts Functional Safety uses the terminology and traceability aspects of Automotive SPICE. However, functional safety also looks at the methods used and reviews the product itself (not only the process). In Fig. 10, for instance, we highlight that Automotive SPICE would expect a software architectural design, while Functional Safety would also check the design methods used and if the design itself fulfils specific criteria (e.g. freedom of interference of safety critical functions/code).

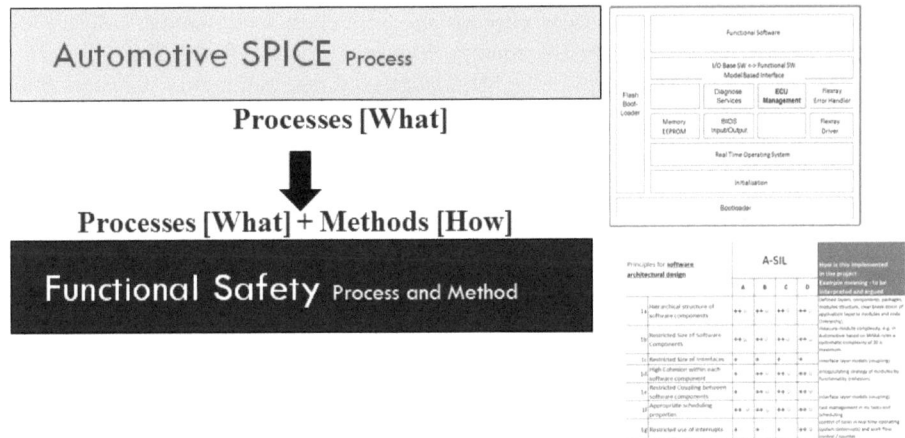

Fig. 10. Integrated Product Engineering Process (PEP) – Level of Detail View

5 Motivation

In the past the role of an Automotive quality manager based on standards like IEC 16949 and the implementation of a quality management system. With the increase of complexity of car functionality and the use of electronics (more than 100 ECUs in cars connected by a bus and each car function mapped onto an ECU cluster) Automotive SPICE (ISO 15504) knowledge is meanwhile an important area of knowledge to assesses Automotive systems which include electronic and software. Most of the manufacturers demand a SPICE level 3 from the suppliers.

Faults of electronic and software can lead to hazards (e.g. blocking wheels, unintended steering, no brake force, etc.) so that a new standard ISO 26262 for functional safety has to be implemented. Systems that might cause a hazard get classified by an ASIL-A to D level. Therefore quality managers that have to release a product to the market must know about functional safety as well. Quality management (also already at IEC 16949) has a responsibility for the entire product cycle, including the production part. Six Sigma is nowadays the most well-known method and statistical tool box for quality control in production. In AQUA we form the picture of a new education "Automotive Quality Manager with AQUA Skills" where we train quality managers for the integrated understanding of the above three methods.

6 Outlook: Future Automotive Quality Manager Certifications

AQUA developed 41 knowledge modules for 11 elements of knowledge. In particular, the integrated views introduced by AQUA are an innovative, practicable input to future engineering strategies in Automotive. In 2014 - in the course of the AQUA project[1] - training and workshops are offered to Automotive industry by partnering Automotive Clusters of Austria, Slovenia, and the Czech Republic. This will lead to a further refinement of the knowledge modules. Automotive Clusters from Austria, Slovenia, Czech Republic and large suppliers in Germany train in 2014 their quality managers based on the AQUA schema. utomotive Quality Managers are offered an AQUA certificate which is managed by the European Certification and Qualification association (www.ecqa.org). The certification is based on the AQUA skills set (developed in 2013) and a set of exam questions managed by the exam systems of ECQA.

7 Acknowledgements for EU Project and SOQRATES Group

The AQUA project is financially supported by the European Commission in the Leonardo da Vinci part of the Lifelong Learning Programme under the project number EAC-2012-0635. This publication reflects the views only of the authors, and the Commission cannot be held responsible for any use which may be made of the information contained therein. We are grateful to the experts who have contributed to the SoQrates Design AK and Safety AK: A. Kaufmann, W. Aschenberger, H. Zauchner (KTM Motorsport), O. Bachmann (SIBAC), S. Habel, I. Sokic, R. Dreves, C. Baer (Continental Automotive), F. König, H. Galle, P. Hagenmeyer (ZF), A. Much (Elektrobit), L. Borgmann (HELLA), K. Dussa-Zieger, B. Sechser (Methodpark), P. Schmidt-Weber (EPCOS), F. Hällmayer (SW Factory), L. Haunert (G&D), G. Griessnig (AVL), P. Schwann, J. Shell (NXP), A. Riel (EMIRAcle), and D. Ekert, R. Messnarz (ISCN).

---

[1] http://automotive-knowledge-alliance.eu/

References

1. Automotive Cluster Austria, AC Quarterly Magazine (February 2012)
2. Riel, A., Bachmann, V.O., Dussa-Zieger, K., Kreiner, C., Messnarz, R., Nevalainen, R., Sechser, B., Tichkiewitch, S.: EU Project SafEUr – Competence Requirements for Functional Safety Managers. In: Winkler, D., O'Connor, R.V., Messnarz, R. (eds.) EuroSPI 2012. CCIS, vol. 301, pp. 253–265. Springer, Heidelberg (2012)
3. Messnarz, R., König, F., Bachmann, V.O.: Experiences with trial assessments combining automotive SPICE and functional safety standards. In: Winkler, D., O'Connor, R.V., Messnarz, R. (eds.) EuroSPI 2012. CCIS, vol. 301, pp. 266–275. Springer, Heidelberg (2012)
4. Kreiner, C., Messnarz, R., Riel, A., Ekert, D., Langgner, M., Theisens, D., Reiner, M.: Automotive knowledge alliance AQUA – integrating automotive SPICE, six sigma, and functional safety. In: McCaffery, F., O'Connor, R.V., Messnarz, R. (eds.) EuroSPI 2013. CCIS, vol. 364, pp. 333–344. Springer, Heidelberg (2013)
5. Messnarz, R., Ross, H.-L., Habel, S., König, F., Koundoussi, A., Unterrreitmayer, J., Ekert, D.: SOQRATES Safety Team. Wiley SPIP Integrated Automotive SPICE and Safety Assessments 14(5), 279–288 (2009)
6. Automotive SPICE an international standard used in Automotive industry, http://www.automotive-spice.com
7. Theisens, D.: How Green Is Your Black Belt? In: Riel, A., O'Connor, R., Tichkiewitch, S., Messnarz, R. (eds.) EuroSPI 2010. CCIS, vol. 99, pp. 257–267. Springer, Heidelberg (2010)
8. Messnarz, R., Sicilia, M.A., Reiner, M.: Europe wide Industry Certification Using Standard Procedures based on ISO 17024. In: Proceedings of the TAEE Conference in Vigo Spain, 2012. Publisher IEEE (June 2012)
9. ISO 26262, Road vehicles — Functional safety
10. SOQRATES Initiative, http://www.soqrates.de
11. HIS: http://www.his-automotive.de

Compliance and Rigour in Process Assessment for Safety-Critical Domain

Timo Varkoi[1] and Risto Nevalainen[2]

[1] Spinet Oy, Finland
[2] Finnish Software Measurement Association – FiSMA ry, Finland
timo.varkoi@spinet.fi, risto.nevalainen@fisma.fi

Abstract. Safety-critical systems are increasingly affecting our lives and welfare. New approaches are being developed to evaluate the abilities related to development of these systems. Process assessment can be applied to increase our trust in safety related systems development. Importance of meeting the requirements of existing safety standards and regulations has increased, but also the quality of the process assessments needs to be ensured. Important features include assessment rigour, and compliance to standards and regulatory requirements. In this paper we discuss the challenges in process assessment with highest safety-criticality and present an approach to manage the assessments by a classification of relevant assessment types. The outcome is evaluated with a domain specific example. We conclude that process assessment has significant limitations in its capability to verify safety requirements, and especially regulatory requirements. On the other hand, process assessments are applicable to certain purposes, like supplier selection, and they can be developed to include a wider coverage of evidence important to the safety-critical domain.

Keywords: process assessment, safety, safety-critical, software process.

1 Introduction

Critical systems are defined as those that in case of an incident or misbehaviour can lead to an accident that will put people or the environment in danger, resulting in injuries and or casualties. Safety is considered as a general quality property of the whole system and so its plans, developments and implementations must follow strict rules in order to prevent failures of the system and their consequences and risks.

Most important references for safety are generic and domain specific safety standards, regulatory requirements and large amount of industrial experience in developing safety critical systems. References typically use classifications, which can include systematic integrity (for example safety integrity level (SIL) in IEC 61508) or safety class or category (for example safety classes 1 – 3 in nuclear power domain).

Generic standards and models have also significant value in safety-critical system domain. Their historical roots can be in safety, even not directly stated in current versions. One good example is software engineering lifecycle standard ISO/IEC

12207 [1]. It´s roots are in military and defence industry. It has changed gradually to be a generic model for software engineering. Similar evolution has taken place also for the CMM and CMMI models, which have roots in the Department of Defense requirements for suppliers. Nowadays CMMI also has a specific safety extension, CMMI+SAFE [2].

Process assessment is highly relevant also in safety-critical system domain. ISO/IEC 15504 [3], known also as the SPICE standard, is mainly based on the ISO/IEC 12207 software life cycle processes. It has also evolved from a quite specific model into a generic and highly abstract set of requirements and models that will be published as the new ISO/IEC 330xx set of standards.

The key question is how process assessments of the system development processes shall be performed to obtain trustworthy assessment results that satisfy the requirements of the safety-critical domain. In this paper we discuss the issues that are related to assessment rigour and compliance to standards and domain-specific regulations. We also propose a new classification for assessment types, which can be applied to meet the requirements of the domain.

In safety-critical system domain special consideration is required also in the assessment process, when using the SPICE standard as a starting point. The requirements in the standard are not enough as such. Important additional features include assessment rigour, and compliance to standards and regulatory requirements. In this paper we discuss these issues. When examples are needed, we use nuclear power domain for that purpose. We have also created a process assessment method called Nuclear SPICE to satisfy a large amount of the requirements set in nuclear standards and regulatory requirements.

Next, in chapter 2 we discuss the compliance and rigour related issues. Chapter 3 presents the Nuclear SPICE assessment process as an example of a rigorous approach. In chapter 4 we propose novel assessment types that can be applied in a safety-critical domain. Chapter 5 presents some results of our evaluation how the regulatory requirements can be met. Finally, chapter 6 summarizes our findings and conclusions.

2 Compliance and Rigour Issues

2.1 Compliance to Standards and Regulations in Safety Domain

A typical case to verify and validate safety requirement is to check compliance with relevant standards and regulatory requirements. Our experience is mainly from the nuclear power domain. The list of relevant nuclear safety standards and regulatory guides is long!

Safety-critical standards have typically some classification scheme. In the generic functional safety standard IEC 61508 [4] it is Safety Integrity Level (SIL), in range 1 – 4. SIL 1 is lowest and SIL 4 the highest integrity level. In higher SIL levels, requirements to use more formal methods and techniques increase.

In the nuclear power domain the most important safety standards are IEC 61513 [5] at system level, IEC 60880 [6] for software in safety class 2 and IEC 62138 [7] in safety class 3 or lower. In nuclear power domain, also another classification Safety

Category is used. It has values A, B and C. Standards IEC 61513 and IEC 60880 are relevant mainly for category A system/software and IEC 62138 for category B and C software.

To demonstrate compliance with relevant safety standard, we have to satisfy classification criteria and requirements. That is a major challenge, because various analyses and evaluations are needed, especially in higher safety levels. Process assessment itself is not enough to satisfy compliance. It needs to be enriched or extended to cover also required analyses. The basic rule is that at higher levels of safety you need more direct product evidences rather than process evidences.

Regulatory requirements are mainly mix of political, historical, technical, legal and administrative requirements. In nuclear power domain, they can be based on global, European or national references. Often also cross-references are used. For example, Finnish nuclear regulatory requirements include also requirements to use "relevant safety standards".

As an example, the Finnish Radiation and Nuclear Safety Authority (STUK) publishes a set of regulatory guidance, the YVL guides [8]. Our main selections for requirements are documents B.1 Safety design of a nuclear power plant and E.7 Electrical and I&C equipment of a nuclear facility. Another important reference is Common Position 2013, a set of requirements for licensing of safety critical software for nuclear reactors [9].

Regulatory requirements are a challenge itself: abstraction level varies a lot; many requirements are difficult – if not impossible – to verify; requirements can have a lot of space for interpretation and judgement. In our work to develop Nuclear SPICE, we used the following independent classifications for regulatory requirements:

- By responsible organisation: licensee, supplier, either licensee or supplier as agreed, general guidance with no specific responsible organisation
- By target: product, system, hardware, software
- By safety class or category: safety class 2, safety class 3, no specific safety class

Of course, a regulatory requirement can belong to many value ranges. Anyway, classification in this case was quite straightforward.

We classified each regulatory requirement also by using the Nuclear SPICE process names. In this exercise we could see that many requirements cover a wide set of processes and are therefore difficult to verify.

2.2 Rigour as a Concept in Safety-critical Software

Rigour in the safety-critical domain is introduced in standard IEC 61508-3:2010 Annex C. It is a relatively new concept and not even defined in part 4 of the standard. Tables in Annex C are classified according to a 3-point ordinal scale of rigour, R1, R2 and R3. R1 is the least rigorous and R3 is the most rigorous. An ordinal scale means that you have to achieve also any lower level of rigour, if you want to achieve the higher level. As an example, to achieve rigour R3 you have to achieve also R1 and R2.

Rigour values R1, R2 and R3 are explained in the following Table 1:

Table 1. Explanation of the rigour values in IEC 61508-3 Annex C [4]

R1	Without objective acceptance criteria, or with limited objective acceptance criteria. E.g., black-box testing based on judgement, field trials.
R2	With objective acceptance criteria that can give a high level of confidence that the required property is achieved (exceptions to be identified & justified); e.g., test or analysis techniques with coverage metrics, coverage of checklists.
R3	With objective, systematic reasoning that the required property is achieved. E.g. formal proof, demonstrated adherence to architectural constraints that guarantee the property.
-	This technique is not relevant to this property

Because the rigour concept is new in the whole IEC 61508 standard, it has no strong statements about how to calculate achievement of any rigour value. Details in IEC 61508-3 Annex C tables give an indication that you have to implement some methods/techniques at lower level of rigour to allow achievement of higher level, but not all of them. There is a mechanism of partial compensation by higher rigour method to achieve also lower level.

Rigour is mainly applied to methods and techniques. Each method or technique gets value R1, R2 or R3, based in its strength as evidence to verify or validate safety-critical software. Rigour of each method or technique is included and interpreted in the properties of systematic integrity. Each safety lifecycle phase can have several properties, and they are not necessarily the same. As an example, properties for software safety requirements phase (or process) are (they are informally defined in Annex F of IEC 61508-7):

- Completeness with respect to the safety needs to be addressed by software
- Correctness with respect to the safety needs to be addressed by software
- Freedom from intrinsic specification faults, including freedom from ambiguity
- Understandability of safety requirements
- Freedom from adverse interference of non-safety functions with the safety needs to be addressed by software
- Capability of providing a basis for verification and validation

Further, each property can be achieved and verified by several methods or techniques. So, a property can potentially get any rigour value R1, R2 or R3. As an example, the method "Application of complexity limits in specification" gives rigour value R2 for the property "Understandability of safety requirements". Because there are a large number of software safety lifecycle phases and properties, the standard IEC 61508-3 Annex C has tens of pages to cover all phases, properties and methods/techniques.

2.3 Assessment Classes in ISO/IEC 33002

Assessments may have a wide range of goals and purposes that depend on the domain and organizational objectives. A process monitoring or improvement oriented assessment may be performed with a light and informal assessment process. Safety-critical domain can provide a contrasting example, where the permission to run a system might depend on the process assessment result. One way to manage the different needs is to define types or classes for the assessments. ISO/IEC 33002 [10] defines three classes of assessment that result in different levels of confidence regarding the assessment results.

The principle is that a process assessment shall be performed according to a class of assessment. Factors that determine the selection of the class of assessment include the following:

a) level of rigour for performing an assessment that is relevant to the assessment purpose;
b) level of confidence required in the assessment results;
c) repeatability of assessment results;
d) relative costs for an assessment in relationship to the needs of the business.

Three classes of assessment and their characteristics are identified in Table 2. This table is based on the working draft of ISO/IEC 33010 and is still work in progress. The independence of the assessment body and personnel performing the assessment shall be classified according to the types of independence.

Table 2. Characteristics of Classes of Assessment

Aspect	Class 1	Class 2	Class 3
Purpose	Results are suited for comparisons across different organizations.	Results indicate the overall level of performance of the key processes in the assessment scope.	Results provide a general indication of process rating.
Requirements for lead assessor	Two assessors who are independent of the organizational unit being assessed, one of whom shall be a lead assessor.	Two assessors, one of whom shall be a lead assessor. Note: It is recommended that the lead assessor is independent of the organizational unit being assessed.	One assessor who shall be a lead assessor.
Minimum number of process instances	A minimum of four process instances for each process within the scope of the assessment.	A minimum of two process instances shall be identified for each process within the scope of the assessment.	No minimum of process instances.

Table 2. (*continued*)

Evidence required	For each process attribute of each Process in the scope of the assessment, across the set of process instances, objective evidence drawn both from evaluation of work products and from testimony of performers of the process shall be collected.	For each process instance, objective evidence drawn both from evaluation of work products and from testimony of performers of the process shall be collected for each Process within the scope of the assessment.	Objective evidence required for evaluating the processes within the scope of the assessment shall be collected in a systematic manner.
Data sources (assessment instruments, interviews and documents)	Requires all three data sources.	Requires only two data sources (one must be interviews).	Requires only one data source.
Type of independence, described in Table 5.2	The type of independence shall be recorded.	The type of independence shall be recorded.	The type of independence shall be recorded.

The main issue with the ISO/IEC 33002 assessment classes is that the class and scope are mixed: only large assessment with many assessors can be considered as a Class 1 assessment. In our experience, in the safety-critical domain the most typical assessment need seems to be related to a specified system or product that is developed by a single team within one organizational unit. Naturally, then the assessment is also quite compact and limited, but has very high demand for confidence. The Nuclear SPICE application of the assessment classes is presented in chapter 4.2.

3 Nuclear SPICE Assessment Process

3.1 Generic Requirements for Process Assessment

Process assessment can be utilized for two purposes: to determine the capability of the processes for particular requirements or to gain understanding of an organization's own processes for process improvement. In this context, our main interest is to ensure product quality by demanding that the systems and software development processes meet appropriate process capability targets.

According to ISO/IEC 33002, the assessment shall be conducted according to a documented assessment process. The documented assessment process shall be capable of meeting the assessment purpose and shall be structured in a manner that ensures that the purpose for performing the assessment is satisfied, in terms of the rigour and independence of the assessment and its suitability for the intended use. The following is a quotation from ISO/IEC 33002:

A documented assessment process addresses the following aspects of the conduct of an assessment:

- *identify the classes of assessment for which the documented assessment process can be applied, and the nature and extent of tailoring associated with each class addressed by the documented process;*
- *define the criteria for ensuring coverage for both the defined organizational scope and the defined process scope for the assessment, in terms of the strategy for collecting and analysing data;*
- *identify the rating method(s) to be used in rating process attributes;*
- *identify or define the aggregation method(s) to be used in determining ratings.*

The Nuclear SPICE assessments are performed to evaluate the capability of systems and software development process applied in systems and software engineering in nuclear industry domain. The domain is safety-critical and presents strict requirements for the capability of the processes.

The Nuclear SPICE assessment process is presented in the diagram below (Fig. 1). The process consists of six activities:

1. Initiating the assessment
2. Assessment planning
3. Data collection
4. Data validation
5. Process attribute rating
6. Reporting the results

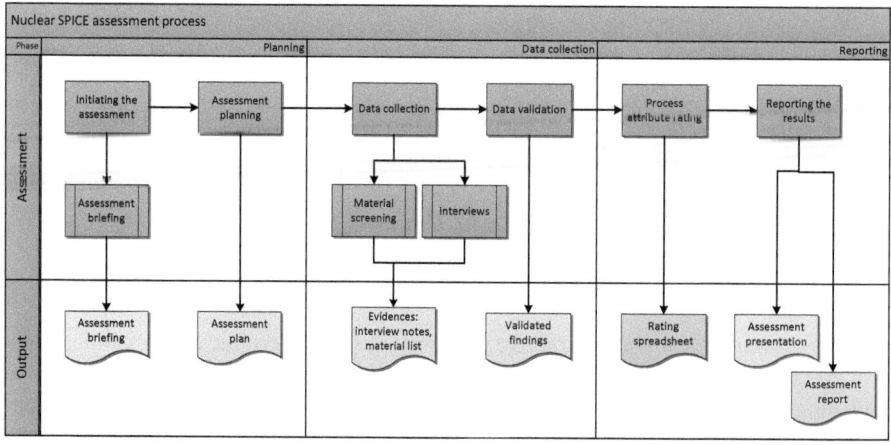

Fig. 1. Nuclear SPICE assessment process

3.2 Requirements for Data Collection and Validation

Data required for evaluating the processes within the scope of the assessment is collected in a systematic manner. The strategy and techniques for the selection, collection, analysis of data and justification of the ratings are explicitly identified and demonstrable.

Each process identified in the assessment scope is assessed on the basis of objective evidence. The objective evidence gathered for each attribute of each process assessed must be sufficient to meet the assessment purpose and scope according to the selected assessment class. Objective evidence that supports the assessors' judgement of process attribute ratings is recorded and maintained in the Assessment Record. This record provides evidence to substantiate the ratings and to verify compliance with the requirements.

Actions are taken to ensure that the data is accurate and sufficiently covers every process instance identified in the assessment scope, including seeking information from first hand, independent sources; using past assessment results; and holding feedback sessions to validate the information collected. Some data validation may occur as the data is being collected.

3.3 Requirements for Competency of Assessors

Proficiency in the models and standards is essential when performing assessments with high rigour. The lead assessor, who is responsible of the assessment team, has the key role in ensuring that the assessment results meet the demands of the domain. The lead assessor guides the assessment team to obtain adequate coverage of the evidences and makes the final decisions about the assessment ratings.

According to ISO/IEC 33001, assessor competence is based on appropriate education, training, skill and experience [11]. Additionally, competence must be demonstrated. Experience and knowledge of the domain is essential when assessing safety-critical application development. The assessor needs to understand impacts of the various techniques and methods that are applied to develop safety-critical systems.

The overall requirements for assessors include personal abilities related to diplomacy, objectivity, trust and authority. Importance of these aspects increase when dealing with issues related to safety.

4 Proposed Assessment Types in Nuclear SPICE

4.1 Introduction

The required assessment in nuclear domain is often related to a specific product or system that is developed within a single organizational unit and by a limited team of experts. In pre-qualification assessment we can collect the required information with 1-2 assessors in a few days. This kind of an assessment could not meet the ISO/IEC 33002 requirements for Class 1 or 2 assessments. Yet, the assessment needs to be performed with high level of confidence. We consider that the concept of rigour in

IEC 61508-3 is a practical and reasonably well defined concept to achieve high level of confidence. For that reason we propose a new classification scheme called "assessment type". It is a combination of assessment class and rigour in safety.

To cover rigour in a systematic manner we need to extend Nuclear SPICE assessment process to include methods and techniques as evidences.

4.2 Proposal for Assessment Types in Nuclear SPICE

Both assessment class and rigour in safety have a 3-point ordinal scale (see chapters 2.2. and 2.3 for details). From those scales we can construct a 3 x 3 matrix, as shown in Figure 2. In that figure also a draft classification of assessment types is proposed and marked with different colours.

	Rigour R1	**Rigour R2**	**Rigour R3**
Assessment class 3	Type 1	Type 2	Type 3
Assessment class 2	Type 2	Type 2	Type 3
Assessment class 1	Type 2	Type 4	Type 5

Fig. 2. A proposal for assessment types, marked also with different colours

The leanest assessment type is a combination of assessment class 3 and rigour R1 (type 1). It allows quick, judgement-based (self-)assessment. That type could be used for process improvement and in internal audits. In Nuclear SPICE context it shall cover also methods and techniques, and gives a reasonably high confidence compared to typical assessments in non-safety domains. The fullest assessment type (type 5) would be a combination of assessment class 1 and rigour R3. That type requires high coverage of evidences and intensive use of formal methods as evidences in Nuclear SPICE. It also requires full independence of the assessors.

Assessment types 2 – 4 are other combinations of assessment class and rigour. They are separate in our proposal mainly to get a full 3 point scale for assessment classes 3 and 1 in the rigour dimension. Other combinations may also be possible.

4.3 Recommended Use of Assessment Types by Assessment Purpose

Different assessment types can be selected when using the Nuclear SPICE method. Also the process scope can be selected. One distinction is whether a lead assessor is required, which depends mainly of the selected assessment type. Sometimes an experienced assessor might be useful in supporting even a self-assessment.

Selection of the assessment type has effects on the required resources: assessor competence and effort, timetable, cost, involvement of assessees, detail of reporting etc. Main driver in selecting an appropriate class are the expectations of the assessment sponsor or, when providing qualification evidence, the requirements of the regulator. Typical Nuclear SPICE assessments by their purpose and recommended types are listed in Table 3.

Table 3. Recommended Nuclear SPICE assessment types by assessment purpose

Assessment purpose	Recommended assessment type(s) when using Nuclear SPICE
Internal SPI (either for utility or supplier)	Type 1 or 2
Supplier selection (by utility)	Type 1 or 2
Pre-qualification of a system in safety class 3	Type 1 or 2
Pre-qualification of a system in safety class 2	Type 3, also Type 2 and Type 4 could be used
Certification of a system in safety class 3	Mainly Type 4
Certification of a system in safety class 2	Type 5

Largest volume of Nuclear SPICE assessments is expected to be in supplier selections and pre-qualifications. We have already run a number of pilot assessments for those purposes.

System certification is not the primary purpose of Nuclear SPICE. In our classification, such assessment would be of Type 4 or Type 5. Further study and development is needed to integrate different approaches for system certification.

Market interest is also in full-scale qualification and support for licensing of safety-critical systems in the nuclear power domain. Nuclear SPICE is not sufficient alone for such a purpose, as discussed further in chapter 5. However, it is possible that the fuller assessment types (mainly Type 4 and 5) could be developed to support full-scale qualifications.

5 Evaluation of Nuclear SPICE Verification Power Against Selected Regulatory Requirements

Our ultimate goal has been to cover most of the requirements in the nuclear domain safety standards and regulatory guides by the extended Nuclear SPICE. In this chapter we explain, to what extent we achieved this goal.

Regulatory requirements YVL B.1 and YVL E.7 have a large number of requirements. Each requirement is well identified by an individual ID and a short text. Some requirements are not relevant from the Nuclear SPICE viewpoint, because they are only explanatory or administrative. Requirements are specified mainly to support the regulator in making license decisions. From the nuclear power company point of view the corresponding activity or process is qualification. That can be further divided into several steps, like pre-qualification and qualification.

The amount of requirements in the selected references is presented in Table 4.

Table 4. Amount of selected requirements in regulatory sources

Regulatory source	# of relevant requirements	...of which belong to Safety Class 2	... of which belong to Safety Class 3	... of which are directly verifiable by Nuclear SPICE[1]
YVL B.1	372	not applicable	not applicable	43
YVL E.7	185	157	127	118
Common Position 2013	337	241	210	109

Most of the requirements are common for both Safety Class 2 and 3. Focus is to some extent more in Safety Class 2 in these selected regulatory sources. That is easy to understand, because also the licensing requirements are tighter in Safety Class 2.

As we can also see from Table 4, about 30 – 50% of YVL E.7 and Common Position requirements could be in principle verified by using Nuclear SPICE. That is not the case in real life. Most requirements are targeted for the licensee organization, whereas real development happens in the technology and/or in manufacturing companies. They are only indirectly interested in regulatory requirements, as a part of the customer requirements. So, we have to classify the requirements further also by the target organization or stakeholder. The result is presented in Table 5.

Table 5. Amount of selected requirements by target stakeholder

Regulatory source	# of relevant requirements	...of which belong licensee only	... of which belong to supplier only	... of which can be agreed between licensee and supplier[2]
YVL B.1	372	not applicable	not applicable	not applicable
YVL E.7	185	64	37	52
Common Position 2013	337	60	64	122

In the case of shared responsibility between the licensee and supplier, the amount of requirements is about 30%. If we use the selection criteria "licensee + supplier + shared", then the coverage of the requirements is considerably higher, almost 80% (156 requirements in YVL E.7 and 246 requirements in Common Position).

We can see that if process assessment is limited to the supplier organization, only approximately 20% of requirements can be directly verified by Nuclear SPICE.

---

[1] Criteria is that max. 3 processes are needed to verify the requirement. Extensive requirements requiring for example whole ENG or DEV categories of Nuclear SPICE are excluded here.
[2] Logic is "either or", meaning that licensee and supplier can in principle agree which organisation has the main responsibility to satisfy the requirement.

6   Conclusions

Process assessment is one of the main approaches to verify the achievement of safety and to evaluate the risks related to the achievement of safety goals. In this article we show, that process assessment has significant limitations in its capability to verify safety requirements, and especially regulatory requirements. This is valid at least in the nuclear power domain, which has been our main focus.

The main reason for limited verification capability is that process assessment is performed mostly for the supplier organisation. Most regulatory requirements are targeted for the licensee organisation, which in most cases is the nuclear power utility. Requirements are only indirectly relevant for the supplier organisation, typically through customer requirements. Considerably higher coverage can be achieved if process assessments are performed in both the licensee and the supplier organisations.

According to our experience, process assessment is more suitable for pre-qualification and supplier selection. That is also one of the original use cases of the ISO/IEC 15504 standard. We can improve the overall relevance of process assessment by increasing its coverage of higher rigour (as defined in IEC 61508-3 Annex C). That can be done by adding methods and techniques as a new evidence type. The target value of rigour can be used to classify Nuclear SPICE based assessments as types 1 – 5. Of course, the fuller an assessment is, the more expensive it also is. Safety demonstration can be performed by using the safety case. One promising area to develop Nuclear SPICE is to use it as a major source of evidence for safety cases. Process assessment can also be used for other similar types of assurance approaches, for example in cyber security context.

Acknowledgements. This work has been partially funded by the Finnish national nuclear safety program SAFIR2014. In its project CORSICA, new approaches and V&V methods have been developed for software safety. The method called Nuclear SPICE implements many of the ideas presented in this article.

References

1. ISO/IEC 12207:2008, Software Life Cycle processes (2008)
2. +SAFE, V1.2, A Safety Extension to CMMI-DEV, V1.2. CMU/SEI-2007-TN-006 (March 2007)
3. ISO/IEC 15504-5:2012, Information technology – Process assessment – Part 5: An exemplar Process Assessment Model (2012)
4. IEC 61508-3 Ed. 2.0, Functional safety of electrical/electronic/programmable electronic safety-related systems – Part 3: Software requirements (2010)
5. IEC 61513 FDIS, Nuclear power plants – Instrumentation and control for systems important to safety – General requirements for system (2011)
6. IEC 60880, Nuclear power plants – Instrumentation and control systems important to safety – Software aspects for computer-based systems performing category A functions (2006)

7. IEC 62138, Nuclear Power Plants – I&C Systems Important to Safety – Software Aspects for Computer Based Systems Performing Category B and C Functions (2004)
8. STUK: New YVL guides, https://ohjeisto.stuk.fi/YVL/?en=on (accessed April 12, 2014)
9. Common Position revision 2013. Licensing of safety critical software for nuclear reactors. Common position of seven European nuclear regulators and authorised technical support organisations (2013)
10. ISO/IEC 33002, Information technology – Process assessment – Part 2: Performing an Assessment (2014)
11. ISO/IEC 33001, Information technology – Process assessment – Concepts and terminology (2014)

The Feature Set of TestSPICE 3.0

Tomas Schweigert[1], Andreas Nehfort[2], and Mohsen Ekssir-Monfared[3]

[1] SQS AG
Stollwerck Str. 11, 51149 Köln, Germany
tomas.schweigert@sqs.com
[2] NEHFORT IT-Consulting KG
andreas@nehfort.at
[3] BDC IT-Engineering, Austria
mohsen.ekssir@bdc.at

Abstract. The paper describes the feature set of TestSPICE 3.0. It explains the overarching structure of TestSPICE 3.0, its main components which are the "Business Life Cycle Process Category", and the "Technical life Cycle Process Category", the measurement framework, the assessment process and the TestSPICE Assessor Training. The paper also deals with the relationship between TestSPICE 3.0 and ISO/IEC 29119 on the one hand and ISTQB® on the other hand and it explains the support of TestSPICE 3.0 for agile projects.

Keywords: TestSPICE, ISO/IEC 29119, Agile, ISO/IEC 15504, Assessment Process, Measurement Framework, Test Process, ISTQB®, Software Testing, System Testing.

1 The History of TestSPICE

The starting point for TestSPICE was an SQS initiative launched in 2009[2]. Its objective was to create a test assessment approach as close as possible to ISO/IEC 15504 (SPICE). The initial architectural decision was just to replace the ENT group of SPICE by a TST Group for TestSPICE[8]. The approach was presented at the SPICE Days 2010 in Stuttgart [1]. At the same place representatives of other SPICE and testing service provider agreed to form a testing special interest group (SIG) and drive the further development of TestSPICE. First publishing was also done in 2010 [4].

The TestSPICE SIG decided some major architectural changes specially regarding technical testing processes[7] and launched TestSPICE 2.0 in 2012[6]. At this point TestSPICE was the only testing PAM that was compliant with ISO/IEC 15504 Part 2 and verified by INTACS. After this launch the TestSPICE SIG started planning for TestSPICE V3.0 with focus on:

- Re-Arrangement of the relationship to ISO 15504-5 à elimination of duplicate processes
- Alignment to the new Test-Process Standard ISO 29119-2
- More attention to the technical testing processes e.g. Test Automation & Test Data Management.

It became also clear, that agile testing approaches like CAT[5] had to be taken into account [9]. Now TestSPICE 3.0 is available for the market!

2 The Overarching Structure of TestSPICE®

TestSPICE 3.0 is a synthesis of several approaches that are available on the market:

- The requirements for process reference models (PRM) and the requirements for process assessment models (PAM) as stated in ISO/IEC 15504 Part 2
- The TestSPICE 3.0 PRM providing process and work product descriptions based on
- Testing best practices as described in the ISTQB® Syllabi (FL, TA, TTA)
- Test process reference model as described in ISO/IEC 29119
- The TestSPICE PAM including the measurement framework as stated in ISO/IEC 15504 Part 2
  - The assessment process as described in ISO/IEC 15504 Part 3
  - Assessor training and certification standard as defined by INTACS
  - The trustworthiness approach as defined by ISO/IEC 15504 Part 7 and supported by intacs

The process descriptions use the following features:

- "Process ID" and "Process name"
- Description of "Process purpose" to provide an understandable direction of the process interpretation
- Description of expected "Process outcomes"
- Description of "Base practices" to be implemented in order to achieve the expected outcomes and to support the fulfillment of the process purpose
- "Work products" (referenced in the process description and described in detail in the work product section)
- "Notes" that give additional information for process assessment and/or process implementation

This feature set was found adequate for the test process description excrcise. During all discussions of the TestSPICE SIG no additional feature was required.

Looking from a user perspective (user might be an organization that wants to have its processes evaluated or an organization that provides assessment services) the following benefits are delivered by TestSPICE 3.0:

- Look and feel: Every organization using any type of SPICE for the evaluation of software or sys-tem development or for service management will receive information about the testing process that fits into the perception because the TestSPICE PAM includes the measurement framework as stated in ISO/IEC 15504 Part 2
- Same procedure for each assessment: TestSPICE uses the assessment process as described in ISO/IEC 15504 Part 3
- Stable quality through standardized and intacs certified assessor training

The TestSPICE 3.0 PRM is structured by 2 process categories: The Business Life Cycle Processes Category and the Technical Life Cycle Processes Category.

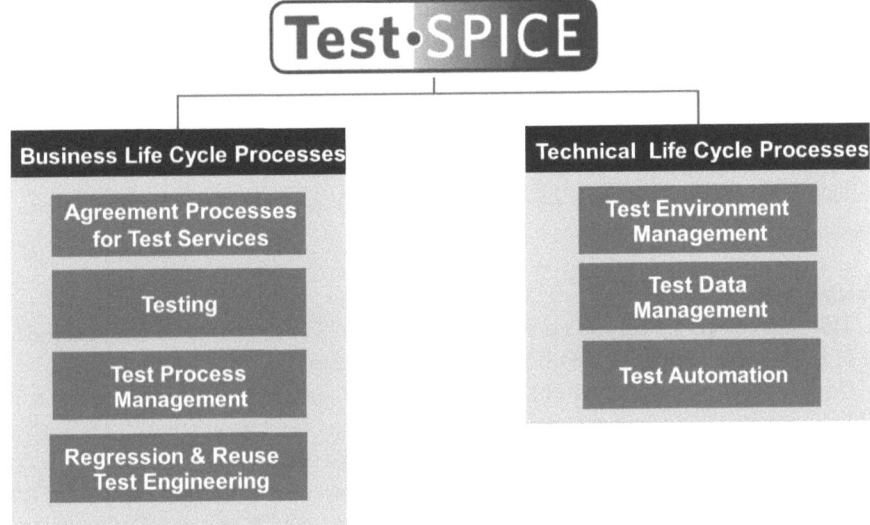

Fig. 1. The overarching structure of the TestSPICE® 3.0 PRM

3 The Business Life Cycle Process Category

The Business Life Cycle Process Category consists of processes that are aimed to support the analysis of the business testing capability.

3.1 Overview

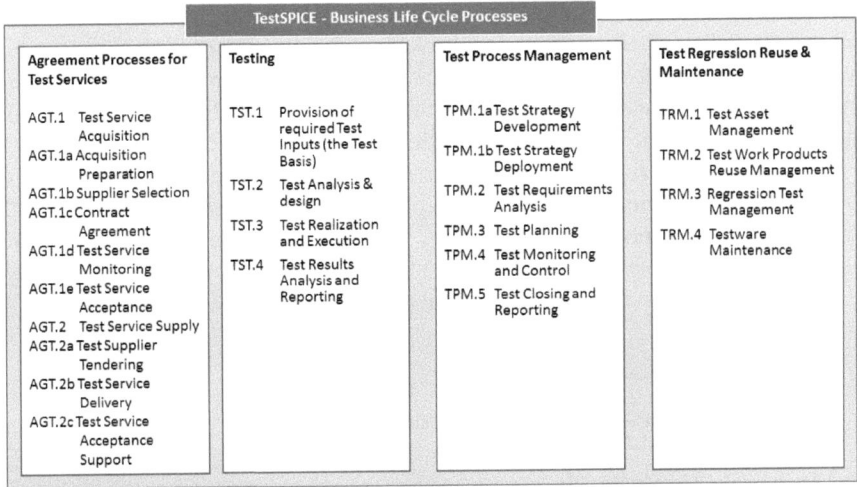

Fig. 2. The content of the Business Life Cycle Category

3.2 Details

Agreement Processes

A growing part of the testing business is performed by external partners (outsourcing of testing activities). From an organisation´s point of view the challenge is to find the right outsourcing partner and as well to establish effective means to control this partner.

Frome the outsourcing partner´s perspective the service supply processes are the key to get into business.

The AGT process group is designed to support customers as well as suppliers of outsourcing deals for testing services.

Testing Processes

This category contains the core testing processes. These processes are designed to fit in ISTQB®as well as in ISO/IEC 29119 environments.

Conformance is assured by changes of outcomes and practices as well as by using additional notes that support process interpretation and implementation.

TST.1 "Provision of required Test Inputs (the Test Basis)" is not a core Testing Process; it is a kind of incoming inspection to check whether the testing team has got appropriate input documents which enable regular testing. Deficiencies in TST.1 lead us to deficiencies in the core development processes which will affect the tests.

Test Process Management Processes

In TestSPICE 3.0 the "Test Strategy" process was split. The reason is that lots of organisations have test strategies in place but fail to deploy them. This issue can't be solved in the PA 3.2 because it makes a difference between deploying a "Test Strategy" process and deploying a test strategy. One decision from TestSPICE 1.0 was to have generic testing processes. This means that test stages were neither transformed to processes nor to activities. The question which test stages are needed and which quality criteria have to be checked is a strategy and/or planning issue. In TestSPICE 3.0 master and stage level planning and test preparation are supported. The details are explained in Annex G of the TestSPICE 3.0 PAM. It was also taken into consideration that testing has to fulfil requirements which are specific for the testing process (e.g. regulatory requirements that require a defined amount of test documentation). As this are no traditional product requirements as stated in ISO/IEC 25010:2011 it can't be assumed that they are handled in the normal requirements management workflow. So TestSPICE 3.0 contains a test requirements analysis process, that supports the organisation in identifying the relevant requirements for testing.

4 The Technical Life Cycle Process Category

The Technical Life Cycle Process Category consists of processes that are aimed to support test execution and test automation.

4.1 Overview

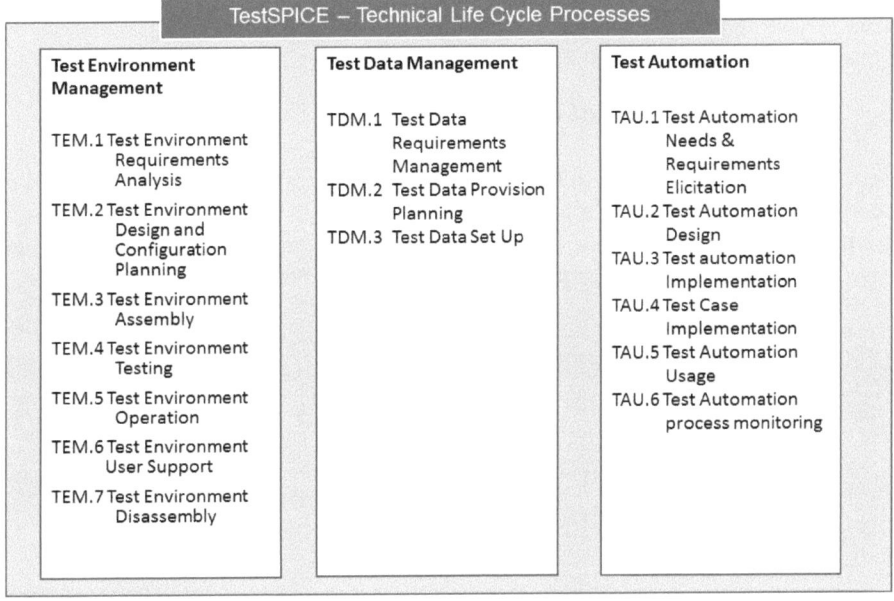

Fig. 3. The content of the Technical Life Cycle Category

4.2 Details

Test Environment Management Process Group
Test environments are becoming more and more a critical point in the testing process. From our experience we can say that test environments issues, e.g. about the necessity and included components, especially interfaces to external systems are discussed frequently. As a result of this trend, the capability of an organisation to agree on the requirements for test envi-ronments and to design and run test environments that fulfill these requirements need in depth checking. Many organisations have outsourced the provision of test environments so the operation of and the user support for test environments need in depth checking as well.

Test Data Management Process Group
The provision of sufficient test data is hampered by growing complexity as well as by safety and security issues. As a result it is often not possible to simply backup and restore test data due to time stamp checks. Organisations which are facing this issue, need guidance what they should do in order to provide sufficient test data that are also usable for regression tests. The "Test Data Management Process Group" provides as basis set of outcomes and activities that will support the implementation of a sufficient test data management.

Test Automation Process Group
Last but not least the capability of an organisation to automate tests might be relevant for the success of a project or a release. TestSPICE 3.0 supports organisations that want to have an in depth analysis of their test automation processes.

5   TestSPICE and ISO 15504-5:2012

TestSPICE V3.0 is designed to be a stand alone assessment. But it is also designed to be used in joint assessments together with processes from ISO 15504 part 5 or part 6. So far TestSPICE can be seen as a complementary offer of process groups and processes to select to the assessment scope of a development project or organization.

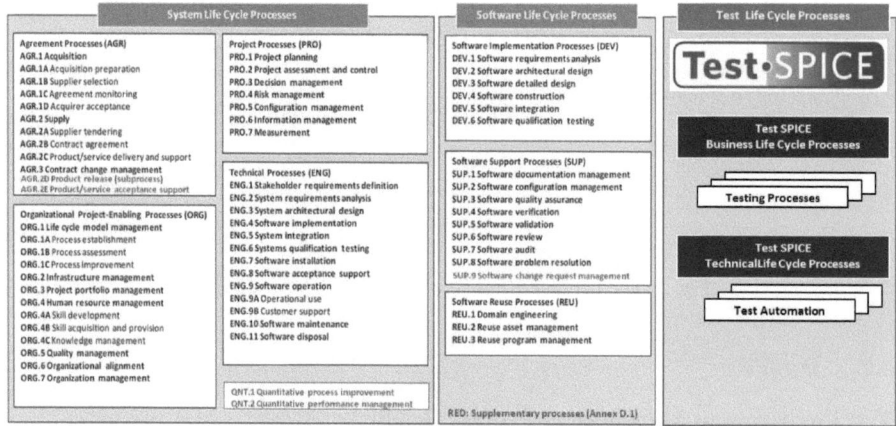

Fig. 4. TestSPICE V3.0 & ISO 15504-5:2012: A joint approach

6   TestSPICE Support for Agile Projects

TestSPICE 3.0 also provides support for agile projects. Due to the draft character of the agile management process group, these processes were not included into the TestSPICE 3.0 PRM but as Annex H into the TestSPICE 3.0 PAM. The agile management processes cover well established practices of agile management

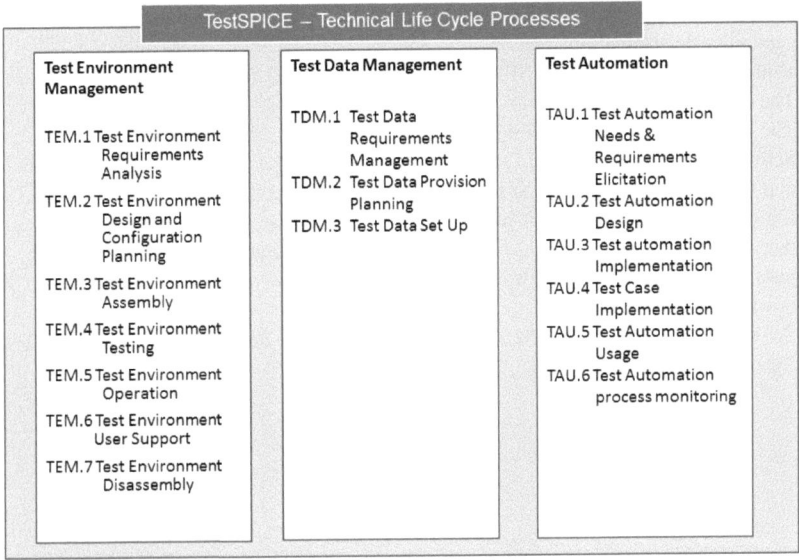

Fig. 5. The content of the Agile Management Process Group (Annex H)

7 Conclusion and Further Work

TestSPICE 3.0 supports business testing as well as technical testing disciplines.

Currently TestSPICE 3.0 is in the final phase of the international review process. Experts from various business domains stated that TestSPICE 3.0 is suitable for their domain.

TestSPICE 3.0 will be published at minimum at the TestSPICE website, www.testspice.info. It will be for public use and free of charge. The Authors and reviewers of TestSPICE cover a various spectrum of markets, e.g. banking, insurance, automotive, aerospace, medicine. It is planned to have pilot assessments in all these markets and in various countries. Due to the results of the preliminary review results, the TestSPICE SIG doesn't expect a need for substantial changes of Testspice but assumes a need for more explanation and examples.

The further development of TestSPICE (TestSPICE 4.0) is depending on the experience of the practical usage of TestSPICE especially in the automotive domain. It might be an option to enhance the agile management group and/or use it as a nucleus for an independent AgileSPICE.

References

1. Blaschke, M., Philipp, M., Schweigert, T.: Get the Test Process under Control The TEST SPICE approach. In: Proceedings of the, Spice Days(el. Published) (2010)
2. Blaschke, M., et al.: The TestSPICE approach, Test Process Assessments follow in the footsteps of software process assessments, Testing Experience 12/2009 S. 56ff

3. ISO/IEC 15504 Part 4:2004 Guidance on use for process improvement and process capability determination
4. Knüvener, C.: TestSPICE – SPICE für Testprozesse, SQ-Magazin 17/2010 S; 26–27
5. The CAT SIG, Certified Agile Tester Manual, Version 2.1, Berlin, ISQI, (2010)
6. The Test SPICE PAM Version (2012), http://www.testspice.info
7. Schweigert, T., Nehfort, A.: Technical Issues in Test Process Assessment and their current and future Handling in Test SPICE. In: EuroSPI Industrial Proceedings, Delta 2011 (2011)
8. Steiner, M., et al.: Make test process assessment similar to software process assessment - the TestSPICE approach. Journal of Software Maintenance and Evolution (2010), published online 2010 at Wiley online library, http://wileyonlinelibrary.com, doi:10.1002/SMR 507
9. Schweigert, T., Blaschke, M., Ekssir-Monfared, M.: TestSPICE® and Agile Testing – Synergy or Confusion

Change Strategy for ISO/IEC 33014: A Multi-case Study on Which Change Strategies Were Chosen

Jan Pries-Heje[1] and Jørn Johansen[2]

[1] Roskilde University, Roskilde, Denmark
janph@ruc.dk
[2] DELTA, Hørsholm, Denmark
joj@delta.dk

Abstract. In the newly published ISO/IEC 33014.2013 [1] standard there is a strategic activity called "Identify the overall change strategy" that includes selecting a change strategy "from among a myriad of available change models". The book [2] on the ImprovAbility model describes a framework of how to select change strategy. There are 10 different change strategies to choose from. But which ones are chosen in practice? To answer that we have analysed data from 49 assessments in 44 organizations that have used the framework. We give a ranking of strategies chosen and we analyse how they adapt the change strategy to their specific conditions. We conclude that the most often recommended organizational change strategy is *Optionality* followed by three other strategies: *Socializing*, *Learning-driven*, and *Specialist-driven*.

Keywords: Organisational change, change strategy, ISO/IEC 33014, process improvement.

1 Introduction

In November 2013 a new standard was published, the ISO/IEC 33014 [1] for process improvement in IT organizations. As can be seen from Figure 1 process improvement operates at three levels; strategic, tactical and operational. At the strategic level an organization are to start with identifying business goals, identifying the scope of organizational change, selecting models and methods and identifying roles, and then identify the *overall change strategy*. This then leads on to the tactical level where the more specific planning takes place.

How do you identify the overall change strategy "from among a myriad of available change models" [2, Table 11-2, p. 198]? The book on the ImprovAbility model [2] gives the answer in the form of an *organizational change framework* of how to select change strategy. There are 10 different change strategies to choose from. One is called "Commanding", another is "Metrics-driven", yet another is "Employee-driven", and so on. The framework includes a description of each strategy and some prescriptions of when to choose the specific change strategy? This prescription was derived using design science research and was built on contingency theory.

Contingency theory arises from a broad array of studies. The core idea in contingency theory is that organizations that want to optimize performance need to adopt the structure that *fits* best with the situation they are in - the contingencies given them. Donaldson [3, p.5] defines contingency theory: "At the most abstract level, the contingency approach says that the effect of one variable on another depends on some third variable …".

As part of their work with the ImprovAbility model the creators describes a framework of how to select change strategy There are 10 different change strategies to choose from and a tool to guide managers in evaluating and choosing which of the ten change strategies that would be most appropriate in an actual organizational setting. What the tool does is that it calculates a *fit* based on contingencies of the situation today and the wished-for change.

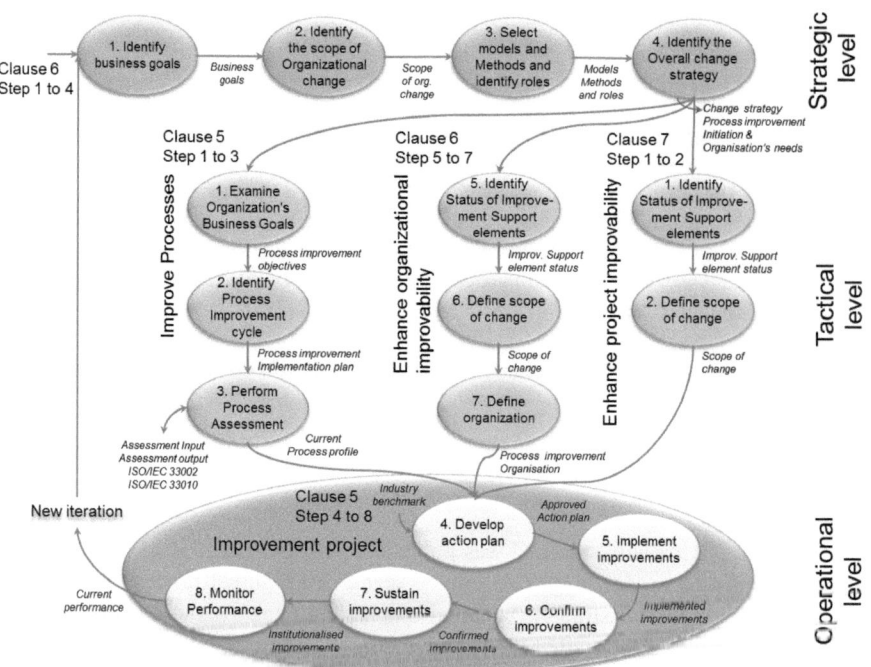

Fig. 1. Overview of the ISO/IEC 33014 model [1]

Thus the framework to be used in connection with ISO/IEC 33014 [1] calculates the fit for each of the ten strategies (a detailed explanation of each strategy can be found in Table 2). So for example the fit in two different organisations may look like Table 1. Fit is calculated on a scale going up to 100% fit. So in Table 1, column 1 on the Housing case, the Specialist driven approach has nearly perfect fit of 96% whereas the optionality change strategy is nearly as good with a fit of 92%.

So within the ISO/IEC 33014 there is framework to help you choose organizational change strategy. Because the calculation of fit is done independently for each strategy more than one strategy can have a good fit. But the real interesting question is *which ones are chosen in practice*? This paper will try to answer that research question.

Table 1. Two examples where the fit is calculated for each of 10 change strategies

	Housing Case	Energy Case
Reengineering	30	40
Optionality	* 92	* 92
Socialization	82	28
Specialist driven	* 96	58
Exploration	21	0
Commanding	8	* 63
Employee driven	23	60
Learning driven	69	0
Metrics driven	58	23
Production organized	63	50

The remainder of the paper is organized as follows. First we describe our research method, how we gathered and analysed data on the use of the organizational change framework. Then we give an overview of existing literature and thinking on organizational change. After that follows a section describing the organizational change framework in more detail. Our study of use covers 44 organizations. The data and analysis from these organizations are covered in the next two sections. Finally the paper concludes.

2 Research Method

To answer the research question, which chance strategies are chosen in practice, we have used the framework for selecting change strategies in 44 organizations. 16 of the organizations were assessed formally by DELTA. Thus DELTA has facilitated the assessment, discussed the contingencies with management in the organization and derived a recommendation based on the calculation of fit. One of the authors of this paper was lead facilitator in most of these assessments. We have gathered the data, the notes taken when assessing, and used it for analysis of what strategy was chosen and why.

The second part of our data set comes from 28 organizations that were taught to use the framework in an Executive Master Program at a University. All participants were managers at project level or higher in their different organizations. Before using the framework the master students were trained for 4 days in organizational change. In the concrete the students were asked to do the following

1. Fill out framework from an organizational perspective
2. Score with the help of the framework
3. Document the recommendation to the Organization – what change strategy to follow. And a detailed plan for doing so
4. Document the rationale for the plan
5. Discuss the utility of the organizational change framework

As a result we had 28 reports each 5-6 pages long. We analysed these reports as we analysed the notes taken from the 18 organizations using Grounded Theory (GT) techniques We used the Strauss and Corbin [4] school of thought where GT analysis is composed of three groups of coding procedures called open, axial and selective coding. The goal of open coding is to reveal the core ideas found in the data. Open coding involves two tasks. The first task is labelling phenomena. The second task is discovering categories and sub-categories of data.

The purpose of axial coding is to develop a deeper understanding of how the identified categories are related. Selective coding involves the integration of the categories that have been developed to form a theoretical framework.

3   Theories and Models for Organizational Change

Since management became a discipline, the study of change has been important. Authors have written about organizational change from different perspectives including psychology, sociology and business. Academic and practitioner contributions to organizational change have been built on empirical work in many organizations. Examples of this include descriptive accounts of change, normative models to guide change processes, theoretical models for understanding and analysing change, typologies of approaches to organizational change, and empirical studies of success and failure.

In terms of the descriptive accounts of change, three different schools of organizational thinking have provided metaphors for organizations. The first school (and oldest) descends back to the end of the 19th century where Taylor, Fayol, and Weber were key figures. Taylor invented "Scientific Management" including the key belief that "it is possible and desirable to establish, through methodological study and the application of scientific principles, the one best way of carrying out any job." (here cited from [5]). The metaphor in this perspective is an organization as a production system where it is possible to optimize its efficiency and effectiveness. Organizational change is about optimizing planning through observation, experimentation, calculation and analysis.

In the 1930s and 1940s the second school challenged the classical view of organizations to provide a new perspective. In relation to change this perspective is characterized by [5, 6] the belief that organizations are co-operative, social systems rather than mechanical ones, where people seek to meet their emotional needs. So the metaphor for an organization is a (large) group of people with an organizational culture and visible communication and interaction processes between them.

The 3rd school of thought has been called the political-emergent perspective [5, 6]. It is characterized by the belief that organizations and change are shaped by the interests and commitments of individuals. It is also characterized by the belief that decisions often arise from power-struggles between special-interest groups or coalitions. "Organizations are not machines, even though some of those running them would dearly like them to be so. They are communities of people, and therefore behave just like other communities. They compete amongst themselves for power and resources; there are differences of opinion and of values, conflicts of priorities and goals" [7].

An interesting approach to combining change strategies is found in Huy [8], who identifies four ideal types of interventions. He distinguishes between episodic and continuous change. Changing formal structures is an episodic change involving something tangible. Thus the ideal type of change will be "commanding". He suggests that every ideal type is relatively more effective than the other ideal types. For example, the "engineering" intervention is relatively best at changing work processes.

Organizational change management thought has now developed so many approaches to change that no one approach can claim that it is suitable for all organizational goals and settings. There is a need for analysis of available approaches in developing a particular organizational change strategy. However, few (if any) comprehensive analytical tools are available to support this analysis. The contingency approach exemplified by Huy [8] provides the right direction, but its two-by-two analytical structure is simplistic compared to the complexity of most practical settings.

4 A Framework for Selecting Organizational Change Strategies

For each of the ten organizational change strategies in Table 2 a number of assertions are formulated that would reveal in a given organizational setting to which degree a condition is present where the strategy would "fit". E.g. for the change strategy called "Commanding," the following assertions are formulated [2, p. 172]:

- Right now we need change to happen fast
- It is primarily organizational structures that need to be changed
- In the past we have had successes in requiring or dictating change

And for the change approach called "Optionality," the assertions formulated are:

- Our employees are self-aware and always have an opinion
- We have very knowledgeable employees that know their areas well
- There are vast differences between the tasks of different employees

Table 2. An overview of the ten organizational change strategies

Change Strategy	Approach definition	Conditions	Literature
Commanding	Change is driven and dictated by (top) management. Management takes on the roles as owner, sponsor and change agents.	*Where* formal structures needs change. *Where* change is needed fast	[8], specifically the approach that is called Commanding. The design and positioning schools as described by [9]
Employee driven	Change is driven from the bottom of the organizational hierarchy when needs for change arise among employees.	*Where* the need for change arises among the employees. *Where* there is no need for a standardized approach; the result is more important than the process. *Where* an open management style that will allow change to arise from the bottom.	[10]on the grass-roots approach. [11] and [12] on participatory design.
Exploration	Change is driven by the need for flexibility, agility, or a need to explore new markets, technology or customer groups.	*Where* dynamic and complex surroundings makes it important to explore	Exploration [13], or the organizational structure called adhocracy [14]
Learning driven	Change is driven by a focus on organizational learning, individual learning and what creates new attitudes and behaviour.	*Where* there is a need for change in attitudes and/or behaviour. *Where* the organization is talented in learning. *Where* relationships between means and goals are unclear.	[8], specifically the approach called Teaching. Also the learning organization [15]
Metrics driven	Change is driven by metrics and measurements.	*Where* there are relatively stable surroundings so measurements from the past can be used to decide the future. *Where* the result of change is measurable.	Total Quality Management thinking, cf. [16]. Six Sigma thinking, cf. [17]
Optionality	Change is driven by the motivation and need of the individual. It is to a large degree optional whether the individual takes the innovation into use	*Where* target group is very diverse and has large individual differences. *Where* individuals that should (could) change are highly educated, very knowledgeable and self-aware.	[18] studied groups that took innovations into use voluntarily. Quite many of the models and techniques in [18] are valid for this change approach.

Table 2. (*continued*)

Production organized	Change is driven by the need for optimization and/or cost reduction.	*Where* you have relatively stable surroundings. *Where* you have many homogeneous resources and workflows.	Scientific Management, [13], [8], specifically the approach called Engineering.
Reengineering	Change is driven by fundamentally rethinking and redesigning business processes to achieve dramatic improvements in critical, contemporary measures of performance, such as cost, quality, service and speed	*Where* a need exists for major change. For example when organization has ground to a halt. *Where* nothing new happens. *Where* decisions are made but not carried out. *Where* a crisis is eminent.	[19], [20], [21], [22], [23], [24], [25], [26]
Socializing	Change in organizational capabilities is driven by working with social relationships. Diffusion of innovations happens through personal contacts rather than through plans and dictates.	*Where* organizational skills and capabilities needs to be developed. *Where* no unhealthy power struggles occur (so people *can* talk). *Where* employees that can be exemplars are available.	[27], and [8], specifically the approach called Socializing.
Specialist driven	Change is driven by specialists, either with professional, technical, or domain knowledge. Examples are a Method or Architecture function	*Where* work has vast complexity and variety so there really is a need for special knowledge. *Where* there is access to necessary specialists, eventually by in-sourcing them.	[28], [14] especially professional bureaucracy, [29], [30], [31], [32]

All of the assertions are formulated in a number of statements which represent expressions of the conditions for implementing change in relation to the organizational setting, the employees, the change ahead, and the current use of metrics. The statements were assembled into a query form where managers on a five level scale can express their degree of agreement or disagreement with the statements. When the query form is filled in by the management of an organization, the conditions for change in that organization can be compared to the conditions for each of the ten change strategies (Table 1). The fit of each is measured by the degree (0-100%) to which these conditions are present in the particular organization.

A fit (score) calculated around 50% represents an indeterminate value. A fit calculated above 70% means that the corresponding change strategy fits the organization well (will be successful). On the other hand a score below 30% means that the corresponding change strategy doesn't fit the organization at all (should not be used).

5   Evaluation of the Framework and Tool

As stated in the Research Method section of this paper we have gathered and analysed data, notes and reports from 49 assessments in 44 organizations. Below you find the analysis and findings from the two-fold study; first from the 16 organizations assessed by DELTA. Then a detailed analysis of one organization in which six assessments took place. And finally a section on the 28 organizations assessed within the Executive Master Program.

5.1   Findings from 21 Workshops in 16 Companies

The organizational change framework was used in 16 different companies as structured workshops. In one of the companies DELTA performed six workshops in different departments of the organization.

The workshops all had the same structure and the workshops were all held for a group of managers in the organization being assessed. The workshop always followed the same process. First, after a presentation of the concept and tools, there was a discussion of and agreement on the scope of change. Then the participants turned to the assertions formulated for each of the 10 change strategies. The assertions were handed out on paper and the participants could agree or disagree, partly or fully, to each assertion. First they did this individually, and then DELTA facilitated a discussion of any major differences brought forth in the individual assessments. For example, if one manager responded "agree" to the assertion "In the past we have had success in requiring or dictating change", whereas another manager said "partly disagree", then we brought out that discrepancy in the discussion and used it as a basis for eliciting an agreed perception within the group. The discussion could lead to a change because of change in view on the statement, or it could end as status quo because there was a different view on the situation from the participants place in the organization.

In table 3 below the best and worst fit of the overall change strategy is listed. The overall conclusion is, that related to the scope of change seen from these 21 groups of managers in Danish companies, the overall change strategy Optionality will fit best, and Metric-driven change and Reengineering will not fit at all. In the following sections we will take a more detailed look at the data.

Table 3. Data from the 16 companies (including 6 departments in one company)

Change strategy	No. of best fit	No. of worst fit
Reengineering		8
Optionality	16	
Socializing	2	
Specialist driven	2	
Exploration		1
Commanding		2
Employee driven	1	1
Learning driven		
Metrics driven		9
Production organized		

If we take a closer look at the 21 dataset from 21 assessments we get a more nuanced picture. The data is shown in Figure 2.

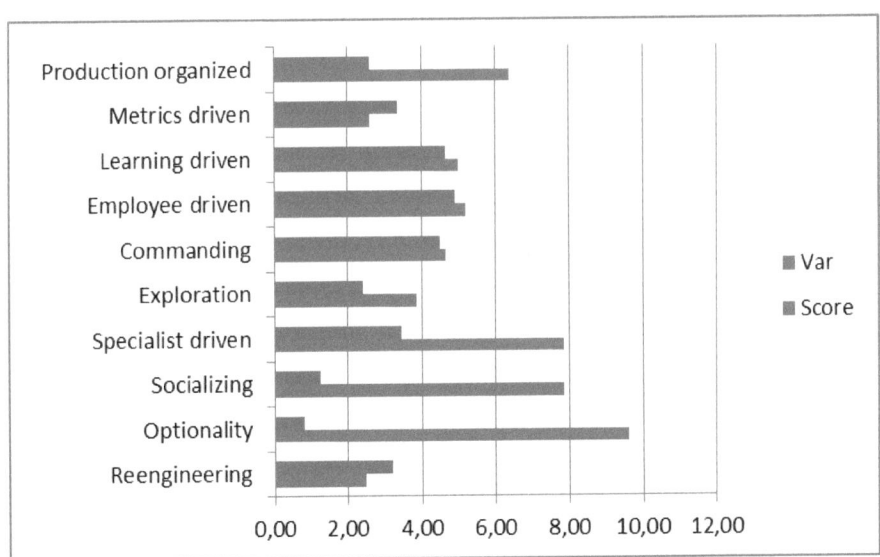

Fig. 2. The distribution of how often an overall change strategy was identified

Score: If 10, it was the given as the best fit in all workshops; if 1, it was not given.

Var: The variance based on the population of the actual overall change strategy.

Although the scope of change has been different for the companies, e.g. starting an outsourcing initiative, change of business, improvement of development processes, implementation of a new organization, it is evident, that there are two overall change strategies, which often fits: Optionality and Socializing. It is stressed by the low variance. Two other overall strategies with an extensive fit is Specialist driven and Production organized, but here the variance is higher and indicates a larger difference in the fit.

The worst fit is dominated by the overall change strategies Reengineering and Metric driven with some variance.

A conclusion from these organizational change strategy assessments are that all participants (of magnitude 100 managers) without exception, was positive and could understand and accept the result. It was expressed by the participants, that they felt the discussions very valuable in relation to obtaining a common view on the scope, the change and to get a common view on an overall change strategy. Normally the participants did not discuss strategy at that level and the responsibility for the change was just delegated. The situation was now much more transparent and the managers had the same view on what was the best overall change strategy, and were able to support it.

5.2 Findings from 1 Organization in 6 Departments

DELTA had the possibility of performing organizational change assessment in six different departments of the same large Danish organization to discuss with it which overall change strategies would fit best to a specific organizational change.

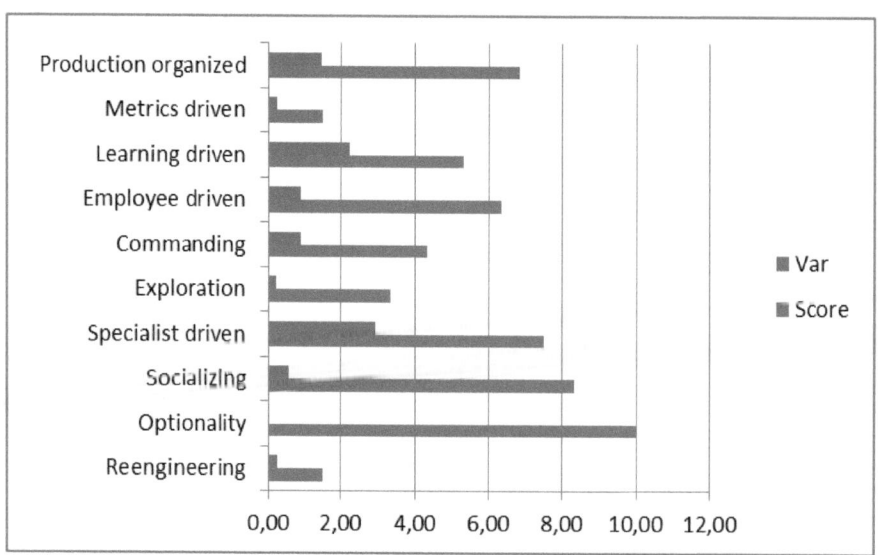

Fig. 3. The distribution of how often an overall change strategy was identified

Score: If 10, it was the given as the best fit in all workshops; if 1, it was not given.

Var: The variance based on the population of the actual overall change strategy.

The departments were related to total different functions, e.g. development of SW or the QA department. The data show a very common view on the organization and its behaviour in relation to the situations described in the tool.

One conclusion is that the model seems to be robust in relation to a different view on a scope for change. The different behaviour and views in departments on the scope of change did not affect the result – the variance is very low. This was also a surprising and joyful conclusion at the workshop.

It is also clear, that there is a strong correlation between the result in this result and the result including all workshops results. The overall strategies which often fit: Optionality, Socializing, Specialist driven and Production organized, all at a low variance, but here the variance.

5.3 Findings from 28 Organizations

As said earlier each of 28 students carried out assessments using the organizational change framework in their own organization. In Table 4 it can be seen for each of the 10 change strategies which came out as the best fit and which came out as the worst fit.

Table 4. Data from the 28 companies

Change strategy	No. of best fit	No. of worst fit
Reengineering	0	5
Optionality	13	1
Socializing	5	0
Specialist driven	5	0
Exploration	1	6
Commanding	1	1
Employee driven	2	3
Learning driven	5	5
Metrics driven	1	7
Production organized	2	2

Optionality was clearly the most popular change strategy recommended as the best fit in 13 out of 28 organizations. Let us give some examples. So here follows the category we coded called 'reasons for choosing optionality'. In a major transport company (#85) the wished-for change was more professional project management. Here optionality was recommended because changes "happen at a personal level" and because they "have to be motivated by the need and motivation of the individual". However, optionality was not chosen alone: "The change cannot be totally optional" says case #85. It has to be combined with commanding (that scored 95).

Another case (#91) is from a teaching institution educating social workers. Here the director fully agrees that they have "Very self-aware employees that always have an opinion. Employees that are very knowledgeable and know their area of work well. And the target group is very diverse and has large individual differences". Interestingly case #91 points out that for changes in the past "that actually succeeded we have been leaning towards the suggested change strategy".

Case #110 is from a Municipality. Here the change concerns the care for elderly people and the change is about implementing electronic patient journals. In this case three strategies have a high degree of fit with optional having the best fit closely followed by socializing and specialist-driven strategies. From this organization it is stated that changes in the past "have had a highly different degree of implementation" and therefore using the organizational change framework "is useful as a tool for creating dialogues with the management group".

In case #104 optionality came out as the worst option. Here a production organised strategy was having the best fit (92%) mainly because "changes are driven by the need for optimized use of resources" and because the Tourist Organization in case #104 have "unified resources and routines" that are centrally located.

Another popular strategy was the learning driven strategy. At a hospital (#88) they wanted to appear and be more professional. Hence the process improvement was more about changing attitude and behaviour than taking a new product into use. The result of having the learning strategy as the best fitting "falls well in line with the development we are undergoing according to the Chief Nurse". Case #88 also says "we were positively surprised over how close the recommended strategy came to plans for change already in place". In that way the organizational change framework functioned as a confirmation of plans.

Understanding and building a relationship to veterans was the change wished-for in case #102. Here the learning driven strategy came out as the best fit (87,5%) again. With the socialization strategy a close second (75% fit). The plan for the actual change was then based on a combination of these two strategies. E.g. teaching employees will give them perspective and nuances in their relationship to veterans. And increased contact will build social capital with the veterans.

In a Bank (#111) where the wished-for process improvement concerned all processes around customer service two strategies came out on top; the explorative and the specialist-driven. "Here I believe that the specialist-driven is preferred. The change we are implementing is very technical and it is important that it is handled by people with specialist knowledge", says case #111.

One strategy – reengineering – was not a best fit in any case. However, reengineering was the worst fit in 5 cases, mainly because the companies assessed were not having an eminent crisis. This point to a potential bias in the data analysed here. A company that sends their employee to an Executive Master and pay for them is not in a crisis where they cannot look (years) ahead and where they cannot spare some thousand Euros for educating their employees for the future.

6 Conclusion

In this paper we have looked at the newly published ISO/IEC 33014 standard in which there is a strategic activity called "Identify the overall change strategy" that includes selecting a change strategy "from among a myriad of available change models". The book on the ImprovAbility model describes a framework of how to select among 10 distinctly different change strategies. We looked at the details of the framework and we phrased the research question: which ones are chosen in practice? The answer that was found in a study of 49 assessments in 44 organizations whom applied the framework was that *Optionality* was a clear number one followed closely by three other strategies: *Socializing*, *Learning-driven*, and *Specialist-driven*. We have showed a ranking of strategies chosen and we have analysed how they adapt the change strategy to their specific conditions. We need to have in mind, that this result is based on workshops performed in Danish companies in Denmark. The result is therefore likely influenced by the Danish culture. So further research may be needed in relation to other cultures in other counties. In conclusion we find that the organizational change framework gives real value to the organizations using it. Nearly all 44 organizations find it to be of high utility and easy to integrate with any wished-for change.

References

1. ISO, ISO/IEC/TR 33014, in Information technology – Process assessment – Guide for process improvement, Geneva, Switzerland (2013)
2. Pries-Heje, J., Johansen, J. (eds.): ImprovAbility: Success with process improvement. DELTA, Hørsholm (2013)
3. Donaldson, L.: The Contingency Theory of Organizations. Sage Publications, Thousand Oaks (2001)
4. Strauss, A., Corbin, J.: Basics of Qualitative Research: Techniques and Procedures for Developing Grounded Theory, 2nd edn. Sage Publications, Beverly Hills (1998)
5. Burnes, B.: Managing Change, 5th edn. Prentice Hall, Finacial Times (2009)
6. Borum, F.: Strategier for organisationsændring (Strategies for organizational change), 2nd edn. Handelshøjskolens Forlag, Copenhagen (2013)
7. Handy, C.: Understanding Organizations. Reprint ed2007. Penguin Books Limited
8. Huy, Q.N.: Time, temporal capability, and planned change. Academy of Management Review 26(4), 601–623 (2001)
9. Mintzberg, H., Ahlstrand, B., Lampel, J.: Strategy Safari: A Guided Tour Through the Wilds of Strategic Management. Financial Times, Prentice Hall, London (2002)
10. Andersen, C.V., et al.: The Grass Root Effort. In: Mathiassen, L., Pries-Heje, J., Ngwenyama, O. (eds.) Improving Software Organizations - From Principles to Practice, pp. 83–98. Addison-Wesley, Boston (2001)
11. Kensing, F.: Methods and Practices in Participatory Design. ITU Press, Copenhagen (2003)
12. Kensing, F., Blomberg, J.: Participatory Design: Issues and Concerns. Computer Supported Cooperative Work 7(3-4), 167–185 (1998)

13. Benner, M., Tushman, M.: Exploitation, exploration, and process management: The productivity dilemma revisited. Academy of Management Review 28(2), 238–256 (2003)
14. Mintzberg, H.: Structure in Fives - designing effective organizations. Prentice-Hall (1983)
15. Senge, P.M.: The fifth discipline: The art and practice of the learning organization. Doubleday, New York (1990)
16. Oakland, J.S.: TQM – Text with Cases, 3rd edn. Butterworth-Heinemann (2003)
17. Pande, P.S., Holpp, L.: What is Six Sigma. McGraw-Hill (2000)
18. Rogers, E.M.: Diffusion of Innovations, 5th edn. Free Press,
19. Bashein, B.J., Markus, M.L., Riley, P.: Preconditions for BPR Success: And How to Prevent Failures. Information Systems Management 11(2), 7–13 (1994)
20. Boudreau, M.-C., Robey, D.: Coping with contradictions in business process re-engineering. Information Technology and People 9(4), 40–57 (1996)
21. Davenport, T.H.: Process Innovation: Re-engineering Work through Information Technology. Harvard Business School Press, Boston (1993)
22. Hammer, M.: Reengineering Work: Don't Automate, Obliterate. Harvard Business Review, 104-112 (July-August 1990)
23. Hammer, M., Champy, J.: Reengineering the Corporation; A Manifesto For Business Revolution. Harper Business (1993)
24. King, W.R.: Process Reengineering: The Strategic Dimensions. Information Systems Management 11(2), 71–73 (1994)
25. Malhotra, Y.: Business Process Redesign: An Overview. IEEE Engineering Management Review 26(3) (1998)
26. Willcocks, L., Feeny, D., Islei, G.: Managing IT as a Strategic Resource. McGraw-Hill (1997)
27. Cohen, M.D., March, J.G., Olsen, J.P.: A garbage can model of organizational choice. Administrative Science Quarterly 17(1), 1–25 (1972)
28. Ciborra, C.U.: From Control to Drift. The dynamics of cooporate information infrastructures. Oxford University Press, Oxford (2000)
29. Simon, H.A.: The Structure of Ill Structured Problems. Artificial Intelligence 4, 181–201 (1973)
30. Simon, H.A.: Search and Reasoning in Problem Solving. Artificial Intelligence 21, 7–29 (1983)
31. Woods, D.D., Hollnagel, E.: Mapping cognitive demands in complex problem-solving worlds. International Journal of Man-Machine Studies 26(2), 257–275 (1987)
32. Woods, Coping with complexity: the psychology of human behavior in complex systems. In: Goodstein, L.P., Andersen, H.B., Olsen, S.E. (eds.) Tasks, Errors and Mental Models, pp. 128–148. Taylor & Francis: London (1988)

Author Index

Amescua Seco, Antonio de 1
Andersson, Jesper 86
Antinori, Alessandra 262
Azevedo, Ana 262

Balcar, Jiří 262
Barafort, Béatrix 48
Biffl, Stefan 73
Biro, Miklos 206
Börstler, Jürgen 86

Calvo-Manzano, Jose A. 194
Casey, Val 36
Clarke, Paul 111
Coleman, Gerry 182
Colomo-Palacios, Ricardo 1
Constantino, Bruno Augusto 170
Cristina, Djenane 170

Delgado, Adelaida 25
de Souza, Adler Diniz 170
Dubois, Eric 48
Duchonova, Natalia 135
Duron, Brenda 123

Ekert, Damjan 262, 285
Ekssir-Monfared, Mohsen 309
Elvang, Morten 246
Escorial Rico, David 99

Fistis, Gabriela 231
Flatscher, Martina 251
Flood, Derek 36, 206

Gasca-Hurtado, Gloria Piedad 123, 194
Gavenda, Marek 262
Georgiadou, Elli 217
Ghazi, Ahmad Nauman 86
Giorgakis, Giorgos 262

Homolová, Eva 262

Ito, Masao 277

Jaakkola, Hannu 60
Johansen, Jørn 317

Kalinowski, Marcos 73
Kishida, Kouichi 271
Kösler, Tobias 251
Kovalenko, Olga 73
Kreiner, Christian 285

Langgner, Michael 285
Laporte, Claude Y. 13

Mas, Antonia 25
Mc Caffery, Fergal 36, 206
Mc Daid, Kevin 206
Mejia, Jezreel 123, 194
Mesquida, Antoni-Lluís 25
Messnarz, Richard 217, 231, 262, 285
Metitiero, Giuseppe 262
Moreno-Campos, Euclides 1
Muñoz, Mirna 123, 194
Mustonen-Ollila, Erja 147

Nehfort, Andreas 309
Nevalainen, Risto 296

O'Connor, Rory V. 13, 111, 135, 182
Osborne O'Hagan, Ann 182

Pais, Marisa 262
Petersen, Kai 86
Photiades, Photis 262
Pries-Heje, Jan 317

Regan, Gilbert 36, 206
Richter, Sven 99
Riel, Andreas 231, 251, 262, 285
Rocha, Ana Regina Cavalcanti 170
Rousseau, Anne 48
Rozman, Tomislav 231

Sanchez-Gordón, Mary-Luz 1
Schweigert, Tomas 309
Serral, Estefania 73
Seth, Frank Philip 147
Siakas, Kerstin 217
Smolander, Kari 159

Taipale, Ossi 147, 159
Thalheim, Bernhard 60

Theisens, Dick   285
Tichkiewitch, Serge   262, 285
Torkar, Richard   86

Valtierra, Claudia   123
Varkoi, Timo   296

Winkler, Dietmar   73

Yilmaz, Murat   111
Yli-Huumo, Jesse   159

MIX
Papier aus verantwortungsvollen Quellen
Paper from responsible sources
FSC® C105338

If you have any concerns about our products,
you can contact us on
ProductSafety@springernature.com

In case Publisher is established outside the EU,
the EU authorized representative is:
**Springer Nature Customer Service Center GmbH
Europaplatz 3, 69115 Heidelberg, Germany**

Printed by Libri Plureos GmbH
in Hamburg, Germany